Frommer's®

W9-BDL-340

1ST EDITION

EXPLORING AMERICA by RV

*Text and Photographs
by Shirley Slater & Harry Basch*

IDG Books Worldwide, Inc.
An International Data Group Company
Foster City, CA • Chicago, IL
New York, NY • Indianapolis, IN

To Janet and Alex Withers

IDG Books Worldwide, Inc.
An International Data Group Company
919 E. Hillsdale Blvd.
Suite 400
Foster City, CA 94404

Find us online at **www.frommers.com**

ISBN 0-02-863696-1

ISSN 1527-165X

Editor: Matt Hannafin

Production Editor: Carol Sheehan

Photo Editor: Richard Fox

Design by Madhouse Studios

Staff Cartographers: John Decamillis, Roberta Stockwell

Additional Cartography by Nick Trotter

Historical photos in chapter 1 courtesy of the David Woodworth Collection

Author photo by Donna Carroll

Special Sales
For general information on IDG Books Worldwide's books in the U.S., please call our Consumer Customer Service department at 1-800/762-2974. For reseller information, including discounts and premium sales, please call our Reseller Customer Service department at 1-800/434-3422.

Manufactured in the United States of America

5 4 3 2 1

CONTENTS

LIST OF MAPS

Major Interstate Highways

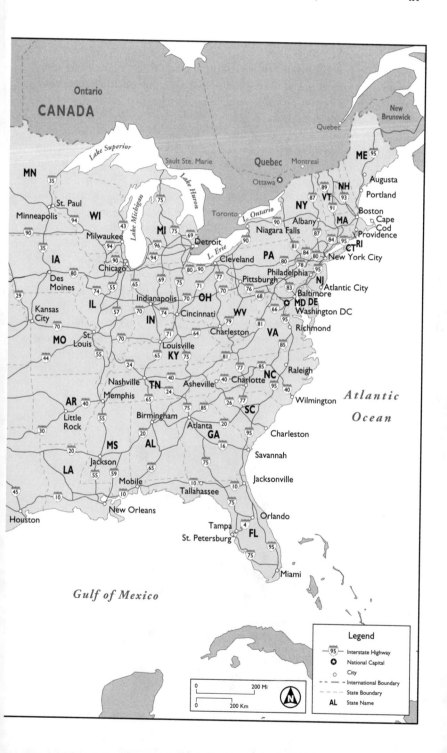

ABOUT THE AUTHORS

Shirley Slater and Harry Basch are a husband-and-wife travel writing team whose books, articles, and photographs have been published internationally over the past 20 years. Former stage, film, and television actors, they have written their syndicated column "Cruise Views" for the *Los Angeles Times* and other major newspapers for more than 15 years, produced six annual editions of the *North American Ski Guide for Prodigy Computer Services,* and written *Shirley and Harry's RV Adventures* (a monthly newsletter) plus four books on Worldwide Cruising.

In 1990, at the 60th World Travel Congress in Hamburg, Germany, the authors were only the third writers (and the first freelancers) ever to receive the prestigious Melva C. Pederson Award from the American Society of Travel Agents for "extraordinary journalistic achievement in the field of travel."

On assignment for publication as diverse as *Bon Appetit* and *Travel Weekly,* they have covered 186 countries by barge, elephant back, hot-air balloon, luxury cruise ship, cross-country skis, paddle-wheel steamer, and supersonic aircraft, but their favorite method of transportation is by RV. In their 27-foot motorhome, they have logged more than 60,000 miles traveling all over the United States, Canada, and Mexico. Aboard other RVs—from mini-motorhomes to 36-foot widebodies with slideouts—they have traveled an additional 60,000 miles exploring the backroads of America.

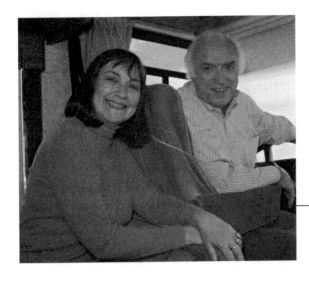

Shirley Slater and Harry Basch inside their RV

Introduction: The RV Life & the Best of the Road

THERE'S SOMETHING QUINTESSENTIALLY AMERICAN ABOUT HITTING the road. You can almost hum along as the wheels eat up the highway— "King of the Road," "Hit the Road, Jack," "On the Road Again," "I've traveled each and every highway . . . I did it my way."

In an RV, you're free of airports, schedules, reservations, shuttles, and public transport. RVers can go anywhere without any advance reservations or preparations and always have a good time discovering something else new, interesting, or weird about the world around us.

"On the road" is shorthand for freedom, independence, discovery, self-reliance—but only if you search out routes that are off the beaten track, with an occasional jaunt over to an interstate to speed through less interesting terrain. As TV's *On the Road* guru, the late Charles Kuralt, once warned, "Thanks to the Interstate Highway System, it is now possible to travel from coast to coast without seeing anything." Leave the freeways to the truckers, the information highway to the computers, and virtual reality to the almost alive. With a folding camping trailer, van, travel trailer, truck camper, or motorhome, an RVer can explore firsthand the famous, infamous, and off-the-wall attractions scattered all over North America, from the legendary Alaska Highway to the challenging run down the Baja Peninsula.

This guidebook picks and chooses overnight oases, from luxurious private RV parks with heated swimming pools and golf courses to quiet, forested campgrounds in state and national parks. You'll also find offbeat places to eat or pick up tasty treats to go, including picking your own farm-fresh fruits and vegetables.

Big cities and world-famous commercial attractions do not fit our travel style—anyone can find them. Instead, we may opt to retrace the route of the Klondike Gold Rush, trying a hand at gold-panning; drop by the California desert museum dedicated to the art of striptease; shuffle off to see the buffalo in Custer State Park; or place a bet at Diamond Tooth Gertie's Casino in the Yukon's Dawson City.

In winter, RVers can learn rock climbing at Joshua Tree National Park or take in the sizzling Terlingua Chili Cook-off in West Texas. In the spring, we set out to catch the dogwood in bloom in the Blue Ridge Mountains or the gray whales migrating along the Baja California coast. Late summer is the time to watch an Alaskan grizzly bear as it fishes for spawning salmon, ride an amphibious Duck vehicle or angle for bass in the lakes of the Ozarks, or go river-rafting on the Colorado. RVers can hang around New Hampshire in the autumn to sample fresh lobster or the dazzling display of red and gold leaves, or head south in time for stone crab season in the Florida Keys.

For some of us, discovering America may happen only after we've had a chance to explore Europe, Asia, Africa, or South America, and that makes the discoveries even richer. And if we repeat ourselves occasionally, it's only to be sure you don't miss something special. While we'd like to think this book is so riveting you'll read it cover to cover at one sitting like a mystery novel, we know you'll dip in and out of chapters at random.

And if we seem partial to KOA-member campgrounds, it's because we've learned through our years of travel that we can rely on a certain standard of excellence, toll-free reservations numbers, and a membership card discount.

The important thing, as Robert Louis Stevenson said, is "to travel for travel's sake. The great affair is to move."

Somebody else said, "Life is what happens while you're making other plans."

You Set the Lifestyle

Our introduction to RVs was during our many years as actors in film and television programs shot in Hollywood and on location, where the self-contained vehicles are used as dressing rooms. So when we leased a Winnebago motorhome in 1992 to research an online ski guide we were producing for Prodigy Services Company™, it was the first time we had been in an RV that actually moved, let alone under our own nervous control.

But what made us even more nervous than operating the machine itself was what we had always heard termed "the RV lifestyle." The suggestion was that by acquiring a recreation vehicle, you bought into a lifestyle—we pictured communal campfire visits, campground pancake breakfasts, and tours of each other's "rigs," culminating in an annual group caravan tour to some scenic area.

Instead, we quickly learned that while you can participate in group and club activities if you're so inclined, you can also use your recreation vehicle to continue whatever lifestyle you already practiced.

Because of our intense, high-pressure work as travel writers and performers, constantly on the move and in social situations, when on vacation we prefer what we call "The Garbo Gourmet Lifestyle." We "want to be alone" with the best food and wine and scenery, to read, go bird watching or hiking, or listen to music. This doesn't mean we don't enjoy exchanging views with fellow RVers, only that we don't want to feel we have to.

It came as a tremendous relief to learn that we were free to do as we pleased. In our first RV journey, 6 weeks on the road all across the United States, nobody came over to urge us to join a club or otherwise identify with some larger group. We did, however, meet some very hospitable individuals, from a campground manager in Independence, Missouri, who taught us, with a flashlight after dark, how to dump the holding tanks we'd been trying to ignore for 3 days, to an exuberant group of hockey fans who shared a keg of beer with us at a campground in LaCrosse, Wisconsin.

The truth of the matter is, there's not one RV lifestyle; there are as many lifestyles as there are people who travel in RVs.

Here are only a few.

TWELVE PERSONALITIES IDEAL FOR RVS

1. **Garbo Gourmets.** They like to be alone together luxuriating in the best life can offer. They dislike tiptoeing through creaky B&Bs or suffering second-rate food and service at expensive five-star hotels and resorts, preferring to carry their own wines and food, sleep in their own beds, and select their own surroundings by serendipity.

2. **Sportsmen.** Skiers, fishermen, surfers, golfers, and mountain bikers want to be in the heart of the action with all the comforts of home, including heating, air-conditioning, and hot showers after a hard workout, plus plenty of storage space to carry fishing rods, skis, golf clubs, and bikes.

3. **Weekenders.** The stressed-out want to get out of the rat race and into the countryside to delete the pressures of the work week from their hard drives. Birdsong replaces Muzak and a campfire flickers in place of a screensaver. Their RV is always packed for a quick getaway, with only a shopping stop to load up on perishables on the way out of town. TGIF!

4. **Families on Vacation.** They offset that visit to a pricey amusement park by traveling with their own budget hotel, with self-serve restaurant at hand around the clock. A comfortable journey for the kids means no more "Are we there yet?," "I have to go potty!," or "I'm hungry!"

Everything they need is in the vehicle. They'll even sit still for an educational journey.

5. **Eco-Tourists.** Go back to nature the easy way, with dawn bird watching, twilight wildlife spotting, photography, and hiking, laying less burden on Mother Earth than heavy hotel and resort infrastructures.

6. **The Ultimate Shoppers.** Hit all the antiques shops, estate sales, and the world's biggest swap meets in comfort and style, with room to take all the treasures back home.

7. **Relatives, Retirees, and Empty Nesters.** An RV is ideal for family visits because you bring your own bedroom and bath along with you and can even entertain your hosts in your own home on wheels. Conversely, when parked at home, the RV doubles nicely as a guest room and bath.

8. **Pet-Lovers.** Take Fifi and Fido along for the ride, enjoy their company, and avoid facing rebellious and destructive pets after a spell of boarding them out. Many (but not all) campgrounds welcome pets.

9. **Disabled Travelers.** If they get impatient with the well-meaning but often bungled accommodations in hotels, from hanging shelves too high to reach to bathroom doors too narrow to navigate, a customized RV can open up the world with familiar and accessible surroundings.

10. **Special Events Attendees.** Day or overnight RV trips to jazz festivals, weekend art shows, outdoor dramas, garlic festivals, football game tailgate parties, jumping frog jubilees, and Civil War reenactments let you sidestep overbooked hotels and restaurants. RVers can take off, even on the spur of the moment, and have bed, bathroom, and breakfast and lunch facilities on the spot.

11. **Snowbirds.** Escaping from minus 10° in Minnesota to the balmy Rio Grande Valley of Texas or heading for the high country to get out of summer's heat, an RV makes you a man (or woman) for all seasons.

12. **Full-Timers.** Whether quitting the rat race for a season or forever, chasing a dream, or discovering America, an RV is the only way to go.

RVS FOR EVERYONE

Of course, for these dozen lifestyle types there are a hundred more that are perfectly accommodated by one or another of the types of RVs available. We've heard about RVers who follow a clothing-optional campground itinerary (yes, Virginia, there are nudist campers, although we've personally never seen any); travel newsletter editors who use their RVs as a combination home, office, and research vehicle; spa goers who toodle from one hot spring to another; singles of both sexes who opt for the wandering life of a loner without a single look back; and leaf peepers who live from one fall foliage tour to the next.

The vehicle adjusts to you and becomes an extension of your own life and travel style. It is simply a means to an end, a very well-designed and comfortable way to access the wilderness, nature, sightseeing, going to the sun, heading for the beach, the mountains, the woods—whatever will make you happy and enhance your life. It's your dream; you call the shots.

Campers have always found a sense of accomplishment in day-to-day survival: cooking food over an open fire, finding a comfortable place to sleep amid rocks and hard ground, protecting yourself from the sun, rain, heat or cold. With RVs, everything is much less work-intensive, without taking away the sense of self-reliance, of having everything you need for survival along with you.

Celebrities from Loretta Lynn to Danny DeVito, Michael Douglas to Pat Boone, John Madden to Bruce Willis are RV owners who use their vehicles for both business and pleasure. More than one film megastar has had a contract sweetened with the perk of a big-bucks motorhome, used for a private location dressing room during the shoot and given as a gift at the end of filming.

Our own favorite RV celebrity is senior golf champion Larry Laoretti, who was interviewed in his motorhome on ABC television during the U.S. Senior Open. After Laoretti won the tournament, sportscaster Brent Musberger asked him if now that he'd won $130,000 at the tournament, he would give up his motorhome to "travel first class." Laoretti retorted that in his opinion, traveling by motorhome *is* going first class, and a six-figure payday wasn't going to change that. We heartily concur.

But much as we love RVing, something we had never really anticipated before we tried it, we also will admit that perhaps not everyone is an ideal candidate for life on the road. If your idea of the perfect vacation is to check into a luxury resort and phone for room service, you may not be ready for an RV—that is, unless you have a mate who loves to wait on you.

A QUICK DO-IT-YOURSELF QUIZ TO TEST YOUR RVC (RECREATIONAL VEHICLE COMPATIBILITY)

1. Do you ever sing along with "My Way," "On the Road Again," or "King of the Road"?

2. Have you ever considered getting a second vacation home but can't decide between the mountains or the seashore?

3. Do you like to putter around the house or spend an entire Saturday morning browsing the shelves of a hardware store?

4. Did you ever envy Jack Kerouac, William Least Heat Moon, or Charles Kuralt, even a little bit?

5. Do you dislike timetables and schedules, the hurry-up-and-wait routine of catching a flight, and bumper-to-bumper commutes?

6. Are you tired of dress codes in chi-chi restaurants that want men to wear a jacket and tie and women to wear a skirt, or vice versa?

RV'ING FOR DISABLED TRAVELERS

RVing, like sailing on cruise ships, makes an enjoyable and easy vacation for disabled travelers, particularly those in a wheelchair, so long as the camping units are configured to take care of the chair's width and turning radius and are free of steps or level differences inside. Among manufacturers providing equipment for disabled RVers are Foretravel, Play-Mor, and Winnebago, listed in chapter 16, "RV Manufacturers: Who Makes What." For a complete list, contact the **Recreation Vehicle Industry Association (RVIA)**, Box 2999, Disabled LST, Reston, VA 20195-0999 (☎ **703/620-6003**), which publishes a free booklet listing manufacturers of RVs or RV accessories for the physically challenged traveler.

Clubs for disabled RVers include **Handicapped Travel Club**, 667 J Ave., Coronado, CA 92118, and **Accent on Information**, P.O. Box 700, Bloomington, IL 61702 (☎ **309/378-2961**). The latter publishes booklets and magazines for disabled travelers. 🚐

7. Do you dislike using public toilets and showers, or wonder who slept in that motel bed just ahead of you?

8. Could you find paradise with "a loaf of bread, a jug of wine and thou / Beside me in the wilderness"?

9. Does the smoky smell of a campfire, a charred hot dog, or a burned marshmallow turn you on?

10. Are you susceptible to serendipity, doing things on a whim like turning down a side road that seems to call to you, buying something offbeat that instantly becomes a favorite possession, or striking up a conversation with an interesting-looking stranger who turns out to be a friend forever after?

If you answered "yes" to any one of the 10 questions, you might consider trying out an RV by rental. See chapter 15, "To Rent or Buy?" for details.

If you answered "yes" to 5 or more of the 10 questions, check out chapter 14, "RV Types & Terms."

If you answered "yes" to all 10 questions, what are you waiting for? Turn to chapter 16, "RV Manufacturers: Who Makes What," for a look at the wide varieties of RVs that are out there for sale.

If you answered "no" to all 10 questions, you still haven't wasted your money. Thumb to one of the following chapters, grab your car keys and a lodging guide or settle down in an easy chair, and set out on one of our roving RV adventures for a fast and funny look at weird, wonderful America.

PART 1

Getting Ready to Hit the Road

Words of wisdom on preparing for life on the road and in the campgrounds

1. Life on the Road: A Personal & Public History of RVing
2. Getting Prepared: RVing Tips & Hints
3. Where to Sleep: Campgrounds & RV Parks

Life on the Road: A Personal & Public History of RVing

AMERICANS ARE A RESTLESS PEOPLE, CONSTANTLY ON THE MOVE, always expecting greener grass and greater opportunities over the next hill, beyond the horizon. For our predecessors, the covered wagon gave them a traveling home despite its lack of luxury. Tent camping provided a little more comfort for exploring America, but still slowed down the footloose.

Once the automobile came into everyday use, pioneering RVers didn't wait for specialty camping vehicles to come off the assembly line—they were creating their own motorhomes just after the turn of the century, in 1901. We discovered RVing in the early 1990s and after an initial shakedown period, learned to love our life on the road. Our only regret now is that we didn't start earlier.

Excerpts from a Road Diary; or, If We Can Do This, Anyone Can

After nearly 20 years on the road as travel writers, we've traveled by just about every mode of transportation known to man, including hot-air balloons, elephant backs, and dugout canoes. But our lives changed when we set out for the first time in an RV, a leased 27-foot Winnebago Brave motorhome, on a 6-week trip to visit more than 100 remote ski areas all over the United States for a computer service guidebook.

In an earlier life, as film and television actors, we had spent many long days in RVs changing clothes and studying scripts—they are routinely used as dressing rooms on film locations and studio sound stages—but we had never been in one that moved. The size we selected was a compromise between how large an inside and how small an outside we could deal with. Here are some notes from that first time on the road, all of them written in the passion of the moment.

August 12

At the California dealer where we are leasing the motorhome, a young man named Daryll, wearing sun-bleached shoulder-length hair and a Persian Gulf War T-shirt, walks us through it, saying how easy everything is and how nothing can go wrong. We nod wisely and make frantic scribbled notes like "circuit breaker and fuses in bedroom" and "generator runs off gas tanks" and "water pump—switch off while moving." When he leaves us alone for a while, we go into a frenzy of measuring and diagram-drawing.

August 14

The day before we are scheduled to leave, we lay out newspaper sections on the floor of our apartment folded to fit the measurements of the RV's cupboards, then set out the items we intend to put there and pack only those items in a box labeled for that section.

August 15

Unfortunately, life isn't that rational and orderly. On packing day, we are forced to double-park in our crowded urban neighborhood and relay boxes of books, cartons of pots and pans, and hangers of clothes back and forth from our apartment to the street, one of us keeping a constant eye out so nothing is stolen, and dumping them anywhere there is space, most of it on the plastic-wrapped mattress and in the bathroom shower.

When Daryll saw us off at the dealer's this morning, he turned on the generator so the rooftop air conditioner could cool down the interior and chill the refrigerator and freezer, but neglected to tell us whether to keep it on while we're driving, or turn it off. Somewhere we remember him saying it's capable of running 16 hours straight with no problem, so we leave it on.

The soothing noise from the air conditioner drowns out many of the small crashes and thuds from the back as our possessions settle in on their own, with only an occasional loud thunk causing us to glance furtively backward.

August 15 (from the Driver's Seat)

The first impression is that you're way above the traffic and at the same time divorced from the road itself. Suddenly you realize you're looking down at the middle of the lane and half your vehicle is in the next lane. To keep from slipping over into an adjacent lane, you have to hug the left-lane line. The back of the vehicle seems to have a mind of its own and wants to turn at a shorter distance than the front end. We soon learned to make wide turns, particularly to the right. Another problem is that at any bump or rut, the vehicle leans to the right or left, then rolls back to the other side. Our fingers and arms are stiff after a couple of hours from white-knuckling the wheel.

August 15 (Nightfall)

It is after dark when we stop for gas in Kingman, Arizona, and Harry goes into a state of shock as he watches the numbers on the tank turn and turn and turn, as gallon after gallon flows in, until the pump turns off automatically at $50 and the tank still isn't full.

Exhausted, we agree it's time to stop. Just in front of us, between the gas station and the freeway, is an RV campground—we can see the sign—but we cannot figure out how to get to it since a used car lot and a strip mall are in the way.

(It is about now that we give up the fantasy of waking to birdsong and the breeze wafting through the pine trees.)

Not far away we find a second campground and something better than birdsong—a space called a "pull-through," which means we can drive the motorhome in one side, plug it in, then drive out the other side the next morning without backing up—something we haven't exactly learned how to do yet.

We begin to speed-read the instruction manual and learn that it is necessary to turn off the generator before plugging in the electricity. That part is a snap—our plug fits into the campground's receptacle.

We make a long, fruitless search by flashlight through all the outdoor storage bins for a hose so we can hook up the water connection. (Harry is positive Daryll pointed one out, but Shirley thinks he has remembered the sewage hose instead, and Harry thinks that maybe we should get a divorce, right now, tonight, or at least go check into a motel with running water. As it turns out, we have plenty of water in the storage tanks without having to use the external hookup.)

We studiously ignore the sewage hookup. The refrigerator has been turned down to the coldest setting—obviously Daryll wanted it to get chilled quickly—and we find frozen romaine, frozen eggs, and frozen chicken breasts inside. Instead of a gourmet dinner, we settle for soup warmed in the microwave.

Stunned, almost stupid with exhaustion, we wash the dishes, close the blinds and curtains, and move back to the bedroom to make up the bed. Clearing it is easier than we expect, since most of the gear piled on the bed has already fallen onto the floor.

We raise the mattress to remove its plastic cover, and the hinged supports lock into the open position, leaving the bed firmly set at a rakish 45-degree angle. By this time we're so tired we probably could have slept in it anyhow, but we get out the toolbox and unscrew the supports so we can flatten the mattress again. Somehow we manage to simultaneously make up the bed and fall asleep in it . . .

August 16

The skies have opened up in the high desert of western New Mexico, dumping so much water in the streets of Socorro that the intersections are flooded ankle-deep. Although our campground guidebook promises there is an RV park in town, we spot the flickering light of a Motel 6 just ahead and, with no discussion whatsoever, pull in just behind a battered truck camper from

Texas. If the veterans can't weather the storm, we amateurs can't be expected to. We check into a $29-a-night room.

August 17
The sun comes out. We stop at a hardware store and buy a water hose, which we hook up, but for some reason it never fills the tank. Later we realize we hooked the water hose to the outside connection that feeds water directly into the system. While we're still not able to make the TV work, we've gotten very good at plugging in the electric, once we realize our large three-prong plug has to fit into a three-prong 30-amp receptacle.

We studiously ignore the sewage hookup.

August 18
While checking out the ski resort at Crested Butte, we make a left turn uphill into the parking garage of the Grande Butte Hotel, which causes the tow-bar connection at the rear of the motorhome to drag and stick fast in the asphalt. The concierge arrives and says a Greyhound bus got stuck there only last week, and should she call the tow truck again? Harry congratulates himself on taking out Auto Club emergency insurance, and the tow truck duly frees us from the driveway. We vow never again to turn into a hotel driveway that heads uphill.

August 19
In the ski town of Breckenridge, we spot a locksmith standing beside his truck talking to a pretty blonde, and ask if he could help us get into our outdoor storage area because either the lock is broken or the key doesn't fit. The locksmith takes one look at the key and says we're using it upside down. From then on it works. At Dillon Reservoir, we settle down to lunch beside the lake, opening a couple of the roof vents for air, when a sudden gust of wind tears across the roof of the motorhome and takes off one of the white plastic roof vents. Harry chases it down and climbs on the roof to replace it, just as the rain begins. At a nearby gas station, we buy a roll of silver duct tape and batten the vent down. We vow never again to open the roof vents on a windy day.

August 20
We get lost in Kansas City looking for Arthur Bryant's famous barbecue restaurant, so it is once again after dark when we check into a small RV campground in the town of Independence, where a kindly campground manager with a flashlight loans us a sewage hose (ours is too short for the hookup) and talks us step-by-step through the dumping procedure for the holding tanks, which have reached their capacity. The same helpful manager shows us where to push a black button that activates the TV set.

Harry, I don't think we're in Kansas anymore.

August 27

It is almost with a sense of relief that we return to Winnie (for some reason we have begun calling the vehicle that lately) after staying overnight in some friends' lavish West Virginia country cottage. Their gardens are lovely, their hospitality warm, but Winnie has become home.

August 29

It has taken us 2 weeks to discover why the bedroom in the back of the motorhome would get so hot while we're traveling, then cool down once we've stopped for the night. It turns out that Harry had kept a control switch on the dash to the left side, thinking it was off, when the left side actually activates the low fan of the bedroom heater.

September 1

There is a great comfort in riding along listening to the sounds in the motorhome behind us. We recognize the sharp clatter of the cutlery drawer suddenly swinging open, the more subdued sounds of the mug of wooden utensils spilling onto the stove top, the rolling thud of the canned food swaying back and forth in its bin, the rattle when the bedroom blinds have come unhooked from their pins and are randomly swaying, the bump when a camera forgotten and left on a chair falls onto the floor and breaks its wide-angle lens, the swishing sound of the cardboard box with its water jugs sliding on the plastic floor covering. (We did not remove the plastic over the carpeting, figuring that was one way to keep it cleaner inside.)

After we have the bed supports repaired, the bed develops a mind of its own and pops up occasionally while we're in transit, as if to have a look around.

September 15

We drive into Yellowstone, suddenly aware of how special it is to travel in a motorhome like this with wide scenic views through the big windows and high seats, as if looking down from a bus. Huge herds of bison shamble around in the roadway, in no hurry to move along, and our vantage point is ideal for photographing them. We stop for lunch by the Yellowstone River in a grove of trees, their leaves turned golden, and for the first time talk about perhaps buying a motorhome of our own.

September 27

Partly because we despair of ever having to unpack Winnie, we buy her from the dealer. That was more than 50,000 miles ago. When not on the road, she resides at a Winnebago dealer's storage area in Carson, California, not far from the Goodyear blimp.

How to Give Backing-Up Directions without Destroying Your Marriage

Whenever possible, request a pull-through campsite and postpone as long as possible the agony of a back-in site.

When no drive-throughs are available, we prefer to start with a quick confab about the broad general aims of the driver, particularly in regard to where the RV will end up, along with some general observations about the presence of boulders, picnic tables, and low-hanging tree limbs. Unfortunately, if the vehicle is blocking campground traffic, the prologue step has to be eliminated.

It is critical to establish a mutual signal that means "Stop immediately before you back into that _____" (fill in as applicable: truck, tree, utility post, fence, fire grate, etc.).

The first step is for the signaler to learn to stand where he or she can be seen by the driver in the side mirror. The same rule applies here as for cameras: If you can see the mirror, the mirror can see you.

Next, the signals should be clear and decisive. The fewer signals that are used, the simpler it usually becomes. We use a two-hand beckoning signal for "keep coming back," a right-hand signal to move toward the right, a left-hand signal to move toward the left, and a dramatic thrust of hand up and palm open toward the driver that means, "For God's sake, stop!" Too many signals or verbiage simply confuses the issue.

If all else fails, you still have a couple of options: Invest in a closed-circuit TV backup system that shows the driver exactly what is behind him as he backs—expensive but effective (although these, too, have their limitations)—or a CB radio system with one unit in the cockpit and the second handheld. Motorola also makes a two-way radio with a 2-watt transmitter good for a 2-mile line of sight ($299 at Camping World). Less expensive walkie-talkies can be had from Radio Shack, but get one with more than one channel. It seems like everybody and his brother has the same one-channel system, and you'll find yourself having overlapping conversations with your neighbors.

Public History: The Tin Can Tourists

They called themselves "Tin Can Tourists." They braved the dust and mud to drive their tin Lizzies across the United States before transcontinental roads were paved, camping by the side of the road, heating tin cans of food on a gasoline stove, and bathing in cold water.

They dressed in their Sunday clothes in the days before jogging suits and running shoes. A photograph of one 1920s camping club shows owners gathered in front of their Weidman Camp Body vehicles, the men in fedoras, suits, and ties, and the women in dresses, cloche hats, stockings, and high-heeled shoes.

"Tin Can Tourist" at Mammoth, 1920

It took ingenuity to travel across the country in those days before the first motel, which opened in 1925 in California. In 1921, for instance, Lee Scoles of Fort Wayne, Indiana, converted his 1916 Federal truck to "a house on wheels" and drove it on an 8-month, round-trip journey to San Francisco with 11 relatives aboard. Such additions as solid rubber tires, a canvas awning, cots, a cookstove, and washtubs added to their comfort, according to his granddaughter Alice Worman, herself a motorhome owner, who chronicled the story in *Lifestyles,* a magazine for Monaco motorhome owners, one of many such publications dedicated to RVing.

According to a story in *RV West* magazine, the family of Charles Ulrich set out for California in 1929 in a General Motors truck body mounted on a Ford chassis, with built-in bunks, overhead wardrobe storage, and a dining table with six folding chairs. The interior was polished mahogany and on the rear was a caboose-type open platform with iron railings. After their "once-in-a-lifetime" trip, which continued on to Hawaii aboard a Matson Line cruise ship, the Ulrichs stored the camper until the 1960s, when it was purchased by a group of hunters to serve as a forest base camp.

A fire-engine red 1929 Ford Model A converted to a mini-motorhome camper complete with pop-up top still carries the Ray Glenn family on trips around the Seattle area, according to *MotorHome* magazine.

Originally, auto camping was regarded as a rich man's hobby. The way had been paved by the well-publicized outings of auto manufacturer Henry Ford, inventor Thomas Edison, naturalist John Burroughs, and tire manufacturer Harvey Firestone, who called themselves "the four vagabonds" as they camped in America's parks. Interestingly, it was the affordability and popularity of Henry Ford's Model T, which made its debut in 1909, that helped bring auto camping to the average American.

THIRTEEN NOTABLE DATES IN RV HISTORY

c. 1901: The first motorhomes are built as special-order units by auto body builders.

1907: Henry Ford introduces the first mass-produced Model T Fords, automobiles with a 2.9-liter, four-cylinder engine that make auto camping affordable for most Americans for the first time.

1910–15: The first manufactured, mass-produced RVs—folding camping trailers—start coming off the line from Los Angeles Trailer Works, Auto-Kamp Trailers in Saginaw, Michigan, and other pioneers.

1917: The first fifth-wheel trailer is built by airplane manufacturer Curtiss-Wright; its name probably originated from the trailer hitch, which is located in the center of the towing truck's bed and could be considered a "fifth" wheel after the four on the trailer unit bottom.

1919: The Tin Can Tourists gather for their first rally, in a Florida campground near Tampa called DeSoto Park, with 20 members present, most of them Model T owners; by the mid-1930s, the club numbered 150,000.

1922: Fifteen million auto campers hit the road, according to the *New York Times,* most of them sleeping on cots, in tents, or in "newfangled houses on wheels."

1923: There are 7,000 free campgrounds in the United States, including Denver's Overland Park, with 800 campsites, piped water, a repairs garage, restaurant, beauty shop, billiards hall, soda fountain, and eight electric washing machines.

1926: Fords equipped with Weidman Camp Bodies are first produced in Tonawanda, New York; the 1929 model sells for $1,900.

1962: John Steinbeck publishes *Travels with Charley* about his RV journey around America with his elderly poodle.

1966: Winnebago becomes the first mass-production motorhome assembly line, turning out its early models (with moldings above the windshield that resembled eyebrows) in lengths of 17, 19, and 22 feet.

1966: David Garvin begins selling RV parts and camping accessories at his family's campground in Bowling Green, Kentucky; by 1993, his chain of Camping World stores (which he calls "Toys R Us for grownups") has become the world's largest retailer of camping supplies with 29 stores, 10 million mail order catalogs distributed annually, and a sales base of $150 million.

1967: Charles Kuralt rents a Dodge motorhome to begin broadcasting "On the Road," his famous series of CBS-TV news features that brought small-town Americans and their stories into the living rooms of people everywhere. During his 27 years on the road, Kuralt used six different motorhomes; the last, a 29-foot FMC motor coach, is installed at the Henry Ford Museum near Detroit.

1976: Winnebago Industries introduces the Heli-Home, a helicopter camper for off-road exploration that could sleep six; we note it's no longer included in their published brochures.

1929 Ford with Weidman Camp Body

Nobody knows more about the early history of recreation vehicles than David Woodworth of Tehachapi, California, who owns the largest collection of antique camping equipment, photography, and literature known to exist. Much of his material appeared in the 1986 Smithsonian Institution's show "At Home on the Road," which he helped produce.

Alaska-born Woodworth attributes his fascination with RVs to his childhood memories, when his family traveled around the country in a Detroiter travel trailer following his carpenter father from job to job.

At RV shows and state fairs around the country, he exhibits vehicles like his art deco–style 1937 Hunt House Car, designed and manufactured by a Hollywood cinematographer and inventor named J. Roy Hunt. (Among Hunt's many screen credits was the classic 1929 film *The Virginian,* starring Gary Cooper.)

The sleek, 19-foot, teardrop-shaped motorhome, crafted on a Ford truck chassis and powered by a Ford flathead V-8 engine, includes a bathroom with hand-pumped shower, lavatory, and toilet (which has to be manually removed to empty); a stove with two burners; an icebox; a sofa and a dinette (both of which convert to beds); and even a kitchen sink.

Woodworth proudly claims membership in the Tin Can Tourists, whose last surviving affiliates have appointed him "Grand Can Opener."

Among the 30 or so antique camping vehicles in Woodworth's collection are 1928 and 1931 Covered Wagon Travel Trailers, manufactured in Detroit; a 1935 York Rambler built in York, Pennsylvania; a Hays from Grand Rapids, Michigan; and a Harley Bowless, created by the builder who oversaw the construction of Charles Lindbergh's historic transatlantic aircraft, the *Spirit of St Louis.* Airstream later used the Harley Bowless as an inspiration for its famous aerodynamic travel trailer back in 1936, Woodworth says.

Early camping club

He can also spout nonstop historic information about auto camping and the early campers. Some of his revelations:

- The first campgrounds were free, built and maintained by cities and towns hoping to attract affluent travelers who would spend money while they were in town. In the days before World War I, only the affluent had the time and money to go auto camping. When Ford's Model T made auto camping affordable for everyone, campgrounds started charging fees to discourage some of the overflow crowds.

- One early pair of auto campers was a couple who were fearful their new travel trailer might pull the rear end off their car, so the husband drove the car and the wife sat in the trailer for the entire journey intently watching the car's rear end to make sure nothing happened to it.

- Highways were notoriously bad in the early days. Woodworth quotes from the memoirs of some 1924 auto campers who termed themselves "Modern Gypsies" and wrote about a local resident telling them, "That's a good road; somebody just made it through there yesterday." Later, he

---

INSIDER TIP

The **Museum of Family Camping** in Bear Brook State Park, Allenstown, New Hampshire (☎ **609/485-3782;** www. channel1.com/users/brosius/museum.htm), includes "typical campsites" of each decade of camping, as well as photo and tape reminiscences of old-timers and a Hall of Fame commemorating such pioneers as Airstream's Wally Byam who organized and led camping caravans all over the world.

says, the travelers commented, "When we left New York for Chicago, we were motorists. When we left Chicago for California, we were pioneers."

Six Common Misperceptions About RVs & Their Owners

As Gary Cooper said in the movie *The Virginian,* "When you call me that, smile!" Because we enjoy our freewheeling life on the road so much, we shudder at every false stereotype that some uninformed person perpetuates. Here, then, are a few common errors, followed by the way it really is.

- **Misperception #1:** We find misperceptions particularly hard to take when the person misperceiving is a fellow travel writer who should know his nomenclature. A writer in a popular national travel magazine writing about driving in Utah said Arches National Park "makes even the most remote rock formations visible to wheezing geezers willing to take a short walk from motorhome to overlook." (The same writer spent much of his story bragging about how much speed his $40,000 Nissan Infiniti made on the empty highways and complaining about the dearth of gas stations and fast-food outlets in southern Utah.) **Reality:** Puh-leeze, wheeze us no geezers! According to a 1994 University of Michigan study, the average RV owner is 48 years old, married with children, owns his own home, and has a household income of around $40,000 a year. During the next decade, the highest RV ownership category by age will be college-educated baby boomers just reaching the age of 45.

- **Misperception #2:** Another writer, describing a lonely highway he drove, says he met "only a few Winnebagos" along the way. **Reality:** While he might have met a series of RVs that were produced by Iowa-based Winnebago Industries, he probably used the term "Winnebago" to mean "recreation vehicles." While all Winnebagos are RVs, not all RVs are Winnebagos. Out of today's 64 million campers, nearly half use a recreation vehicle. When Death Valley tabulated its overnight campground stays in 1988, a total of 61,743 overnights were made in tents, 249,726 in recreation vehicles.

- **Misperception #3:** A real estate developer friend inquiring politely about our RV passion asked about our "mobile home" and was startled to be so instantly and vehemently corrected. **Reality:** Our motorhome is not a "mobile home." The latter is not a recreation vehicle but manufactured residential housing that is infrequently moved after initially being set in place.

- **Misperception #4:** Well-meaning greenies like to say that unlike backpacking and tent camping, RVing pollutes the environment and guzzles gas and water resources. **Reality:** Having graduated from the ranks of backpackers and tent campers, we're acutely aware of this "purist" attitude toward RVing. A recent RVIA (Recreation Vehicle Industry Association) poll shows that 98% of all RVers practice one or more forms of "green" RVing. In our case, our low-water toilet and quick showers use much less water than public facilities in the parks. We put all waste water into holding tanks, which are then properly disposed of at dump stations, rather than pouring anything on the ground or into streams. We never build a campfire that leaves layers of pollution hanging in the atmosphere, never dig up the ground or tie anything to trees and bushes, and always recycle everything possible.

- **Misperception #5:** According to the University of Michigan study, some 14% of all potential RVers believe their state requires a special license to drive an RV. **Reality:** No state requires a special license of any kind to operate an RV; your normal driver's license is all you need. At present, one of every 10 motor-vehicle-owning families in the United States has an RV. In the 35–54 age group, it's one out of every 9. In fact, the RVers between 35 and 54 outnumber the over-55s.

- **Misperception #6:** When city officials of the former naval base town of Port Hueneme in southern California proposed to bolster the town's sagging economy by building an oceanside luxury RV resort, the proposal passed, despite a vociferous handful of residents at a town meeting that claimed "typical" RVers are "homeless, jobless, use drugs, commit crimes, belong to gangs and desecrate any area they happen to park in," according to a journalist on the scene. Wow! And we thought our neighbors in the next campsite were just toasting marshmallows!

❷ Getting Prepared: RVing Tips & Hints

THE FIRST TIME WE SET OUT IN AN RV, WE DEVOTED AS MUCH attention to it as the Allies planning the Normandy landing, and had about as much success as Napoleon at Waterloo. These days, we can decide on the spur of the moment to go away for a few days, pick up the RV keys, and set out. In this chapter we'll discuss some of the nuts and bolts of life on the road so that you, too, can overcome disorganization and inefficiency and have the guts to just hit the road anyway.

Driving Schools

While most confident (or overconfident) drivers pick up RV-wrangling fairly quickly, if you want to acquire some certifiable professional RV driving skills, contact the **RV Driving School,** 1512 E. 5th St., #149, Ontario, CA 91764 (☎ **909/984-7746**). Instructor Dick Reed has 20 years of RV driving experience as well as being a teacher of truck and RV driving. He covers use of mirrors, driving defensively, courtesy, backing into campsites, safety checks, and braking and control. Students may learn on their own rigs or his. He also offers driving seminars at the Los Angeles RV Show each October at the Fairplex in Pomona.

Learning Your Vital Statistics

As beginners, our lack of technical knowledge was most frightening the first time we encountered a narrow, rickety, one-lane bridge near New Harmony, Indiana, with a small sign noting its weight limit was 5 tons. But how much did we weigh? We didn't know. Finally, since there was no way to turn around and go back, and the traffic was beginning to build up behind us, we gingerly inched our way across, holding our breaths until we made it.

Later, we studied the brochure that detailed our floor plan and learned that our maximum weight, fully loaded and with passengers, could be just over 12,000 pounds, or 6 tons.

The moral is, memorize your height, weight, and width before getting behind the wheel.

- **GVW (Gross Vehicle Weight):** Total weight of a fully equipped and loaded RV with passengers, gas, oil, water, and baggage; must not be greater than the vehicle's GVWR.

- **GVWR (Gross Vehicle Weight Rating):** The amount of total loaded weight a vehicle can support; determined by the manufacturer, this amount must not be exceeded.

- **Dry Weight:** The weight of the RV without fluids such as gas, oil, and water added.

Making a List, Checking It Twice . . .

It's a good idea for beginning RVers to make up some sort of checklist to follow when packing for a trip, preparing the vehicle for a trip, or when setting up and breaking up camp. Some veterans suggest laminating the list, then checking off the items in grease pencil or erasable felt pen so it can be wiped clean to use again.

If you don't want to write out your own, the **"RV Check List"** from MARCOX Products, Box 7815, Moreno Valley, CA 92552 (☎ **909/242-1248**), covers all the preparation and safety details in a three-ring binder ($11.95) or a paperback with spiral binder ($8.95). Add $2.95 for shipping; deduct $2 by adding your Good Sam membership number.

What Kind of Wardrobe Is Right?

Like most RVers, we have a wardrobe always stowed in our motorhome that can cover any situation we may encounter on the road, from an impromptu dinner in a fine restaurant to an outfit for cold-weather camping or white-water rafting.

Since wardrobe and drawer space is fairly limited, except on the largest motorhomes and fifth-wheels, you'll want to confine your carry-along wardrobe to a few carefully selected basics, adding seasonal or special apparel when the journey requires it.

We concentrate on basic clothing that is machine washable, stretchable with elastic waists and a comfortable but loose fit, in styles and colors that will harmonize with the other items in the closet. For cold-weather camping, even in parts of the California desert in winter, a set of **silk long underwear** is invaluable to wear under sweatshirts and pants. A loose cotton gauze or linen shirt and a pair of **shorts** are always on hand for unusually hot weather, like the heat wave we encountered in New England last summer.

A spare pair of **hiking or jogging shoes** is handy to have, along with a comfortable pair of **slippers** to wear in the evenings after outside chores are finished. We each take one pair of slightly worn but acceptable **dress-up shoes,** along with one business or **evening outfit,** in case of an important appointment en route. Anyone planning to use the public showers in the campground should also take a pair of **rubber shower shoes.**

Several changes of underwear, socks, and pajamas, along with a bathrobe, are folded and tucked into nightstand drawers beside the bed. We even carry spare bottles of **prescription medication** and a full supply of **toiletries** so we can slip away on the spur of the moment yet still have everything we need aboard the RV.

Knit clothes that can be folded and stacked rather than put on a hanger take up less room and don't need ironing. We often take travel- or sample-size toiletries, stowing them at home in a special "Winnie-box" that's ready to be taken along on the next RV trip.

On our initial 6-week journey, we took far too many clothes, forgetting that a lot of campgrounds have laundromats and that items of clothing can be worn more than once. The other thing to remember is that in a campground, nobody pays much attention to what anyone wears anyhow.

Stocking the Larder

Because we use our RV year-round, we keep it stocked with non-perishables that are always ready to go and need only be supplemented with fresh food, ice, and water before we set off for a weekend. But since even canned goods should not be stored for a long period of time, we mark the date of purchase on top of each can with an indelible marker and use the cans in order of age.

Particularly in warm weather, we try to avoid leaving open cardboard packages of crackers, flour, or cornmeal in the RV. We usually store small amounts of dried beans, rice, and grains in screw-top jars or plastic zip-lock bags, along with coffee beans and sugar. Open bottles of olive oil, mustard, or mayonnaise are brought back home at the end of each outing, to be replaced by another small, unopened container on the next trip. All wines are returned home at the end of every trip, but liquors can usually be stored in the vehicle between trips.

Because we both enjoy cooking for ourselves after so many years of dining out, we include among our permanent equipment a food processor, spice rack, and pots of fresh herbs (which go back home between journeys).

A large, French enameled cast-iron soup pot, which doubles as a spaghetti pot, is the biggest item in our cookware collection. It is accompanied by several smaller, nonstick enameled cast-iron skillets and pans, a

A cook's kitchen on the road may have fresh herbs and a food processor.

small whistling teakettle, an earthenware teapot that always travels in an old-fashioned, padded tea cozy, and several Pyrex microwavable measuring cups and dishes.

For eating, we have a set of sturdy French bistro plates, soup bowls, and wine glasses, plus two oversized ceramic mugs that fit nicely into the beverage-carrier on the cockpit dash. New dish towels double as place mats and/or napkins, then become dish towels after a few washings. We try to avoid using disposable paper products, preferring to recycle.

A large wooden cutting board, padded with a rubberized mat on the bottom, doubles as a cooktop cover when we're traveling; it keeps the burners from rattling. In the microscopic workspace between the double sink and cooktop, we have the food processor, electric can opener, knife block, spice rack, wooden box with cooking utensils, and glass canning jar of coarse salt.

Optional appliances we've taken with us at one time or another include a toaster oven (indispensable if you don't have a regular oven, handy if you dislike the bending it takes to light the regular oven), sorbet maker (we found you need a freezer that can be set extra-low), and bread maker (as handy and easy to use on the road as at home).

AN ODE TO BUBBLE WRAP

Mel Brooks, in the classic comic routine "The 2000-Year-Old Man," lauded plastic wrap as the greatest invention of the past two millenniums, but we'd have to say bubble wrap is a close second, at least in the wonderful world of RV cupboards.

The cylinder-shaped bubble wrap containers that come around bottles in airport duty-free shops make great sleeves for mugs and glasses, while the flat sheets that come in packing boxes are easy to slide between plates or pots and pans to protect them. You can also buy commercially produced plastic foam sleeves for glasses and pan protectors in camping supply stores such as the Camping World chain.

Alternately nesting baskets and metal bowls keeps down the clatter from the cupboards as well. And lining the bottoms of drawers and cupboards with waffle-patterned rubber matting, available by the yard at RV dealers and camping stores, makes a non-skid surface for dishes.

We store fragile items like tulip-shaped champagne glasses in their original boxes and use other boxes or shaped Styrofoam packing protectors that come around appliances to wedge them firmly in the cupboard. Whenever possible, we use real dishes and utensils and cloth napkins that are recycled instead of disposable paper and plastic products.

A DOZEN DELICIOUS, QUICK & EASY ONE-POT MEALS

The following are some of our favorite quickly assembled meals after a day of driving or hiking, made with ingredients that are easy to keep on hand. Each involves one pot and a few simple preparation steps. On some, there are vegetarian and/or low-fat adaptations of the original recipe.

Quick Tortilla Soup

The cook controls the spiciness in this dish with the ratio of enchilada sauce to chicken broth. Makes 2 to 4 servings.

> 1 8-ounce can mild enchilada sauce
>
> 1 to 2 14-ounce cans of low-sodium, low-fat chicken broth (for milder flavor, use more broth)
>
> 1 15-ounce can of beans, drained and rinsed (black, red, or pinto beans)
>
> 2 seeded and chopped fresh tomatoes
>
> Cut kernels from 2 ears shucked fresh corn

Combine enchilada sauce, chicken broth, beans, and tomatoes in a saucepan. Heat thoroughly, then stir in the kernels cut from two ears fresh corn that have been shucked and washed. Stir and let warm through briefly. Remove from heat and serve with any or all of these optional toppings: corn chips, grated cheese, sliced green onions, fresh cilantro, cooked chicken breast slivers.

Easy Fried Rice

With planned-ahead leftover cold cooked rice, this is a tasty hot main dish that takes less than 15 minutes. Makes 2 main- or 4 side-dish portions.

> 4 slices bacon chopped in 1-inch pieces
>
> 1 green pepper, seeded and chopped
>
> 2 green onions, washed, trimmed, and chopped

2 tbsp. fresh Italian parsley, washed and chopped (optional)

2 cups cold cooked rice

2 beaten whole eggs, blended with 2 tbsp. bottled soy sauce

Arrange bacon in large nonstick frying pan. Cook over medium heat until the bacon browns, then remove to drain on paper towels, leaving the fat in the pan. Still over medium heat, in the same pan, sauté green pepper, green onions, and parsley until tender but not browned. Stir in rice. Continue stirring until heated through. Then pour eggs with soy sauce evenly over the top of the mixture. Cook over medium heat, stirring constantly, until eggs are no longer runny. Sprinkle the cooked bacon on top and serve at once.

Variation: Low-Fat Fried Rice
Omit the bacon from the recipe above. Instead, lightly spray the pan with no-stick cooking oil or heat ¼ cup vegetable or chicken broth in the pan. Sauté the vegetables and follow the recipe above until the addition of the eggs. Or, instead of two whole eggs, add one whole egg and two egg whites beaten with the soy sauce.

Three-Bean Tuna Salad
For lunch on a warm day after a hike, this is ideal. Makes 4 to 6 portions.

1 15-ounce can kidney or white cannelini beans

1 15-ounce can black beans and garbanzo beans

1 6-ounce can of solid tuna in water, well-drained

¼ cup finely chopped red or green onions

2 tbsp. minced parsley, basil, oregano, or other fresh herb (optional)

Juice of 1 large lemon or lime

1 to 2 tbsp. olive oil

Drain and rinse beans in cold water. Combine beans in a mixing bowl. Add tuna, onions, parsley, lemon or lime juice, and olive oil. Toss gently and serve atop lettuce leaves. Can be prepared as much as a day ahead and refrigerated, tightly covered, until serving time.

Easy Low-Fat Oven-Fried Chicken
This is good hot or cold or in sandwiches. We sometimes make a double recipe and refrigerate part of it for another meal. Makes 4 portions.

4 boneless, skinless chicken breasts (about 1 pound)

½ cup vermouth, dry white wine, or chicken broth

1 minced clove of garlic

½ cup bread crumbs

2 tbsp. cornmeal

½ tsp. each cumin, ground cayenne pepper, and crumbled dry sage or
    thyme

Rinse chicken and pat dry. Marinate for 30 minutes in a mixture of vermouth
(or wine or chicken broth) and garlic.

Remove from marinade and dip each piece in a mixture of bread
crumbs, cornmeal, and a mixture of cumin, cayenne, and sage or thyme.
Arrange in baking pan that has been sprayed lightly with no-stick cooking
oil and bake at 450°F about 20 minutes or until no longer pink inside.

Campground Pizza

A special lunchtime treat for a lazy day in camp. Makes 6 to 8 slices.

1 large prepared pizza shell (Boboli and Contadina are two brands in
    the non-refrigerated deli section of the supermarket)

1 envelope (6–8 ounces) of prepared pizza sauce

Tomatoes, thinly sliced (optional)

Onions, thinly sliced (optional)

Pepperoni, thinly sliced, or low-fat turkey salami (optional)

Grated low-fat mozzarella and/or nonfat mozzarella (optional)

Preheat regular or toaster oven to 475°F. Following baking directions on the
package, put prepared pizza shell on a pizza tile, baking sheet, or large
piece of heavy or doubled aluminum foil. On the shell, smear prepared
pizza sauce. Top with thinly sliced tomatoes, thinly sliced onions, thinly
sliced regular pepperoni or low-fat turkey salami, and/or grated low-fat
mozzarella, mixed with nonfat mozzarella if desired. Cook following baking
directions for the shell, usually 10 to 12 minutes, and serve at once.

Microwave Fish Dinner

*We like this when we're driving along the coast and spot a fish market. Makes
2 main dish portions.*

2 skinless, boneless fresh fish fillets or steaks

1 cup diced, unpeeled red potatoes, parboiled until almost tender, then
    drained

1 cup thin spears of fresh asparagus or zucchini

Salt

White pepper

Juice of ½ to 1 fresh lemon

1 to 2 tbsp. olive oil

Arrange fish fillets side by side in the center of a Pyrex pie dish. Arrange peeled red potatoes around the edges of the dish. On top of the fish place asparagus or zucchini. Sprinkle lightly with salt and pepper and lemon juice, to taste. Drizzle olive oil across the top. Cover tightly with plastic wrap and microwave at high for 11 minutes. Serve with slices or chunks of fresh sourdough bread (optional).

Rest Area Huevos Rancheros

On a driving day, we like to start early in the morning with only some fruit or juice and a cup of tea, then stop later at a highway rest area for something more substantial. This dish takes less than 30 minutes from the start of cooking through cleanup after the meal. Makes 2 portions.

   2 to 4 corn tortillas

   ½ tbsp. butter

   2–4 eggs

   ¼ to ½ cup prepared salsa or canned enchilada sauce

Sauté tortillas in a nonstick skillet sprayed with no-stick cooking oil. When hot, remove to serving plates. Melt butter in the same pan. Fry eggs overeasy or as preferred. Put the cooked eggs atop the tortillas. Then add salsa or canned enchilada sauce to the same pan. Heat through and spoon atop eggs.

Low-Fat Huevos Rancheros

Warm the tortillas without oil in a nonstick skillet, at the same time poaching the eggs in water in a second pan. Remove tortillas, put drained poached eggs atop, and spoon over the heated salsa as directed above.

Quick Posole

This low-fat version of a full-meal, traditional winter soup from Mexico and New Mexico is easy to put together and good enough for guests. It's even better reheated the next day. Makes 4 to 6 portions.

   2 pounds of boneless, skinless chicken thighs, chopped into 1-inch
      pieces

   2 quarts chicken broth, canned or made from bouillon cubes or
      powder

   3 cloves minced garlic (optional)

   1 yellow onion, peeled and chopped

   1 teaspoon ground New Mexico chili (optional)

   1 sprig fresh or 1 tsp. dried thyme or oregano

   2 14-ounce cans of white or yellow hominy, drained and rinsed

Mix chicken, chicken broth, garlic, onion, chili, and thyme or oregano in a large soup pot. Simmer for an hour or so, then add hominy. Simmer until heated through. Serve in soup bowls with any or all the following toppings:

Thinly sliced raw radishes

Thinly sliced green cabbage

Diced avocado

Prepared corn chips

Lime wedges

Chopped red or green onions

Sprigs of fresh cilantro

Eggplant Parmesan

This dish can be prepared in a regular oven or a 650-watt microwave. Makes 2 to 3 main-dish servings, 4 to 6 side-dish servings.

1 medium eggplant cut into ½-inch slices, then diced

2 seeded, diced fresh tomatoes

1 to 2 cloves minced garlic

2 tbsp. chopped fresh basil or parsley (optional)

1 tbsp. olive oil

½ cup grated mozzarella

2 tbsp. freshly grated Parmesan cheese

Combine eggplant, tomatoes, garlic, basil or parsley, and olive oil in a baking dish. Cover tightly with aluminum foil and bake in 400°F regular oven 1 hour.

Uncover and sprinkle with mozzarella and Parmesan. Return to oven and bake 5 minutes or until cheese has melted.

To prepare in a microwave oven, put the cheeses on top of the eggplant/tomato mixture, cover tightly with plastic wrap, and microwave on high for 5 minutes.

One-Pot Garlic Spaghetti

This vegetarian dish contains heart-healthy olive oil and garlic. Makes 2 to 4 portions.

Spraying the cooking pot before adding the water keeps the spaghetti from sticking to the bottom, making the pan much easier to wash.

1 to 2 tbsp. salt

¼ pound dry spaghetti for each serving

¼ cup olive oil for two portions, ½ cup for four

4 to 6 cloves minced garlic

Minced fresh parsley, basil, and/or oregano (optional)

Parmesan cheese, freshly grated

Spray a very large cooking pot with no-stick cooking oil, fill with water, and add salt. When water is boiling rapidly, add spaghetti. Cook until *al dente* (just soft enough to bite through easily but not soft and flabby), then drain and rinse with hot water. Wipe out the spaghetti pot with a paper towel and return to the heat. Put in olive oil and garlic. Cook until garlic begins to sizzle, then stir in minced fresh parsley, basil, and/or oregano (optional) to taste. Return spaghetti to the pot and toss over heat until warmed through. Serve at once with optional freshly grated Parmesan cheese. A big green salad goes well with this, along with fruit and cheese for dessert.

French Vegetable Soup

This soup from the south of France is incredibly delicious, although it is simple and easy to make. It is even better with a spoonful of pesto stirred in just before serving. Makes 6 to 8 portions.

2 quarts water or chicken broth

2 cups unpeeled red or new white potatoes chopped into ½-inch cubes

2 cups green beans, cut into 2-inch pieces

2 to 3 zucchini, washed and sliced

2 cups tomatoes, preferably Roma, seeded and chopped into small pieces

4 ounces dry spaghetti, broken into short pieces

1 15-ounce can garbanzo beans or cannelini beans, drained and rinsed

Salt

Pepper

Parmesan cheese, grated, or pesto sauce (optional)

In a large soup pot, combine water or chicken broth, potatoes, green beans, zucchini, and tomatoes. Bring to a boil, lower heat, cover and simmer for one hour, then add spaghetti and garbanzo or cannelini beans. Cook until spaghetti is tender, season to taste with salt and pepper, then serve in wide soup bowls. Top each portion with optional grated Parmesan cheese or pesto sauce.

Microwave Polenta with Mushrooms

This trendy Italian dish technically takes two pots, one for the microwave and one for the top of the stove. We like this when we find fresh wild mushrooms in farmers' markets or supermarkets. The microwave eliminates all the tedious stirring from the traditional recipe, as well as cutting down the time considerably. Any leftovers can be put in a dish or small loaf pan and refrigerated to slice and sauté later for a side dish. Makes 2 to 4 portions.

4 cups water

1 cup yellow cornmeal

1 tsp. salt

1 pound wild or cultivated mushrooms (preferably a mix of several such as oyster, portabello, chanterelle, or shiitake)

1 tbsp. unsalted butter or margarine

1 tbsp. olive or other cooking oil

1 clove garlic, peeled and minced

2 to 3 tbsp. fresh sage leaves, chopped, or 1 tsp. dry sage

To make the polenta, mix water, cornmeal, and salt in a Pyrex microwavable bowl or large measuring bowl. Microwave uncovered for 12 minutes, stirring once about halfway through. Remove from microwave and let stand 3 minutes, then spoon onto serving plates.

While the polenta is cooking, prepare the mushroom sauce. Clean, trim, and slice the mushrooms. In a large nonstick skillet, melt butter and olive or cooking oil. Over medium heat, sauté the mushrooms until tender and lightly browned, about 5 to 8 minutes. Remove and keep warm. Sauté the garlic and sage in the same pan in the drippings.

Spoon polenta on warm serving plates, and top with mushroom sauce and herbs.

Don't Drink the Water

When there's no bottled water available in the fishing villages of Fiji or the mountainside inns of the Himalayas, we brush our teeth with scotch whiskey. We veto street-food vendors in Madras, Mazatlán, or Manhattan, and always skip summer shellfish salads, rare hamburgers, and anything with custard in it.

As veteran world travelers, we're cautious—some of our friends say overly cautious—but with a schedule that requires us to be on the road 60% of the time, we can't risk getting sick even for a day.

So, we decided long ago that whenever we're on the road, we'd stick with **bottled water** for drinking and cooking, and always use **bags of commercial ice,** using the campground water supply and the surplus stored in our tank only for washing and flushing. While most of the city water in North America is probably safe to drink, a constantly changing mineral content when you're making 1-night stands can throw your system off. We pick up 2 or 3 gallons at a time at a supermarket, convenience store, or campground store, put one in the galley and the others below in outside storage, and store a 7-pound plastic bag of ice cubes in the freezer.

People who have a restricted sodium intake would also be wise to use **sodium-free bottled water,** which is available in most supermarkets, since the sodium content of water varies widely from one campground area to the next.

A solution for RVers who don't want to buy ice and water is to use a **water filter**—either one that's permanently installed in the kitchen sink or one you temporarily hook up to the hose system when filling the tank initially.

Even more thorough is a **water purifier** that not only removes sediment from the water the way a filter does, but also takes out bacteria and delivers clean, good-tasting drinking water. (We use one in our kitchen at home for drinking water and the icemaker, but the cost is such that for the RV we'd just as soon stay with bottled water for daily use.)

A number of the new upscale motorhomes have a built-in water filter that serves both the kitchen and refrigerator ice maker. We also saw, at the Los Angeles RV Show, a Rexhall motorhome that was equipped with an optional water exchange, with which you could separate your own fresh water source for drinking and cooking and use the campground plug-in source for washing and flushing only.

It's wise to use **biodegradable toilet paper and holding-tank chemicals,** both available from camping supply stores and many campground stores. Follow the RV instruction booklet or the directions on the chemical container.

When you're driving every day, you rarely need to use your **water heater,** since the engine heat keeps the water hot.

Trimming Costs: Eight Money-Saving Tips for the Road

1. **Buy local produce.** Shopping at roadside fruit stands or farmers' markets will usually net the freshest and the cheapest local produce and give you a chance to chat with the locals.

2. **Watch for pick-your-own farms and orchards in season,** where a few minutes of work can save a lot of money on luxuries like fresh raspberries and cherries. One national park campground in Utah is set in the midst of fruit orchards where campers pick their own. (See chapter 6, "Utah's Parks and Canyons.")

3. **Clip coupons locally.** Pick up local newspapers or free throwaways in towns where you overnight and use the ads and supermarket discount coupons to save grocery money.

4. **Take advantage of capitalism.** If you see a local gas station having a price war with a neighboring station, turn around and go back and fill up your tank. You'd be surprised how many times that happens along the road.

5. **Cash or charge?** Some gas stations charge more when you use a credit card than when you pay cash. Keep your eye out for stations that list

the same price for credit or cash. If there's no sign that says so, ask before filling the tank.

6. **Don't skimp on service.** Spend that extra bit of money for regular engine and vehicle upkeep on a long haul. This saves a lot of money in the end.

7. **Be rational about your campground needs.** When overnighting in campgrounds that charge based on hookups and facilities used, opt for the most basic, since RVs are designed to be self-contained. (For more campground money-savers, see chapter 3, "Where to Sleep: Campgrounds & RV Parks.")

8. **Buy out of season** (antifreeze, for instance, in summer) and in quantity. When canned or paper goods are on sale in bulk, buy two or three for the house and two or three for the RV.

Safety, Sanity & Insurance

DRIVING TIPS

To combat glare, fog, snow, or oncoming headlights when driving after dark, slip on a pair of yellow glasses (sold in ski shops as ski goggles) or clip a pair over your regular glasses.

Binoculars for the navigator solve that ever-present problem of changing lanes with a large vehicle when approaching an on-ramp for an interstate. It's easy to look ahead to see if the entrance is from the left lane or the right lane.

The AARP (American Association of Retired Persons) puts out an excellent booklet called *Safety in RVs: A Moving Experience,* that is available free from the **Recreation Vehicle Industry Association (RVIA),** P.O. Box 2999, 1896 Preston White Dr., Reston, VA 22090. They point out various ways driving an RV is different (not more difficult) from driving your family car. Adjusting to the vehicle, taking care in inclement weather, and anticipating difficult situations ahead are stressed in the booklet. A separate chapter on towing and a detailed explanation of equipment and how to handle emergencies is also included.

SPEEDERS BEWARE

While exceeding the speed limit is never laudable, it can also be extremely inconvenient for residents of California, Alaska, Hawaii, Montana, Oregon, Michigan, and Wisconsin, states that are not signatories to the Non-Resident Violators Compact.

What it means is that drivers with license plates from these seven states are subject to having their driver's license confiscated and being required to go to the nearest office of a judge, sheriff, or justice of the peace to appear before an officer, post bond, and/or pay a fine. If said officer is not

AIN'T MISBEHAVIN': ROAD ETIQUETTE

1. **Don't hog the highway;** pull over at turnouts or into slow-moving lanes to let vehicles behind you have a chance to pass. In some states it's against the law for a slow-moving vehicle not to allow following vehicles to pass at the first opportunity when five or more are trailing.

2. **Keep in the right lane except when passing a car,** and when you do pass, make sure you have the speed and space to do it quickly and easily.

3. **As with your car, dimming your RV headlights for an approaching car is a must.** It is also a good idea to do the same when driving into a campground after dark.

4. **It seems customary to make a friendly wave to an oncoming RV as you meet,** particularly if it's a make and model similar to your own.

5. **Always signal your intention to turn or change lanes well ahead of time** so the driver in back of you has plenty of warning. Your vehicle is not as agile as those around you.

6. **Use binoculars to check out the road signs ahead** to make it easier to change lanes in heavy traffic. They are especially useful when trying to determine whether the interstate entry ramp will require being in the right or left lane, since changing lanes in a big vehicle takes additional time and distance.

7. **Keep your headlights on.** More and more states are requiring the use of headlights in the daytime. We think it should be mandatory throughout the country. It's amazing how some cars can blend into the roadway and suddenly appear headed your way, particular when you're planning to pass another car. Headlights on in the daytime can be a life-saving factor.

available, the individual may be jailed until a court appearance can be arranged, which may be several hours later.

SHOULD YOU CARRY A GUN IN YOUR RV?

If you want to start a lively argument around a campground, try this as an opener. We personally would never carry a firearm of any sort in our motorhome, but then we would never have one at home, either. While many frequent and full-timing RVers agree, just as many others disagree, sometimes vociferously.

Entering Mexico with a firearm of any sort can land an RV owner in jail—and did, in one famous case in 1993. A veteran RVer had bought a semi-automatic rifle at an Arizona gun show and stowed it, along with 500 rounds of ammunition, under the couch in his travel trailer. When the Mexican police found the AK-47 in the trailer and a pistol in his truck, they confiscated the vehicle, firearms, and ammunition, and put him in jail in

Hermasillo. Jailed in May, he spent months incarcerated with no bedding or regular meal service, both optional luxuries the prisoner's family members are expected to pay for, before his attorney could bring the case to trial. (See chapter 5, "Baja Bound: From Tijuana to Los Cabos.") Canada also prohibits entering the country with guns.

Despite our feelings that our motorhome is indeed our home, the law in many states considers the RV a motor vehicle when moving and a home only when parked in camp. Therefore, any firearms carried must be unloaded and the bullets kept separately from the weapon when in transit.

Firearms are also prohibited in many state parks.

If we did choose to carry a firearm, we would make it a point to keep abreast of the regulations in every state, which can differ radically the minute you cross a state line.

Firearm Laws of the Fifty States by J. Scott Kappas (60 pages, $9.95, published by Traveler's Guide, P.O. Box 2156, Covington, KY 41012, ☎ **606/647-5100**), delineates the firearm laws for each state and deals with carrying a firearm in a vehicle.

SHOULD YOU CARRY A CELLULAR PHONE IN YOUR RV?

We always do, but it provides almost as much frustration as assistance. The places we like to drive and camp are frequently, if not always, in a border-line or "no service" area, even though we have (and are willing to pay a siz-able sum for) a Follow Me Roaming system that theoretically can forward our calls to almost anywhere in the U.S. and Canada we happen to be. Our editors have been able to reach us in the wilds of British Columbia or when we're driving down an interstate in west Texas, but can't seem to get through to us when we're on a 2-day outing in a national park in San Diego or Santa Barbara counties, only a hoot and a holler from our Los Angeles base.

We find cellulars most helpful for dialing ahead for a campground reservation or for returning business calls we've picked up from our answering machine when the campground or highway pay phones are too noisy. And we are certainly happy to have one in case of an emergency, which we have had to deal with on occasion.

The technology leaves something to be desired, with voices fading in and out when you're in a fringe reception area. The cost is almost prohibitive because you pay for connecting to the roamer system as well as the elapsed time for any calls whether incoming or outgoing. Some new pricing plans include long distance and roaming charges throughout the United States for a flat fee for a certain number of minutes, but these plans are costly unless you plan to make a lot of calls.

A 1,185-page guide promising **all you need to know about roaming** is available for $19.95 from Communications Publishing, Box 500, Mercer Island, WA 98040 (☎ **800/927-8800;** www.telecompublishing.com). It includes areas with maps, rates, instructions on sending and receiving for many cities, and roaming agreements.

If you are reluctant to invest in a cellular phone, be aware that most private campgrounds and many public campgrounds have a pay phone on the premises.

SIX OFF-THE-WALL TIPS FOR RV AILMENTS

1. **To remember to lower your TV antenna** before pulling out of the campground, put some sort of label or tag—one RVer suggests a spring-loaded clothespin—on the antenna crank in the travel position. When the antenna is up, put the same tag or device on the gearshift or steering wheel. Then as you prepare to move out, the item will remind you the antenna is still raised.

2. **To get unstuck** when mired in snow, mud, or sand, one Canadian RVer suggests using two strips of metal plasterer's lath, available in hardware stores, approximately 10 by 30 inches each, either in front of or behind the drive axle wheels to extricate the vehicle. The lath can be hosed off and stored flat to be reused as many times as needed.

3. **To get rid of mice,** tuck sheets of Downey fabric softener around the sofa, under the sinks, and near the furnace.

4. **When lights or turn signals on a tow vehicle fail to work,** spray white vinegar on the electrical connectors.

5. **When sensors on holding tanks for gray and black water do not read properly,** a Prodigy online bulletin board subscriber suggests filling the problem tank half full of water and adding a half cup of Dawn liquid dish detergent before leaving home, then emptying the tank on arrival at the campground. He suggests repeating the technique if the first effort doesn't fix it.

6. **To do the wash,** a Nevada man reminds us of the hero in *The Accidental Tourist* with his suggestion: Put hot water, dirty clothes, soap, and a tennis shoe (to act as an agitator) in a large beverage cooler and strap the whole thing to the rear bumper of the motorhome. At lunchtime, empty the soapy water in an appropriate spot, refill the cooler with clean water, and drive on into the afternoon. In camp, set up a clothesline and hang the clean laundry out to dry.

RV INSURANCE

We were pleasantly surprised to find our RV insurance was very affordable, even in costly southern California. Safe driving records, a shorter use period during the year, and slightly older drivers on the average mean less risk for the insurer. Before buying, check your own automobile insurance carrier as well as specialized RV insurance carriers, such as **Good Sam Club's National General** (☎ 800/234-3450), **Foremost Insurance Company**

(☎ 800/545-8608), **AARP Insurance** (☎ 800/541-3717), **RV Alliance America** (☎ 800/521-2942), and for Mexican insurance, **Sanborn's** (☎ 800/222-0158) or **Oscar Padilla** (☎ 800/258-8600). Towing insurance in case of a breakdown is a good idea; in many cases, AAA members can extend that company's towing coverage to their RV. For a more extensive discussion of coverage and insurers, see *The RV Money Book,* by Bob Howells, a *Trailer Life* book, $29.95 (under "Financing," in chapter 15).

The Community of Man: Getting Together with Other RVers

CARAVANS & RALLIES

RVers who would prefer to travel or camp with a group can join up with any number of like-minded people for a paid vacation tour that they make in their own rig instead of a tour bus, or a friendly get-together with other owners of the same brand of RV. Caravans are the RV equivalent of a group tour with structured itineraries, sightseeing, communal meals, and many group social functions.

Popular caravan destinations include Mexico, Alaska, and New England at autumn foliage time. To find out about caravan and club tours, read general monthly RV publications such as *Trailer Life* and *MotorHome,* available by subscription or from most magazine racks; *Family Motor Coaching Magazine; Highways* (for Good Sam Club members); or other club or RV manufacturing company publications.

RV CLUBS

American Sunbathing Association. For nudist RVers; has RV parks in many states. Call ☎ **407/933-2064** for information.

Baby Boomers. For RV enthusiasts born between 1940 and 1960. P.O. Box 23, Stoneham, CO 80754.

Escapees Incorporated. Founded in 1978 by veteran RV writers Joe and Kay Peterson, Escapees is a support system for full-timers. Membership numbers more than 33,000. Members have pooled resources to build their own nonprofit RV parks across the country, as well as creating a new CARE program that provides parking facilities and support services for temporarily or permanently incapacitated full-timers. % Cathy Carr, 100 Rainbow Dr., Livingston, TX 77351. ☎ **409/327-8873.**

Family Motor Coach Association. For owners of self-propelled, self-contained vehicles with cooking, sleeping, and permanent sanitary facilities in which the living quarters can be accessed directly from the driver's seat. Members number around 170,000 families, each with its own ID number. The group provides a handsome monthly magazine and other benefits, including insurance. Costs are $35 for a family, including initiation fee and first year dues. 8291 Clough Pike, Cincinnati, OH 45244. ☎ **800/ 543-3622.**

Good Sam Club. A broad-range club with insurance, campground affiliates, financing, and other services. Members number nearly a million, and the club also has special-interest chapters for hobbyists, computer aficionados, singles, the deaf, and others. ℅ Susan Bray, 2575 Vista Del Mar Dr., Ventura, CA 93001-3920. ☎ **800/234-3450.**

Handicapped Travel Club. For disabled individuals who enjoy traveling and camping; also welcomes the non-handicapped. For membership requirements, send self-addressed, stamped, long-form envelope with first-class postage to 5929 Ourway, Citrus Heights, CA 95610. ☎ **916/961-1611.**

Loners on Wheels. Now 25 years old, Loners on Wheels is a club for single RVers, numbering around 3,000 widowed, divorced, or never-married members. While members who subsequently give up traveling alone turn into non-members, they are welcomed back at special anniversaries and rallies. P.O. Box 1355, Poplar Bluff, MO 63902. Fax **314/686-9342.**

RV Birdwatchers Club. With caravans for birders. ☎ **812/295-2729.**

RV Elderhostel. Offers study groups for RV owners at universities or on the road in caravans along a historic route. 80 Boylston St., Suite 400, Boston, MA 02116. ☎ **617/426-7788.**

Vagabundos del Mar. A club of RV travelers who spend a lot of time in Mexico. Also provides Mexican auto insurance and information on RV parks south of the border. 190 Main St., Rio Vista, CA 94571. ☎ **707/374-5511.**

Wandering Individual Network. For single RVers born after 1926. The group has a newsletter and rallies. P.O. Box 2010, Sparks, NV 89432. ☎ **800/445-1732.**

COMPUTER ONLINE SERVICES

Online RV bulletin boards on computer services such as AOL allow RV enthusiasts or "wannabe" RVers to exchange dialogue, give helpful hints, and discuss the pros and cons of the various vehicle brands.

The greatest use of on-board computers is for e-mail connection to the rest of the world. More and more campgrounds provide phone jacks to connect to your Internet service, some without charge, some for a modest charge if it is a local call to connect. Some upscale campgrounds now have phone connections at the site for those newer motorhomes that have phone lines built into the wiring system.

Where to Sleep: Campgrounds & RV Parks

THE ANSWER TO THE QUESTION OF WHERE TO SLEEP IN YOUR RV IS "Almost anywhere." There are more than 16,000 campgrounds in the United States that can accommodate RVs, some offering hookups, others for self-contained or "dry" camping.

A few are free, but many more are lavish resorts that may cost $25 a night and up for full hookups, cable TV, phone service, spas, swimming pools, tennis courts, playgrounds, and miniature or par-three golf courses.

If you prefer ranger hikes and scenery to horseshoe pits and pancake breakfasts, head for one of the 29,000 campsites in our national parks and monuments. The national forest service has 4,000 developed campgrounds in 155 forests, and the Bureau of Land Management oversees 270 million acres of scenic outdoor sites, many with free camping.

Mini-motorhome in a tree-shaded campsite near Anacortes, WA

For watery wonderlands, check out the Corps of Engineers projects, with 53,000 campsites near oceans, rivers, and lakes, with fishing, boating, swimming, and water-skiing on tap.

Bird watchers can overnight in many of the nation's wildlife refuges to get the drop on feathery friends, and game watchers can take advantage of the optimum spotting times of dawn and dusk. (See "The Best Campground Directories," below, for how to get a full listing of wildlife refuge camping, as well as guides for all the other campgrounds.)

Campground Glossary

Black water: Waste water from the toilet.

Boondock: To camp without electrical or other hookups.

Dual electrical system: An RV system in which lights and other electrical systems can run on 12-volt battery power, 110 AC electrical hookup, or gas generator.

Dump station: Also called sanitary dump, disposal station, and so on; this is where an RV dumps the gray water and black water from its holding tanks.

Gray water: Waste water from the sinks and shower.

Hookups: Umbilical cords that connect your RV with electrical power, water, and sewer service. (*Full hookups* are sites furnished with all three connections. *Partial hookups* are sites furnished with one or two of the three connections.)

Propane or LPG: Liquefied petroleum gas used for heating, cooking, and refrigeration in RVs.

Pull-through: A campsite that allows the driver to pull into the site to park, then pull out the other side when leaving, without ever having to back up—a boon for beginners.

Spirit level: A device for determining true horizontal or vertical directions by the centering of a bubble in a slightly curved glass tube or tubes filled with alcohol or ether. Some RVs come with built-in levels. If yours does not, small spirit levels can be purchased in hardware stores or RV supply centers.

Three-way refrigerator: An RV refrigerator/freezer that can operate on LP gas, electrical hookup, or gas generator.

Should You Sleep by the Side of the Road?

While more than half the states permit some overnight parking in highway rest areas, except where posted, we feel there have been too many recent incidents of violence in these areas and would not consider parking overnight in our RV in a rest area, shopping mall parking lot, truck stop, or by the side of the road. Some of our friends frequently do, however, and consider us money-wasting wimps for insisting on overnighting at a secure private or public campground.

The thing that constantly amazes us is how many owners of very expensive motorhomes take the risk of sleeping free in a parking lot or by the side of the road when the cost of their vehicle advertises how much in cash, credit cards, and expensive electronics might be inside. All this to save $12 or $15? Campground fees are a modest enough investment in security and peace of mind. Besides, unlike RVers, the poor truckers with whom you share the road have few other options when they need to take a rest. Why take up their space?

Campsites: The Good, the Bad & the Ugly

As backpackers, we would set up camp at any clearing that didn't have too many rocks where we planned to spread out the ground cloth and sleeping bags.

As tent campers, we looked for scenery, shelter, and seclusion, but not too far away from the water source and facilities.

Now, as RV campers, we have a long list of Ls:

- **Location:** We want to be away from the highway and campground entrance and not too near the swimming pool, bath facilities, garbage dumpster, playground, or dog-walking area.

- **Large:** It must be big enough to back our 27-foot motorhome in and park it, and still have space for chairs, table, and charcoal grill.

- **Level:** There's a lot of running back and forth to check spirit levels inside and outside the vehicle; sometimes we have to wedge wooden blocks under the tires until that pesky little bubble hits the center. Hydraulic jacks make this procedure much easier. (What happens if it's not level? Something dire and expensive befalls the refrigerator.)

- **Length:** The umbilical cords from the vehicle to the electric, water, and sewer connections (where applicable) must reach comfortably.

- **Look out:** Watch for any low-hanging branches or wires that could damage the roof air conditioner or TV antenna; for a potentially noisy neighbor; for wet or marshy ground that could mire you down if it should rain all night.

A rustic private campground on Michigan's Upper Peninsula

A campsite may or may not contain a picnic table, grill, or fire ring. What is critical for tent campers becomes an added luxury for an RVer, who already has a table, chairs, and cookstove inside the vehicle. While we all want to overnight in the very best campgrounds, we find that campground ratings—for example, those in the popular *Trailer Life Campground/RV Park & Services Directory*—do not always seem to relate to us. The guide, issued annually, rates campgrounds very specifically according to a detailed form that scores in three areas: facilities, cleanliness (particularly of toilets and showers), and visual or environmental appeal.

Since we always use our own toilet and shower facilities, we are not concerned with the campground's, and we rarely if ever take advantage of a TV lounge, swimming pool, Saturday night dance, or children's playground.

Therefore, for us, a highly rated campground may have less appeal than a remote area in a national forest or state park, or a simpler family-run park in the country.

Occasionally, in both private and state park campgrounds, you may encounter what we call a **"parking lot" design,** with rows of paved spaces fairly close together. The up side is that you're usually level and don't have to spend time checking spirit level bubbles and putting ramps (otherwise known as wedges) under tires. The down side is that your dining room window may be 2 feet away from your neighbor. The saving grace is that with an RV you can close your curtains or blinds, turn on some soft music, and be all alone in the universe.

On the other hand, we are always thrilled to find those enlightened campground owners who have spent extra time and money to create **terraced areas** with landscaping that gives a sense of space, light, and privacy.

Using the Directories to Find a Campground

While we frequently are at odds with campground ratings, we find the directories, especially the one from *Trailer Life*, invaluable when traveling, particularly when we're making one-night stands and need to find a place to overnight. Being able to call ahead for reservations is also helpful; you won't have to drive 5 miles off the route only to find there are no campsites left. This is where a cell phone comes in handy (see discussion in chapter 2, "Getting Prepared: RVing Tips & Hints").

Careful reading of an entry can also tell you the site width (important if you have an awning or slideout); if there are pull-throughs; if you can expect any shade trees; if the campground is open year-round or only seasonally; and if there's a dump station on the premises.

THE BEST CAMPGROUND DIRECTORIES

Bureau of Land Management, 270 million acres of public land. Ask for camping information from BLM, Department of Interior–MIB, 1849 C St. NW, Room 5600, Washington, DC 20240. Free.

KOA, 615 campgrounds in the U.S., Canada, and Mexico. You can receive a guide free, or send $3 for an annual guide from Kampgrounds of America Executive Offices, P.O. Box 30558, Billings, MT 59114-0558.

National Forest Service, 4,000 campgrounds. Write to U.S. Department of Agriculture Forest Service, Public Affairs Office, P.O. Box 96090, Washington, DC 20090-6090. Free.

National Park Camping Guide, 440 campgrounds. U.S. Government Printing Office, Superintendent of Documents, Washington, DC 20402-9325. Ask for stock #024-005-01080-7. $4.

A luxurious private RV park in Bend, OR

CAMPGROUND COSTS

A family of four can vacation in a family campground for less than $200 a week, and a snowbird can spend the entire winter in a full-service warm-climate resort for less than $2,000, according to the National Association of RV Parks and Campgrounds.

National Wildlife Refuges, 488 refuges. For free publications write to U.S. Fish and Wildlife Services, Public Affairs Office, 1849 C St. NW, MS-5600/MIB, Washington, D.C., 20240 (☎ 202/452-5125).

Trailer Life Campground/RV Park and Services Directory, 2575 Vista del Mar Dr., Ventura, CA 93001 (☎ 800/234-3450), covers 12,500 campgrounds in the U.S., Canada, and Mexico. Available at bookstores and camping stores, or write to above address. $20.

U.S. Army Corps of Engineers, 53,000 campsites near oceans, rivers, and lakes. For free publications write to U.S. Army Corps of Engineers, OCE Publications Depot, 2803 52nd Ave., Hyattsville, MD 20781-1102 (☎ 301/394-0081).

Wheelers RV Resort & Campground Directory, Print Media Services, 1310 Jarvis Ave., Elk Grove Village, IL 60007. $12.95.

Woodall's Campground Directory, 28167 North Keith Dr., Box 5000, Lake Forest, IL 60045-5000. $16.95.

Yogi Bear's Jellystone Park Campground Directory, Leisure Systems, Inc., 6201 Kellogg Ave., Cincinnati, OH 45230. Free.

Ten Ways to Save Money on Campgrounds

1. **Never pay for more park than you'll use.** Posh playgrounds with swimming pool, spas, tennis courts, and miniature golf are usually pricier than simple, clean mom-and-pop campgrounds. The latter are adequate for an overnight stay. If there is a charge per hookup, take the electric and water and forgo the sewer unless you really need it.

2. **Remember, you can camp without hookups comfortably for several nights** as long as you don't insist on using the TV, air conditioner, or microwave. Read a book or listen to a tape for entertainment, and cook on your gas cooktop or outdoors on a grill. You'll still have running water, lights, refrigeration, heat, and hot water for dishes and shower.

3. **If you're on a tight budget, watch out for campground surcharges** such as extra fees for running your air conditioner or hooking up to

cable TV, a surcharge for 50-amp electricity, or "extra person" charges for more than two people when you're traveling with your kids. Some of the campgrounds that accept pets may also levy a fee on Fido's head.

4. **Join membership clubs that offer a discount to member campgrounds,** such as KOA (Kampgrounds of America) and Good Sam, which usually discount 10%. KOA promises the discount whether you pay by cash or credit card; Good Sam usually grants the discount only if you pay cash. In most cases, you can join up right at the campground when you register.

5. **Take advantage of age.** If one of you is over 62 and applies for a free Golden Age Passport with proof of age at a national park visitor center, your vehicle enters the park, national monument, recreation area, or wildlife refuge free, and gets a 50% discount on overnight camping areas administered by the federal government.

6. **Look for free campgrounds,** such as those in the southwestern desert, administered by the Bureau of Land Management.

7. **Invest in a current campground guide** or request a state tourism office's free campground listings. County, city, and national forest campgrounds range from free to considerably less expensive than most privately owned campgrounds, although they do not often offer the luxury of hookups.

8. **If you arrive late at a campground, ask about staying overnight self-contained in an overflow area at a reduced price.** Some owners are amenable, some are not.

9. **Stay longer than a week and you can negotiate discounts,** usually from 10% to 20% or even more, depending on the season and length of stay.

10. **Consider volunteering as a campground host** if you're interested in staying a long time in one area. You can camp free and may pick up a bit of pocket change in exchange for performing specified duties on the premises. (See "How to Become Campground Hosts" later in this chapter.)

Membership Campgrounds

Membership campgrounds and resorts are sort of like time-share condos, meaning that once an RVer is a member, he can stay at any of the areas participating with the group. Joining something of this sort has to be weighed carefully against the initial cost, the amount of time you'll stay in the various resorts (note the locations and your access to them), and the amenities they offer.

BEWARE OF MEMBERSHIP SCAMS

A recurring scam affecting people advertising campground memberships for sale goes like this: An individual contacts the seller, says he has a buyer, then sends an official-looking contract with buyer name and purchase price by Federal Express. All the eager seller has to do is send back a certified check for $500 or so by return FedEx. You can guess what happens next—nothing.

For example, we recently checked out two upscale membership RV resorts affiliated with **Outdoor Resorts of America** in the Palm Springs area (see chapter 4, "The California Desert & Las Vegas," for details), the older of which is owner-operated and mostly owner-occupied. We were quite impressed with the cleanliness and security, as well as the landscaping. A great many expensive motorhomes and fifth-wheels, as well as a few more modest travel trailers and mini-motorhomes, are parked seasonally or permanently on the sites, many of them owned by southern Californians who use them as a weekend home in the desert.

While a few owners make their sites available for overnighters or transient RVers, most seem to keep their vehicles based there. The base lot price in the newer park limited to motorhomes is $36,900 to $51,900 for a 35- by 69-foot site, plus a monthly fee of $180.

There are about 450 membership resorts nationwide for RV travelers who want a range of indoor and outdoor activities. Most sell memberships for a one-time fee, much like a country club, plus an annual or monthly fee. One such company, **Thousand Trails/NACO,** based in Bellingham, Washington, and owned by U.S. Trails in Dallas, Texas, estimates it has 150,000 members in North America, with about 10,000 using the campground chain year-round as full-timers. Members who use the campgrounds for fewer than 50 nights a year pay no surcharge, said a spokesman for Thousand Trails, while those who use them more than 50 nights a year pay a $2 fee for each additional night. Except during peak travel seasons, RVers can usually find a spot without advance reservations. Call Thousand Trails at ☎ **800/288-7245** for details and reservations, which can be made up to 90 days in advance.

INSIDER TIP: GATHERING INFORMATION

Always stop at the tourist information offices or welcome centers when you enter a new state on an interstate highway. You can pick up everything from maps to campground booklets to individual flyers for private RV parks that may offer a discount for visitors—all of it free.

In general, the spokesman said, the cost of joining a membership campground has dropped considerably from a peak of $5,000 to $10,000 a few years ago. Thousand Trails members currently pay $1,500 membership with annual fees of $429. Thousand Trails/NACO membership campgrounds offer potential members a chance to try out their product with no obligation to buy or attend a sales presentation. A 2-night stay in any of the company's 62 campgrounds costs $29.95

On all membership campgrounds, memberships can be sold after a specified period of time, but it appears to be a buyer's market with a lot of members opting to sell.

Because some membership resorts in the past have been plagued by bankruptcies and undelivered promises, potential buyers should check with the local Better Business Bureau, the state attorney general's office, and members of the prospective resort before signing up or making a payment.

Avoid resorts that use high-pressure sales tactics and promise big prizes for buyers who sign up right away. And be wary of resorts that seem reluctant to provide information unless you make a personal visit. If you're interested in buying someone's membership, check the classified ads each month in RV magazines such as *Trailer Life* and *MotorHome.*

Special Camping Situations

CAMPING WITH KIDS

Children make great campers.

Veterans of family camping suggest involving children in the preliminary planning, assigning regular duties at the campsite, assigning seats in the car or RV en route to the campsite, and curfew and campfire times, taking into consideration any special evening events from ranger talks to movies and dances at the campground. Older children might also be assigned a last-minute duty at home before leaving, whether locking doors and windows or removing perishable food from the refrigerator.

Even infants can happily go camping. Experts recommend taking along a backpack for a toddler or a chest pack for an infant for hikes, as well as a folding stroller and playpen, mosquito netting and a baby guardrail for the bed to use in camp. A baby seat that clamps to a picnic table will also allow the child to participate with the rest of the family at meals or game time.

Sunscreen to protect a baby's delicate skin is essential, along with a gentle insect repellent like Avon's Skin So Soft skin lotion. (That works for adults as well; we've used it successfully in buggy places like the jungles of Honduras.)

CAMPING WITH PETS

Six percent of all traveling dog owners take their pets with them on vacation, but only 1% of cat owners do, according to the Travel Industry Association of America. Here are 10 tips that'll keep you and your campground neighbors from wishing that figure was lower.

- **Keep the cat's litter box in the shower or tub, encased inside a 30-gallon plastic trash bag.** Put the bottom of the box in the trash bag, dump a 10-pound bag of kitty litter inside, and snap on the litter box cover. The same cat owner who suggested this to us carries a folding cat cage so her pets can enjoy the outdoors.

- **Put a throw rug or two on top of the carpeting** in a motorhome to protect it from little cat (or dog) feet. They can be taken out and shaken when necessary, and washed and dried in the campground laundry.

- **Decide whether or not to use a kennel crate.** Owners get into lively debates about whether to keep dogs and cats sheltered in airline-type kennel crates when the RV is in motion, or to let them lie about on the floor, furniture, or dash. The lie-about school suggests the pet could protect itself better from possible injury in an accident if he's free, while the kennel crowd (many of them professional dog handlers) assert just as doggedly that the pet (and the driver) are much safer enclosed en route.

- **Always carry plastic baggies to pick up after your pet,** even in camping and hiking areas (or should we say especially in camping and hiking areas?).

- **Never leave your pet alone in the RV for more than 10 minutes in any weather,** and less than that in summer when heat can cause great discomfort or even death.

- **Feed pets at night only** (especially if they're susceptible to motion sickness), so they will have digested the food before the next day's drive. Give only water during the day, preferably bottled water, which you have introduced at home several days before leaving.

- **Check in a campground guide to ascertain whether the campground will accept pets.** While many do, some assess a surcharge, and all require that dogs be kept on a leash. When in doubt, call ahead. (See "The Best Campground Directories," above, for a list of campgrounds.)

AIN'T MISBEHAVIN': CAMPGROUND ETIQUETTE

1. **No claim jumping.** Anything marking a campsite, from a jug of water on a picnic table to a folding chair set out in the parking space, means that site is occupied and the campers are temporarily away in their car or RV. You may not set it aside and move into the site.

2. **Mind your fellow campers' personal space.** Teach your kids never to take a shortcut across an occupied campsite, but to use the road or established pathways to get where they're going.

3. **Keep your pets from roaming.** Never let your dog roam free in a campground. It should be walked on a leash and exercised in a designated pet area.

4. **Avoid using your generator whenever possible,** even within designated generator-use hours, to keep from disturbing other campers with the noise and fumes. If using electrical appliances such as microwaves and TV sets is that important, go camping in a private campground with hookups.

5. **Avoid loud and prolonged engine revving** in the early morning and late evening hours.

6. **Don't play radios, TVs, or boom boxes loudly at any time in a campground.** Many of your fellow campers are there to enjoy the peace and quiet.

7. **Never ever dump waste water from holding tanks, even gray water, on the ground.** While some old-timers claim it's good for the grass, it can also contain virulent salmonella bacteria if raw chicken has been rinsed in the sink, or bits of fecal matter from diapers. This matter can be transferred to anyone touching or stepping on contaminated ground. Gray water, like black water, belongs only in a dump station.

8. **Do not cut trees for firewood.** Most campgrounds sell firewood at special stands or the camp store. Even picking up or chopping dead wood is forbidden in many parks.

9. **Watch what you throw in the fire.** Never leave aluminum foil, aluminum cans, bottles, or filter-tipped cigarette butts in a campground fire ring or grill. They do not burn but remain as litter. And never crush out cigarettes on the ground without picking up the butts and putting them in the garbage.

10. **Don't leave porch or entry lights on all night in camp;** they may shine in someone else's bedroom window.

- **Bring familiar bedding and toys for the pet,** and spend some time regularly for about a week ahead of setting off on its first trip just sitting with your pet in the RV to help accustom him to it.

- **Bring along your pet's shot records and extra leashes and collars,** as well as flea treatment products that will kill not only live fleas but eggs and larvae as well.

- **Good Sam Club members can take advantage of the club's Lost Pet Service.** They provide a tag imprinted with a toll-free number to call so your pet can be returned during rather than after the trip.

WINTER CAMPING

Some of our best RVing adventures have been in winter in snow-covered campgrounds in national parks such as the Grand Canyon and Bryce Canyon, as well as at various ski resorts. Skiers on a budget will find that many good ski areas permit free, or low-cost, self-contained RV parking overnight in their parking lots—Killington and Aspen Highlands, for example—while other resorts such as Breckenridge, Deer Valley, and New York's Holiday Valley have RV hookups or year-round RV campgrounds at or near the site. California's Sierra Summit has free RV hookups for skiers.

Many RVers enjoy snowmobiling, sledding, cross-country skiing, skating, and ice fishing in winter. Besides being able to stay toasty warm with a propane heater that does not require a hookup, winter RVers can enjoy hot meals, hot showers, and a snug, cozy feeling despite ice and snow all around.

We've found winter a good time to visit and photograph national parks, particularly in the Southwest, where a light dusting of snow highlights the vivid red canyons and green pines. Another bonus is the wildlife, especially deer and elk, that comes down into lower elevations in winter for better feeding. (See chapter 6, "Utah's Parks and Canyons.")

Ten Tips for Cozy Winter Camping

1. **Don't connect your water hose to an outdoor faucet overnight** unless you want to create a 12-foot Popsicle. Use water from the RV's supply and refill when necessary.

2. **Add antifreeze to holding tanks** to keep drains from freezing.

3. **Don't park under trees** where branches heavily weighted with snow and ice could break off and fall on your RV.

4. **Watch battery strength;** the colder it gets, the faster it will discharge.

5. **Open one window slightly for fresh air when using a propane heater;** we use the window above the kitchen sink.

6. **Leave the bathroom door open at night** so the heat from the main living area can circulate inside this normally unheated room.

7. **Keep a pair of après-ski boots handy** for good traction on even short walks through the snow, especially to a photo opportunity.

MAKING CAMPSITE RESERVATIONS BY PHONE

You can call ☎ **800/280-2267** for campsite reservations in national forests and U.S. Army Corps of Engineers Campgrounds—although the line is usually busy or applicants wait on hold for a long time. The line is operative daily from 7am to midnight eastern standard time. Their Web site is **www.reserveusa.com**.

8. **Carry chains** or have snow tires for your tow vehicle or motorized RV.

9. **Don't let snow accumulate** on the refrigerator roof vent or exhaust ports.

10. **Drive with extreme care.** Even an experienced driver will find handling a motorhome or pulling a towable trickier in snow and ice. A heavy motorhome can be difficult to stop on an icy surface.

Plugging in Your Rig

ELECTRICAL HOOKUPS

Many older campgrounds, especially in state parks, may have 15- or 20-amp electrical hookups, for which modern RVs with a three-prong plug will need an adapter. When we first encountered this, we happened to be at a Texas state park that loaned out adapters, but we soon acquired one of our own. You can use the lower amperage so long as you remember not to run the air conditioner, microwave, and TV set at the same time. Otherwise, you'll blow a fuse.

Each manufacturer issues a list of the amperage used by the various appliances, such as TV, refrigerator, microwave, and air conditioners. The total amperage of those units in use should not exceed your campground hookup amperage limitation, which is 15-, 20-, 30-, or 50-amp. If you do exceed it, the power goes off, which is not so much a problem if you are in a campground with circuit breakers. But older campgrounds still using fuses will make resetting more difficult. Learn when to turn off one appliance when turning on another to keep from going over the limit.

CABLE TV

Many private RV parks offer cable TV connections as an option, sometimes with an added dollar or two on the nightly fee. If you don't have a built-in exterior cable connection, you can use a length of coaxial cable hooked to the campground connection at one end, then routed through a window to your RV's TV set. You can also use an alternative outdoor entertainment area hookup as the connector. It's best if you carry your own cable, since the campground often does not provide it. Don't forget to turn off the switch to your roof antenna. (It usually has a little red light beside it.) It is also wise to have a male and female connector since campground cable connections vary.

SATELLITE TV

Newer models of RVs now have satellite dishes mounted to the roof of the vehicle with internal wiring to the control box, which is usually installed near the TV set. The software for whatever program system you use is usually included with the package. (The two major systems are DISH and DirecTV.) One disadvantage in the mounted dish is that in many campgrounds there is inevitably a tree in the direct path of the satellite signal, requiring you to move the vehicle to make a connection. If you have such a system, it is wise to mention it when checking in so the registrar can assign you a site that might be tree-free.

We carry a portable dish on a tripod using a secondary control box from our home, which means we don't have to have a separate account for the RV. We've found that it is a simple matter to make a connection to the satellite by being able to move the dish to an open viewing area. Satellite dishes are particularly advantageous when you travel in rural areas with little or no local TV reception, or when you plan to stay in one area for several days.

Remember, your dish programming is set on your home time, so as you move to other time zones, programs are still based on your home time. West Coast travelers RVing on the East Coast will find their 8pm programs can't be seen until 11pm.

PART 2

RV Adventures

Hitting the road on ten great RV excursions

4

The California Desert & Las Vegas

ACTUALLY, THERE'S NOT ONE DESERT IN CALIFORNIA, BUT MANY—**Death Valley's** low desert with its sizzling heat records, the **Mojave's** high desert with its ghost towns and mines, and vast **Anza Borrego,** the biggest state park in California with 600,000 acres of cactus and canyons. Death Valley and Joshua Tree, previously designated national monuments, were recently turned into national parks by Congress after 9 years of petitioning.

And then there's The Desert: **Palm Springs** and vicinity, where Beverly Hills goes to desiccate, safe and circumspect once again after its own Desert Storm action when the late celebrity-mayor Sonny Bono outlawed teen spring-break frivolities and put Palm Canyon Drive back in the hands of the Waxworks. It's where 10,000 swimming pools and countless lawn sprinklers, waterslides, and misting outdoor air conditioners turn once bone-dry air damp; where cows are allotted 1,000 acres of feeding area apiece to browse on vitamin-rich desert spinach; and where the Manson Family hid out at a run-down movie ranch rehearsing murder and mayhem.

The California deserts gave us trail mix and date milk shakes, the state's first nudist bed-and-breakfast hotels, the world's first broken sound barrier, 20-Mule-Team Borax, and the Twentynine Palms Outhouse Race.

It's where Wyatt Earp retired, where Al Capone took the waters, where Lawrence of Arabia rode his camel across the dunes, where General Patton left his tank tracks, and where Paul Newman, Steve McQueen, and James Garner learned how to drive race cars.

It's where Elvis and Priscilla Presley honeymooned, where Frank Sinatra lived on Frank Sinatra Drive, and where old-time radio favorites Jack Benny, Amos and Andy, and Fibber McGee and Molly beamed their shows out to a kinder, simpler nation.

RVers can find the Hullabaloo World Tobacco Spitting Championships in Calico every Palm Sunday, visit an endangered desert pupfish in Anza–Borrego State Park, go to camel and ostrich races in Indio during the National Date Festival in mid-February, and go sand-sailing on a dry lake at speeds up to 70 m.p.h.—with no brakes.

California Desert Highlights

Amargosa Opera House ❸
Antelope Valley Indian Museum ⓫
Barstow Station ❼
Cabazon Dinosaurs ⓮
Calico ghost town ❻
Casa del Zorro ㉔
Coachella Valley Preserve ⓲
Cottonwood Visitor Center, Joshua Tree National Park ⓬
El Mirage dry lake ⓬
Exotic World, The Strippers' Hall of Fame ❽
Furnace Creek Inn and Ranch Resort ❷
General Patton Memorial Museum ㉑
Hadley Orchard ⓰
Heartland, the California Museum of the Heart ❹
Hotel Nipton ❹
Ingleside Inn ⓰
Jiberto's Taco Shop ㉔
La Mancha ⓰
La Quinta Resort and Club ⓳
Legoland California ㉗
The Living Desert ⓱
The Mad Greek's ❺
Marriott's Desert Springs Resort and Spa ⓱
Morgan's ⓳
Murph's Gaslight ⓳
Nate's Deli ⓰
The Noriega Hotel ❿
Nudist bed-and-breakfasts ⓰
Oasis Date Gardens ⓴
Ocotillo Wells State Vehicular Recreation Area ㉓
Palm Springs Follies/Plaza Theatre ⓱
Ritz-Carlton ⓱
Roy Rogers/Dale Evans Museum ⓭

San Diego Wild Animal Park 26
Scotty's Castle 1
Shields Date Gardens 19
Simba's Ribhouse 15
Taqueria 16
Two Bunch Palms Resort and Spa 15
Willow Springs International Raceway 9
World's tallest thermometer 5
Zzyzx 6

RVing in the California Desert & Las Vegas

A lazy loop around California's deserts can be made in one long haul or on a series of shorter drives from a central base. From the Palm Springs area, the route fans south and east as far as the Arizona and Mexico borders. From San Bernadino, it radiates east to the Colorado River, northeast to Las Vegas, and north to Death Valley. From Lancaster/Palmdale, it runs north into the Owens Valley east of the Sierra Nevada. The whole circuit is about 1,000 miles, plus side trips, but can be divided into a number of shorter trips.

Stay on roads and trails at all times, whether driving or walking. The desert terrain is fragile and slow-growing, and one careless off-road driver can destroy vegetation decades old.

HITTING THE HIGHLIGHTS

If you divide your time between Death Valley, the Palm Springs area, Joshua Tree National Park, and Anza–Borrego State Park, you should get to know the California desert fairly well. Allow 4 days in Death Valley, then drive south through Baker, Barstow, and Calico or detour into Nevada for a fling at the gaudy casinos of Las Vegas or Laughlin. Allow 2 or 3 days in Joshua Tree, longer if you want to make day trips over into nearby Palm Springs. Anza Borrego State Park is south from Indio and Coachella, then west on Route 78 through Ocotillo Wells.

If you're flying in and renting an RV, either Los Angeles or San Diego makes a good base.

GOING FOR THE LONG HAUL

If you want to spend a winter among the snowbirds in the California desert, you could explore all three major desert areas, take a leisurely attack on the suggested side trips, then settle in around the Palm Springs area if you're affluent or on the BLM Lands (see "Trimming Costs: Eight Money-Saving Tips for the Road" in chapter 2, "Getting Prepared: RVing Tips & Hints") if you're strapped.

Most recreation areas, state parks, and forest service campgrounds have posted camping limits, often around 14 days, but you can check out and then check in again on a later day. Or you could become a VIP (Volunteer in Parks) and camp free all season long as a campground host.

Travel Essentials

WHEN TO GO

Winter is ideal in California's desert country, balmy and warm days with cool nights. Early spring and late autumn are also good. Summer in the low desert is only for mad dogs and Englishmen, as well as Germans, Swiss, and

Calico's bottle house

Japanese, who dote on traveling in Death Valley in August when the temperature can top 115°.

WHAT TO TAKE

Binoculars, a camera and plenty of film, and a tripod if you plan to shoot cactus, wildflower portraits, or dazzling sunsets. Carry a strong sunscreen and a canteen or water carrier for hikes.

WHAT TO WEAR

In the desert, lightweight and light-colored natural fiber fabrics are best. Stout-soled hiking shoes and tough-fabric pants are essential to repel cactus spikes if you're hiking in cactus country. Winter evenings cool down quickly once the sun sets, so be prepared with a down vest or jacket, windbreaker, or heavy sweatshirt. A wide-brimmed hat, preferably one that can be tied down, is best in the strong desert sun.

TRIMMING COSTS ON THE ROAD

Ask any snowbird turned desert rat how to live off the land—or rather, the Bureau of Land Management—and he'll tell you about "the Slabs" or one of the other Long-Term Visitor Areas (LTVAs) in the southern desert.

Here's how it works: You can buy a Golden Eagle Passport for $50 that gives you a camping discount good for 1 year. Prices and discounts vary depending on season, state, and camping area. To make an advance purchase, call one of the district offices listed below and they'll supply a permit by mail. If you want to spend only a few days, you can buy a short-term permit from campground hosts in each camp area.

Don't expect hookups, paved parking (except at "the Slabs," which were once cement pads for military buildings), water, or sanitary dump sites. What you get is plenty of desert, some solitude if you wish, and all the warm sunshine you can handle.

The sites are generally located off I-8 or I-10 west of Yuma and in Arizona at Quartzite on U.S. 95 off I-10. The most established areas are Hot Spring, off I-8 east of El Centro at Highway 115; Imperial Dam, off I-8 at Winterhaven, then west on Senator Wash Road; Pilot Knob, off I-8 at Sidewinder Road 5 miles west of Yuma; Dunes Vista, off I-8 at Ogilby Road, 10 miles west of Yuma; La Posa at Quartzsite, Arizona, on both sides of Route 95; Midland, off I-10 at Lovekin Boulevard; and Mule Mountain, off I-10 at Wiley's Well Road, then north 9 miles. To get more information, call the **California Desert District Office of BLM** in Riverside (☎ **909/697-5200**), or the **Yuma District Office** in Arizona (☎ **602/726-6300**).

WHERE TO GET TRAVEL INFORMATION

The following organizations can supply you with any visitor info you need for your desert trek.

- The **Borrego Springs Chamber of Commerce,** 622 Palm Canyon Dr., Borrego Springs, CA 92004. ☎ **800/559-5524;** www.borregosprings.com.

- **California Division of Tourism,** 801 K St., Suite 1600, Sacramento, CA 95814. ☎ **916/322-2881;** www.gocalif.ca.gov.

- **Inland Empire Tourism Council** (providing info for Riverside and San Bernadino counties), 301 E. Vanderbilt Way, Suite 100, San Bernadino, CA 92408. ☎ **909/890-1090;** www.ieep.com.

- **Las Vegas Convention and Visitors Authority,** 3150 Paradise Rd., Las Vegas, NV 89109. ☎ **702/892-0711;** www.lasvegas24hours.com.

- **Palm Springs Desert Resorts,** 69–930 Highway 111, Suite 201, Rancho Mirage, CA 92270. ☎ **800/41-RELAX** or 760/770-9000; www.desert-resorts.com.

- **Palm Springs Tourism,** 333 North Palm Canyon Dr., Suite 114, Palm Springs, CA 92262. ☎ **800/34-SPRINGS;** www.palm-springs.org.

DRIVING & CAMPING TIPS

- **Leave an itinerary with friends.** Never head out on back roads in the desert without telling someone where you're going and when you expect to return.

- **Carry water**—at least 1 gallon per person per day.

- **Carry good detailed local maps** (desert access guides are available for $2.50 each from the Bureau of Land Management, California Desert District Office (☎ **909/697-5200**).

- **Never trespass on private desert land**—some of the "desert rats" don't take kindly to strangers.

- **Be aware of where you set up camp.** Set up at least 200 yards away from a man-made water source for wildlife and no more than 300 yards from the road. Don't set up camp in a wash where flash floods could literally wash you away.

The Best Desert Sights, Tastes & Experiences

OFF-THE-WALL ATTRACTIONS

The Palm Springs Follies. Retired chorus girls aged 50 to 80 with great gams still kick 'em high at the city's nostalgic Plaza Theatre, 128 S. Palm Canyon Dr. Call ☎ **760/864-6516** for information, 760/327-0225 for tickets (around $25). Daily matinees at 1:30pm, nightly performances at 7pm, winter season only.

Nudist bed-and-breakfasts, Palm Springs. We haven't run across many of these anywhere, but Palm Springs has a selection. **The Terra Cotta Inn,** 2388 E. Racquet Club Rd., is a clothing-optional 17-room resort for couples, open year-round. From $79 summer, $115 winter (☎ **800/SUNNY FUN;** www.sunnyfun.com). **Desert Shadows Inn,** 1533 Chaparral Rd., also welcomes naturists with 74 year-round units (☎ **800/292-9298;** www.desertshadows.com). Other small, clothing-optional boutique hotels in Palm Springs cater to gay male or female clientele. For a full hotel list, contact Palm Springs Tourism at ☎ **800/347-7746.**

The Roy Rogers/Dale Evans Museum, Victorville. An eclectic compendium of everything the cowboy film stars ever saw, received, or touched. A collector's set of 1950s western tableware; a Pontiac decorated with horns, pistols, and silver dollars; and dioramas about the family's life are only a minuscule part of the assortment. Roy's horse Trigger and Dale's horse Buttermilk, along with several family dogs, survive as models of taxidermy. 15650 Seneca Rd. in Victorville. Exit Interstate 15 at Roy Rogers Drive, keep left, and make a left on Civic Drive. ☎ **760/243-4547;** $3 entrance fee.

Exotic World, The Strippers' Hall of Fame, Helendale. At 29053 Wild Rd. in Helendale, former headliner Dixie Evans, better known as "the Marilyn Monroe of Burlesque," commemorates the days when disrobing seductively was a work of art for once-famous stars like Lili St. Cyr, Blaze Starr, and Tempest Storm. See Gypsy Rose Lee's cape, Jayne Mansfield's dressing room ottoman, and an urn with the ashes of Jennie Lee, who started this museum before she died of cancer. Call ahead for an appointment at ☎ **760/243-5261;** admission $10.

Roy Rogers' horse Trigger announces the location of the Roy Rogers/Dale Evans Museum in Victorville.

The moving rocks of Death Valley. They skitter along the desert floor at Racetrack Playa, leaving behind a clear trail of their route. Scientists suspect rain-slick clay allows the wind to push the rocks back and forth at speeds of up to 2 m.p.h., but no one has ever seen them in motion. Death Valley National Park, at state highways 127 and 190 (☎ **760/786-2392**).

Amargosa Opera House. The ballerina dances for an audience of painted figures if no live ones show up at the Amargosa, at the intersection of Highways 127 and 190, where dancer Marta Becket painted in 250 spectators for her dances and pantomimes scheduled on winter weekends. Call ahead for tickets at ☎ **760/852-4441.**

The roadside dinosaurs at Cabazon. Located about 40 to 45 miles northeast of Palm Springs on I-10, the dinosaurs appeared in the film *PeeWee's Big Adventure* and serve to promote a chow stop at the Wheel Inn, where no less a gourmet authority than Gault-Millau praises the huge helpings of homemade desserts, from strawberry shortcakes to bread puddings. While we were not lured by their "famous" cream pies, we adored the gift shop in the belly of the biggest dinosaur. Since a pair of fast-food purveyors moved into the neighborhood, you have to look twice to spot the dinosaurs.

Long-eared owls and short-eared owls. If you've ever wondered what the difference is (beside the obvious), take a winter's day drive on the dry side to Harper Lake, 25 miles east of Barstow via Highway 58, then 5 miles north to the dry lake. The long-eared owls hang out in woodland thickets, while the short-eared owls stay close to the marsh. One veteran birder reports seeing 300 short-eared owls feeding in a single field. Bureau of Land Management (☎ **909/697-5200**).

The world's tallest thermometer, Baker. It soars above the Bun Boy restaurant in the Mojave Desert town of Baker, showing 1 foot for each degree of temperature, up to the hottest recorded day in history at Death Valley (July 10, 1913, when it hit 134°). You can see it as you drive along I-15, with the current temperature recorded both day and night. The restaurant dates from 1926, and has a mini-museum about Death Valley in the entrance. The intriguingly named Bun Boy Motel is next door. Baker Area Chamber of Commerce (☎ **760/256-8617**).

Scotty's Castle, Death Valley. A lavish $2-million Moorish mansion built by a Chicago insurance executive and his radio evangelist wife (but named for a former performer in Buffalo Bill's Wild West show who also lived there), the castle has an unfinished 270-foot swimming pool, 25 rooms with tapestries and fireplaces, and a 26-foot clock tower. Johnson and his friend Walter Scott (Scotty) rejected designs submitted by Frank Lloyd Wright in favor of an unknown architect who did not go on to fame and fortune. Guided tours led by costumed docents are so popular that you can expect a wait of an hour or two in season. Scotty died in 1954, and his entire estate consisted of one well-worn cowboy hat. On Scotty's Castle Road in Death Valley National Park. You can get there from Highway 190. Look for a sign. You can also take Highway 95 to 267-S and take Scotty's Castle exit. ☎ **760/786-2331.**

Coachella Valley Preserve covered-wagon tours. If you've always yearned for the rugged pioneer life, hop into a genuine bone-crusher of a prairie schooner, drawn by draft mules, with an optional campfire and barbecue also on the agenda; $55 for adults, $27.50 for kids. Located north of I-10 and about 6 miles east of Thousand Palms at the north end of Washington Street on the Coachella Valley Preserve. ☎ **800/367-2161** or 760/347-2161.

Antelope Valley Indian Museum, Lancaster. This whimsical and eclectic place, built in the style of a Swiss chalet, is filled to the brim with giant kachinas, bird claw fishhooks, grass skirts, and some unlikely illustrated Indian legends; a second-story cave is open on weekends only, October through mid-June, at 15701 E. Ave. M in Lancaster. It was hand-built by a romantic, self-taught artist in 1928. ☎ **661/942-0662** or 661/946-3055.

Barstow Station. East of Barstow on East Main Street (off Interstate 15), the station looks like several small railway cars by the station from the outside, but inside it's one huge, rambling shop with an astonishing collection of

Barstow Station

great tacky souvenirs, from life-sized plaster of Paris howling coyotes to plastic cacti and personalized mugs for every Tom, Dick, and Lupe that happens by. Things dangle from the ceilings and are stacked precariously on random shelves and counters around the premises. A tour bus rest stop, the station also has a McDonald's and various take-out food counters. We were fascinated with the 42 jellybean flavors, including jalapeño, piña colada, buttered popcorn, strawberry cheesecake, cotton candy, and toasted marshmallow, not to mention the life-sized plaster American eagles and the Marilyn Monroe cookie jars. Barstow Tourism Marketing Council (☎ 888/4-BARSTOW; www.barstowca.com).

Heartland, the California Museum of the Heart, Palm Springs. Walk through a giant model of a human heart, record your heartbeat, or step into a pulsating coronary artery to observe plaque formation, all in a wing of the Heart Institute of the Desert at 39–600 Bob Hope Dr. in Palm Springs. While there, you can catch a healthy snack at the Heart Rock Cafe or watch a heartwarming film at the Happy Heart Cinema. Free admission, but voluntary donations suggested. From Highway 111, take the Country Club exit and make a left on Bob Hope Drive; the first right takes you to the Heart Institute. ☎ 760/322-8889.

Naked hiking. Take a moonlight desert hike au naturel with Desert Safari's Moonlight Hiking Expedition. Contact ☎ 888/TO-SAFARI or www.desert-safari.com. The hikes are conducted in "secret remote locations" outside Palm Springs each month on the night of the full moon and the day before and after it.

PUTTING YOURSELF IN PERIL, AT SPEED

Aside from heat, desert daytimes offer just about any extreme you could dream up. Here are three of the better ones.

Willow Springs International Raceway. Willow Springs Raceway offers an appointment in the fast lane, a chance to watch or take part in fast track racing. You can watch a race, take a lesson on handling your own car from an expert at any of several schools, or book a formula car racing session, just as many movie star drivers like Paul Newman and James Garner have in the past. 3500 75th St. West, in Rosamond. From Highway 14 north, exit west on Rosamond Boulevard. Continue for 5 miles to the track. ☎ **661/256-2471.**

El Mirage dry lake. El Mirage, in the eastern Mojave, is a haven for sand sailors on windy weekend afternoons. In the right wind, their sand sail craft—T-shaped tubular frames 6 feet wide and 10 feet long with a triangular sail on a 17-foot mast—let them get speeds of up to 70 m.p.h.—but there are no brakes. Get there via Avenue P in Lancaster, which turns into El Mirage Road, then turn north on El Medio road (unpaved) 5 miles to the lake.

Parachutes over Palm Springs. Parachutes over Palm Springs arranges free-fall parachute jumps where you have both the parachute and the instructor strapped to your back. It's called tandem parachute jumping, and it looks a little like Superman taking Lois Lane for a whirl. It costs $179 to jump from 8,000 feet, or $10 more per 1,000 feet up to 14,000. ☎ **800/535-JUMP.**

THREE DESERT SPLURGES

1. **Furnace Creek Inn and Ranch Resort.** Furnace Creek, Highway 190 in Death Valley National Park, has a dazzling, cerulean swimming pool and palm garden that look like a mirage from the 1930s, with stone arches framing distant views of snow-capped mountains beside a lush oasis shaded by palms. From $95 a night for two. ☎ **760-786-2345;** www.furnacecreekresort.com.

2. **Desert Adventures of Palm Springs.** A bouncy jeep ride along private dirt roads with this outfit lends insights into everything from lifestyles and rituals of the local Cahuilla tribes to fascinating facts about desert flora and fauna. Try to catch a ride with Morgan Wind-in-Her-Hair Levine, a mile-a-minute talker and one of the company's co-owners. Tours range from 1 to 4 hours and cost $35 to $99 for adults. Call ☎ **760/324-5337** to book. Reservations are required.

3. **Ingleside Inn in Palm Springs.** Sit under the shade trees on the grassy lawn by the pool at the circa-1935 Inn, 200 W. Ramon Rd. in

Palm Springs, on the corner of Highway 111 and Ramon, where Howard Hughes used to check in under the name "Earl Martyn," along with Ava Gardner as "Mrs. Clark." In the hotel's Melvyn's Restaurant, you can still dine on 1950s-style martinis, shrimp cocktails, and steak while overhearing remarks like, "Sheila, you look wonderful; not even in the light can you tell!" From $100 for two. ☎ **800/772-6655** or 760/325-0046; www.inglesideinn.com.

GREAT TAKE-OUT (OR EAT-IN) TREATS

Murph's Gaslight, Bermuda Dunes. The pan-fried chicken can be ordered to take out with all the trimmings—black-eyed peas, mashed potatoes, cornbread, hot biscuits, country gravy, and fruit cobbler—if you call ahead. Murph's is open 11am to 3pm and 5 to 9pm daily except Sundays, when the hours are 3 to 9pm, and Mondays, when the restaurant is closed. You can also feast family-style at a table inside on a first-come, first-served basis; the platters of chicken keep on coming. 79–860 Ave. 42, by the airport in Bermuda Dunes. ☎ **760/345-6242.**

The Mad Greek's, Baker. The hummus and homemade pita bread and the falafel sandwich with tahini are good choices to go at The Mad Greek's at 72112 Baker Blvd. in Baker, where an unautographed photo of Zsa Zsa Gabor hangs over the door. Truckers like the $5 ham-and-three-egg breakfast also pictured on the wall. Take Highway 127 to Baker exit. ☎ **760/733-4354.**

Hadley Orchard, Cabazon. The original recipe for trail mix, concocted 20-some years ago by an employee of Hadley Orchard, is still for sale in the freeway farmstand, along with dried fruits and nuts and what appears to be the world's largest assortment of fruit-and-nut gift packs. Take the Apache Trail exit from I-10 near Palm Springs. ☎ **800/854-5655.**

Morgans, La Quinta. The yummy peanut-butter pie at Morgans in the La Quinta Hotel, 49–499 Eisenhower Dr., La Quinta, is surprisingly light and delicate, with a brushing of chocolate on the crisp crust before the filling is mounded on, then topped with whipped cream and sliced almonds. Even in a take-out carton, the pie slice is artistically nestled on a base of chocolate stripes, which helps justify its $3.95 tariff. Open 6am to 10pm. ☎ **760/564-4111.**

Taqueria, Palm Springs. The vegetarian enchiladas, burritos, tamales, and tacos at Taqueria, 125 E. Tahquitz Canyon Way, Palm Springs, come with your choice of refried, black, or ranch beans and a big dollop of rice. This charming cantina with its bright colors and big patio also features a selection of margarita specialties. Open daily from 11:30am to 10pm. ☎ **760/778-5391.**

Fresh dates, Indio. Dates are harvested between September and mid-December around Indio; check **Shields Date Gardens,** 80–225 Highway 111, dating back to 1924, for Royal Medjool–Super Jumbo dates, the world's biggest. Open daily. ☎ **760/347-0996.** The **Oasis Date Gardens** in Thermal on Highway 111 give you a free date milk shake at the end of their free 20-minute tour and an enlightening video on the sex life of the date. ☎ **800/414-2555** or 760/347-0996.

Simba's Ribhouse, Palm Springs. The best barbecued ribs in the desert can be found at Simba's, located in a former bank building at 190 N. Sunrise Way in Palm Springs, along with down-home versions of chicken and dumplings, black-eyed peas, barbecued beans, cornbread, hush puppies, and sweet potato pie. Call ahead at ☎ **760/778-7630** for takeout or reservations.

Nate's Deli, Palm Springs. The corned beef sandwiches from Nate's Deli, 100 S. Indian Canyon south of Tahquitz Way, Palm Springs, are virtually guilt-free because the beef is so lean. A big serving of crunchy, fresh, kosher dill pickle slices comes alongside. The $7.95 sandwich is big enough for two. ☎ **760/325-3506.**

The Noriega Hotel, Bakersfield. A family-style Basque restaurant, the Noriega Hotel is always worth a detour. Founded in 1893 by Faustino Noriega and operated since 1931 by the Elizalde family, it's open daily except Mondays, with breakfast ($7) served between 7 and 9am, lunch ($8) served promptly at noon, and dinner ($15) at 7pm. Breakfast, tailored to the appetites of the Basque sheepherders who've always eaten here, include fried eggs or omelets; Basque sausage; bacon or ham; California jack cheese; sheepherder bread; salsa; coffee; and wine. At lunch and dinner, the long tables are set with tureens of hot soup, platters of salad, beans, a couple of meats (chicken, lamb, pork chops, liver and onions, corned beef and cabbage) and vegetables, bottles of house red wine, loaves of sheepherder's bread with butter, and dishes of blue cheese. It's located at 525 Sumner St., near the intersection of Golden State Avenue and Union Avenue. Call ☎ **805/322-8419** for reservations, even only a few minutes ahead of time. The hotel has a medium-sized parking lot; large RVs will also find adequate street parking within a block or two.

Jiberto's Taco Shop, Borrego Springs. Ensenada-style fish tacos, carne asada burritos, or Sonoran chimichangas (a sort of fried burrito) can be found at Jiberto's, 655 Palm Canyon Drive in Borrego Springs. Call ahead for take-out. It's open daily 7am to midnight. ☎ **760/767-1008.**

WILDLIFE WATCHING

Dusk and dawn are the best wildlife-watching times in the desert, especially where there's a water source. But stay downwind so the animals can't smell you.

Besides the **bandit coyotes** that lurk around all day, you might spot the elegant little **desert kit fox** or the malevolent **sidewinder** in the sand dunes around Stovepipe Wells at dawn or dusk. **Roadrunners** are everywhere, looking exactly like the "beep beep" cartoon version.

California's endangered state reptile, the **desert tortoise,** can often be seen in its own Mojave Desert sanctuary near California City. Chances of sighting one are best from mid-March to mid-June, but if you spot one moving slowly across the highway, don't touch him or pick him up. He'll panic and lose the precious water he's hoarding from those rare winter showers.

One of the best places to see **desert bighorn sheep** is on the manicured lawns of the posh Ritz-Carlton Hotel in Rancho Mirage. They hoof down from their adjacent hilltop wildlife sanctuary to feast on the foliage, and don't seem to mind tourists and cameras.

Another good spot to look for bighorns, especially rams, is in Anza Borrego State Park on road S22 between markers 12.5 and 13.5. The best time is in the morning; pull your vehicle off the road completely and do not disturb them.

In Death Valley, you can spot the endangered **desert pupfish** from a wooden boardwalk at Salt Creek Interpretive Trail off 190 south of Stovepipe Wells.

Both the pupfish and the rare **fringe-toed lizard,** who can shut off all his body orifices and "swim" through sand dunes, can be found in the Coachella Valley Reserve and may be glimpsed on one of several easy walking trails radiating out from the visitor center. Take Thousand Palms Canyon Road off Ramon Road north of I-10 near Palm Springs.

The Living Desert is a 1,200-acre wildlife and botanical park located at 47–900 Portola Ave., off Haystack Road in Palm Desert, showcasing captive and wild-roaming desert species year-round. Look for road runners, quail, desert tortoises, desert pupfish, rattlesnakes, desert kangaroo rats, Peninsular bighorn sheep, coyotes, golden eagles, Mexican wolves, bobcats, mountain lions, javelina, and rare naked mole rats. It's open daily 9am to 5pm. ☎ **760/346-5694.**

On the Road

ACTIVE ADVENTURES IN ANZA BORREGO

In the 600,000 acres of California's largest state park, tent campers can set up almost anywhere as long as they follow the park's guidelines, spelled out in a free publication at the visitor center in Borrego Springs.

Campers will have to carry their own water in and all trash and garbage back out.

The earth-covered "underground" **visitor center,** on S22 (a.k.a. Palm Canyon Drive) 2 miles west of the town of Borrego Springs, provides a good introduction to the flora and fauna of the park, including the endangered desert pupfish.

More organized camping is available at **Borrego Palm Canyon Campground,** part of the state park system, with full hookups and 30-amp electrical capacity. Sites are unshaded and not particularly attractive, but the surroundings are pretty. Hot showers and flush toilets are on-site, and a self-guided nature trail sets out from the campground area. It's located on S22 2 miles west of Borrego Springs (☎ **760/767-5311**).

The best time to visit is during the winter months. With good January rains, expect to see blossoms in February when the flowering Mojave yucca breaks out in cream-colored bursts from spiny stalks, ocotillos take on sprays of tiny red flowers, and beavertail cactus are topped with big jaunty pink blooms. And don't be surprised to see 10,000 other like-minded visitors. Check on conditions in advance by calling the visitor center.

East of Anza Borrego on the north side of Highway 78, just west of the San Diego County border with Imperial County, is the **Ocotillo Wells State Vehicular Recreation Area,** where owners of 125s with knobbies can play pretend-moto and new owners of 4×4s can check out the equipment without offending the neighbors.

Campground Oases Around Anza Borrego

Palm Canyon Resort and RV Park. Palm Canyon Resort in Borrego Springs makes a good family getaway, except on major winter holiday weekends when so many RVs are so close together it looks like gridlock. With 130 full hookups (30-amp), cable TV, modem capability, heated pool and spa, and an Old West–style resort hotel adjoining, the park is appealing despite its fairly narrow 20-foot sites. Located at 221 Palm Canyon Dr., Borrego Springs. From Highway 86, take S22, then make a right on Palm Canyon Drive. Call ☎ **800/242-0044** for reservations.

Fountain of Youth Spa Campground. On Coachella Canal Road near Salton Sea, 15 miles north of Niland off Highway 111, Fountain of Youth Spa Campground has 546 RV sites with full hookups, flush toilets, showers, natural artesian steam rooms, hydrojet pools, masseur, laundry, barber shop, beauty parlor, propane, groceries, and church services for Catholics, Protestants, Mormons, and Adventists. Huge and almost mind-boggling, Fountain of Youth says it's for over 55s. If it sounds like your sort of scene, you can call for information at ☎ **760/354-1340** or reservations at ☎ **888/8000-SPA.** $20 and up.

Desert Campgrounds

Black Rock Campground **16**
Borrego Palm Canyon Campground **20**
Boulder Creek RV Resort **1**
Bullhead RV Park **6**
Calico Ghost Town **8**
Circusland RV Park **3**
East Shore RV Park **14**
Fishermen's Trailer Lodge **6**
Fountain of Youth Spa Campground **21**
Furnace Creek Campground **2**
Great Times RV Resort **15**
Jumbo Rocks Campground **17**
Las Vegas KOA **3**
Malibu Beach RV Park **13**
Needles KOA Kampground **7**
Orange Grove RV Park **11**
Outdoor Resorts of America, Cathedral City **18**
Outdoor Resorts of America, Indio **19**
Palm Canyon Resort and RV Park **20**
Primadonna RV Village **4**
Red Rock Canyon State Park **10**
Riverside RV Park **5**
Saddleback Butte State Park **9**
Silver Creek RV Park **6**
Valencia Travel Village **12**

ELSEWHERE IN SAN DIEGO COUNTY

Kids and their parents adore the new **LEGOland California** theme park, opened in 1999 off I-5 in Carlsbad, 1 hour south of Disneyland, 30 minutes north of San Diego. Created by the Danish company that makes the brightly colored interlocking plastic building blocks called LEGO, the 128-acre family theme park has 40 interactive rides and attractions. While the prices seem to be pegged on Scandinavian rates—$32 for adults and $25 for seniors and kids 3 to 16—most attendees make a day of it and enjoy the low-key, relaxed sense of fun and creativity. It's particularly good for smaller children who are sometimes intimidated by bigger, noisier theme parks. To get more details about it, call ☎ **760/918-LEGO** or visit their Web site, www.legoland.com.

San Diego Wild Animal Park makes another good family getaway for a day. Located in Escondido at 15500 San Pasqual Valley Rd., just off Route 78, the park is an offshoot of the famous San Diego Zoo, with safari trails through the forest, savanna, and wetlands to see more than 200 exotic animals in their natural habitats. ☎ **619/234-6541.**

PALM SPRINGS

Every other one of Palm Springs' checkerboard lots belongs to the Agua Caliente band of Cahuilla Indians, who control 42% of the land in the Coachella Valley and are the richest tribe in North America. The **Spa Hotel & Casino & Mineral Springs** at 100 N. Indian Canyon Dr. is one of the tribal ventures, offering 24-hour poker, slots, and Spa-21, which we interpret as a healthy version of blackjack.

While many of Palm Springs' senior celebrity residents are irreverently referred to as The Waxworks, there's nothing sedentary about the area. You can go skydiving with **Parachutes Over Palm Springs** (☎ **800/535-JUMP**); catch a polo match or try a version of golf cart polo at **Eldorado Polo Club,** 5950 Madison, Indio (☎ **800/525-7634**); splish-splash in California's largest wave-action pool or ride an inner tube down a 600-foot white-water river at the **Oasis Waterpark,** on Gene Autry Trail between Ramon Road and East Palm Canyon Drive in Palm Springs (☎ **800/327-0499** or 760/GO-SURF); float above the cactus with **Balloon Above the Desert** (☎ **760/776-5785;** www.pshotairballoons.com); ride the **Aerial Tramway** from the desert floor to the cool crest of 8,516 feet in 15 minutes (take I-10 west to Indian Avenue exit, turn left at exit, then make a right on San Rafael; ☎ **760/325-1391** or 888/515-TRAM, www.pstramway.com); or lope out into the desert astride a camel with **Ship of the Desert Camel Tours** (☎ **760/398-2000**).

For couch potatoes, we'd recommend more sedentary amusements— watching **Fun in the Sun Candies** make Nutcorns at their factory store at 68–845 Perez Rd. (☎ **800/922-6390**) is really riveting, as is sampling microbrews at the **Palm Springs Brewing Company,** 5055 Calle San Raphael (☎ **888/327-BREW**), by appointment on Tuesdays through Thursdays.

Ruddy's 1930s General Store Museum on the Village Green makes nostalgic browsing for anyone who remembers Uneeda Biscuits, Rinso, sarsaparilla, and silk stockings. It's open weekends only in summer, Thursday through Sunday in winter 10am to 4pm (☎ 760/327-2156).

Wind Farm Tours, 62–950 20th Ave., west of the Indian Avenue exit on the north side of I-10, North Palm Springs, takes tourists around in electric vehicles powered by the wind to see the forest of giant windmills that dominate the desert landscape around Palm Springs. One-and-a-half-hour tours leave four times a day in winter—9 and 11am and 1 and 3pm—and sometimes less frequently in summer. Reservations are encouraged, although they do accept walk-ins, space providing; call ☎ 760/251-1997.

"How could you travel to California and not see the San Andreas Fault?," your neighbors back home might well ask. Two different companies hawk them in Palm Springs. **Jurassic Expeditions** (☎ 760/862-5540) sells a 3-hour "Indiana Jones" motorcoach eco-adventure tour with guide Murray Rodkin and his dog Seismo, while **Eco Tours** (☎ 760/322-6029) takes a more educational approach and requires reservations for the twice-daily, Wednesday-through-Sunday excursions.

RVing golfers who carry along their clubs (and even their carts, in some cases) can book a round at one of the nearly two dozen **golf courses** in the Palm Springs area. Tee times are obviously easier to come by in summer than in the winter high season, and as long as you get on the course by 6am to play 18 holes, you'll survive before the worst of the dry heat hits.

Most private golf courses require you play with a member; however, the following do not: **Palm Springs Country Club,** 2500 Whitewater Club (☎ 760/323-2626); **Rancho Mirage Country Club,** 38–500 Bob Hope Dr. (☎ 760/324-4711); **The Golf Center at Palm Desert,** 74–945 Sheryl (☎ 760/837-9553); **Date Palm Country Club,** 16–200 Date Palm, Cathedral City (☎ 760/328-1315); and **Indian Wells Golf Resort,** 44–500 Indian Wells (☎ 760/346-4653).

A 1-hour **Celebrity Bus Tour** (☎ 760/770-2700) drives past 30 to 40 homes where the rich and famous once lived, while a 2½-hour tour adds the Eisenhower Medical Center, the Sinatra and Annenberg Estates, and The Springs and Rancho Mirage Country Clubs plus a rest-and-refreshment stop at Edwards Date Shoppe. Reservations are required and no credit cards accepted. $15 adults, $13 seniors, $7 students under 16 for the hour tour; $20, $17, and $9 for the 2½-hour tour.

To see stars in a different light, the **Desert Memorial Cemetery** offers a free guide to their graves, listing locations and birth and death dates for such big names as Frank Sinatra, Sonny Bono, songwriters Jimmy van Heusen and Frederick Lowe, director Busby Berkeley, actors William Powell (*The Thin Man*) and Cameron Mitchell (*How to Marry A Millionaire*), and actor/bon vivant Charlie Farrell, who founded the Palm Springs Racquet Club. The cemetery is open daily 7am to 7pm; ask in the office for the guide or refer to a copy posted outside when the office is closed. It's located at 69–920 Ramon Rd. at Da Vall Road; enter from Da Vall. ☎ **760/328-3316.**

Special events in the desert worth planning ahead for include the **Palm Springs PolkaFest** in January (☎ **760/324-3483**); the **Indio Date Festival camel and ostrich races** in mid-February (☎ **760/863-8247**); **Nude Recreation Week** in early July at the Terra Cotta Inn, a 17-room, clothing-optional couples resort (☎ **760/322-6059**); and the **Indio International Tamale Festival** the first weekend in December (☎ **760/347-0646**).

Palm Springs Nightlife

The **Rat Pack Room** in Mayo's Supper Club on El Paseo is a private dining room with a Sinatra soundtrack, larger-than-life photographs of Sinatra and his buddies Dean Martin, Sammy Davis Jr., Joey Bishop, and Peter Lawford, and a digitally enhanced photo of Bob Mayo, the club owner, "singing" with the guys at the Sands in Las Vegas. The bistro is at 73–990 El Paseo Dr. in Palm Desert (☎ **760/346-2284;** www.mayos.com).

The hottest new club in town is **Muriel's Supper Club** at 210 S. Palm Canyon Dr. Reminiscent of a vintage New York supper club, the new spot offers "eclectic world cuisine"—desert talk for "whatever our chef knows how to cook"—along with nationally known entertainers like Nancy Sinatra and Paula Poundstone. They actually serve dinner as late as 11:30pm, a desert first. Call ☎ **760/416-6876** for reservations.

Just like Branson and Pigeon Forge, Palm Springs promises a respite to performers who are tired of touring but don't want to give up show biz. Noted entertainer Jim Bailey appears as Barbra Streisand, Peggy Lee, Judy Garland, and Phyllis Diller, among others, at whichever seasonal venue he redubs the **Jim Bailey Theater** during the winter season. And **Frankie**

Lush greens and fairways in the middle of a desert

Palm Springs

Desert Memorial Cemetery 14
Desert Shadows Inn 4
Eldorado Polo Club 27
Fun in the Sun Candies 17
Great Times RV Resort 10
Heartland, the California Museum
  of the Heart 18
Indian Wells Golf Resort 22
Ingleside Inn 12
La Mancha 7
La Quinta Resort and Club 24
Marriott's Desert Springs Resort
  and Spa 19
Morgan's/La Quinta Hotel 24
Muriel's Supper Club 9
Murph's Gaslight 23
Nate's Deli 9
Oasis Date Gardens 28
Oasis Waterpark 13
Outdoor Resorts of America,
  Cathedral City 15
Outdoor Resorts of America,
  Indio 26
Palm Springs Aerial Tramway 3
Palm Springs Brewing Company 11
Palm Springs Country Club 5
Palm Springs Follies/Plaza Theatre 9
Rancho Mirage Country Club 18
Rat Pack Room/Mayo's
  Supper Club 20
Ritz-Carlton 16
Ruddy's 1930s General Store
  Museum 8
Shields Date Gardens 25
Simba's Ribhouse 7
Spa Hotel & Casino 6
Taqueria 7
Terra Cotta Inn 21
The Living Desert 21
Two Bunch Palms Resort and Spa 2
Wind Farm Tours 1

Randall sings his heart out in a musical tribute titled "Sinatra, My Way," also at a local theatre in season. Check listings in the current copy of the *Desert Guide,* free at information racks all over town.

Campground Oases in & Around Palm Springs

Outdoor Resorts of America. Outdoor Resorts of America has two Palm Springs–area RV parks, one for motorhomes only, that are well-landscaped, individually owned sites made available to travelers when space is open. With lavish spa facilities from swimming pools to par-3 golf courses, the full-hookup sites cost around $45 a night. Call ☎ **800/453-4056** (or 800/841-3131 in California) for the Cathedral City property, 69411 Ramon Rd. (use the Date Palm Drive exit south from I-10), open to both motor-driven and towable RVs. Call ☎ **800/892-2992** for the Indio location, off Jefferson Street on Avenue 48 (reached from the Jefferson Street exit south 3.3 miles from I-10), open only to type A and type C motorhomes.

Great Times RV Resort. So new it's not yet on the maps, Great Times just opened at 28393 Somers Rd. in Murrieta, off I-215 at Clinton Keith exit, then north on Antelope Road to Somers. Resort facilities such as clubhouse, billiard and fitness rooms, putting greens, breakfast cafe, bicycle rentals, and fishing make it appealing to RVers who like a busy schedule. There will be 79 RV sites and 12 or so tent campsites. Call ☎ **909/679-6562** for reservations.

THE MOJAVE DESERT & JOSHUA TREE NATIONAL PARK

The Mojave is dotted with twisted green Joshua trees, which explorer John C. Fremont, never a happy camper, considered "the most repulsive trees in the vegetable kingdom."

Explorers, immigrants, and miners alike endured rather than adored the high desert, but latter-day desert rats get rapturous about such ersatz doings as chili cook-offs, tobacco-spitting contests, and burro biscuit tossings.

Cynics forget that **Calico,** for example, was a real ghost town before it became an artificial ghost town re-created by Walter Knotts of Knotts Berry Farm. Silver was mined there in the late 1880s, and a dog named Dorsey used to carry the mail from Calico to Bismarck, a half mile away. Take the Calico exit off I-15 between Barstow and Yermo.

You may notice the exit markers from I-15 for **Zzyzx,** where Dr. Curtis Howe Springer, a radio evangelist and health-food vendor, developed a health resort for refugees from Los Angeles' Skid Row. After 30 years of tending the urban ill free of charge, the Springers were suddenly evicted by the Bureau of Land Management in the 1970s for trespassing. The site, which was nearly destroyed by vandals during the years, was rescued and restored not long ago by the California Desert Studies Consortium, who welcome visitors.

At nearby **Nipton** (pop. 26), the four-room **Hotel Nipton,** 107–355 Nipton Rd. (☎ **760/856-2335;** from $60), recalls the days when silent film

Calico in the late afternoon sun

star Clara Bow and cowboy-actor husband Rex Bell had a ranch nearby. An outdoor hot tub lets you soak under the stars while listening to the mournful whistle of a passing freight train. Nipton is about 70 miles from Las Vegas near the California-Nevada border. Take I-15 east to Nipton Road. Continue for 10.1 miles to the railroad tracks, then make a right to the hotel. Address: Nipton Road, Nipton.

Joshua Tree National Park is a tumbled wonderland of bizarre boulders and glorious gardens of cactus ideally visited by RVers who can tent or stay overnight in a self-contained recreational vehicle; there are no hookups or water available. At all but two of the park's campgrounds (Cottonwood and Black Rock Canyon), campers must bring in all the water and firewood they plan to use, and toilet facilities are primitive. Jumbo Rocks, our favorite campground, is also a top draw for rock climbers. (See "Campground Oases in the Mojave Desert," below for details.) Joshua Tree is one of the world's most popular climbing areas, with more than 3,500 climbing spots for every degree of ability.

JOSHUA TREE CAMPSITE TIP

If you visit Joshua Tree in early to mid-winter or on a weekday, you'll be able to choose a great site on a first-come, first-served basis, but if you arrive on weekends or during the prime rock-climbing season in early spring, you'll have to take any vacancy you can find. See "Campground Oases in the Mojave Desert," below for campground listings.

Parts of the park still bear scars from four lightning-ignited fires that swept through during the 1999 Memorial Day weekend, the largest wildfire in the park's history. The 13,894 acres damaged by the fires are in the park's northwestern corner, between the West Entrance Station past Hidden Valley Campground to Ryan Campground and Keys View road and a smaller area around Covington Flat off the main roadways.

Cottonwood Visitor Center is 7 miles north of the Joshua Tree National Park exit from I-10 (☎ **760/367-7511**).

While vehicles of all sorts can negotiate the main roads in the park, four-wheel-drive vehicles, motorcycles, and bicycles are best for exploring unpaved roads. Rules require all bicycles and motor vehicles to stay on established roadways. Good **backcountry roads** include Pinkham Canyon Road, 20 miles from Cottonwood Visitor Center to an I-10 service road; Covington Flats, which accesses some of the best Joshua tree stands, 4 miles from Covington Flats picnic area to Eureka Peak; Geology Tour Road, 5.4 miles from Jumbo Rocks to Squaw Tank; or Black Eagle Mine Road, up through the canyons in the Eagle Mountains. Alert freewheelers may spot roadrunners, coyotes, kangaroo rats, jack rabbits, golden eagles, and sidewinders.

Birders will find good watching at Cottonwood Spring, while photographers and wildflower enthusiasts will want to set out from there to walk Lost Palms Oasis Trail in early spring to find dozens of native desert wildflowers.

The **General Patton Memorial Museum** at 2 Chiriaco Rd. in Chiriaco Summit, a marked exit just off I-10 about 50 miles east of Palm Springs, is built on the site of Camp Young, the World War II desert training center. While you won't see George C. Scott lurking around in his Patton uniform, you will see memorabilia, boots, and saddles, and plenty of tanks and war film footage. Open daily 9:30am to 4:30pm; $4 adults, $3.50 seniors, under 12 free. ☎ **760/227-3483.**

Campground Oases in the Mojave Desert

Black Rock Campground. Located at the northern end of Joshua Tree National Park, Black Rock Campground has 100 sites with piped water and flush toilets. Sanitary dump available. $10 for RVs up to 32 feet long. Good hiking. Open October to May only. Take I-10 east to Highway 62 east to Yucca Valley. Turn right on Joshua Lane. Follow signs 5 miles to the campground. Call ☎ **800/365-CAMP** for reservations.

Jumbo Rocks Campground. Located in the middle of Joshua Tree National Park near Twentynine Palms, Jumbo Rocks Campground has 125 sites, pit toilets, some evening ranger programs, and rock climbing (sites are surrounded by huge boulders). No hookups, no water, no fee. It's easiest to find space in winter when nights are nippy; early spring weekends are chock-a-block with rock climbers and desert flower photographers. Take

Highway 62 to Park Boulevard exit. Enter at west entrance. Continue for 23 miles to campground. ☎ 760/367-5525 or www.joshuatree.org will put you in contact with the Joshua Tree National Park Association, an educational support group.

Calico Ghost Town. This San Bernadino County campground, located in the canyons just steps from the commercialized but genuine silver mining town of Calico, near Baker, has 220 sites, 46 with full hookups (30- and 50-amp), some grills, picnic tables, showers, flush toilets, and sanitary dump. Up to $22 a night with hookups. Reservations essential on weekends. ☎ 760/254-2122. Take Calico exit off I-15 between Barstow and Yermo. There are restaurants, shops, and attractions in Calico, and groceries, propane, and laundry facilities nearby. Families with children, ghost town collectors, and rock hounds will especially like the area.

Saddleback Butte State Park. Located off Highway 14, 17 miles east of Lancaster; use Avenue J turnoff. Once called Joshua Tree State Park, it has well-preserved stands of Joshua trees, rocky buttes, and excellent hiking trails. Fifty sites accommodate self-contained RVs up to 30 feet and have piped water, flush toilets, and a sanitary dump, but no hookups. No reservations except for groups. $10. ☎ 805/942-0662.

Red Rock Canyon State Park. Red Rock Canyon park has 50 primitive sites with no hookups. Water and sanitary dump available. No reservations. Ranger campfire programs in summer and fall, hiking trails, dramatic geologic formations, and archaeological displays at visitor center. Occasional winter snowfalls, cool to cold nights. Nesting falcons, hawks, owls in spring. Take Highway 14 for 25 miles. The turnoff to the campground is well marked. ☎ 805/942-0662.

Campground Oases Around Los Angeles & Elsewhere
East Shore RV Park. East Shore RV Park, in San Dimas, is perched atop a hill overlooking Pomona's Fairplex, site of the Los Angeles County Fair, with cool breezes even on the hottest days. Large, grassy sites, mature shade trees, and some lakefront locations make East Shore a reliable getaway year-round. Reserve ahead, especially on weekends or holidays, by calling ☎ 800/809-3778. Exit I-10 via Fairplex Drive and follow the signs.

Malibu Beach RV Park. Located on Pacific Coast Highway in Malibu, Malibu Beach RV Park overlooks the sea, and the beach is only a short walk downhill and across the road from your campsite. In winter, you may see whales migrating along the coast. Sites are small but the views are great; call ☎ 800/622-6052 for reservations.

Valencia Travel Village. Valencia Travel Village, on Route 126 off I-5 north of Los Angeles near Magic Mountain, offers shade trees, a swimming pool,

and a quiet, convenient location only an hour from Los Angeles. Call
☎ **805/257-3333** for reservations.

Orange Grove RV Park. Off Highway 58 east of Bakersfield at Edison
Road, 122 sites are nestled in an orange grove, with pick-your-own privileges, a pool, recreation room with big-screen TV, playground, country
store, hot showers, air-conditioned rest rooms, cable TV, laundry, propane.
$23 a night. ☎ **800/553-7126.** Nearby: Bakersfield's famous Basque
restaurants.

DEATH VALLEY NATIONAL PARK

If publicists had been around during wagon train days, Death Valley would
have been named Golden Sands or Shimmering Haze or maybe Rancho
Mirage. Instead, it took nearly a century to shake off the bad-mouthing the
pioneers gave it. It wasn't until stalwart, sincere Ronald Reagan brought TV's
"Death Valley Days" into our living rooms that it became a tourist destination.

Now, as a national park with an additional 1.3 million acres, it's busy
even in summer, when European tourists flock here to experience the
hottest, driest, lowest, loneliest, and so on.

Tent campers and self-contained RVs (no hookups available) will find
comfortable spots to spend a winter weekend at **Furnace Creek
Campground,** which has shade trees and some privacy, plus flush toilets,
hot showers, and dump station. (See "Campground Oases in & Around
Death Valley National Park," below.) Bigger, less attractive camping areas
include **Stovepipe Wells** and **Sunset Campground** (☎ **800/365-2267**),
located near the **Furnace Creek Visitors Area,** Highway 190, 30 miles
east of Death Valley Junction at State Road 127 at Highway 190 (☎ **760/
786-3244**).

Bicyclists can tour the mostly flat terrain of Death Valley quite comfortably in winter. Rain is rare, but winds can come up to hinder your progress.
Use touring bikes on paved roads, mountain bikes on sandy or rocky routes.
The 13-mile, paved **Artists Palette Road** is particularly scenic, a winding,
narrow one-way with a lot of up and down. A 9-mile paved route from
Furnace Creek to Zabriskie Point is best at daybreak, but a 7-mile loop to
the sand dunes from Stovepipe Wells is easy any time of day.

___COYOTE TIP___

Keep an eye out for the bandit coyotes of Stovepipe Wells, a trio
(when we last visited) of brazen animals who come out at midday alongside the highway to stop traffic in hopes of scrounging
food handouts. Don't encourage them by giving them food or
the rangers will banish them to the far-off regions of the park.

Campground Oases in & Around Death Valley National Park

Furnace Creek Campground. Located in the community of Furnace Creek in Death Valley, the grounds have 136 sites, most large enough for an RV, at $16 a night. Spacious campsites look across open desert terrain. No hookups, but flush toilets, hot showers, fire grates, drinking water and sanitary disposal station, general store, restaurant, and propane available nearby. Get there early on winter weekends or holidays or you'll be banished to the overflow campground across the road, which has much less ambience. Take Highway 190 to Furnace Creek Visitors Center; the campgrounds are less than a mile north of the center. ☎ **800/365-2267.**

Boulder Creek RV Resort. At 2550 S. Highway 395, a few miles south of Lone Pine, this handsome modern campground has campsite views toward Mt. Whitney and makes a great year-round stop for travelers driving to Death Valley or Yosemite. Buffet breakfasts and dinners are available on occasion. It's the RV headquarters for the Lone Pine Film Festival every October, saluting the western films shot in Lone Pine's scenic Alabama Hills. Call ☎ **800/648-8965** for reservations.

LAS VEGAS

Las Vegas welcomed 30.6 million visitors in 1998, issued 1.2 million marriage licenses, and raked in $5 billion in gross gambling revenue, representing an average gambling budget of $469 per person per trip—and for that very reason, we always feel a little guilty about the place because if it were anywhere else and financed by any other activity, its eccentric, over-the-top architecture would bring us joy and delight. But gambling holds no appeal for us, hotel pyrotechnics and gee-whiz magic shows leave us cold, and huge buffets, however cheap, fail to tempt our palates. We liked it a little better back in the days when people dressed to go to shows and restaurants rather than donning shorts and tank tops or jogging suits and shoes.

The average nightly room rate in Las Vegas in 1998 was $66, making the typical RV campground hookup site at $18 look like a real bargain. Plus, by visiting Vegas in your own RV you can come home to peace and quiet rather than crossing a jangling hotel lobby casino filled with secondhand smoke.

Because Las Vegas traffic is heavy on the under-reconstruction I-15, the traffic-clogged downtown, and the often-gridlocked strip, RVers will probably want to leave their rigs on hookup IVs in the campground and commute by city bus, casino shuttle, towcar, or rental car (some campgrounds—Las Vegas KOA, for instance—have car rentals available on the premises). Shuttle buses are provided by the campgrounds and/or casinos. Hours vary, but some run all night. Inquire locally.

Las Vegas Hotel Casinos

Since you're in your RV and don't need a hotel room, you're free to wander along the Strip and enjoy all the fantasy venues. In addition to those we've

New York, New York Hotel, Las Vegas

listed below, plans at press time, pending zoning approval, called for a **Titanic Resort** to be built in the shape of the tragic luxury liner (but twice the size) with a 1,800-seat showroom encased in an iceberg.

- **Bellagio** is lush and lavish, with an art gallery starring millions of dollars worth of masterpieces by such artists as Monet, van Gogh, and Picasso; a glassed-in garden conservatory; and 1,200 fountains splashing to synchronized classical music.

- **The Venetian** offers gondola rides along a canal in a Venice replica, complete with singing gondolier.

- **New York, New York** has the Manhattan Express roller coaster that zips you around past the Statue of Liberty and the city skyline.

- **The Las Vegas Hilton Star Trek Experience** offers a future fantasy that includes being beamed up into the starship *Enterprise* to blast across the galaxies and battle the Klingons in the 24th century. You can even arrange a wedding ceremony on the spaceship's bridge with a couple of Star Trek characters for witnesses.

- **Circus Circus** is roller coaster heaven, with the world's only indoor, double loop, double corkscrew coaster and an unlimited-rides wristband admission.

- **Stratosphere Tower,** the tallest freestanding observation tower in America at 1,149 feet, offers a thrill ride to the top. In daytime you get a panoramic view of the desert, at night the twinkling lights of Vegas.

- **Rio** has a free Mardi Gras parade daily. You can also don a costume and ride a float for only $10.

Las Vegas

NEVADA

Las Vegas

0 — 1/4 Mi
0 — .25 Km

Cincinnati

Sahara Av.

Karen Ct. Lynwood Van Patten Sherwood

Karen Ave.

Wet 'n' Wild Water Park

Circus Circus

Riviera

Las Vegas Country Club

Edna

Las Vegas Convention Center

Convention Center Dr.

Stardust Rd.

Desert Inn Rd.

Fashion Show Mall

Desert Inn Country Club

Mountain Rd.

Emerson Av.

Burbank

Vegas Plaza

Sands Av.

Tram

(The Strip)

Central Park Cir.

Dauphine

Westchester St.

Manhattan St.

Albert

Dunes Rd.

Flamingo Rd.

Las Vegas Blvd. S.

Monorail

Audrie

Deckow La Cienaga Sadie Salton Lana

Fredda Charlotte

University of Nevada Las Vegas

Harmon

Burke

Monterey Monterey Cir.

Grand

Naples

Paradise Rd.

MGM Theme Park

Deckow

Bermuda

People Mover

Tropicana Av.

Reno

Giles

Paradise Rd.

McCarran International Airport

Hacienda

Industrial Rd.

Bellagio ⑩
Circus Circus ③
Circusland RV Park ③
Flyaway ⑤
Luxor ⑫
Mirage ⑧
New York–New York ⑪
Open-air neon museum ①
Rio ⑨
Stratosphere Tower ①
**The Las Vegas Hilton
    Star Trek Experience** ④
The Liberace Museum ⑭
**Mandalay Bay Resort
    and Casino** ⑬
The Sahara Speedworld ②
Treasure Island ⑥
The Venetian ⑦

- **Treasure Island** has a free Mutiny Bay pirate battle with sailing ships, pirates, and firing cannons every 90 minutes from 4 until 10pm, later on weekends.

- **Paris** presents the Eiffel Tower, L'Opera, the back streets of old Paree, and a pop-rock version of *The Hunchback of Notre Dame.*

- **Mirage** has an erupting volcano that spews nightly every 15 minutes from 6pm to midnight. Feel the blast when the volcano erupts, with flames leaping into the air.

- **The Mandalay Bay Resort and Casino** has a sandy beach—but it's open only to hotel guests.

- **Luxor** features the Sphinx, a glass pyramid, and King Tut's tomb, just like Howard Carter found it in 1922, along with an IMAX theater.

Off-the-Wall Las Vegas

The Liberace Museum displays a king's ransom in sweetly innocent rhinestone-beaded capes, piano-shaped knickknacks, ornately gilded bibelots, mirror-covered pianos, and one-of-a-kind decorated automobiles. "Donations" to enter (their phrasing) are $6.95 for adults, $4.50 for seniors, $3.50 for students, and $2 for children 6 to 12. The museum is at 1775 E. Tropicana (☎ 702/798-5595; www.liberace.org).

The newly opened **Elvis-a-Rama Museum** displays $3 million in artifacts and memorabilia, including a 1955 Cadillac limousine, the King's winter dress army uniform, his Social Security card, a peacock jumpsuit, his customized purple Lincoln, and a whole lot of shakin' goin' on in interactive

Luxor Hotel, Las Vegas

games and concert clips. It's open daily from 9am to 7pm at 3401 Industrial Rd., 1 block off the Strip via Spring Mountain Road (☎ **702/309-7200**). Admission is $9.95 adults; $7.95 seniors, residents, and students; under 12 free.

Ethel M Chocolates fulfills that childhood fantasy of touring a chocolate factory, then getting to pick out a free sample. The tour is self-guided and free, both in the chocolate factory and in the adjacent cactus gardens. The factory is open daily from 8:30am to 7pm with spacious parking lots able to handle RVs easily. Take exit 64 at Sunset Road to the junction with Mountain Vista Street and follow the signs. ☎ **800/438-4356** or 888/627-0990; www.ethelm.com.

A bit more mysterious is the **Cranberry World West Visitor Center,** since we've never seen anything like a cranberry in the greater Las Vegas area. Nevertheless, if you come, they will build it. The free tour covers a plethora of multimedia exhibits, the anatomy of a cranberry (you might compare it to the Palm Springs date), samplings of as many as 10 different juice products, and a gift shop with more than 600 different cranberry-themed gifts. Located at 1301 American Pacific Dr., off Gibson Road, Henderson, NV. Free admission; open Monday to Saturday 9am to 5pm, closed Sunday. ☎ **800/289-0917** or 702/566-7160; www.lasvegas.nv.com/cranworldwest.

The **open-air neon museum,** best seen at night, preserves the vintage signs that no longer have a hotel to cling to—Chief Hotel Court from 1940, The Flame from 1961, Aladdin's Lamp from 1966, the Hacienda horse and rider of 1967, and dairy mascot Andy Anderson from 1956. Other signs are in the process of being restored; look for them near the Fremont Street Experience between 4th Street and Las Vegas Boulevard.

The **Clark County Heritage Museum** shelters indoor and outdoor collections of railway cars, vintage furnished bungalows from the 1930s and 1940s, ranching displays, and a ghost town. It's at 1830 S. Boulder Hwy. in Henderson, just north of where Highway 582 meets Route 93/95, with plenty of RV parking space. Open daily from 9am to 4:30pm, the museum charges adults $1, children and seniors 50¢ (☎ **702/455-7955**).

You can fly like Peter Pan without the wires, like a full-sized Tinkerbell, at **Flyaway.** You go into a chamber where a covered and protected airplane engine is mounted below a grid floor, then flap about suspended in the blast of air. Prices begin at $35; it takes 20 minutes of instruction to train, then you can fly. Your height and weight must be in proportion. It's open daily at 200 Convention Center Dr. near the Stardust (☎ **702/731-4768**).

Campground Oases in & Around Las Vegas

Circusland RV Park. Located behind Circus Circus Casino, Circusland is the only RV park on the Strip, but with so much construction and renovation going on, you can't expect much peace and quiet. The 384 spaces are served with 30- and 50-amp electric (you'll need it in summer for the air-conditioning), a swimming pool, sauna, and hot tub. Call ☎ **800/444-CIRCUS** or 702/734-0410 for reservations, or check out the Web site at www.circuscircus-lasvegas.com.

Las Vegas KOA. Located away from the casino noise at 4315 Boulder Hwy., off Route 93/95 at Exit 170, the Las Vegas KOA is a busy year-round park with a lot of pavement, which makes a hot day seem even hotter, but it's courteously run with frequent shuttle service to the Strip. Rates are on the high side ($25 to $30 for two adults with hookup). Call ☎ **800/ KOA-7782** for reservations.

Primadonna RV Village. 35 miles south of Las Vegas on I-15, adjacent to Buffalo Bill's and Whiskey Pete's Casinos at the California–Nevada border in Primm Valley. Essentially a paved parking lot with hookups, the RV park is only steps from these two casinos, a roller coaster, Fashion Outlet mall, and two 18-hole championship golf courses, and is only 35 miles from Las Vegas. With 198 30- and 50-amp hookups, 24-hour security, showers, dump, heated pool, and spa, it's a bargain stopover at $12 or so. Just don't expect a quiet, scenic state park. Call ☎ **800/FUN-STOP** for reservations, or visit the Web site at www.primadonna.com.

Campground Oases in Laughlin, Needles & Bullhead City

Riverside RV Park. Riverside RV Park in Laughlin is another huge parking lot RV park with 900 full hookup sites (30-amp electric). There's a 24-hour shuttle to the Riverside Resort Casino, but advance reservations are required. Located at 1650 Casino Dr., Laughlin. ☎ **800/227-3849.**

Bullhead City, Arizona. Bullhead has a number of RV parks across the river from Laughlin with a little less flash and noise and a lovely distant view of the bright lights from the casinos. Three good choices: **Fishermen's Trailer Lodge,** on the river at 491 Moser St. off Route 95 (☎ **520/754-3846**); **Silver Creek RV Park** at 1515 Gold Rush Dr. off Route 95 (☎ **520/763-2444**); and **Bullhead RV Park,** 3 miles south of the junction of highways 95 and 68 on 95 (☎ **520/763-8353**).

Needles KOA Kampground. This park bills itself as the closest KOA to Laughlin, Nevada. It's at I-40 and the West Broadway River Road exit, then north a half mile on Old Trails Highway. Some 81 of the 95 sites are pull-throughs, and there are some 50-amp hookups, so it's definitely a big-rig-friendly campground. The Cactus Kafe serves meals for times you don't feel like cooking. Reservations, ☎ **800/562-3407;** average price around $24.

Ten Scenic Side Trips

1. **The California poppy trail.** (About 50 miles.) When the winter has the right amount of rain, early spring looks like Dorothy's dream in *The Wizard of Oz,* except the poppies are orange instead of red. Drive California 138 between Gorman and Lancaster, turning south on Avenue I to the Antelope Valley California Poppy Reserve (☎ **805/ 724-1180**). While there's an admission fee to the reserve, you may, as we did one year, see more poppies in bloom along the roadsides than in the reserve itself. Call ahead to determine bloom time, usually best March through May.

2. **The Alabama Hills Loop, Lone Pine.** (About 10 miles, unpaved.) Make a dusty circle through this wacky terrain where countless good guys in white hats have headed off bad guys in black hats at endless passes, not to mention where Cary Grant's 1939 classic *Gunga Din,* Humphrey Bogart's *High Sierra,* and James Stewart et al's *How the West Was Won* were shot. The rounded, sculpted rocky outcroppings that resemble fantasy animals, castles, temples, and skyscrapers are best viewed in early morning or late afternoon light. If you leave signposted Movie Road, pay close attention to your route or you could get lost forever in this weird place. North of Lone Pine off Highway 395. Contact Lone Pine Chamber of Commerce (☎ **760/876-4444;** fax 760/876-9205; www.cris.com/lpcc).

3. **The road to Bodie.** (13 miles, some of it unpaved.) Bodie was one of the rip-roaringest gold towns in California, with some 12,000 residents in its heyday between 1876 and 1880. Today, the remaining houses, school, and mines exist in a state of arrested decay preserved by the state park system. Schoolbooks lie open on wooden desks and rusting tins of food line the grocery store shelves. It's best not to attempt the road in bad weather, since the last 3 miles become a dirt washboard road. Best time to go is summer or early fall. Take Highway 270 east off U.S. 395, 7 miles south of Bridgeport. Bodie State Historic Park (☎ **760/647-6445**).

4. **The bristlecone pine forest.** From late June through October, a narrow, winding, paved road is often (but not always) open to an enclave of the world's oldest living creatures, the oldest more than 4,300 years old. The tough, twisted trees have only a few limbs but sturdy trunks that grow about an inch a century. From U.S. 395 at Big Pine, turn east on Route 168; a sign will be posted within half a mile that will tell you whether the 25-mile road to the trees is open. If you're in a motorhome or towing a travel trailer, you should go no farther than Schulman Grove, where the pavement ends. From here, a ranger station offers maps and self-guiding walking trails leading into the pines. Call Inyo National Forest in Bishop (☎ **760/873-2458**).

5. **Along the Salton Sea.** (41 miles plus side trips.) From Niland to the evocatively named Mecca, Route 111 skirts the Salton Sea National Wildlife Refuge, great for spotting Canada geese, snowy egrets, snow geese, and pelicans, with an occasional glimpse of the endangered Yuma clapper rail. Thousands of migratory birds winter here, filling the air with noise as they chatter or argue back and forth. You'll have to leave the main road at marked intervals and proceed on short, sometimes rough, unpaved stretches to the observation areas. Salton Sea National Wildlife Refuge (☎ **619/348-5278**).

6. **The desert rat's road to Randsburg.** This offbeat mining town never quite became a ghost town, and today still has a small but hardy population, a museum, and some antiques shops. The Hard Rock Cafe is a piker compared to the Hard Rock Dinner in the town's museum— eggs, pie, sausage, cauliflower, potatoes, even (yes!) hamburgers—all of it actually natural rocks and minerals that just look like food. You can swing 5 miles northeast of California City (itself about 10 miles from Highway 14 at the California City exit), following Randsburg Mojave Road to the marked entrance, 5.5 miles from town, to pay homage to the endangered desert tortoise at a 38-square-mile sanctuary. The best time for sightings is mid-March to mid-June.

   A loop of roughly 100 miles from the Lancaster area on Route 14 could include Red Rock Canyon State Park and Mojave Airport, with its huge grounded fleet of resting or retired jets from commercial airlines near the junction of 14 and 58. The town of Mojave was also the terminus of the 20-mule-team borax wagons from Death Valley. Randsburg "Living" Ghost Town (☎ **800/847-4830**).

7. **Along the Lower Colorado River.** A 150-mile loop from Needles can snare you a camping, gaming, and watersports excursion. First go north by U.S. 95 and Route 163 to bustling Laughlin, Nevada, where every casino welcomes RVers with open arms. Then head south on State Road 95 via Oatman, Arizona, on old Route 66, where wild burros roam the colorful main street. Farther south is Lake Havasu City, Arizona, where London Bridge spans the Colorado. Go west again on Parker Dam Road to Route 62 into Earp, a minuscule California desert town where the famous marshal retired to try his hand at mining instead of shooting.

8. **The Barstow Triangle.** Despite certain similarities to the more infamous Bermuda Triangle, you won't have to worry about dropping out of sight here so long as you stay off the desert's back roads. Start in the town of Barstow and its Desert Information Center, on Barstow Road between Virginia Way and Kelly Drive (☎ **760/256-8617**), for a quick read of the Mojave Desert, then check out the Barstow Station, the ultimate curiosity shop built in and around a 1900s railway station.

Head east on I-15 to Yermo and the thriving ghost town of Calico (see "Campground Oases in the Mojave Desert," earlier in this chapter), where mining lore shares the spotlight with archaeology and the Early Man site excavated by Dr. Louis Leakey. A few miles east of Barstow on I-40 is the 1860s town of Daggett where you can take a self-guided walking tour. Then head west on Route 58 into the triangle, brushing Edwards Air Force Base (where space shuttles often land—and some say UFOs as well) at Four Corners before dropping south to Victorville and the ever-popular Roy Rogers/Dale Evans Museum. (For more about the Roy Rogers Museum and Barstow Station, see "Off-the-Wall Attractions," earlier in this chapter) Barstow Tourism Marketing Council, ☎ 888/4-BARSTOW; www.barstowca.com. Roy Rogers Museum, ☎ 760/243-4547.

9. **The I-8 to Yuma.** The 171 miles between San Diego and the California–Arizona border could whiz by in a blur, but not if you take these detours: Desert View Tower at the In-Ko-Pah Park Road exit near Jacumba gives you a great view of what's ahead, plus some eccentric carved stone animals lining the trail; Calexico, separated by a fence from its Mexican neighbor Mexicali, is mysteriously chock-a-block with Chinese restaurants; and the Imperial Sand Dunes Recreation Area, where retakes of the film *Lawrence of Arabia* were shot, draws off-road-vehicle types between October and May. Allow some sightseeing time for the Yuma Territorial Prison, now a state park but once "the hellhole of Arizona." Imperial Sand Dunes (☎ 760/352-3681); Yuma County Chamber of Commerce (☎ 520/782-2567).

10. **East Mojave National Scenic Area.** This "wannabe" failed to get full national park honors in the recently passed California Desert Protection Act, ending up instead with a "preserve" status, a designation heavily lobbied for by the National Rifle Association because it will allow hunting to continue in this 1.2 million acre high desert reserve. Cattle grazing, as well, will go on. In Kelso, visit the singing dunes—the sand you dislodge when you walk on a dune makes moaning and humming sounds as it slides. Head north from Kelso on Kelbaker Road to see the cinder cones and lava beds where astronauts trained for the 1969 moon landing. When you join I-40, drive east to the Essex Road exit, then north 16 miles to Mitchell Caverns in Providence Mountain State Recreation Area, where rangers lead tours into the caves and self-contained camping is available. North on Black Canyon Road, Mid Hills and Hole-in-the-Wall campgrounds, with 63 sites between them, are connected by 11-mile Wild Horse Canyon Road, a scenic unpaved backcountry byway. Mojave National Preserve, Barstow (☎ 760/733-4040 or 760/255-8801).

Travel Quiz: Astronaut Underwear

Almost everybody knows where to find a full-scale skeleton of a dinosaur or a big collection of Norman Rockwell art, but some of America's small, off-beat museums contain some unique, eccentric, or downright peculiar exhibits. Here are the items, the museums, and a hint about why things are located where they are. See if you can match which goes with which.

1. Astronaut underwear is only one of the riveting exhibits in this space museum, which also displays a slice of Moon Rock Number 15555. It's located in the midwestern home town of two former astronauts.

2. G-strings and feather boas, sequins and pasties, autographed pictures of famous strippers such as Sally Rand, a cape that once belonged to Gypsy Rose Lee, and an ottoman that was Jayne Mansfield's decorate Exotic World: The Burlesque Hall of Fame. Hint: It's located in the desert retirement home of the late Jennie Lee, founder of the Exotic Dancers League of America.

3. The world's largest rhinestone (at 115 carets, weighing 50 pounds), a piano crafted from 10,000 toothpicks, a Norwegian blue fox cape weighing 136 pounds, and a uniform worn by Czar Nicholas II were prized possessions of this museum, named for Liberace, the musician who owned them.

4. A tumor from Grover Cleveland's jaw, a piece of John Wilkes Booth's thorax, and a collection of 139 skulls are only part of the gruesome and grotesque on display at the Mutter Museum, located in the College of Physicians in a major city.

5. A replica of George Washington's toilet from Mount Vernon, plus an historic one-piece toilet unit designed for jail cells and some early "indoor outhouses" are highlights of the American Sanitary Plumbing Museum, which is located in the home town of the late Charles Manoog, a major plumbing distributor.

a. Helendale, California

b. Las Vegas, Nevada

c. Philadelphia, Pennsylvania

d. Jackson, Michigan

e. Worcester, Massachusetts

5

Baja Bound: From Tijuana to Los Cabos

BAJA IS WHERE JOHN WAYNE, DESI ARNAZ, AND BING CROSBY USED to go fishing and where Orson Welles, Prince Ali Khan, and Mickey Rooney used to come partying in the fifties, where boxer Jack Dempsey ran a hotel and bar during Prohibition, and where Raquel Welch got married.

Back in the 1840s, the United States offered to purchase Baja California in a $25 million package with California, but after conquering it during the Mexican-American War, decided it wasn't worth keeping. In 1864, a cash-poor Benito Juárez leased two thirds of the peninsula to an American named Jacob P. Leese for purposes of real estate development, but the lease was cancelled when Leese turned out to be a fraud.

For many Americans, particularly Californians, the bumpy highway down the long, skinny Baja Peninsula is a rite of passage, no matter that the once almost-impassable highway has been paved (if not always well maintained) since 1973 and that, despite a number of closed or abandoned service stations along the way, the danger of running out of fuel is less than it once was. Chances of getting lost are quite slim since there is only one road (Highway 1) down the peninsula until you hit Highway 19 near Todos Santos.

Who makes the rite of passage? Based on our observation, a lot of people, many of them young men. One after another, the motorcyclists zipped past our 27-foot motorhome so fast we might be standing still—not the hulking cliche bikers of legend but trim, yuppie riders on touring bikes, wearing helmets and neatly zipped red leather jackets. Later, there were the bicyclists, two young men pumping diligently along a roadway that runs endlessly into the Vizcaino Desert with no shade in sight as far as the horizon.

And on our way back north, when we turned off the highway to return along some crisscrossed sandy trails to a favorite beachfront picnic spot, we found ourselves behind a driver in his late thirties in a brand new four-wheel-drive vehicle loaded with a surfeit of shiny new camping and fishing gear. He wasn't sure where he was going, he told us, just somewhere to camp and fish, but he planned to spend a month or more along the road— and when he hesitated, the unspoken phrase "to find myself" hung in the air for a moment.

As for the rest of us, Baja has its own unique attractions—isolated beaches, fresh shrimp and abalone, world-class fishing, charming colonial towns still living in an earlier time, and, for driving the highway, a strong sense of pride and accomplishment. Anybody with the price of a plane ticket can get to Los Cabos; freewheelers do it the hard way.

RVing on the Baja Peninsula

Paving was finally completed on Baja California's notorious Transpeninsular Highway in 1973, and the next year the former territory won statehood, divided into Baja California (or Baja California Norte) and Baja California Sur.

It starts off impressively at the border if you opt to bypass Tijuana and take the toll road, a smooth divided highway with frequent ocean views, south to Ensenada (tolls for our motorhome came to around $20). Your RV will purr along at top speed, and you'll find yourself thinking, "This is gonna be a piece of cake."

Only after you get south of Ensenada do you see the real road you'll be driving, rough despite its paving, filled with potholes and dropping off pre-cipitously on the shoulders as if someone has been nibbling at the pave-ment. This is the real Highway 1, the only highway until you get down around Los Cabos. Everything is pretty much along this highway and easily found from the road.

Don't expect to make more than 40 miles an hour anywhere along the route, and sometimes considerably less.

When you see a rare billboard in English that says the highway is "designed for economic development, not high-speed driving," you can be sure the road ahead will improve.

For RVers, the Baja route is still an adventure anytime you leave the paved roadway looking for a beach or campground. **Off-road routes** that were marked during our journey may have subsequently lost the signposts; new tracks through the sand may carry signage that was not there before. It's always best to ask locally.

Because Mexico uses the **metric system,** you'll buy gas in liters (4 equals a little more than 1 gallon) and count distances in kilometers (10 kilometers equals 6 miles). When shopping, a kilo equals 2.2 pounds, and 100 grams is about a quarter pound.

As a rule of thumb, the **RV parks** throughout Baja do not provide picnic tables at hookup sites. The electricity is most often 15 amps, inadequate to operate air-conditioning simultaneously with TV or microwave oven. Expect to pay an average of $12 to $15 a night for campsites with hookups. Parking

Baja Peninsula Highlights

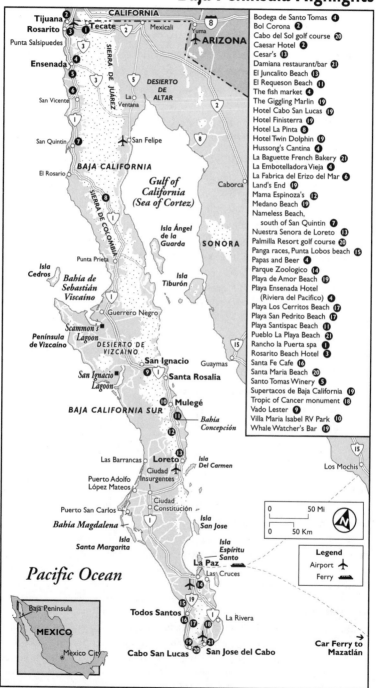

Bodega de Santo Tomas ④
Bol Corona ②
Cabo del Sol golf course ⑳
Caesar Hotel ②
Cesar's ⑬
Damiana restaurant/bar ㉑
El Juncalito Beach ⑬
El Requeson Beach ⑪
The fish market ④
The Giggling Marlin ⑲
Hotel Cabo San Lucas ⑲
Hotel Finisterra ⑲
Hotel La Pinta ⑧
Hotel Twin Dolphin ⑲
Hussong's Cantina ④
La Baguette French Bakery ㉑
La Embotelladora Vieja ④
La Fabrica del Erizo del Mar ⑥
Land's End ⑲
Mama Espinoza's ⑫
Medano Beach ⑲
Nameless Beach,
    south of San Quintin ⑦
Nuestra Senora de Loreto ⑬
Palmilla Resort golf course ⑳
Panga races, Punta Lobos beach ⑮
Papas and Beer ④
Parque Zoologico ⑭
Playa de Amor Beach ⑲
Playa Ensenada Hotel
    (Riviera del Pacifico) ④
Playa Los Cerritos Beach ⑰
Playa San Pedrito Beach ⑰
Playa Santispac Beach ⑪
Pueblo La Playa Beach ㉑
Rancho la Puerta spa ①
Rosarito Beach Hotel ③
Santa Fe Cafe ⑯
Santa Maria Beach ⑳
Santo Tomas Winery ⑤
Supertacos de Baja California ⑲
Tropic of Cancer monument ⑱
Vado Lester ⑨
Villa Maria Isabel RV Park ⑩
Whale Watcher's Bar ⑲

without hookups usually averages $5 to $10. U.S. currency is accepted all over Baja California.

RVers who wheel into an established waterfront RV park in winter will usually find all the oceanfront sites taken by seasonal or permanent residents, most of whom have put up *palapas* (thatch shelters), walls, and storage sheds blocking off anyone else's view of the sea. You are frequently not only viewless but also breezeless. Many parks shunt transient RVers off into a paved overflow parking lot.

The 2,000-mile round-trip cost us $800 in gasoline and tolls for our 27-foot Winnebago Brave motorhome, which averages around 9 miles to the gallon.

HITTING THE HIGHLIGHTS

It's possible to make a round-trip drive from Southern California to Los Cabos and back in a week (we've done it), but it doesn't leave much time for fishing, swimming, lazing in the sun, and sampling the fresh seafood and local beer. If you have only a week for a round-trip, consider going only partway down—say, as far as Bahia de Los Angeles or Bahia Concepción—so you have time to enjoy the water and scenery.

If you have 2 weeks, you can do the full drive and opt for a couple of the side trips detailed at the end of the chapter.

Travelers headed for Cabo San Lucas will find that the newer, faster Highway 19 cuts about 90 minutes off their drive. It follows the Pacific Coast rather than going over the mountains through small mining villages. But the latter are so interesting, RVers making the round-trip should cover them both, one way in one direction, and the reverse in the other.

GOING FOR THE LONG HAUL

If you want to turn snowbird and spend the winter in Baja, you could stay the whole season at a single RV resort (reserve and preferably check it out personally ahead of time, since facilities can change rapidly) or move along at a freewheeling pace, when you are ready, stopping where you like. A four-wheel-drive vehicle will be invaluable for exploring, although a sturdy pickup with two-wheel drive can accomplish most or all the side roads on our list. You can also rent small boats locally for fishing or book a deep-sea fishing trip out of most Baja seaside towns.

If you want to splurge on your extended trip, plan to spend part of your stay in one of the resorts around Los Cabos.

Travel Essentials

WHEN TO GO

Spring and fall months offer the best temperatures because it can be too cool to swim in the north in winter, and very hot inland in summer in the south. However, the climate is fairly dry, so if summer is the only time you can go, you shouldn't be too uncomfortable. Just make sure your RV or four-wheel-drive van is air conditioned. From Christmas through February or early March is the high season in Los Cabos, when hotels are full and prices at their highest.

RENTING YOUR WHEELS

San Diego–based **M&M Jeeps** rents two- or four-wheel-drive Ford Explorers for a one-way drive up or down the Baja Peninsula with no drop-off fees. You can pick up the vehicle in either San Diego or Los Cabos, and drop it at the other end. Unlimited mileage is part of the deal, and the vehicles have radios, luggage racks, and a tow capable of handling a travel trailer or boat. Call them at ☎ **619/297-1615.**

WHAT YOU NEED TO ENTER MEXICO

You'll need **Mexican vehicle insurance,** which can be purchased on the U.S. side of the border, as well as **proof of citizenship** (a passport, birth certificate, or naturalization certificate), and, if you're going to be there more than 72 hours, a **tourist card** (*forma migratoria turista* or FMT), which can be obtained free from a Mexican consulate or tourist office, from the airline if you fly into Mexico, from many travel agencies who deal with Mexican tourism, or at the border. If you're going in and out of Mexico more than once, request a multiple-entry tourist card from a Mexican consulate. When you enter Mexico, you must have your tourist card validated by a Mexican immigration officer. This is done most easily at the border.

You will also need a valid driver's license, valid registration or title for the vehicle, and, to enter the Mexican mainland, an auto permit that requires a security deposit on an international credit card or cash in the amount of the value of the vehicle, as well as a nonrefundable additional service fee. This permit is good for 6 months of multiple entries into and out of Mexico. It is not required in Baja California.

If you take a **rental vehicle** into Mexico, you will need a rental agreement or letter authorizing you to take that vehicle out of the United States.

For more detailed information and prices, you might call one of the big Mexican insurance companies doing business in the United States, such as **Sanborn's** (☎ 800/222-0158; www.sanbornsinsurance.com) or **Oscar Padilla** (☎ 800/258-8600).

PHONING MEXICO

To call ahead to Baja from the United States, first dial the international access code (**011**), then the country code (**52**), then the phone number with area code (which is what we've listed in this chapter). All told, it'll look something like this: ☎ **011-52-657/0-0000.**

BAJA TRAVEL TIP: THE HEAD TAX

On July 1, 1999, a newly imposed head tax of $15 per person entering Mexico went into effect. The tax is not imposed on visitors staying less than 72 hours or visitors who do not travel farther into the interior than 16 miles from the border. It is also not in effect at this writing for visitors to Baja California (tourism businesses in Cabo San Lucas vociferously opposed it), but it's a good idea to double-check with a Mexican consulate or tourism office prior to your trip.

WHAT TO TAKE

Insect repellent, cameras and film, binoculars, detailed road books, and maps. Bottled water and clean, commercially produced ice are available along the route, as are very basic groceries, but it's a good idea to take along as much food as you can comfortably pack. For the RV, a tool kit, spare fan belts, hoses, and filters are a good idea. Some of the mechanics along the way are good at jerry-rigging spare parts if something breaks down.

WHAT NOT TO TAKE

Under no circumstances should you carry a firearm of any kind into Mexico; it is against the law. Not long ago, a longtime RVer and traveler to Mexico was found in possession of a firearm in his vehicle and summarily thrown into jail.

WHAT TO WEAR

Comfortable, all-cotton clothes are best, along with a couple of bathing suits, since the beaches along the way are tempting. If you plan to stay in one of the resort hotels at Cabo San Lucas, you may want to take along some dressier resort clothing; otherwise, don't bother.

TRIMMING COSTS ON THE ROAD

If you're heading for Los Cabos, don't go down in high season—roughly Christmas through Easter—because hotels and restaurants are crowded, prices higher, and traffic heavier.

Instead of stopping at RV parks with hookups, ration those out for only when absolutely necessary and stay self-contained in the popular beach spots around Bahia de la Concepción. Due to heavy resort development, there are no accessible free beachfront campsites left on the main road between Cabo San Lucas and San Jose del Cabo, even though Mexico's beaches are all public. You'll have much better luck finding a place along Highway 19 north of Los Cabos, although the Pacific is generally too chilly and rough for much swimming.

WHERE TO GET TRAVEL INFORMATION

The **Mexican Government Tourism Office,** 2401 W. 6th St., 5th floor, Los Angeles, CA 90057 (☎ **213/351-2069;** www.mexico-travel.com), offers recorded information about taking your vehicle into Baja California.

DRIVING & CAMPING TIPS

- **If you have a breakdown, pray to the Green Angels.** The *Angeles Verdes* are government employees who patrol the highway in green-and-white pickup trucks. There are always two, and one usually speaks English. They carry spare parts, gas, oil, and water and make minor repairs free of charge; you pay only for the parts. If you have a breakdown, you should not have to wait more than a few hours before they find you. You can also dial toll-free ☎ **91-800-90239** from within Mexico to reach English-speaking operators to get help or give advice.

- **Be aware of your gas needs.** Because our gas tank holds 60 gallons, we were able to make the journey without needing to carry extra gasoline containers. The longest single stretch we had to drive without lead-free gasoline (*magna sin* in the green pump) available was the 219 miles between El Rosario and Guerrero Negro, plus the 84-mile side trip over to Bahia de Los Angeles and back.

- **Look out for road hazards.** Warnings of washouts or bumps may be marked by clusters of whitewashed rocks or an occasional empty plastic water jug, less often by red plastic traffic cones, which are apparently a rare commodity on the peninsula. Watch for wandering animals in the road.

- **Never, never, never drive at night,** because big trucks whose drivers know every bump and curve come barreling down the road at high speed, hitting any cows who happen to be standing there, which is what those vultures you see perched on the cactus are waiting for.

- **Pay the man.** At various intervals along the highway, you may be flagged down by volunteers wearing armbands and collecting money for the Red Cross or other organizations. The easiest thing is to give them some pesos and take the tab they give you for your windshield. It shows you already contributed if and when you drive past again.

- **Avoid overnighting in remote or isolated beach areas,** especially around San Quintin, which has had several episodes of night robbery of campers by armed intruders.

- **Don't get stuck in the sand.** Although we were careful and did not get stuck in Baja sand (having weathered being stuck in Quebec mud), that's a potential hazard for RVers who want to camp near the water. Some experts suggest letting some or most of the air out of the tires, which increases the traction. To reinflate them, take along an inexpensive tire pump, available from auto stores, that works off a vehicle cigarette lighter connection.

The Best Baja Sights, Tastes & Experiences

OFF-THE-WALL ATTRACTIONS

The unique boojum, or cirio cactus. Found around Bahia de Los Angeles and nowhere else in the world, boojum are 30-foot-tall stringy vegetable giraffes draped with parasitic mosses, scowling and hunching toward the road like demented animated trees from a Disney cartoon.

The infamous Vado Lester. Located between Santa Rosalia and San Ignacio, it's one of only two highway washouts in Baja that has its own name and danger sign, a red-and-black warning in addition to the usual whitewashed rocks.

Hussong's Cantina, Ensenada. Hussong's, Avenida Ruiz 11 (☎ 61/78-3210), is a century-old Ensenada watering hole that hasn't gentrified its original sawdust-floor despite its new T-shirt and souvenir empire nearby; it's still an obligatory rite of passage for many California teens under drinking age, and still reeks of disinfectant in the mornings. You may love it or hate it, depending on your own age and tolerance for tequila-driven noise. A newer star on the party-hearty circuit is **Papas and Beer,** at the corner of Avenida Lopez Mateos and Avenida Ruiz.

The Rosarito Beach Hotel. Dating from the 1920s when it was Hollywood's hideaway, the Rosarito, at the south end of Boulevard Juárez, has fiercely devoted fans and equally adamant detractors, but it's sold out on weekends, probably since the days when Mickey Rooney, Ali Khan, Larry Hagman, and Vincent Price used to arrive—although not at the same time, of course, or even necessarily in the same decade. ☎ 800/343-8582 or 661/2-1111.

The mid-afternoon panga race at Punta Lobos beach. North of Todos Santos, local fishermen rev their motors and ride ashore on the crest of the right wave, hitting the sand with boats full of fish.

The Giggling Marlin in Cabo San Lucas. The big giggle comes from hoisting bar patrons upside down with a block and tackle to pose for friends' cameras trophylike beside a cutout of a grinning fish holding a deep-sea rod. Located on Calle Matamoros near Boulevard Marina. ☎ 114/3-1182.

The sombrero-wearing "zebras" of Tijuana. They're burros with painted white stripes, but who cares? You'll find them on Tijuana street corners waiting for tourists to climb aboard and be photographed.

ROAD GAMES

If the children (or adults) get bored on the road, you can play "What's that foodstuff lying beside the road?" If it's dark red and you're around El Rosario, it's drying chile peppers. If it's mounds of bright yellow and you're around Ciudad Insurgentes, it's probably cornmeal. If it's white and glistening and you're around Guerrero Negro, it's likely to be salt.

The Parque Zoologico, Santiago. This eclectic zoo on the levee road south of La Paz mixes macaws and monkeys with pigs, cows, roosters, a cat, and a dog.

The former Playa Ensenada Hotel, Ensenada. The Playa Ensenada, later called the Riviera del Pacifico, opened as a casino managed by boxer Jack Dempsey, which lured movie stars in the early 1930s. It closed when Mexico outlawed gambling in the late 1930s. Rumors say it may have been owned by Al Capone. Now the handsome building, sans the hotel wings, serves as the more sedate Civic Center of Ensenada, on Boulevard Costero in downtown, with a history museum, open daily except Mondays. ☎ 617/7-0594.

La Fabrica del Erizo del Mar. This cooperative sea urchin processing plant in Uruapan, off the edge of Highway 1 to the east, sends its spiny little products exclusively to Japan. Visitors are sometimes permitted, and there's an adjacent picnic and camping area.

TEN BEST BEACHES

1. **El Requeson on Bahia de la Concepción.** Unbearably alluring, a sugar-white curved sandspit with intensely blue water on both sides and bright blue sky beyond. Self-contained camping is permitted; there's usually someone collecting a fee, which can vary depending on the whim of the collector. Off Highway 1.

2. **Playa Santispac on sheltered Bahia Coyote.** A part of the larger Bahia de la Concepción, the beach lies just off the highway with a steep road downhill to the beach that should not be attempted by larger RVs and trailers. Palapas provide shade, and a person is on hand to collect a parking fee at this very popular beach. A natural hot spring can be found a short stroll away. On Highway 1 between kilometers 114 and 115.

3. **Playa de Amor, Cabo San Lucas.** You can hire a local boatman to take you, your lover, and a picnic lunch to this sandy beach and cove tucked into the rocks where the waters of the Pacific meet the waters of the Sea of Cortez. Have him come back to pick you up several hours

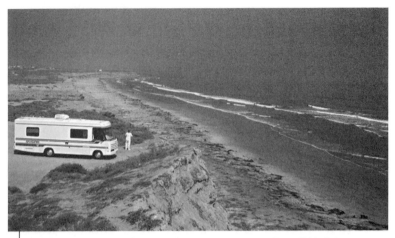

An empty beach south of Quintin makes an ideal lunch stop for an RV in Baja.

later; don't pay in advance. And don't expect to have the beach all to yourself, especially when a cruise ship is in port.

4. **The beach with no name, south of San Quintin.** A sand road crosses one-quarter mile or so over to the cliffs and dunes, where flocks of pelicans and seagulls may be your only company. These sand roads (there are numerous ones south of San Quintin) are just two tracks that go off into the wild, with no designation—you just take your pick and hope that it goes somewhere. If you find the right road into the dunes, you can look back toward San Quintin and see surfers and swimmers on the beach to the north, then look down at an empty, nameless beach below.

5. **Playa San Pedrito, south of Todos Santos.** About 4 miles south of Todos Santos on Highway 19, then 1.6 miles down a dirt road, Playa San Pedrito has a large grove of coconut and Washingtonia palms and a nice sandy beach. (There may be a sign, but don't count on it: The locals know where the beach is and don't care if anyone else is able to find it.) Don't plan to swim, however; as with most beaches near the cape, the surf can be rough.

6. **El Juncalito, south of Loreto.** South of Loreto on Highway 1 and off the highway via a half-mile dirt road (look for a sign to the nearby village east of the highway) are sand, palms, and a quarter-mile beach with some phosphorescence in the water. A fishing village nearby offers *pangas* (open boats with outboard motors) for rent.

7. **Playa Los Cerritos, south of Todos Santos.** Off Highway 19 south of Todos Santos via a 1.4-mile dirt road is a sheltered beach with good surfing and views of the coastline.

8. **Santa Maria Beach, Los Cabos.** On a secluded cove off Highway 1, by the Twin Dolphin Hotel between Cabo San Lucas and San Jose del Cabo, Santa Maria Beach is good for swimming, snorkeling, and diving. One catch: It's a public beach but reached by crossing through Twin Dolphin's private property; beachgoers are not permitted to park in Twin Dolphin's lot.

9. **Pueblo La Playa, San Jose del Cabo.** Also sometimes called La Playita and located about a mile east of downtown San Jose del Cabo, Pueblo La Playa has traditionally shared its stretch of beach with local fishermen and a seafood restaurant that buys its catch fresh from the boat.

10. **Medano Beach, Cabo San Lucas.** This busy, popular beach right in Cabo San Lucas has water-skiing, Jet-Skiing, snorkeling, canoeing, sailing, and windsurfing. A beachside restaurant called The Office serves grilled snapper or shrimp in garlic sauce, and the view is of the rock arch at Land's End.

TEN SPLURGES IN BAJA CALIFORNIA

1. **Hit the trendy Santa Fe Cafe.** In gentrifying Todos Santos, on Highway 19 north of Cabo San Lucas, the Santa Fe Cafe has grilled or steamed fish, super salads, and elegant desserts. It's on Calle Centenario facing the plaza, and is open daily, except Tuesdays, noon to 9pm, closed in mid-October during fiesta. ☎ 114/5-0340.

2. **Order the seafood platter at Cesar's in Loreto.** It's under a big thatched palapa roof near the intersection of Calle Zapata and Calle Benito Juárez. One platter is big enough for two unless you're starving. ☎ 113/5-0203.

3. **Take a dive at Land's End in Cabo San Lucas.** Divers should book an excursion to the unique underwater sandfalls and 900-foot canyon first explored by Jacques Cousteau at the tip of Land's End in Cabo San Lucas; bring along your certification. Get tanks and equipment from Cabo Aquadeportes at the Hacienda Hotel (☎ 114/3-0117) or Amigos del Mar across from the Marina (☎ 114/3-0505).

4. **Chow down on langouste (spiny lobsters) in Puerto Nuevo.** Puerto Nuevo, 30 miles south of Tijuana off the toll road (Highway 1D, paralleling the free Highway 1), via Exit 44, specializes in a local cooking style that splits them and grills them in oil with garlic and pepper. The most famous are served at five Ortega family places, including The Original Ortega Lobster House from 1954, but all are similar. With the lobster ($15 to $30, depending on size) comes rice, refried beans, fresh flour tortillas, and salsa and chips; cold beer or soda is readily available. Because of area overfishing in recent years, your lobster may be imported.

5. **Check into the lavish Hotel Twin Dolphin in Cabo San Lucas.** Come here either for a meal like garlic and peppered Brie or Thai grilled shrimp, or for a luxurious stay overnight. The driveway and parking lot can handle your RV, but call ahead (☎ 800/421-8925) since the road into the hotel is unmarked except for a sign that says PRIVATE PROPERTY.

6. **Check into the Rancho la Puerta spa.** Extend your visit long enough to take in a healthy and slenderizing week at Tecate's splendid Rancho la Puerta, a vegetarian spa with tennis courts, swimming pools, and famous early morning walks. ☎ 800/443-7565.

7. **Make an expedition to see prehistoric rocks.** The pretty white Hotel La Pinta, Highway 1, kilometer 174 (☎ 61/76-2601, or in the U.S. 800/336-5454), in the middle of Catavina's boulder fields, offers guided expeditions to the prehistoric carved and painted rocks, as well as claiming the best margaritas in the state of Baja California Norte.

8. **Search for the best margarita in Cabo San Lucas.** Claimants for the best margaritas in the southern half of the peninsula include the Whale Watcher's Bar in the Hotel Finisterra, a quietly romantic spot with a drop-dead view, and the beachfront bar in the lavish Hotel Cabo San Lucas.

9. **Take a deep-sea fishing trip.** Day trips leave from Cabo San Lucas, which boasts the biggest deep-sea fishing fleet in the world. Two local companies you can call ahead are Solmar Fishing (☎ 800/344-3349) or Fishing International (☎ 800/950-4242). Expect to pay around $300 and up for a full day with large boat, guide, and tackle; $120 a half day for a panga (smaller outboard).

10. **Go golfing.** There are some great new golf courses along the Highway 1 tourist strip between Cabo San Lucas and San Jose del Cabo, including two designed by Jack Nicklaus, one at posh Palmilla Resort (☎ 800/637-CABO), the other at the brand new Cabo del Sol (☎ 114/3-3149).

GREAT TAKE-OUT (OR EAT-IN) TREATS

La Baguette French Bakery, San Jose del Cabo. We consider their tasty sesame-seed whole wheat bread Cuban-style rather than French, but the whole wheat is luscious. Boulevard Mijares 10 in San Jose del Cabo.

The local liqueur called Damiana. Thought to be an aphrodisiac, it's served in a special margarita at the classic Damiana restaurant/bar in San Jose del Cabo, where fresh abalone is also on the menu. ☎ 114/2-0499.

Organic vegetables and strawberries. Sometimes for sale at the booths at Rancho Nuevo Villa on Highway 19 south of Todos Santos at kilometer 60.

Mama Espinoza's, El Rosario. The lobster burritos at Mama Espinoza's are not as good as they were in the old days before the road was paved, but

A BAJA ROAD GLOSSARY

"No hay magna sin hoy": "No lead-free gas today," a phrase you may hear at any station along the highway when your tank is running low

Alto: Stop (often interpreted by local drivers as "yield")

Autopista: Superhighway (don't expect to see this south of Ensenada)

Cuoto: Toll

Curva peligrosa: Dangerous curve (when this sign appears, it signifies a serious curve)

Llantera: Tire repair shop

Magna sin: Lead-free gasoline (usually designated by a green highway sign and a green pump at Pemex stations)

No rebase: No passing

Tope: An unmarked speed bump

Vado: Dip in the road

Vibradores: Speed bumps

they're still pretty tasty. Although the cafe is clean and attractive, it doesn't serve alcohol, so get your food to go if you want a cold Tecate to sip along with it. Located on Highway 1, near the Motel El Rosario.

Bags of oranges, mangos, and avocados. For sale at the roadside booths in the lovely old mining town of San Bartolo.

The fish market, Ensenada. The famous fried fresh fish tacos at Ensenada's fish market, doused with hot sauces and salsas and squirted with fresh lime juice, still cost under $1.

Bol Corona, Tijuana. The gigantic burritos at Bol Corona on Tijuana's Avenida Revolucion between Comercio and Benito Juárez are on sale between 7am and 4pm.

Supertacos de Baja California, Cabo San Lucas. The octopus tacos at Supertacos are doused with fresh salsa and rolled up in a hot fresh tortilla. It's located on Calle Morelos between Calle 20 de Noviembre and Calle Revolucion. No phone.

Caesar Hotel, Tijuana. The original Caesar salad, invented by and still served in the restaurant of the Caesar Hotel in Tijuana, will please hold-the-anchovies types; the original recipe does not call for those salty little fish. Located on Calle #5 at Avenida Revolucion. ☎ **668/8-2744.** Open daily for dinner.

Tijuana's huaraches. A staple of Tijuana's street food, this unique specialty is named after the flip-flop woven sandals. The thick oval tortillas are topped with ground beef, cheese, onions, and chiles. Look for them around the corner of Calle 1 and Avenida Revolucion and Calle 2 and Avenida Constitucion.

The fresh shellfish cocteles of San Felipe. They're tall glasses filled with any combination of shrimp, octopus, and clams in a tart, spicy salsa marinade. Served at brightly painted stalls along the main street in San Felipe.

Villa Maria Isabel RV Park, Mulege. Nab some of the baked goods at Villa Maria Isabel RV Park in Mulege, especially the chocolate chip cookies and the cheese onion rolls.

BAJA ADVENTURES

Several eco-tourism companies offer natural history expeditions around the Sea of Cortez, led by naturalists who also organize hiking, snorkeling, and diving. Oldest is **Baja Expeditions** (☎ **800/843-6967**) in La Paz, which also books 1-day summer diving and snorkeling trips to Los Islotes, where there's a sea lion rookery. **Natural Habitat Adventures** (☎ **800/548-7555**) can take you on a variety of trips, and **Oceanic Society Expeditions** (☎ **415/441-1106**), in San Francisco, leads boating expeditions from San Diego.

WILDLIFE WATCH

Along the Baja Highway, coyotes pad calmly along the roadsides like dogs, and birds of prey, mostly turkey vultures with red wrinkled heads and calculating eyes, sit atop tall cardoon cactus to check the terrain for any roadkill.

Porpoises play in the clear blue waters of the Sea of Cortez. In Cabo San Lucas, small boats take you out to the rocky arch and close to pelicans sunning on the rocks and sea lions cavorting in the water or snoozing in the sun.

Between January and March, **Amigos del Mar** (☎ **114/3-0505,** or in U.S. and Canada 800/344-3349) offers trimaran tours for whale watching from Cabo San Lucas. Snorkeling is especially good in Santa Maria Cove near Hotel Twin Dolphin.

The islands in the Sea of Cortez offer fantastic bird watching, with nesting blue-footed boobies, elegant long-tailed tropic birds, soaring frigate birds, brown pelicans, red-billed Heerman's gulls, and royal terns.

On the Road

TIJUANA & THE BORDER

If you're headed south from California on I-5, you'll cross the border at Tijuana and find plenty of insurance offices on the U.S. side of the border. Agricultural inspections also occur in several spots along the Baja Highway; the inspectors may ask to look in your refrigerator and pantry.

Tijuana is the foreign city most visited by Americans, and is the fifth largest city in Mexico, with nearly a million people. **Tijuana Cultural Center,** Paseo de los Heroes at Avenida Independencia, with sight-and-sound show, a

Baja Campgrounds

Benito Juarez Trailer Park ❼
Club Cabo Motel
 Campground ⓰
El Arco RV Resort ⓰
El Dorado Ranch ❺
El Padrino RV Park ❽
El Palomar Hotel and
 RV Park ❹
Estero Beach Hotel and
 Resort RV Park ❸
Guillermo's Trailer Park &
 Villa Vitta Hotel and
 Trailer Park ❻
La Paz RV Park ⓭
Loreto Shores ⓫
Mallarimo Restaurant,
 Bar and Trailer Park ❼
Oasis Hotel Suites and
 RV Resort ❶
Orchard Vacation Village ⓾
RV Park Brisa Marina ❻
RV Park Las Palmas ❾
San Felipe Marina Resort and
 Spa ❺
San Pedrito RV Park ⓮
The Tecate KOA (aka
 Rancho Ojai RV Park) ❷
Tripui Trailer Park ⓬
Vagabundas del Mar ⓯
Villa Maria Isabel ⓾
Villas de Loreto RV Park ⓫

museum, and IMAX scenic film, offers one good introduction to the country. **Mexitlan,** a 3.4-acre architectural theme park with 150 scale models of Mexico's most famous sites, is another. Here you can visit miniature versions of the silver city of Taxco, Mexico City before the conquest, or the famous Maya ruins of Yucatán. It's located on Avenida Ocampo between Calles 2 and 3, and is open 9am to 5pm. ☎ **66/38-4101.**

Shopping is another major Tijuana attraction (so long as you remember labels are not necessarily what they seem), along with horse and dog racing, jai alai, and bullfighting.

As in any large urban area, be extremely careful where you park your RV as well as where you walk around day or night. Avoid the raffish and sometimes dangerous **Zona Norte,** which is north of Calle 1 toward the border. Also, the city is not an easy one to maneuver in with an RV. RV campgrounds are to the south in Rosarita.

Campground Oases near Tijuana

Oasis Hotel Suites and RV Resort. Oasis, at Rosarito, is off the toll road at the El Oasis exit if you're going south; if you're headed north, take the Rancho del Mar exit and then cross over to the south to the El Oasis exit. Some 44 sites offer full hookups with 50-amp electric, patios, city water, satellite TV, and lots of activities. Tents and pets are not permitted. It's fairly pricey, with rates of $45 to $53. For reservations, call ☎ **888/709-9985** or book via e-mail at oasis@telnor.net.

The Tecate KOA (a.k.a. Rancho Ojai RV Park). Open year-round, the Tecate KOA is 13 miles east of Tecate on Highway 2 on a working ranch surrounded by oak trees. The 41 full hookup sites offer 30- and 50-amp electricity. Horseback riding and hayrides are available, as well as horseshoes, nature trails, and a playground. Call ☎ **664/4-4772.**

BAJA CALIFORNIA NORTE

About five million years ago, the San Andreas Fault ripped open along the west coast of Mexico, separating the slender, finger-shaped, 850-mile-long Baja Peninsula from the mainland. Most people who have only flown over it think of the peninsula as one big desert flanked by beaches on both sides, but there are also huge boulder fields around Catavina, lush groves of palm trees around San Ignacio, and a spine of mountain ranges almost the length of the peninsula.

Through much of Baja, the air is clean and sparkling clear, the sea and sky intensely blue. You may run into local coastal fog in areas marked *Zona Neblina* (foggy zone).

Despite its aridity, Baja California produces a surprising variety of agricultural products. Baja has been producing wine grapes since they were introduced in 1687 by the Jesuits. The **Santo Tomas Winery** south of

Ensenada was founded in 1888 in fields where vines had been planted a century before. You can go on a tour and tasting in the Bodega de Santo Tomas in the middle of Ensenada at Avenida Miramar (☎ **617/8-2509**), daily for a small fee, or sample the company's finer wines in their wood-paneled restaurant, **La Embotelladora Vieja,** built in a converted aging shed at Avenida Miramar at Calle 7 (☎ **617/4-0807**).

Past Santo Tomas, the agricultural Camalu Valley produces tomatoes, peppers, and squash. The tourist town of **San Quintin** and its beaches can be crowded, but farther south, Pacific waves splash on beaches empty except for the shadows of swooping pelicans and gulls.

Bright red splotches on the hillsides turn out to be drying red chile peppers. To eyes accustomed to easier terrain, the cactus begins to take on a life of its own after a day or two, turning into trees and people and distant landmarks. In the **Catavina boulder fields,** a tumble of smooth granite stones sets off the prickly flora as if ordered up by a set designer for Hollywood westerns. Especially weird are the knobby gray **elephant trees** with their peeling, scaly bark.

Campground Oases, Baja California Norte

Estero Beach Hotel and Resort RV Park. Six miles south of Ensenada off Highway 1 in Estero Beach. Gate-guarded resort with hotel, swimming pool, outdoor restaurant with lounge and music, sailing, windsurfing, Jet-Skis and water-skiing, snorkeling, diving, and fishing. There are 39 full-hookup sites, many by the estuary with 30-amp electricity and good wading-bird watching. Fire pits, flush toilets, showers. For reservations, dial ☎ **617/6-6230.**

El Palomar Hotel and RV Park. In Santo Tomas, on Highway 1 at mile 31, El Palomar has 47 sites, some shaded, with 20-amp electricity, tennis, swimming pool, and barbecue pits. It's located downhill from the main road near

RV Park Las Palmas in Santa Rosalia

The beautiful spit of sand at El Requeson on Bahia de la Concepción

vineyards, mission ruins, and olive trees. Across the road is a restaurant selling lobster tacos and a store selling olives from the grove. ☎ **615/3-8002.**

El Dorado Ranch. On the Sea of Cortez in San Felipe, El Dorado is a membership park that provides 100 full-hookup sites (30-amp electricity) with ocean views, saltwater fishing, and a heated pool. Drive 8 miles north of San Felipe on Highway 5 to a dirt road marked EL DORADO RANCH, then 1 mile east to the campground. ☎ **657/7-1277.**

San Felipe Marina Resort and Spa. San Felipe Marina is also a condo park but offers 143 paved full-hookup sites with 30- and 50-amp electricity, security, laundry, food service, and satellite TV. Interior roads are paved, tents are not permitted, and rates average $22. Call ☎ **657/7-1435** or e-mail: sanmarina@telnor.net.

BAJA CALIFORNIA SUR

The Eagle Monument at State Line, the dividing point between Baja Norte and Baja Sur, is stuck right in the middle of the highway, looks like a tuning fork, and can be seen for some distance. There's an obligatory stop here at an agricultural inspection station; any home-grown fruits that may have Mediterranean fruit fly infestations will be confiscated.

Guerrero Negro is a burst of civilization after the long, dry trek south, replete with pizza joint, disco, *supermercado,* and, most important, a Pemex station at the end of the long road into town. Watch for the unmarked *topes* in town. There's usually a long line at the gas station, so be prepared to wait. The major industry here is salt, hardly surprising since Las Salinas de

Guerrero Negro are the largest salt flats in the world. You'll see some of the evaporating ponds on the road into town.

There's a big new brouhaha at this writing because Japan's Mitsubishi Industries is proposing a joint venture with the Mexican government to build the world's largest saltworks on San Ignacio Lagoon, a World Heritage site and the last undisturbed breeding and calving ground of the California gray whale. The 116-square-mile area would contain a million-ton salt stockpile, fuel and water tanks, and 17 pumps operating 24 hours a day to draw 6,600 gallons of saltwater per second from the lagoon into the evaporation ponds.

A winter side trip to **Scammon's Lagoon** for whale watching is possible for four-wheel-drive vehicles and smaller RVs, but not trailers; see "Seven Swell Side Roads to Explore," later in this chapter.

Charming little **San Ignacio,** a couple of miles off the main highway, is worth the detour to see the rose-colored Dominican church finished in 1786. The Jesuits had earlier established a mission here in 1728. The *zócalo* (town square) across from the mission is shaded with fine old trees, and there are usually several impromptu RV parks nestled among the date palms on the edge of town.

In **Santa Rosalia,** the main sight is a prefabricated Eiffel church originally destined to be shipped to Africa, made from galvanized iron to dispel termites. It is cool and graceful and surprisingly modern inside. The one-way streets are wide enough for all but extra-wide RVs. The handsome balconied wooden buildings, made from imported timber, date from the late-19th-century days when a French syndicate built and operated the old copper smelter on the north edge of town.

Lush, tropical **Mulege** has several RV parks in a canyon down by the river, but they can be close and hot in summer. Rather than stay here, we'd recommend pushing south a few miles to the beautiful beaches around **Bahia de la Concepción** if you're in a self-contained RV. If you need something organized, **RV Park El Coyote,** 18 miles south of Mulege on Highway 1, has flush toilets, drinking water, and showers.

Looking a little like Puerto Vallarta did a long time ago, Mulege draws gringo dropouts, surfers, and divers. The mission church here was founded by the Jesuits in 1705 and built in its present style in 1766.

Campground Oases, Guerrero Negro to Loreto

RV Park Brisa Marina. By following a battered sign in Bahia de Los Angeles several years ago, we happened onto this park, 1.8 miles from Bahia de Los Angeles on a very rough track (it couldn't be called a road) marked by road signs advertising "150 sites." The derelict park was once a government RV park. Signs say "Parking $5," and there were no working hookups, plumbing, or water connections. But it was a quiet place by the Sea of Cortez with incredible moonlit nights, concrete pads for chairs and folding tables, and plenty of level space for parking. Sometimes someone came out from the village to collect, sometimes they didn't. We're not sure it's still there, but it's worth a look.

Guillermo's Trailer Park & Villa Vitta Hotel and Trailer Park. In Bahia de Los Angeles, if you can't locate the Brisa Marina (or don't want to), these are your two parking lot standbys, both in town. Guillermo's (☎ **665/0-3207**) has 22 full-hookup sites (15-amp electricity in the evenings only), and Villa Vitta (☎ **760/741-9583**) has 40 parking places in front of the hotel but no hookups.

Benito Juárez Trailer Park. Benito Juárez is located on Highway 1 beside the Eagle Monument and the Hotel La Pinta in Gerrero Negro, on the border separating North and South Baja. It has 60 sites with 15-amp hookups when the electric generator is working, which is 6am until 11am and again 5 to 11pm. There is no phone; the park looks like one the government built, then let go, like the Brisa Marina in Bahia de Los Angeles.

Mallarimo Restaurant, Bar and Trailer Park. Also in Guerrero Negro, a mile west of the junction of Highway 1 and Guerrero Negro Highway, located on the latter road. There are 36 full hookups with 15- and 20-amp electricity. They also offer whale-watching tours. Call ☎ **115/7-0250** for information and reservations.

El Padrino RV Park. Located on San Ignacio Road, 1.5 miles south of Highway 1 in San Ignacio, El Padrino has 20 dirt sites, some of them shaded and 10 with 20-amp electricity and full hookups. Call ☎ **115/4-0089.**

RV Park Las Palmas. On Highway 1, about 2 miles south of Santa Rosalia, RV Park Las Palmas is a welcome sight in this area of sparse RV accommodations. The recently developed park has 30 full hookups with 20-amp electricity and shade palapas, and a laundry and recreation room with a pool table (at least it had one when we stayed there). Phone ☎ **115/2-2070.**

Orchard Vacation Village. Mulege is a long-time tourist destination with several established RV parks, including this one, prettily landscaped and set in a tree-lined valley by a river about a half mile east of town on Highway 1. There are 35 full hookups with 30-amp electricity, rest rooms, and showers. Call them at ☎ **115/3-0300.**

Villa Maria Isabel. Villa Maria Isabel, also in Mulege, is on Highway 1 a mile and a half south of town, with 24 hookup sites with 30-amp electricity and a laundry. Call them at ☎ **115/3-0246.**

LORETO TO LA PAZ

The primary sight in town is the lovely old mission of **Nuestra Senora de Loreto,** founded in 1697 and the first mission and permanent European settlement in the Californias. The mission was badly damaged by a hurricane in 1829, and the town began restoring it in the past decade.

What used to be the best hotel in town, the Stouffer Presidente Loreto, closed down for a couple of years for lack of business and reopened as the Diamond Eden Resort from Allegro Resorts, for adults only with a clothing-optional beach.

South of Loreto, the **Sea of Cortez** is breathtaking in the light of dawn with the sun rising behind the islands. The road climbs steeply up around torturous curves, with the sawtoothed mountains of the Sierra Giganta plunging straight down into the shimmering, ink-blue sea. Don't get too caught up in admiring the scenery, however, since around each one of the curves you can expect to meet a huge truck barreling along well above the speed limit.

In the southern desert, roadside cacti double as billboards, with signs tacked on them saying LONCHERIA, BEER, and TYRE RIPER (tire repair). Along the sides of the roads, dead animals, mostly cows but some burros and dogs, have been shoved over out of the traffic and lie, still and swollen, legs stretched out taut. The vultures (locals call them *zopilotes*) study them with a proprietary eye but won't start to work until they ripen a bit more. After the feast, there will be nothing left but scraps of desiccated hide. Even the bones disappear.

The splats on the windshield here are not the usual fat bugs but butterflies, both fluttering yellow ones and smaller white ones.

At Insurgentes and Ciudad Constitucion, farmers have learned from Israeli agricultural experts how to get optimum yield out of irrigated desert, and the sprawling acres of agribusiness farms sport conspicuously new housing units for farm workers.

La Paz, the capital and largest city in Baja Sur, with a population of around 170,000, has a giant sculpted dove of peace dominating a traffic circle as you enter town, and a neat grid of manageable streets until you get into the old part of town near the waterfront.

This was once a major pearling center. The pearls were first discovered by sailors who survived a mutiny on the ship *Concepcion,* sent out by

RV TRAVEL WARNING

The worst road surface along the entire route is the stretch south from Loreto most of the way to Ciudad Insurgentes. This is also an area with the most beautiful scenery, so proceeding slowly is a good idea. This was the area where the bumpy road caused a lid from a jar of peanut butter in the refrigerator to come unscrewed and the roll of toilet paper in the bathroom to unwind into a long ribbon on the floor.

Hernán Cortés in 1535. The greedy Cortés was so pleased at the booty that he joined a return expedition personally, claiming the place for Spain and attempting to colonize it with a group of settlers. They stuck it out for 3 years before giving up for lack of food and water. The area wasn't permanently settled until 1811.

In 1853, an American general named William Walker from the Mexican-American War invaded La Paz on the grounds that it should have been part of the treaty that gave the state of California to the United States after the war. Seven months later he left after learning the Mexican Army was on its way and his own government did not support his claim. Undaunted, he went south to Nicaragua, made himself president, and ultimately was executed by a firing squad.

South of La Paz, just below the town of Santiago, is a turnoff to the spherical **Tropic of Cancer monument,** a good place for a "we were here" photo.

Campground Oases, Loreto to La Paz

Villas de Loreto RV Park. Probably the best in Loreto, Villas de Loreto is east of Highway 1's Loreto exit off Pedro de Ugarte road on Calle Francisco Madero. They do not accept tents, but do provide 12 full hookups with 20-amp electricity. They also have food service, a pool and playground, rest rooms, and showers, and are by the sea. Call ☎ **113/5-0586.**

Loreto Shores. Also on Calle Francisco Madero, Loreto Shores has 36 full hookups and 20-amp electricity, security, saltwater fishing, swimming, and boat rentals. ☎ **113/5-0629.**

Tripui Trailer Park. Located 16 miles south of Loreto off Highway 1 (¼ mile east of the Puerto Escondido exit, near a nautical park development with marina), Tripui Park draws mostly seasonal or permanent resident Americans, with only 31 transient spaces in an overflow gravel lot. The park itself has flush toilets, showers, swimming pool, tennis courts, and lovely landscaping, but overnighters may feel like poor relations. ☎ **113/3-0818.**

La Paz RV Park. Just northeast of La Paz (1.7 miles from the junction of Highway 1 and Boulevard Las Garza, then 1.2 miles down an unmarked dirt road to the right), the park is located by the sea with 48 full hookups (20- and 30-amp), swimming pool, clean flush toilets and showers, Jacuzzi, paperback book swap, cable TV, squash court, laundry, and restaurant. Call ahead for reservations at ☎ **112/2-8787.**

LOS CABOS

Los Cabos ("the Capes") is a new tourism and marketing name given by the government for the two old settlements at the tip of the Baja Peninsula, sedate and colonial **San Jose del Cabo** and kicky, booming **Cabo San**

Lucas. The 20 miles between the two is turning into a golf course– and hotel-lined resort strip far too fast to suit veteran visitors.

Traffic is bumper-to-bumper now on most of Cabo's streets, even those narrow, bumpy, sandy lanes that still crisscross most of the town. Our 27-foot motorhome, a palatial shelter along the drive down, turned into a clumsy behemoth in the beeping tourist traffic, especially in the bedlam between the two towns in the vicinity of the modern international airport.

In general, Baja's not much for **nightlife,** but aside from golf and beaches, Los Cabos is almost nothing but. Van Halen's **Cabo Wabo nightclub** in Cabo San Lucas is sure to please young rockers with its live bands, as will the tequila shooters at **Squid Roe,** one of the raucous Grupo Anderson restaurants. **Iguana Grill & Bar** is back in San Jose del Cabo with dancing under the stars to live music, and **Senor Sushi's** in Cabo San Lucas provides good happy-hour people-watching.

For us, the beginning of the end of Cabo San Lucas's appeal was the first time we sailed into the bay and saw the gigantic, ugly, pinky-orange Plaza Las Glorias, looking like a transplant from Malaga or Marbella, squatting and glowering where there used to be bobbing fishing boats and a view to the hills.

Anyhow, the air is still dazzlingly clear and the sky bright blue.

Campground Oases, Los Cabos

San Pedrito RV Park. Five miles south of Todos Santos on Highway 19, then 2 miles west on a dirt road, San Pedrito has 51 RV sites, hookups (20-amp), satellite TV, showers, flush toilets, laundry room, restaurant, swimming pool, and beach. Call ☎ 112/2-4520.

Vagabundas del Mar. Just north of Cabo San Lucas on Highway 1 (at kilometer 3.5, about ¾ mile east of the junction of Highway 1 and the Highway 19 bypass), Vagabundas del Mar has 95 spaces, most with full hookups and 30-amp electricity, plus a swimming pool, shade trees, paved interior roads, flush toilers, showers, and laundry. Most of the inhabitants are seasonal or full-time residents and members of a club by the same name. To join the club, call ☎ 707/374-5511. For park information, call ☎ 114/3-0290.

Club Cabo Motel Campground. Near Cabo San Lucas, Club Cabo is off the junction of Highway 1 and the Highway 19 bypass about a mile down a side dirt road. The ten full hookups offer 20-amp electrical connections, and the campground also has rest rooms, showers, heated pool and spa, security, and laundry. Call ☎ 114/3-3348.

El Arco RV Resort. Two miles east of the junction of Highway 1 and the 19 bypass on Highway 1, El Arco offers 90 full hookups with 20-amp electric, food service, and a pool. Call ☎ 114/3-1686.

COMING HOME

While it takes little or no time to cross into Mexico at Tijuana, the wait coming back into the United States can be an hour or more. Consider crossing back into California at Tecate, southeast of San Diego, or Mexicali, south of Calexico. Both connect to I-8.

Seven Swell Side Roads to Explore

1. **Take the road to Bahia de Los Angeles.** The bay is stark and surreal, flat and smooth as a mirror, dotted with bare islands that shine blue in the gathering twilight, and a full white moon in the blue sky. The town itself isn't cute or historic, just a scruffy fishing town with a half-dozen turkey vultures perched around the dump. RVers will find the Villa Vita Trailer Park and adjacent Guillermo's Trailer Park, both little more than waterside parking lots, in town. The road (marked BAHIA DE LOS ANGELES and heading off Highway 1 at kilometer 280) is rough in spots, with some serious *vados* that have washed out, and it's lined with acres of spooky boojum cacti.

2. **Follow Route 3 to Tecate from Ensenada into vineyard country.** You can stop at the Pedro Domeq winery and taste or buy the modest local wines. Treats: Olive trees on the hillsides, coyotes along the roadside, and very inexpensive clay pottery in Tecate. If you want to cross the border into California, Tecate is simplicity itself compared to Tijuana, where the line of cars is long and slow.

3. **Head for San Felipe.** The other end of Route 3 between Ensenada and San Felipe, also paved, will take you up a steep climb (not recommended for those pulling fifth-wheels or long trailers) out of Ensenada. On the downhill side and the second uphill climb you'll see a heavy concentration of barrel cactus. Turn south on Highway 5 to the fishing and beach town of San Felipe, which can be rowdy and crowded during holiday weekends and spring break. There are a number of RV parks around San Felipe (see "Campground Oases, Baja California Norte," above), as well as fishing boats and deep-sea charters. And there is a very loud and lively all-terrain-vehicle crowd using dune buggies.

4. **Take a whale-watching detour from Guerrero Negro.** California gray whales use Scammon's Lagoon as a nursery when the mouth is not silted up too much for them to get in. A 16-mile side trip to the lagoon from the highway south of GN is marked LAGUNA OJO DE LIEBRE on a washboard sand road across the desert. You'll find some primitive campsites and whale-watching boats at the end of the road. Whale sightings are possible December through May.

Vultures perch atop a
cardoon cactus to survey
the landscape.

5. **Visit Baja's old 19th-century gold and silver mining towns.** The
   drive along Highway 1 from the junction of 1 and 19 to Los Barriles at
   the coast goes through El Triunfo and San Antonio, where roadside
   vendors sell handwoven baskets and bags of fresh oranges and avocados. The route to the coast over the wooded Sierra Laguna mountains is beautiful. Las Barriles is the windsurfing capital of Baja, with
   some RV camping in the vicinity, most of it down washboarded sand
   roads.

6. **Stop by Santiago, home of Baja's one and only zoo.** Highway 1
   from San Jose del Cabo to Los Barriles passes through the little town
   of Santiago, which has the only zoo in Baja California, and near where
   the Tropic of Cancer monument is located. Once you are south of it,
   you're officially in the tropics.

7. **Go snorkeling and diving in Cabo Pulmo.** The road from Highway 1 to La Ribera and south to Cabo Pulmo is gradually being
   improved and paved, although it runs slightly inland from the original
   dirt East Cape route. Cabo Pulmo has the best snorkeling and diving
   in Baja (partly because it has the only live coral reefs) as well as beautiful beaches, some of which were clothing-optional the last we heard.
   There are several areas suitable for self-contained camping along the
   route, including the beaches at the north and south end of Bahia
   Pulmo. Ask locally before trying to finish the loop into San Jose del
   Cabo; the road is heavily washboarded and subject to erosion.

Travel Quiz: Name That Road

The bouncy road to Baja has been called many names, some of them unprintable, but the following highways also have nicknames for distinctive characteristics, some of them flattering, some of them not. See if you can match up the road names with the route numbers below.

1. *Life* magazine may have been derisive when it called this "The Loneliest Road in America," but now proud signs along the route brag about it.

2. Alligator Alley's eponymous reptiles may be spotted along this road, but you'll need to get out of your RV to see them.

3. The Million Dollar Highway is so-called because, some say, it's paved with silver-bearing ore; others say the name comes from a 3-mile stretch that in 1883 cost more than $1 million to build.

4. Nicknamed the Alcan, this highway has only 20% of its roadway in the state it's named for.

5. Killer Highway, the Hard Ride, and Blood Alley are a few of the nicknames given to this road.

6. Top of the World Highway has few road signs and no guard rails or pavement.

a. British Columbia's Route 97, Yukon's Highway 1, and Alaska's Route 2

b. Colorado's U.S. 550 between Ouray and Ironton Park

c. Route 93 from Phoenix, Arizona, to Wells, Nevada

d. Nevada's U.S. 50 between Fernley and Ely

e. Yukon's Route 9 and Alaska's Route 5 between Dawson City and Eagle

f. Florida's I-75 between Ft. Lauderdale and Naples

ANSWERS: 1 (d); 2 (f); 3 (b); 4 (a); 5 (c); 6 (e)

6

Utah's Parks & Canyons

UTAH CONTAINS AN UNPRECEDENTED FIVE NATIONAL PARKS, SEVEN national monuments, seven national forests, two national recreational areas, one national historic site, and forty-five state parks.

Utah is where Butch Cassidy and Etta Place rode a bicycle in *Butch Cassidy and the Sundance Kid,* where Thelma and Louise drove off the cliff into the canyon, and where Max von Sydow delivered the Sermon on the Mount in *The Greatest Story Ever Told.*

It's where the California gull is the state bird, where the world's most famous automobile commercial was filmed, and where Brigham Young took his 27th wife.

America's first department store was unveiled in Salt Lake City in 1868, Philo T. Farnsworth (the little-heralded inventor of television) was born in Beaver in 1906, and the first licensed franchise for Kentucky Fried Chicken—still serving up finger-lickin' chicken today—is located on State Street in Salt Lake City.

Mountain man Jim Bridger tasted the waters of the Great Salt Lake and thought he'd reached the Pacific; mountain man Robert Redford, shooting the film *Jeremiah Johnson,* sniffed the clear, clean air of the Wasatch Mountains and thought he'd reached Nirvana; and countless wandering hobos dreamed of licking the Big Rock Candy Mountain.

Early-day tourists flocked to take the waters at Schneitter's Hot Pots, later turned into The Homestead Resort, and to gawk at the wild man of Borneo, a pair of Siamese twins, and an alligator pit at the fantasy towers of Saltair, the Coney Island of Salt Lake, whose ghost pavilion still lurks off I-80 some 17 miles west of Salt Lake City.

> *"This is the most beautiful place on earth."*
> —Edward Abby,
> Desert Solitaire, 1968

Utah Highlights

Anasazi Indian Village State Park ⑩
Arches Vineyards ⑲
Big Rock Candy Mountain ⑫
Bumbleberry Inn ⑥
Capitol Reef Inn and Cafe ⑬
Charlie Steen's dream house/Sunset Grill Restaurant ⑳
Circleville, Butch Cassidy's boyhood home ⑪
College of Eastern Utah Prehistoric Museum ②
Cowboy's Smoke House ⑨
Delicate Arch ㉒
Dick's Cafe ③
Dodge City's Main Street ⑦
Eddie McStiff's Brew Pub ⑯
Electric Jim's Cafe ⑥
Fat City Smokehouse ⑱
Fisher Towers ㉑

Grafton Ghost Town ⑥
Hole N' the Rock Home ⑰
John Wesley Powell River History Museum ⑤
Kolob Canyons ⑤
Kolob Reservoir ⑧
Monument Valley Navajo Tribal Park ⑭
Natural Bridges National Monument ⑮
Newspaper Rock State Historical Monument ⑭
Petrified Forest State Park ⑩
Price City Cemetary ⑫
Sauropod Track Site ④
Snow Canyon State Park ④
Vernal dinosaur garden ㉒
Wolfe Ranch ④
Zion IMAX ⑥

Countryside around Zion National Park

This is where dinosaurs roamed 500 million years ago, where the Anasazi, or Ancient Ones, planted corn 2,000 years ago, and where Chinese miners at Silver Reef put food on family graves a century ago (giving local Paiutes a taste for Chinese cuisine).

Utah has the highest literacy rate, largest average household size, second highest birth rate, and second lowest death rate in the 50 states. The average citizen lives to be 75.76 years old, and the average age is 25.7. More than 70% of the state's population are members of the Church of Jesus Christ of Latter-day Saints, also known as Mormons.

THE MORMONS

In the spring of 1830, a devout young man in Fayette, New York, named Joseph Smith, published the Book of Mormon and founded the Church of Jesus Christ of Latter-day Saints, a charismatic religion claiming to be a restoration of the original church. Among its tenets were polygamy and an active program of proselytism, neither of which found favor in the neighborhood.

Chased from New York and then Ohio, Smith and his followers settled in Nauvoo, Missouri, where they developed a city of 20,000. But the new neighbors were no more hospitable than the old ones, burning and killing until Smith decided in 1844 it was time to move again. In the meantime, however, he declared himself a candidate for president of the United States and said that if elected he would not move West.

> *"This is the right place!"*
> —Brigham Young in 1847, on first seeing Salt Lake Valley

When members of the church smashed a printing press they believed was publishing libel against them, Smith and his brother were jailed, then taken from prison by a mob and killed.

The man who succeeded Smith as church leader was Brigham Young. At the end of 1845, when the state of Illinois repealed the city charter for Nauvoo, he organized an advance party to go West looking for a new settlement. Beginning in early 1846, church members loaded their goods onto covered wagons, hitched up their horses, and led them down to ferries on the Mississippi River. The great Mormon exodus had begun.

That year they got as far as Iowa, and the next year Brigham Young and his company of pioneers entered the Salt Lake Valley on July 24, 1847. The migration continued, with thousands of the devout literally walking and pulling their possessions in handcarts, until by 1900 the Mormons had established 500 settlements in and around Utah, many of them in arid, inhospitable desert.

Certainly the most dramatic moment was at Hole-in-the-Rock in 1879, when 230 Mormons blasted a hole through a 50-foot cliff at Glen Canyon and lowered their 80 wagons by chains and ropes to the river 1,800 feet below, where homemade rafts waited. They went on to found the town of Bluff, which today claims a population of 250—20 more than its founding fathers. Today boaters and four-wheel-drive travelers can see the spot where the hole was blasted in the rock.

The Mormon cause was severely set back in 1857 when some xenophobic members, fearful of federal interference and anxious to keep out both miners and eager new settlers, triggered the infamous Mountain Meadows Massacre, where Mormon militia members and local Indians together slaughtered 120 of the 137-member Fancher wagon train party bound for California. The only survivors were 17 children under the age of 7. Ironically, the Fancher party had taken the southern route despite warnings of possible friction in Utah because all had heard the terrible stories of the Donner Party tragedy crossing a northern route a decade earlier. A marker off Route 18 near the town of Central in southwestern Utah identifies the massacre site.

It took almost 50 years and the church's outlawing of polygamy before Utah achieved statehood in 1896.

RVing Utah's National Park Country

Early on an October morning, the snowcapped Henry Mountains glisten against a blue sky. Down every wash a stalwart line of cottonwoods has turned a glowing gold. Flocks of tiny Berwick's wrens, exuberant after the rain, flutter up past our windshield and across the Bicentennial Highway. Water shines from holes and grooves in slickrock, and snow dusts the red mesas and buttes and throws twisted black junipers into sharp relief. As we

> ### RV TRAVEL ADVICE
>
> It was 4pm, and the Canyonlands park ranger, standing by a sign saying CAMPGROUND FULL, suggested we might drive around anyhow and check for space. We discovered a couple packing up to check out and nabbed the last free space in the park. Moral: Don't give up without a try.

begin to climb toward Natural Bridges National Monument, the whole desert forest of piñon pines and sagebrush is covered with puffy white clumps of snow. Everything is indescribably, breathtakingly beautiful.

Because so much of Utah is public land, it makes an ideal getaway for RVers, especially those who enjoy self-contained camping in parklands and the wilderness. Driving through the state, we always try to imagine the pioneers and early Mormon settlers moving slowly through the incredibly eerie terrain with plenty of time on their hands and a little creative daydreaming. It's the only way some of the geological landmarks could have been named. We stare in vain at spots like Capitol Reef's Capitol Dome or Zion's Great White Throne and wonder who on earth could have thought that particular rock really looks like a dome or a throne.

The state tourism people have divided southern Utah into four different areas—**Color Country** in the south central and southwest, including Zion and Bryce Canyon National Parks; **Canyonlands** to the southeast, including Canyonlands and Arches National Parks; **Panoramaland** in the west central region, including Capitol Reef National Park; and **Castle Country** in the east central sector, the terrain where Butch Cassidy used to ride.

Northern Utah is divided into **Golden Spike Empire,** named for the spot where the first transcontinental railroad was finished in 1869, the extreme northwest corner reaching from the Nevada border east to Ogden; **Bridgerland,** named for mountain man Jim Bridger, the small northeastern corner surrounding Logan; **Great Salt Lake Country,** which includes Great Salt Lake, the Bonneville Salt Flats, and Salt Lake City; **Mountainland,** with Utah's best ski country and Sundance Resort; and **Dinosaurland,** notable for dinosaur digs, Green River rafting, and dude ranches. You'll need to remember the divisions when using the otherwise excellent state travel guides.

One of the newest recreation areas in Utah is **Grand Staircase–Escalante National Monument,** so designated in September 1996 and the first monument to be administered by the Bureau of Land Management instead of the National Park Service. Gateways to the new national monument are Escalante and Boulder on Route 12 and Kanab on Route 89, all in the south central area of Utah. With world-class paleontological sites and a panoramic geologic sampler, Escalante attracts adventuresome hikers and four-wheel-drive explorers. Very few services and facilities are available yet inside the monument.

I-70 is the only paved road accessing the spectacular scenery of the **San Rafael Swell,** Utah's most inaccessible wilderness area. We've done the drive in both directions, and strongly urge you to go west to east for the most dramatic impact. There are numerous scenic turnouts on the 100-mile route between Salina and Green River, but no services, so be sure to top off the gas tank before crossing the reefs.

Utah state parks accept advance reservations if you phone ☎ **800/ 322-3770** or 801/322-3770 weekdays between 8am and 5pm mountain time. For Utah national forests, phone ☎ **800/280-2267.**

HITTING THE HIGHLIGHTS

The roads are generally very good in Utah, so you'll be able to move along as briskly as necessary, except when the first snow begins to fall in late October or early November. The highlights could be covered in as little as 7 days, but you'd have very little time to hike and explore.

Zion and Bryce Canyon National Parks require a minimum of a full day each, with 2 days in each allowing time to hike a bit as well.

RVers who choose not to take the tunnel route from Zion to Bryce can return to I-15, make the short detour into Kolob Canyons from the interstate, then exit at Cedar City to drive through Cedar Breaks and along Route 143 past Panguitch Lake, a very scenic route, before turning south on U.S. 89 to connect with Route 12 to Bryce.

Although geology buffs will enjoy the dead-end scenic drive that delves more deeply into **Capitol Reef National Park,** travelers pressed for time can skip it. But everyone should take the time to drive into the orchards and campground area at **Fruita,** as well as make roadside stops along the way at the old schoolhouse and the cliff petroglyphs.

If time permits, swing south from the junction at Hanksville to drive **Bicentennial Highway,** which allows you a good look at Glen Canyon National Recreation Area at Hites Crossing and a visit to Natural Bridges National Monument. Otherwise, head north to I-70 and take U.S. 191 south at exit 180 to drop down in Moab, Arches, and Canyonlands.

Allow a full day each for **Arches, The Needles,** and **Islands in the Sky,** adding to the latter a side detour into Dead Horse Point State Park.

GOING FOR THE LONG HAUL

We ran across quite a few people in Utah who came out on a vacation and never went home, so consider yourself warned. One could certainly spend a long, happy season RVing, hiking, and biking in and around the public lands with an occasional hop into town to restock the larder, fill up with gas, top off the water, and dump the holding tanks.

Two weeks in each park or national monument, taking into consideration the 14-day camping limit, would give plenty of time to explore each, and a week or two on a houseboat in **Lake Powell** would provide pure pleasure. Add another 2 weeks at particularly scenic BLM areas, such as the **Colorado River** outside Moab, and you'll find an entire season filled with appealing things to do.

The temporary employment scene in Moab is usually active, so full-timers can find seasonal shops looking for clerks and restaurants hiring waiters. In winter, ski areas are good sources of seasonal employment.

Travel Essentials

WHEN TO GO

Any time of year, some part of Utah is in its prime. In winter, skiers flock to "the greatest snow on earth," Utah's champagne powder. Most of its dozen major ski areas are clustered to the east of Salt Lake City, but Brian Head ski resort, nearly 10,000 feet with a long snow season, is 12 miles off I-15 at Parowan, near Cedar City. St. George in the southwest's Dixie area is mild in winter. Fall and spring are the ideal times for RVers to visit Utah's national parks; summer is hot in the lower elevations, but cooler at Brian Head, Cedar Breaks, and Bryce Canyon. All the national parks, however, are jam-packed in summer with Americans and Europeans.

WHAT TO TAKE

Sunblock, a sun hat, good walking or hiking shoes, an adequate supply of favorite spirits, a camera, and at least twice as much film as you'd expect to use (it's that photogenic!).

WHAT TO WEAR

Take layered clothing for all of Utah's parks. In late fall and winter, you'll want heavy parkas and boots or shoes with snow-safe treads. We encountered considerable snow in mid-October at Bryce Canyon and Cedar Breaks, while Zion, Canyonlands, Arches, and Capitol Reef still had sunny, shirt-sleeve weather. In summer's heat, natural fibers help absorb perspiration.

TRIMMING COSTS ON THE ROAD

As a state, Utah is much less expensive than many, although sparsely settled southern Utah does not offer frequent or varied shopping opportunities. Keep your larder well stocked and your gas and water tanks topped off when venturing into less-traveled territory.

With so much of southern Utah's most scenic terrain under Bureau of Land Management (BLM) administration, RVers will find some no-fee undeveloped campsites where camping is permitted under the following conditions: camping in one site is limited to 14 days; campers must pack out all trash; campfires may not be left unattended; and camping is not permitted within 300 feet of springs or ponds so that water is accessible to wildlife.

Self-contained RVs meet with BLM's regulations as long as dumping of gray or black water takes place only in designated sanitary dump stations and never on the ground. Call the **BLM** in Salt Lake City at ☎ **801/539-4001** for information.

WHERE TO GET TRAVEL INFORMATION

All of the following park offices will be able to provide you with travel information:

- **Utah Travel Council,** ☎ 800/200-1160, fax 800/538-1399, www.utah.com
- **Arches National Park,** ☎ 435/259-8161
- **Bryce Canyon National Park,** ☎ 435/834-5322, www.nps.gov/brca
- **Canyonlands National Park,** ☎ 435/259-7164
- **Capitol Reef National Park,** ☎ 435/425-3791, www.infowest.com/ garfield
- **Cedar Breaks National Monument,** ☎ 435/586-9451, www. utahsplayground.org
- **Dead Horse Point State Park,** ☎ 435/259-2614
- **Glen Canyon National Recreation Area,** ☎ 435/826-4315
- **Grand Staircase of the Escalante National Monument,** ☎ 435/ 826-4291, www.blm.gov/utah//monument
- **Natural Bridges National Monument,** ☎ 435/692-1234
- **Zion National Park,** ☎ 435/772-3256

DRIVING & CAMPING TIPS

- **Use the plat system.** Brigham Young directed Utah's early Mormons to lay out street plats like a giant checkerboard, with streets running true north and south and true east and west from a central meridian point. If an address is 500 South 700 East, for instance, you drive 5 blocks south from the center and then 7 blocks east. Blocks are laid out in increments of 100. Whether you're in Salt Lake City or Moab, the plan holds true. They were also instructed to make streets "wide enough for a team of four oxen and a covered wagon to turn around."

- **Bring along tapes or CDs.** Otherwise you'll have to listen to the car radio, and on the radio in Utah you can get only three sounds day or night: the Mormon Tabernacle Choir, country music, and Rush Limbaugh.

- **Be aware of Utah's mysterious liquor laws.** Utah's liquor laws allow purchases of wine and spirits by the bottle in state liquor stores in many areas except on Sundays and holidays. Beer with 3.2% alcohol can be purchased in grocery and convenience stores 7 days a week. Licensed restaurants may serve alcohol by the drink, but neither drinks nor a wine list can be offered by the server; the patron must request them. In some areas, alcohol by the drink can be served only if patrons "join" a private club by paying a small fee. Lounges and taverns serve only beer. "Brown-bagging," bringing your own alcohol for consumption in a location, is no longer permitted.

- **Don't break the cryptobiotic crust.** The direst thing you can do in southern Utah is to walk, bike, drive on, or otherwise break the cryptobiotic crust, a fragile and ancient covering that looks dark brown and crumbly and nurtures virtually all desert life, both flora and fauna. One careless step can destroy crust that will take 50 to 100 years to recover. Always stay on the trail or roadway. As locals say, tiptoe through the crypto.

The Best Utah Sights, Tastes & Experiences

OFF-THE-WALL ATTRACTIONS

The Big Rock Candy Mountain. Located on Highway 89 south of Richfield, off I-70, exit 23 to Sevier, it really does look a little like a mound of caramel. Neither folk singer Burl Ives nor songwriter Harry McClintock ever saw it, but that didn't stop them from making money out of a hit song about it. Folk experts John Lomax and Charles Seeger said the original version, with its "lemonade springs" and "lakes of stew," was sung by old-time hobos to lure young farm boys into a life on the road.

The Vernal dinosaur garden. Sculpted by Elbert Porter at the Utah Field House of Natural History State Park in Vernal, the garden displays 13 critters, from woolly mammoths to triceratops. The park is at 235 E. Main St. in Vernal (☎ **435/789-3799**). Utah is also home to the largest dinosaur egg found so far, discovered at the Cleveland-Lloyd Dinosaur Quarry south of Price and exhibited in the **Prehistoric Museum** of the College of Eastern Utah, 200 E. 100 North, in Price (☎ **435/637-5060**).

Hole 'n the Rock Home, South of Moab. Not to be confused with the place where the Mormons crossed Glen Canyon, the Hole 'n the Rock Home in Moab is a 5,000-square-foot drilled-out cavern that was home for Albert and Gladys Christensen beginning in 1952. It has 14 rooms, a 65-foot chimney, a built-in deep fryer, and a bathtub carved from a rock. During the 12 years Albert spent creating it, he also had time to paint a Sermon on the Mount and carve the head of Franklin D. Roosevelt in the rock above the house. After Albert died in 1957, Gladys continued to run their cafe and gift shop until her death in 1974. Now their family operates it as a museum and memorial, and the gift shop sells souvenirs. It's on U.S. 191 south of Moab; admission $2.50 adults. ☎ **435/686-2250.**

The Zion IMAX big-screen theater. It's hard to believe, but near the entrance to Zion National Park is a new IMAX big-screen theater purporting to show "the Zion you came to see—the real Zion." Since we didn't succumb to the come-on and pay $6.50 a ticket for a 37-minute film, we are not sure what it shows that we missed by driving into the park itself. If your curiosity causes you to stop by when leaving the park by the Springdale exit, the theater promises to refund your park admission if you buy a movie ticket.

The John Wesley Powell River History Museum, Green River. This has to be the only museum in America dedicated to river-rapids runners, with some 15 Hall of Fame members to date. Admission is free but donations are appreciated. The handsome new museum commemorates Powell, the one-armed Civil War veteran who first mapped the Grand Canyon and navigated the Colorado River seated in a chair lashed atop a pine rowboat. Located at 885 E. Main St. in Green River. ☎ **435/564-3427.**

Circleville, boyhood home of Butch Cassidy. Circleville, on U.S. 89 about 25 miles south of I-70, was the boyhood home of Butch Cassidy, and where he came on his return from Bolivia (if, indeed, he ever went there), to meet with his mother for the last time in 1925. The family shared a blueberry pie, said Butch's sister, Lula Parker Betenson, who wrote a book about her famous brother. The outlaw's real name was Robert LeRoy Parker. What remains of their two-room log cabin is still standing south on U.S. 89.

Charlie Steen's dream house, Moab. Now the Sunset Grill Restaurant, the dream house sits perched atop the tallest hill in Moab, north of town on Route 191. (Locals opine that the view considerably surpasses the food, mostly steaks, pasta, and seafood.) Charlie was, you may remember, the Texan who became an overnight millionaire in the uranium market during the Cold War days of the 1950s. He struck pay dirt in 1952, and the rush of miners that followed quadrupled the population of Moab. His mine, named Mi Vida, brought him $60 million in a few short years. The house became a restaurant in 1974 when Charlie ran into bad tax and mining luck. Call the restaurant at ☎ **435/259-7146.**

HOT ROCKS

Moab's boundless bounty of uranium was first noted by France's Madame Curie when she used radioactive ore from Moab to develop radium in 1896 (some say she traveled to Utah and conducted experiments on-site). The supply finally bottomed out in the late 1960s.

Indian petroglyphs at Newspaper Rock State Historical Monument

Newspaper Rock State Historical Monument. Located 12 miles off U.S. 191 via Route 211 west, Newspaper Rock is an Indian-era billboard made up of petroglyphs (carvings incised on rock surfaces). Most of the drawings date back 1,000 years, attributed to prehistoric Indians and early Utes, with additions by white pioneer settlers and, unfortunately, a few contemporary vandals. A primitive, attractive, ten-site campground is here among the aspens, with two spaces for RVs up to 40 feet, along with grills and picnic tables but no water or hookups. Call the Bureau of Land Management for camping information at ☎ **435/259-6111.**

Price City Cemetery. The Price City Cemetery is the final resting place for a body shot by a proud posse in 1898, identified as Butch Cassidy, and laid out with great fanfare before burial. One of the many visitors couldn't stop laughing when viewing the corpse. Later, when a Wyoming lawman made a positive identification of the body as another outlaw, people realized the amused stranger had been Cassidy himself. The whole story is carved on the stranger's tombstone. Price is at the junction of U.S. 6 and U.S. 191 in the center of the state.

The Sauropod Track Site. Eight miles south of I-15 on U.S. 191 and north of the Arches National Park entrance, then 2 miles down a dirt road, is where four dinosaurs tramped through a damp river channel some 150 million years ago, leaving only footprints (but probably not taking pictures). Discovered in 1989, the footprints of the single brontosaurus are 2 feet wide, and one of the carnivores, probably an allosaurus, leaves evidence of having a limp. Don't attempt the trip in an RV during or after a rain or you may end up as a sightseeing attraction yourself for some future tourists.

Wolfe Ranch, in Arches National Park. Civil War veteran John Wesley Wolfe came here with his oldest son Fred searching for a place to raise cattle. His wife and three younger children remained in Etna, Ohio. Eventually, in 1906, his daughter Flora, with her husband and two children, came to stay, and talked her father into gentrifying the ranch. For her sake, he built a new cabin with a wood floor (the one you see today), ordered a 100-piece set of blue china dishes from the Sears Roebuck catalogue because she disliked tin plates, and bought her a camera and developing kit, with which she made one of the earliest known photographs of Delicate Arch. To get there, turn east off the main road onto Wolfe Ranch Road and continue to the parking area. A short walk leads to what's left of the ranch. A little farther up the trail you'll see some Ute petroglyphs.

SEVEN SITES OFFERING DÉJA VU ALL OVER AGAIN

1. **Grafton.** This picturesque ghost town, set against the towering rock walls of Zion National Park, is where Paul Newman and Katherine Ross rode a bicycle to the music of "Raindrops Keep Fallin' on My Head" in the film *Butch Cassidy and the Sundance Kid.* Turn south (200 East) on Bridge Road in Rockville, near the entrance to Zion National Park on Route 9, cross an old iron bridge, and follow a 4-mile dirt road to the old cemetery and town. Larger motorhomes and trailers might find it a tight squeeze in some spots, so we'd recommend pulling off at the tunnel information/scenic view turnout on Route 9 west of Rockville for an overview of the area.

2. **Fisher Towers.** History's most famous TV car commercials were shot outside Moab at a pair of 1,500-foot looming spires called Fisher

Lake Powell at Hites Crossing

Towers. A Chevrolet, lowered by helicopter, was shown sitting all alone atop a tall, narrow pinnacle rising high into the air, surrounded only by desert and craggy red rocks in all directions. The first commercial was such a big hit in 1964, a second one was shot in 1974 to wow a new buying generation. The towers are on Scenic Route 128 east from Moab at mile 21, with a road sign identifying them. A hiking trail to the towers and a picnic table are also at the site.

3. **Delicate Arch, Arches National Park.** All the book covers and posters you've ever seen about Utah leap to life at Delicate Arch. Early cowboys called the much-photographed 45-foot-high red sandstone arch "The Schoolmarm's Drawers," but to us it most closely resembles the bottom half of a bow-legged cowboy wearing chaps. The hike, the park's most popular walk, is a strenuous 480-foot ascent over a huge rock mountain similar to Australia's Ayers Rock; it seemed to us much longer than the 3-mile round-trip the park literature claims, especially on the uphill part. Once there, many visitors sit and stare in awe at the arch (trying, perhaps, to catch their breaths) while photographers clamber over precarious rocks for an ever-better angle. Late afternoon is best to photograph the golden light against the stone. The walk sets out from the Wolfe Ranch parking lot off the park's main road.

4. **Movie location in Moab.** Pick up a free "Moab Movie Locations" brochure in the Moab Information Center, Center and Main streets, and you can head for all your favorite movie locations in the area. An Indiana Jones fan? See where scenes for *Indiana Jones and the Last Crusade* (1988) were shot in Arches National Park. South Park Avenue is where the late River Phoenix (playing the young Indiana) and his Boy Scout companions were seen in the opening of the film, and The Windows area was also used in the early scenes. At Canyonlands' Island in the Sky, Max von Sydow as Christ delivered the Sermon on the Mount in *The Greatest Story Ever Told* (1963); he stood facing the Green River at the Green River Overlook on a rock to the left of the fence. Two thousand years later in cinema time, Thelma and Louise, in the film of the same name (1990), drove off the cliff under Dead Horse Point 10 miles down the Shafer Trail (also called Potash Road), an unpaved road off Route 279, located 19 miles south of Moab. Earlier in the film, at Arches' Courthouse Towers, they locked a pursuing police officer in his patrol car trunk, and several chase scenes were filmed in the La Sal Mountains outside the town of La Sal off Route 46. West of Moab is the little town of Thompson, off exit 185 from I-70, where the Silver Grill diner and its pinball machine and pool table scored prominently in *Thelma and Louise*.

For Western movie fans with long memories, in *Rio Grande* (1950), John Wayne rescued kidnapped cavalry children from a pueblo just off

Utah Scenic Byway 128, a half mile up a dirt road from milepost 19, and located the hideout in *The Comancheros* (1961) nine-tenths of a mile east of milepost 21. In *Cheyenne Autumn* (1963), cavalryman Richard Widmark chased the Cheyenne across a flat area south of the Arches' South Park Avenue. And Devils Garden in Arches served as the site where an Indian ambush trapped the U.S. cavalry in the truly terrible *Taza, Son of Cochise* (1953), starring Rock Hudson and Barbara Rush.

5. **Monument Valley Navajo Tribal Park.** Located in southeastern Utah on the Arizona border, Monument Valley Park is bisected by Highway 163. Famous for its appearances in a host of John Ford films, Monument Valley stood in for Texas in *The Searchers,* Arizona in *My Darling Clementine,* and New Mexico in *Stagecoach,* the classic film that introduced a tall, rangy actor named John Wayne to a larger audience than his previous B westerns had reached. Visit the **Visitor Center** (☎ **435/727-3287**), east on Monument Valley Road off Route 163, open daily for a self-guided driving map and information. The **Navajo Tourism Department** (☎ **520/871-6436**) will mail a guide for tours from 2 hours to a full day.

   Goulding's Monument Valley Campground & RV Park has nightly shuttle service to the company's historic lodge and trading post for a sound-and-light show. Open mid-March to the end of October, the park's 66 RV sites provide satellite TV, full hookups with 30-amp electric, and a heated pool. Take 163 south to Monument Valley west; go 2 miles. Reservations: ☎ **435/727-3235;** gouldings@gouldings.com.

6. **Snow Canyon State Park.** Northwest of St. George, Snow Canyon State Park is where Robert Redford in *The Electric Horseman* (1979) freed his stallion at the end of the film; Jane Fonda and Willie Nelson co-starred in the Sidney Pollack contemporary western set in Las Vegas.

7. **The Main Street of Dodge City.** The very main street where Marshall Dillon in TV's long-running series *Gunsmoke* faced gun battles weekly still stands in Johnson Canyon, 9 miles east of Kanab off Highway 89 on Johnson Canyon Road. Sometimes the set is open to visitors for a fee; otherwise, you can see it from the roadway with binoculars.

TEN MACHO THINGS TO DO IN UTAH

1. **Go mountain biking.** The tiny town of Brian Head, reached via Route 143 from exit 78 on I-15, offers 12 different routes rated "easy" to "advanced." Because the area is at 10,000 feet, it's cool enough in summer to enjoy biking but usually snow covered from November through May. Expect a rich variety of flora and fauna in the four life zones:

TALKIN' UTAH: A GLOSSARY

Butte: An isolated hill or mountain rising suddenly out of flat land.

Desert varnish: A dark, glossy finish on rock created by heat-loving bacteria that draw iron and manganese from airborne dust.

Gentile: In Latter-day Saints usage, any non-Mormon.

Hoodoo: An eroded pillar of sandstone topped with a hard rock cap and sculpted into eerie shapes.

LDS: Church of Jesus Christ of Latter-Day Saints, also called Saints or Mormons.

Mesa: A flat-topped, steep-walled land area; a table mountain.

Natural arches: Water-cut rock formations that stand on the skyline.

Natural bridges: Water-cut (including snow melting and refreezing) rock formations in the bottoms of canyons.

Petroglyphs: Carvings incised on rock surfaces.

Pictographs: Pictures drawn on rock surfaces.

Slickrock: A smooth, slippery rock formation burnished by "desert varnish."

Wash: The dry bed of a sometimes stream; never camp in these areas, and avoid them during rainstorms.

alpine, subalpine, Canadian, and transitional. You can get essential detailed maps locally. There are five bike-rental shops are in town: **Brian Head Bike Rentals,** 508 N. Hwy. 143 (☎ **435/677-3838**); **Brian Head X-C,** 223 Hunter Ridge Dr. (☎ **800/BIKE-SKI** or 435/677-2012); **Brian Head Resort** (☎ **800/27-BRIAN** or 435/677-2035); **Brian Head Sports,** 329 S. Brian Head Blvd. (☎ **435/677-2014**); and **George's,** 612 S. Brian Head Blvd. (☎ **435/677-2013**).

Local shuttle services or chairlifts can ferry you to the top of the hill and you can ride down. The nearest camping is in Cedar Breaks.

2. **Go white-water rafting and four-wheeling.** One-day expeditions that combine white-water river rafting and four-wheel-drive land tours are offered by Navtec Expeditions of Moab (☎ **800/833-1278;** www.navtec.com). A morning sports boat ride goes along the Colorado River gorge just underneath Dead Horse Point State Park, stopping to see dinosaur tracks, petrified wood, and Indian rock art. A buffet picnic lunch is served, then a transfer to 4×4s for a tour up Long Canyon and Gemini Bridges. Cost is around $75 for adults, $58 for kids up to 17.

3. **Go trail riding.** Trail rides from Pack Creek Ranch near Moab can be as short as an hour or two or as long as a 4-night pack trip into the backcountry. Previous riding is not necessary for the short rides, which start at $25 and can accommodate kids 6 and over. Morning and evening rides into Courthouse Wash in Arches National Park are also available in summer for $20 an hour, $35 for 2 hours. Meals and cabin or bunkhouse lodging are also available at the ranch, but reservations

need to be made well ahead of time. Call the ranch at ☎ **435/259-5505** (e-mail: pcr@packcreekranch.com; Web site www.packcreelramch.com).

4. **Go cross-country skiing or snowshoeing at Bryce Canyon.** Bryce Canyon in winter offers extraordinary views of bright red Navajo sandstone sprinkled with snow and sparkling in the sunlight against a clear blue sky. Cross-country skiing or snowshoeing are two excellent ways to see it. Self-contained RVs can stay in the park's North Campground near the visitor center during winter, although water is cut off and the sanitary dump closed down. There are no hookups. The 11-mile Rim Trail with its level terrain and sensational views down into the canyon is a good place to start. Snowshoer-wannabes can borrow a pair free from the rangers at the visitor center (at the north end as you enter the park), leaving a credit card or driver's license as a deposit, and set off in the snow. Call ☎ **435/834-5322** (www.nps.gov/brea).

5. **Go mountain biking on the Slickrock Trail.** From Moab, the North American capital of the sport, you can start on the 10-mile Slickrock Trail, tackled by 100,000 eager sprocketheads a year. Beginners are advised to start with Gemini Bridges or Hurrah Pass, each 14 miles long. In town, six bike shops, each with its obligatory espresso machine, rent or sell anything you might need, from maps to machines: **Chile Pepper Bike Shop,** 702 S. Main St. (☎ **888/677-4688** or 435/259-4643; fax 435/259-4643; e-mail: chilebikes@aol.com); **Dreamrides,** 96 E. Center St. (☎ **888/662-2882** or 435/259-6419; fax 435/259-8196; www.mountainbiketours.com); **Kaibab Mountain Bike Tours,** 391 S. Main St. (☎ **800/451-1133** or 435/259-7423; fax 435/259-6135; e-mail: kaibabtour@aol.com); **Nichols Expeditions,** 497 N. Main St. (☎ **800/648-8488** or 435/259-3999; fax 435/259-2312; www.nicholsexpeditions.com); **Poison Spider Bicycles,** 497 N. Main St. (☎ **800/635-1782** or 435/259-7882; fax 435/259-2312; www.poisonspiderbicycles.com); and **Rim Tours,** 1233 S. Hwy. 191 (☎ **800/626-7335** or 435/259-3349; www.rimtours.com).

6. **Take a 1-day river run through Gray Canyon.** A run on the Green River with Moki Mac River Expeditions in Salt Lake City is a quick, easy option for beginners. They'll pick you up at your campground in the Green River area off I-70 and take you through six or so splashy rapids and some rugged scenery on an oar-powered expedition that costs $45 for adults, $35 for children. Call them at ☎ **800/284-7280** for information and reservations (e-mail: mokimac@mokimac.com; www.mokimac.com).

7. **Run the Green in Desolation Canyon.** Desolation Canyon, with its calm waters and peaceful put-in point, is a favorite for first-timers and families. But with more than 60 rapids and an ultimate Class III rating, the river challenges experienced river rafters and kayakers as well.

Contact **Adrift Adventures** in Canyonlands (☎ 800/874-4483), **Adventure Bound Trips** (☎ 800/423-4668), **Red River Canoe** (☎ 800/753-8216), or **Western River** (☎ 800/453-7450).

8. **Take a snowmobile tour.** One-and-a-half-hour, half-day, or custom tours set out from Brian Head during ski season and are priced from $40. Kids 10 and under travel free. Cedar Breaks National Monument, gorgeous against a bright blue sky when decorated with winter snow, is nearby. Call Crystal Mountain Recreation at ☎ **800/BIKE-SKI** or 801/677-2012.

9. **Rent a houseboat and go exploring on Lake Powell.** Explore ancient Anasazi caves, photograph remote Rainbow Bridge, and swim and picnic at a deserted beach—all from the comfort of home. Houseboating on Lake Powell, second-largest man-made lake in North America, is something akin to having your RV walk on water. Sizes from 36 to 59 feet are available for rent year-round from four perimeter marinas in Glen Canyon National Recreation Area—Bullfrog, Hite Marina, Wahweap, and Halls Crossing. Between October and May, houseboats can be reserved for trips as short as 1 or 2 days. The rest of the year, minimum rental requirements are longer. Call ARAMARK (☎ **800/528-6154**) for reservations, well ahead of time in summer.

10. **Go horseback riding along the scenic rim of Bryce Canyon.** Alternatively, head through the Butch Cassidy country or through a 1,600-year-old bristlecone pine forest. Any of these can be booked through Ruby's Inn at the entrance to Bryce Canyon (☎ **800/679-5859** or 435/679-8761; fax 435/679-8778). All rides are guided and range from an hour to all day. On the longer rides, there is an age and weight limit—no less than 8 years old and no more than 220 pounds on the all-day ride, 6 years and 250 pounds on the half-day. Big-game hunting is also available in season.

TAKE-OUT (OR EAT-IN) TREATS

Bumbleberry Inn, Springdale. Bumbleberry pie is the house specialty at the Bumbleberry Inn, 97 Bumbleberry Lane in Springdale, gateway town to Zion National Park. While the house hands out a whimsical description of its fruit—"burple and binkel berries that grow on giggle bushes"—it's a black-red berry like loganberry or boysenberry in a cornstarch-thickened sauce and fairly thick crust. A wedge to go costs a pricey $2.95. (☎ **800/828-1534**).

Capitol Reef Inn and Cafe, Torrey. The Capitol Reef Inn and Cafe, at 360 W. Main St. in Torrey, just west of Capitol Reef National Park, may or may not be the only restaurant in southern Utah serving fresh vegetables, but it's the best bet in the area for vegetarians as well as carnivores. The former can feast on 10-vegetable salad and stir-fry vegetables atop steamed brown rice, while the latter can tuck into fresh local rainbow trout, grilled rib-eye steak, or charbroiled lemon hickory chicken. Beer and wine are available. Breakfast-eaters get hearty omelets with optional bacon or smoked trout, or an order of French toast or pancakes. It's a good idea to call ahead (☎ **435/425-3271**).

Fat City Smokehouse, Moab. Fat City Smokehouse, at 36 S. 100 W. in Moab, not only dishes up pit-style barbecue ribs in what was once a turn-of-the-century dance hall, but also turns out fine vegetarian sandwiches from grilled eggplant, zucchini, onions, and green peppers with fresh tomato pesto. Prices are modest, and you can save time by calling ahead on orders to go (☎ **435/259-4302**). Open daily at 4pm.

Green River melons. The town of Green River is famous for its melons, which reach their peak in late summer and early fall. We tried Dunham's fruit stand on the east end of town and found their honeydew, Crenshaw, and cantaloupe were all delicious. They grow watermelons, too.

Bear Lake raspberries. Perfumed dark red Bear Lake raspberries, which grow in the tiny northeastern Utah town of Bear Lake on the lake of the same name, are the world's most delicious—and aficionados arrive the last week of July and the first week or two of August to eat them fresh from the vine at Hildt's Famous Bear Lake Raspberry Stand, or have them whirled into milk shakes at Le Beau's or Raspberry and Yummy Things Bakery. The rigorous climate limits the vines to one instead of the usual two annual crops, and locals believe that packs in more flavor intensity. If you can't make it to Bear Lake, taste the fresh Bear Lake raspberry ice cream at Snelgrove's local chain of ice-cream stores in Salt Lake City.

Electric Jim's Cafe, Springdale. The Virgin Burgers from Electric Jim's Cafe in Springdale by the entrance to Zion National Park are world-famous, the cafe claims, probably because the park attracts people from all over the world, some of whom undoubtedly get hungry after a hike. Jim's also claims the best shakes in the West. Since the Mormons are not supposed to drink coffee, tea, soft drinks, or alcohol, Utah is heaven for milk shake freaks.

Eddie McStiff's Brew Pub, Moab. Moab's Eddie McStiff's offers several unique boutique brews, including a jalapeño beer, a spruce beer with the foresty tang of spruce needles and bark, light blueberry and raspberry wheat beers, cream ale, amber ale, chestnut brown beer, and full-bodied stout. You'll find it at 57 Main St., and all food and beer is available to go (☎ **435/259-BEER**).

The Cowboy's Smoke House, Panguitch. Closed during the winter but otherwise open from early morning for breakfast (we got the sausage biscuit to go, a huge crumbly biscuit with a spicy sausage patty inside) till the last of the barbecued beef, chicken, and ribs is gone and the last of the customers have left in the evening. Some of the mounted animal heads around the room were bagged by Smokehouse employees, like the elk "shot down by Panguitch Lake" by one of the waitresses. Located at 95 N. Main St. in Panguitch (☎ **435/676-8030**).

Arches Vineyards, Moab. Arches Vineyards is Utah's only winery, and offers tastings of its red and white table and dessert wines daily from 11am to 7pm, but never on Sundays. Located at 420 Kane Creek Blvd. (☎ **435/ 259-5397**).

Dick's Cafe, St. George. Dick's serves huge T-bone steaks amid a heap of western kitsch amassed by owner Dick Hammer during his days as a champion rodeo rider and movie stuntman. Located at 114 E. St. George Blvd. in St. George (☎ **435/673-3841**).

WILDLIFE WATCHING
Mule deer are almost everywhere in southern Utah, especially in Bryce Canyon, Capitol Reef around the Fruita campground, Dead Horse Point State Park, and Natural Bridges National Monument.

Unexpected glimpses of **Shiras moose,** as well as elk and Great Basin mule deer, are possible in the Hogan Pass area along Route 72 between I-70 at Fremont and the town of Loa 32 miles to the south, with the best possibility between the pass and Loa.

Buffalo have been re-established in the Henry Mountains around Hanksville. A resident buffalo herd, some of them in enclosures and thereby guaranteed to be seen, can be visited on Antelope Island, reached by the Route 127 causeway off I-15 at Syracuse, north of Salt Lake City.

We saw lots of inquisitive **Utah prairie dogs,** a threatened species of this ubiquitous western rodent, popping up from holes beside the road on Route 211 into the Needles area of Canyonlands.

Along the Colorado River, keep a lookout for river otter, beaver, and birds. **Bald eagles** winter in the area around Fremont Indian State Park, and Canyonlands offers glimpses of soaring **peregrine falcons** and other birds of prey.

On the Road
ZION NATIONAL PARK
The national park, which began its official life as Mukuntuweap National Monument in 1909, dates from 1917 with the name Zion, given to it by Mormon settlers in the area who did not like the Paiute name. Its early description as an "extraordinary example of canyon erosion" fails to do justice to the rich palette of colors in the canyon, which range from creamy white to burnished copper and dark rose.

Southern Utah Campgrounds

Beaver KOA **3**
Bryce Canyon KOA **6**
Bryce Canyon North Campground **8**
Bryce Canyon Sunset Campground **8**
Butch Cassidy Campground **1**
Calf Creek Recreation Area **14**
Capitol Reef National Park campground **15**
Circleville RV Park and Country Store **4**
Dead Horse Point State Park **21**
Devil's Garden Campground **20**
Fremont Indian State Park **2**
Goulding's Monument Valley
   Campground & RV Park **23**
Kodachrome Basin State Park **12**
Lake Powell Resorts & Marinas,
   Lake, Bullfrog **16**
Lake Powell Resorts & Marinas,
   Halls Crossing **17**
Lake Powell Resorts & Marinas,
   Wahweap **13**
Moab KOA **22**
Mukuntuweep RV Park and Campground **11**
Point Supreme Campground **5**
Red Canyon RV Park **7**
Ruby's Inn campground **8**
Shady Acres RV Park **19**
Snow Canyon State Park **9**
South Campground **10**
Spanish Trail RV Park and Campground **24**
Squaw Flat **18**
Watchman Campground **22**
Willow Flat **10**

Dramatic, accessible, and beautiful, Zion is Utah's most-visited national park, with more than two and a half million visitors a year. Some 800 species of wildflowers bloom here, and 75 species of mammals, 271 birds, 32 reptiles and amphibians, and 8 varieties of fish are native to the park, including the unique (and endangered) Zion snail. More than 100 varieties of plants in the park were introduced after European settlement began in the mid-1800s and are presently being eliminated. A wide range of elevations, temperatures, water, and sunlight create microenvironments that showcase diverse flora and fauna, from hanging gardens with "weeping" rocks watering cascading ferns to forested canyons and arid mesas.

Despite its hot summers, Zion's mild spring, autumn, and winter weather makes the park a year-round destination for RVers. There may be some snow in winter but the roads are plowed, and one campground is open at the south entrance.

Zion National Park's top attraction is the 7-mile **Zion Canyon Drive,** which has been notoriously traffic-clogged during the past decade and so has been designated to be served by a propane-fueled shuttle-bus system beginning in the year 2000. When the shuttle is fully operative, no private vehicles will be allowed in the canyon. Hikers and bicyclists are still permitted into the canyon, as are visitors with confirmed reservations at Zion Lodge. But anyone else arriving between March and October will be expected to board buses into Zion Canyon. Motor vehicles, including RVs, are still permitted on the park's eastern side and in the campground area at the south entrance from Springdale. Parking is available at various areas in the town of Springdale and at the new visitor center, scheduled to be completed early in 2000, just inside the south park entrance at Springdale.

Based on our experience, RVs, particularly trailers and motorhomes, never had adequate turnaround or parking space at popular points along the canyon road anyway, so we've always supported the optional shuttle system, which has been in place for several years. Should implementation of the new shuttle system be delayed, previous restrictions will still be in effect. RVs more than 19 feet long are prohibited from entering the Weeping Rock and Sinawava parking areas because of limited turnaround space. The tram service should be used; RVs can be parked in the Zion Lodge vicinity.

There are four **driving entrances** into Zion, only two of which connect—the Route 9 south entrance at Springdale and the east entrance on Zion–Mt. Carmel Highway. The 25-mile dead-end drive along Kolob Terrace Road from the town of Virgin to the Kolob Reservoir winds in and out of the park's western boundaries through varying terrain, and the not-to-be-missed Kolob Canyons Road enters the northernmost part of the park from I-15 south of Cedar City. For more about both, see "Ten Scenic Side Trips" at the end of the chapter.

The best way of all to see the canyon is to use **hiking trails.** Hikers are cautioned to arrive early in the morning to the trailheads since most parking areas fill by midday. Permits are required for all overnight hikes, and can be applied for at the visitor center any time after 8am the day before the hike begins. Permits require a fee of $5 per person.

Among the park's most popular hiking trails are several that are short and/or easy. **Weeping Rocks trail** is a fairly steep quarter-mile climb leading to an enormous rocky ledge covered with mosses and plants with a constant stream of "tears" dripping from it. It's also a cool place to linger on a hot summer day.

The 2-mile **Emerald Pools trail** loop is not too demanding if you go uphill via the right-hand trail after crossing the footbridge by the parking lot, climb to the Middle Pool, and then take the other trail, somewhat rougher and steeper, back downhill.

The **Lower Emerald Pool trail** and the **Gateway to the Narrows trail** at the Temple of Sinawava are wheelchair-accessible if a companion is along to help with the rough spots along the cement paving. The latter trail is a fairly level 2-mile loop that goes through the hanging gardens area, bright with wildflowers in spring and early summer.

Dedicated hikers like to strike out along the 10-mile **West Rim trail** between the canyon and Lava Point, but those starting from the canyon are cautioned not to try to make it uphill to Lava Point on a 1-day hike. The **Zion Narrows trail,** which splashes through the icy waters of the Virgin River at some points, requires a free hiking permit for the 2-day, 32-mile round-trip. (Permits can be obtained from a ranger station in the park, and you have to apply in person.) Fall is best, when water levels in the river are lowest; take along a dry change of clothing in a sealed plastic bag.

ZION RV RESTRICTIONS

RVs entering Zion National Park are subject to parking and tunnel restrictions that do not cause any major inconveniences but must be adhered to. A fee of $10 is required for any RV wider than 7 feet, 10 inches (including side mirrors) or taller than 11 feet, 4 inches to drive through the 1.1 mile tunnel on the Zion–Mt. Carmel road. This is because the vehicle has to proceed through the middle of the tunnel without oncoming traffic, which is controlled by park rangers posted at either end. The tunnel is open to RVs under 13 feet high between 8am and 8pm March through October; to pass through any other time, call ☎ 435/772-3256 to make advance arrangements. The fee is collected at the park's entrance, where drivers are issued a yellow receipt to display on the windshield.

It is not essential to go through the tunnel if you don't want to; simply arrive and leave the park by the same Springdale gate.

Zion National Park

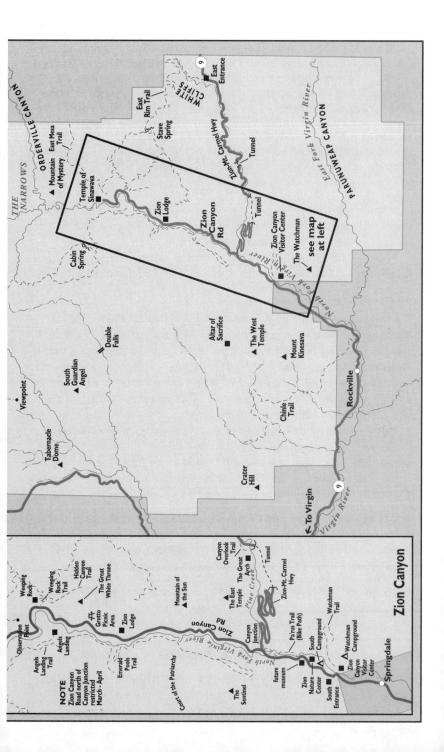

THE HISTORY OF UTAH—AND A TASTY DINNER, TOO

Down in St. George, southwest of Zion off Interstate 15, the outdoor musical drama *Utah* is open summer nights between June and September, with a cast of 80, along with lightning bolts, floods and waterfalls, burning cities, Indian raids, galloping horses, coyotes that howl on cue, and a full-fledged fireworks display. Call ☎ **800/746-9882** for reservations; adult tickets are $14.50 to $26.50, and kids under 12, $9 to $16. An optional western Dutch-oven dinner is served at $7.95 for adults, $5.95 for children, but must be reserved at the same time tickets are booked. The theater is 10 miles from St. George at Tuacahn, off Route 300 near Snow Canyon State Park. 🚐

Bicyclists are limited to paved roads in the park, and are not permitted to ride through the Mt. Carmel tunnel. Rangers will transport your bicycle through the tunnel free of charge, however.

Photographers should try to visit the canyon in early morning and again in late afternoon to take advantage of the dramatic light that models the contours of the rocks.

Campground Oases in & Around Zion National Park

Watchman & South Campgrounds. The two campgrounds in Zion suitable for RVs can be found just beyond the park's Springdale entrance: **Watchman Campground** with Loops A, B, and C (229 sites), and adjacent **South Campground** (140 sites). The sites, without hookups, are generally widely spaced with some shade trees. All have metal picnic tables and cooking grills; some of the nicest are along the Virgin River at the edge of Loop A. Campgrounds have flush toilets but no showers, and a 14-day limit on a first-come, first-served basis except for some sites at Watchman. Many sites are handicap-accessible. All spaces fill before noon in summer. A sanitary dump station and water are located at the entrance to Watchman (☎ **800/ 365-2267** or 801/772-3256; http://reservations.nps.gov).

Mukuntuweep RV Park and Campground. Located near Mount Carmel on Route 9 just outside the east entrance to Zion National Park, Mukuntuweep has more tent sites (120) than RV sites (30, all with full hookups and 20 or 30 amps). Reservations: ☎ **435/648-2154;** e-mail zionpark@ expressweb.com.

Beaver KOA. This KOA in Beaver is convenient to both Zion and Bryce and makes a handy stopover for travelers en route between Salt Lake City and Las Vegas. It's reached from I-15, exit 112, and is open March through October with 65 pull-through sites offering water and 30-amp electric; 27 sewer connections available. Reservations: ☎ **800/KOA-2912** or 435/438-2924.

Snow Canyon State Park. Snow Canyon, near St. George in Utah's Dixie district, has 14 sites with water and electrical hookups and picnic shelters lined up in a row, plus 22 non-hookup sites that are more spacious and tree-shaded. The park has flush toilets, showers, a sanitary dump station, and hiking trails through spectacular scenery. It's open year-round and the weather is mild, although summer can be hot; the canyon was named for a pioneer family's surname, not the falling white stuff, which rarely falls here. Take exit 6 (Bluff Street) from I-15 and drive northwest of St. George on Route 18 10 miles, then 2 miles southwest on Route 8. The ¾-mile hike to Johnson's Arch is the park's most popular, although some visitors take flashlights and explore the lava caves near the north end of the park. Reservations: ☎ **800/322-3770** or 435/628-2255.

BRYCE CANYON NATIONAL PARK

Bryce Canyon—"a hell of a place to lose a cow," in the words of one early rancher—is a collection of needlelike red limestone *hoodoos* (see "Talkin' Utah: A Glossary," above), jewellike eroded spires seen at their best in early morning or late-day light or, best of all, after a snowfall, when puffs of white snow dust the bright red rocks. Local Paiute legend has it that they were men turned into stone by an angry god.

Winter can be a rewarding time to visit if you enjoy cross-country skiing or snowshoeing; the park lends snowshoes to visitors free of charge at the visitor center (at the north end as you enter the park) if you leave a credit card or driver's license for deposit.

Mule deer are plentiful and easily spotted, especially in winter. Elk are also present but more rarely seen. With 172 species of birds identified in the park, you'll have a good chance of spotting something; a checklist is available at the visitor center.

Snow in Bryce Canyon

BRYCE CANYON RV RESTRICTIONS

RV restrictions abound in Bryce Canyon National Park, but should not inhibit RVers from sampling some of the park's best and most distinctive scenery. Vehicles towing trailers are not permitted beyond Sunset Point turnoff, but after a winter snowfall the road is usually closed off at this point, anyhow. Travel trailers may be left in designated parking areas at the visitor center or Sunset Campground. RVs longer than 25 feet are not allowed at Bryce Point or Paria Point at any time because of extremely limited turnaround space.

A number of **hiking trails,** a total of 61 miles, wend their way down into the canyons among the hoodoos. The most popular half-day trek is a combination of the Queens Garden and Navajo Loop trails, a 3-mile round-trip jaunt through the most dramatic part of the amphitheater. Just remember that every trail that goes down in the early part of the hike when you're fresh and eager comes back up later when you may be tired; don't overestimate your ability.

Bristlecone Loop trail from Rainbow Point takes a 1½-mile circuit through a pine forest. If a level walk sounds ideal, the **Rim trail** follows an 11-mile route with smooth paved walking areas accessible for wheelchairs between Sunrise and Sunset Points. Naturalists offer morning walks daily in summer, as well as moonlight hikes on the 3 evenings a month preceding a full moon.

The reconstructed **Bryce Canyon Lodge (☎ 435/834-5361**), a National Historic Landmark, echoes some of the 1920s feeling of the original. **Ruby's Inn,** just north of the park entrance on State Highway 63, dates from 1919 but has suffered so many fires over the years that it has lost its period look. There is a private campground at Ruby's Inn with hookups; closed in winter (☎ **435/834-5301**).

The most direct connection to Bryce Canyon is from Zion National Park north on U.S. 89, then east on Route 12—one argument in favor of paying the $10 RV tunnel fee on the Zion–Mt. Carmel Road. Otherwise, you can access U.S. 89 from the west via Routes 14 or 20 from I-15, or from the north via I-70. Red Canyon on Route 12 is a particularly scenic approach, with rock tunnels and bridges framing the road ahead.

Campground Oases in Bryce Canyon National Park

Bryce Canyon National Park. Bryce has two campgrounds, both near the entrance, open from late spring to early fall, with some limited winter camping. **North Campground** offers 105 sites and **Sunset** has 111, none with hookups. A sanitary dump station (fee), showers (fee) at Sunset, and flush

Bryce Canyon National Park

0   2 Mi

0   2 Km

12

Parking for
Bryce Shuttle

Mossy Cave
Trail

63

PINK CLIFFS

PINK CLIFFS

Fairyland
Point

Visitor Center

BRYCE CANYON

Bryce
Point

see inset map
at left

Hat
Shop

Dixie
National
Forest

Swamp
Canyon

Under - the - Rim Trail

Dixie
National
Forest

Farview
Point

Natural
Bridge

Grand Staircase-
Escalante
National
Monument

East Fork
Sevier River

Agua
Canyon

Under-the-Rim
Trail

Ponderosa
Canyon

Rainbow
Point

Riggs Spring
Loop Trail

Yovimpa
Point

Bristlecone
Loop Trail

Fairyland
Point

Fairyland
Loop Trail

Rim Trail

Visitor
Center

North
Campground

General Store
Laundry
Showers

Dump
Station

Nature
Center
Lodge

Sunrise Point

Queen's
Garden
Trail

Sunset
Point

Navajo
Loop Trail

Sunset
Campground

Peekaboo
Loop Trail

Inspiration
Point

Rim Trail

Bryce
Point

Paria
View

Under-the-
Rim Trail

0   1/2 Mi

0   .5 Km

Salt Lake City

UTAH

Bryce Canyon NP

🦅 Picnic Area
■ Point of Interest
△ Campground
• Overlook

1-0940

SAFETY TIPS

Be careful to allow a day or two to acclimatize to the area's elevation—in Bryce, 6,500 to 9,100 feet—before setting out on a major hike. And if a lightning storm comes up, stay away from the canyon rims, particularly the iron railings.

---

toilets are available. Picnic tables, fireplaces, and piped water are supplied. Bring your own firewood. There's a 14-day camping limit; pets are permitted on leash. Reservations are not taken, but to check ahead if there's space for the night, call the visitor center at **435/834-5322** (Bryce Canyon National Park, P.O. Box 170001, Bryce Canyon, UT 84717).

Bryce Canyon KOA. This fairly new RV park, at 555 S. Main St. in the town of Panguitch, about 25 miles from Bruce Canyon, has big level sites, 30- or 50-amp hookups, and lots of camping cabins. Reservations ☎ **800/KOA-1625** or 435/676-2225; www.zionkoa@color.country.net.

Red Canyon RV Park. Red Canyon, a Good Sam member in Panguitch, has 31 sites, many suitable for big rigs. Located 15 miles from Bryce Canyon on Highway 12, 1 mile east of the junction with 89; open mid-March through mid-November. Reservations: ☎ **435/676-2690;** fax 435/676-2765.

Kodachrome Basin State Park. Named by the National Geographic Society for its colorful, penis-shaped rock formations called chimneys, Kodachrome Basin is off Route 12 on an unnamed road 7.3 miles south of the junction of Highway 12 and Main Street in Cannonville (look for the sign for Kodachrome Basin), with 27 sites for RVs and a sanitary dump station but no hookups. Reservations: ☎ **435/679-8562.**

CEDAR BREAKS NATIONAL MONUMENT & CEDAR CITY

The "breaks" in the park name comes from early settlers in the region, who called any terrain too steep for wagon travel "breaks" or "badlands." The same folks thought the junipers and ancient bristlecone pine trees growing on the rim of the redrock amphitheater were cedars.

Similar to Bryce Canyon but even more vivid in color, Cedar Breaks is less visited, despite its convenient location only 23 miles from I-15 via Route 14.

A huge rock amphitheater with trails leading 3,400 feet down into the gorge, it offers a special challenge to hikers in good shape. Two special 2-mile walks for those already acclimated to the elevation are the **Alpine Pond Trail,** a fairly easy jaunt to a pond and forest glade, and the **Spectra Point Trail,** a good place to see bristlecone pines. There are also ranger-led nature walks, geology talks, and campfire programs in summer. Information on these activities is listed in the free handout newspaper you receive when entering the park.

Snowy overlook at Cedar Breaks National Monument

Although roads are closed by snow in winter, visitors can come into the park by cross-country skis or snowmobile, entering via **Brian Head ski resort.** A campground inside the monument is open June through September only. The **Rim Drive** along Scenic Byway 148 goes through the monument when weather permits.

The **Utah Shakespearean Festival** in nearby Cedar City, going strong for more than 30 years, presents three classic plays in repertory every summer in the outdoor Shakespearean theater, as well as three contemporary plays in a smaller indoor theater. The season runs from early July through September, and playgoers come early to enjoy the evening's Greenshow of jugglers, puppeteers, and vendors dressed in Elizabethan costume. They can also dine at a lively Renaissance Feaste. Call ☎ **800/PLAY TIX** for reservations or more information about the festival.

Campground Oases in the Cedar Breaks/Cedar City Area & North off Interstate 15

Point Supreme Campground. One mile north of the Cedar Breaks National Monument visitor center on Highway 148, Point Supreme Campground offers 30 sites suitable for RVs, with picnic tables, piped water, and flush toilets. Because the elevation is above 10,000 feet, the campground is open mid-June through mid-September only. No reservations are taken, there are no hookups, and a fee is charged. ☎ **435/586-9451.**

Circleville RV Park and Country Store. Located a half mile south of Circleville on Highway 89, the park is in the heart of Butch Cassidy country and has paved sites, some pull-throughs, and full hookups with 30- and 50-amp electric. Reservations: ☎ **435/577-2437;** e-mail: crvpark@aol.com.

Fremont Indian State Park. Near Richfield, this former Fishlake National Forest campground, previously called Castle Rock and located a couple of miles off I-70 near the junction of I-15, was shifted over to state park status to supplement the park, where part of a large Fremont River Indian village has been excavated. The little-known Fremont River Indians, who preceded the Anasazi, vanished before the first Spanish arrived. We found the campground quiet and uncrowded (we shared its 15 sites with one other RV one moonlit October night). The camping fee also includes admission to the museum. Sites are well spaced out, many shaded by aspens, all with tables; there are flush toilets but no hookups or dump station. Open year-round to RVs 30 feet or under. ☎ **800/322-3770.**

Butch Cassidy Campground. A Good Sam member, Salina's Butch Cassidy Campground is reached by taking exit 54 from I-70 and driving north seven-tenths of a mile on Route 89. With 50 tent sites and 40 RV sites, the year-round campground offers 20-, 30-, and 50-amp electric hookups and a heated swimming pool. Reservations: ☎ **800/551-6842** or 435/529-7400.

CAPITOL REEF NATIONAL PARK
Little-known and little-visited Capitol Reef lies about halfway between Bryce Canyon and Canyonlands on Route 24. The park is notable primarily for its unique **Waterpocket Fold,** a 100-mile wrinkle in the earth's crust formed by enormous pressures deep inside the earth that caused ancient rock beds to buckle. After a rain, pockets in the fold hold water and serve as residence and nursery for the unique spadefoot toad, which lays eggs in the water as soon as it rains so they can hatch into tadpoles, perhaps even make it to adulthood, before the puddles dry up.

Early settlers thought a white sandstone formation in the park resembled the Capitol Dome in Washington and that the Waterpocket Fold looked like a coral reef (although few of them had ever seen either). Ergo, the park is named Capitol Reef.

A 10-mile, one-way **scenic drive** is accessible to small to medium-sized RVs; pick up a self-guided trail map at the beginning of the drive to follow the different layers of rock that tilted, folded, and eroded to create today's dramatic formations. While we confess to a certain shortsightedness in recognizing every Egyptian Temple, Golden Throne, Castle, and Chimney dotted on the map, we admire the general structure of them. Let's face it—the old-timers had more leisure to sit and contemplate what they resembled than we do.

Fifteen **hiking trails,** from a tenth of a mile to 4½ miles, are designated as very easy, easy, moderate, and strenuous. A trail to **Hickman Bridge,** a natural bridge, is 1 mile each way and termed moderate, while a strenuous climb to **Cassidy Arch** is 1¾ miles each way.

Capitol Reef National Park

Legend
- ⊼ Picnic Area
- △ Campground
- ■ Point of Interest
- ▲ Mountain Peak
- 4WD Road

> ## TRAVEL TIP
> Always take drinking water with you, especially in summer, when hiking or exploring in Capitol Reef National Park. There's no reliable source of water outside the Fruita settlement near the Visitor Center.

Petroglyphs on the canyon walls on the main drive near the visitor center are only a few short steps from the turnout.

In 1900, eight to ten Mormon families lived here, planting orchards, operating a blacksmith shop, and teaching in a one-room log schoolhouse. The last of the community's residents moved away in 1960, and now the park maintains the village as a restored historic site known as the **Fruita settlement.** The park campgrounds are built in and around the orchards, which are open for visitors to pick their own fruit—you pay by weight at a scale and honor cashbox. Browsing mule deer are common in the campgrounds, especially at dawn and dusk.

Butch Cassidy and his gang used to hang out in the neighborhood. Cassidy Arch, on the Grand Wash road off the Scenic Drive, was named for the famous outlaw.

Even more fascinating is the **Behunin Cabin,** a tiny one-room rock cabin where an early Mormon settler raised ten children. The historical plaque beside it says they ate their meals outdoors, which is only logical, since it would be hard for all of them to be inside at the same time. What we can't imagine is where they all slept.

Campground Oases in & Around Capitol Reef National Park

Capitol Reef National Park campground. The only RV campground in Capitol Reef park is among the orchards at the Fruita settlement, less than a mile from the park's visitor center. The 63 RV sites are mostly level, grassy, and tree-shaded, with gorgeous red rock cliffs on all sides and grazing mule deer at dawn and dusk. It's open year-round. There are no hookups, no reservations, a 14-day limit, flush toilets, and a sanitary dump station. One wheelchair-accessible campsite in Loop B is held until 6pm nightly. ☎ **435/425 3791** (Capitol Reef National Park, HC70, Box 15, Torrey, UT 84775).

Calf Creek Recreation Area. This campsite, near Escalante, lies in a river bottom canyon surrounded by red cliff walls and has 11 well-spaced sites, some of them adequate for RVs up to 25 feet. Trout fishing is nearby. There are no hookups, a 14-day camping limit, and only primitive toilets. A 5-mile trail leads to lovely Calf Creek Falls. Operated by the Bureau of Land Management and closed late November to mid-March, the park is 15 miles northeast of Escalante off Route 12. ☎ **435/826-5499** or 435/826-4291.

CANYONLANDS NATIONAL PARK

The pristine serenity of Canyonlands has been protected for more than a century, largely because early white settlers deemed the land totally worthless. The Anasazi had lived and farmed the region until 1200, when they mysteriously left, perhaps because of drought, tribal warfare, or the arrival of hostile strangers.

Canyonlands National Park is divided into three separate areas, each self-contained and reached only by exiting one area of the park and re-entering elsewhere. **The Maze,** a dense, impenetrable mass of convoluted rock described as "a 30-square-mile puzzle in sandstone," lies southwest of the confluence of the Green and Colorado rivers. **The Needles** is southeast of it, and **Island in the Sky** is north of it. A trail leads to the confluence of the rivers from the road's end at Big Spring Canyon Overlook in The Needles.

Only experienced hikers with good topographic maps and compasses should venture into The Maze, the most remote and forbidding part of Canyonlands, a dense and complex system of chasms and ravines and dead-end routes. Two roads suitable only for four-wheel-drive vehicles enter it from the west, but only after a very long and rough journey from Route 24 near Goblin Valley State Park.

Spired sandstone walls, some as high as 400 feet, characterize The Needles in the southern part of Canyonlands, 75 miles from Moab, 49 miles from Monticello, and 31 miles off U.S. 191 via Route 211. Less visited than its northern counterpart, The Needles has a particularly scenic drive outside park perimeters as an introduction.

Island in the Sky, the mesa that composes much of the northern part of Canyonlands, is outlined in a V-shape as the Colorado and the Green rivers meet at the park's belly button. This area is reached by Route 313 off U.S. 191 north of Moab.

CAMPING AT GLEN CANYON NATIONAL RECREATION AREA

If you're heading into the Glen Canyon National Recreation Area, **Lake Powell Resorts & Marinas** provide RV camping with full hookups at Wahweap, Bullfrog, and Halls Crossing in Glen Canyon (reservations: ☎ 800/528-6154). A national park campground at Lees Ferry has no hookups but does have a dump station, showers, and a coin laundry, with sites available on a first-come, first-served basis. Bullfrog Campground has a laundry and showers; Halls Crossing Campground has a dump station, laundry, and showers; and Wahweap Campground, a laundry and showers.

ABOUT EDWARD ABBEY

You won't travel far in southeastern Utah without running across the ghost of the late Edward Abbey, a tough-minded, combative outdoor writer and environmentalist who spent several seasons as a park ranger in Arches.

He was best known for comments like, "You can't see anything from a car; you've got to get out of the goddamned contraption and walk, better yet crawl, on hands and knees, over the sandstone and through the thornbush and cactus. When traces of blood begin to mark your trail, you'll see something, maybe. Probably not." Nevertheless, he wasn't above poking fun at himself as he railed against overuse of his beloved Utah desert. On an early trip into The Maze, the most remote part of Canyonlands, he and a friend stopped to look at an almost-new hiker register.

"Keep the tourists out," a tourist from Salt Lake City had written, to which Abbey added, "As fellow tourists we heartily agree."

Later, still at The Maze, he wrote in the log, "For God's sake leave this country alone—Abbey," to which his friend added, "For Abbey's sake leave this country alone—God."

Pick up a copy of his book at any of the park visitor centers. It makes a good companion on the journey.

Views are memorable, especially in early morning or late afternoon when the landscape is gilded with red and gold. **Upheaval Dome,** a short walk from the parking lot at the end of the road at Holman Spring Canyon Overlook, may have been formed when struck by a meteorite—at least that's the explanation we prefer of the two possibilities offered by the information sign at the overlook. The other, much less sexy reason is underground salt buildup that eroded until a crater appeared.

Here at the edge of Canyonlands' Island in the Sky, not at what most viewers assumed was Grand Canyon, is where Thelma and Louise, in the film of the same name, drove their Thunderbird convertible off the cliff.

Both bobcats and mountain lions are occasionally seen in the park, as well as mountain sheep in the White Rim area.

Four-wheel-drive vehicles and backpackers can get much more deeply into the park than RVs and family cars, and there are primitive campsites dotted at intervals along the routes. Throughout Canyonlands, campers are expected to carry their own water and firewood. The only water supply in the park is at the Squaw Flat campground in The Needles, and it is not operative in winter.

Campground Oases in Canyonlands National Park

Squaw Flat. Squaw Flat, in The Needles section of Canyonlands, has 26 well-separated sites, many snuggled into rock-surrounded coves with trees, and some, but not all, are adequate for RVs up to 28 feet. Each site has fire grates and a table, and there are pit toilets and water available by the bucketful

Canyonlands National Park

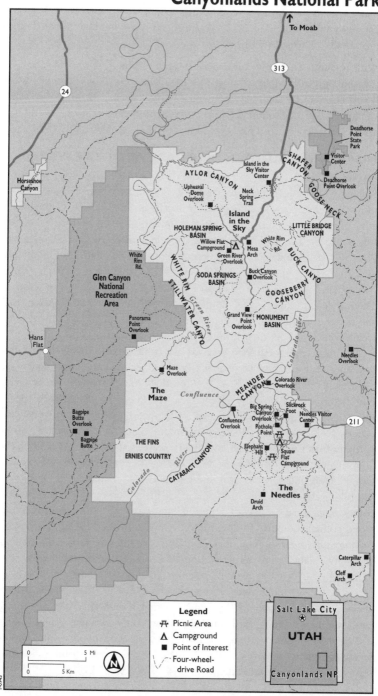

To Moab

313

24

Deadhorse Point State Park

Horseshoe Canyon

AYLOR CANYON

Island in the Sky Visitor Center

SHAFER CANYON

Visitor Center

Deadhorse Point Overlook

GOOSE NECK

Upheaval Dome Overlook

Neck Spring Trail

Island in the Sky

LITTLE BRIDGE CANYON

HOLEMAN SPRING BASIN

Willow Flat Campground

White Rim Rd.

BUCK CANYON

White Rim Rd.

Green River Overlook

Mesa Arch

Buck Canyon Overlook

WHITE RIM TRAIL

SODA SPRINGS BASIN

GOOSEBERRY CANYON

Glen Canyon National Recreation Area

STILLWATER CANYON

Grand View Point Overlook

MONUMENT BASIN

Panorama Point Overlook

Green River

Colorado River

Hans Flat

Needles Overlook

Maze Overlook

Colorado River Overlook

The Maze

Confluence

MEANDER CANYON

Big Spring Canyon Overlook

Slickrock Foot

Needles Visitor Center

211

Bagpipe Butte Overlook

Confluence Overlook

Potholes Point

Bagpipe Butte

Elephant Hill

Squaw Flat Campground

THE FINS

ERNIES COUNTRY

River

CATARACT CANYON

Colorado

The Needles

Druid Arch

Caterpillar Arch

Cleff Arch

Legend

⛺ Picnic Area

△ Campground

■ Point of Interest

⌁ Four-wheel-drive Road

Salt Lake City
★

UTAH

Canyonlands NP

0   5 Mi
0   5 Km

1-0945

from a water wagon. If you need to top off your RV tank, follow signs to a water hose connection on Cave Spring Road near Wooden Shoe Arch. The campground is located at 2282 S. W. Resource Blvd. in Moab. From U.S. 191 take Utah 211 west to The Needles.

Willow Flat. The only campground in the Island in the Sky area of Canyonlands accessible to most RVs is Willow Flat, down a rough washboard dirt road off Highway 313, with 12 primitive sites for smaller RVs only (under 25 feet). Unfortunately, gnats are a problem much of the summer. There are pit toilets and fire grates but no water. ☎ **435/259-7164.**

MOAB, THE MOUNTAIN BIKE CAPITAL OF THE WORLD (AND MORE)

Suddenly this faded uranium-prospecting town, best known as a Western-movie location area, has become the mountain bike capital of the world, attracting as many European yuppies as American outdoorsmen to its gentrified streets. The **Moab Slickrock Bicycle Trail,** which begins on Sand Flats Road, 2.3 miles from the intersection of the Sand Flats Road and Millcreek Drive in Moab, and follows a 12.7-mile loop through orange Navajo sandstone, is for experienced bikers with only a little time to spare. The big deal, though, is the 128-mile **Kokopelli's Mountain Biking Trail,** still under construction, between Moab and Grand Junction, Colorado. Ask locally when you get there to see if it's been finished.

The mid-October **Fat Tire Festival** brings hundreds of bikers to join both fun and semi-competitive events. Leading manufacturers of bikes and equipment are there to show off their products and hosts parties. The weekend before the Festival, Granny Gear Productions (☎ **304/259-5533;** www.grannygear.com) organizes an endurance race for four-person teams called "24 Hours of Moab." For more information, contact **Moab Information Center,** Center and Main streets in Moab (☎ **435/259-8825**).

An itemized list of things to do in the Moab area, detailed in the town's visitor guide, includes aerial tours, backpacking, campouts and cookouts, dirt biking, hiking, horse and llama pack rides, hot-air balloon rides, helicopter rides, boating, cross-country skiing, four-wheel-drive and all-terrain tours, golfing, hunting, fishing, motorcycling, mountain biking, picnicking, photography, river running, rock climbing, rock hounding, rock-art hunting, shopping, sightseeing, skateboarding, swimming, snowmobiling, tennis, touring movie locations, wildlife watching, and windsurfing.

Later, the writer added others—watching the local **sound-and-light show** called "Canyonlands by Night," taking a jet-boat cruise, kayaking, canoeing, hang gliding, bird watching, stargazing, and painting.

We were intrigued during our most recent visit at the large numbers of young Germans, and noted that **"authentic" German food** was being served at the Grand Old Ranch House (☎ **435/259-5753**).

The uranium miners wouldn't recognize the town with its trendy business names, everything from **Poison Spider Bikes,** 497 N. Main St. (☎ 800/635-1792), with its espresso bar, to **Honest Ozzie's** (a pun on Anasazi—get it?), 60 N. 100 West (☎ 435/259-8442), probably the only restaurant in Utah recommended in a French truck-drivers' guide. The **Moab Brewery,** a boutique brewery with a dozen flavors on tap, is at 686 S. Main St. (☎ 435/259-6333), next door to an art gallery promising "an eclectic mix of fun, folk art and funk." Also in town is a tasting room for Utah's only winery, **Arches Vineyards,** at 420 Kane Creek Blvd. (☎ 435/259-5397). It is currently turning out a vintage chardonnay. Can merlot and chipotle mayo be far behind?

Campgrounds in & Around Moab

Dead Horse Point State Park. Dead Horse Point park makes an excellent alternative to the campgrounds at Canyonlands or Arches (see above and below) when they are full, which is most of the time. There are 21 campsites with 20-amp electric hookups, covered cooking/eating areas and windbreaks, metal picnic tables, and concrete pads for RVs. A sanitary dump station is available. A family of mule deer are often seen grazing in the area. The campground is open year-round. The park is located off Route 313 northwest of Moab. Call the park office at ☎ 435/259-2614. Reservations: ☎ 800/322-3770.

Spanish Trail RV Park and Campground. South of Moab on U.S. 191, Spanish Trail RV Park offers 55 sites with 20-, 30-, and 50-amp electric, cable TV, and city water. Reservations: ☎ 800/787-2751 or 435/259-2411; e-mail: spanishtrail@moab-utah.com.

Moab KOA. Also south on U.S. 191, Moab KOA has 103 spaces with 20- and 30-amp electric, city water, and cable TV, as well as an innovative miniature golf course. Reservations: ☎ 800/KOA-0372 or 435/259-6682.

ARCHES NATIONAL PARK

Arches National Park boasts the world's largest concentration of natural stone arches, perhaps as many as 2,000 by the most recent tally. To qualify as an arch, the formation has to pass light through an opening at least 3 feet wide.

Some are visible from the paved roadway, others are reached by short or medium hikes from ¹⁄₁₀ of a mile to 7 miles long. Daily **ranger-guided hikes** are also available; check schedules at the visitor center, located just inside the entrance gate. The Fiery Furnace, for instance, in a labyrinth of red sandstone cliffs and narrow passageways, can be visited only with a ranger; hikes are scheduled twice a day in season and must be reserved in person ahead of time at the visitor center.

See "Seven Sites Offering Déjà Vu All Over Again" for the park's most popular long hike, a half-day trip to **Delicate Arch.**

Rock climbers also love the Arches for its cliffs, walls, towers, and cracks in the rock, coupled with incredible views. Modern techniques in rock climbing often avoid the old system of pounding pitons into the rock, then ascending by nylon ladders. Today the goal is to do "free" climbing, either *face climbing,* in which the climber grasps or steps on natural holds in the rock, or *crack climbing,* by wedging part of the body into cracks in the rocks. Women can often outdo men in their dexterity in rock climbing.

If you're hiking or camping here, be sure your gas tank is adequately full, and take along your own water, food, and firewood, since nothing is available in the park.

Campground Oases in & Around Arches National Park

Devil's Garden Campground. Located in Arches National Park, Devil's Garden is situated amid red rocks and green pines near the end of an 18-mile road, with 53 first-come, first-served sites. We would suggest that if campground space is still available when you enter the park, no matter what the time of day, that you drive straight to the campground, pick out a spot, and register, then go back out to do your sightseeing. The fee is $10 a night, and sites include tables and grills, with flush toilets and piped water. While all the pads are paved, RVs owners will need to check the level, since many of them are uneven. There is no camping fee when the water is turned off, usually from the end of October until mid-March. Call the park office at ☎ **435/259-8161.** Reservations: ☎ **800/322-3770.**

Shady Acres RV Park. Located in the town of Green River at 360 E. Main St. (Business Route 70), it's a favorite of river rafters, fishermen, and melon aficionados (for the festival in late September). Some 56 paved pull-throughs, an RV car wash, cable TV, and 30- and 50-amp electric make this popular with big rigs. Reservations: ☎ **800/537-8674** or 435/564-8290.

SALT LAKE CITY

In the early 19th century, itinerant fur traders trapped beavers along the waterways of the Wasatch Mountains, but by mid-century Mormon colonists, following the commands of Brigham Young, had established farms and settlements in the "vast desert" of the Great Salt Lake Valley with irrigation and a lot of hard work. Many of the colonists who walked to Utah, pulling handcarts filed with their possessions, were immigrants recruited in Europe by Mormon missionaries. Settlers fought off hostile Indians, bad weather that destroyed the crops, and clouds of locusts. Flock of seagulls flew in and devoured the locusts, and to this day you'll see large numbers of California gulls, the state bird of Utah, all around the Great Salt Lake.

Northern Utah Campgrounds

Antelope Island State Park ❹
Bear Lake KOA ❶
Camp VIP ❺
Century Mobile Home & RV Park ❷
Cherry Hill ❸

In **This Is the Place State Park** in Emigration Canyon, west of Salt Lake City on Sunnyside Avenue, a monument marks the spot where Brigham Young stopped on July 24, 1847, and proclaimed he'd found the haven that would shelter his 148 weary followers from persecution because no outsider would covet this barren basin with its saltwater lake.

Today's RVers will enjoy Salt Lake City's wide streets and easy layout. Primary tourist goals are **Temple Square,** where the Mormon Tabernacle Choir's Thursday night rehearsals and Sunday morning broadcasts are open to the public, as well as daily organ recitals. Two **visitor centers** are open on the square with tours of the Temple Square area starting by the flagpole every few minutes.

You can even search out your family roots at the **Family Search Center** in the famous genealogy files of The Church of Jesus Christ of Latter-day Saints. For more information on tours and events, call ☎ **800/537-9703.**

Winter visitors to Salt Lake City can take advantage of Utah's famous champagne powder snow at easy-to-reach smaller ski resorts like **Brighton** (☎ **800/873-5512**) and **Solitude Mountain** (☎ **800/748-4754**), both in Big Cottonwood Canyon some 30 miles east of town by exit 7 from I-215. And the 2002 Winter Olympics loom large on skiers calendars, despite charges of undue influence peddling by Olympic boosters.

Tastebud treats abound in this legendary sweet-tooth town, from **Snelgrove's ice cream** at locations all over town to **Cumming's Studio Chocolates,** 679 E. 900 S. (☎ **801/328-4858**), from **Peppermint Place candy factory** tour at 155 E. 200 N. in Alpine (☎ **801/756-7400**) to the **Deli Lama Tony Caputo's** downtown, 308 W. 300 S. (☎ **801/531-8669**).

Campground Oases in Northern Utah

Century Mobile Home & RV Park. Located off I-15 at exit 346 in Ogden, near three local ski areas. It's open year-round and offers pull-throughs, big-rig, and full-hookup sites with 30- and 50-amp electric and cable TV. Reservations: ☎ **801/731-3800.**

Bear Lake KOA. This KOA is on U.S. 89 in Garden City in Utah's northeast corner, en route to Yellowstone and adjacent to Bear Lake, home of the world's most delicious raspberries. Only a mile north of town, the campground is open from May 1 through October 31, but book well ahead for the end of July raspberry season. There are 100 pull-through sites with 30-amp electric and water hookups; 56 of them also have sewer hookups. Reservations: ☎ **800/KOA-3442.**

Antelope Island State Park. Antelope Island is in the Great Salt Lake, accessible by the Route 127 causeway, and has several parking-lot RV "campsites" by the beach and at White Rock Bay. No hookups. Fees are $6 for day use and $8 for overnight stays. Reservations: ☎ **801/773-2941.**

Cherry Hill. Cherry Hill, 20 minutes north of Salt Lake City in Kaysville, provides splashy summer fun for the family between early April and early November with its water park, miniature golf, hamster haven, aeroball, and batting cages, plus 240 RV campsites with 30- and 50-amp electric hookups. Note, however, that the amusements are closed on Sunday. Reservations: ☎ **888/4GO-CAMP;** fax 801/451-2267; www.cherry-hill.com. From the junction of I-15 and U.S. 89, take exit 326 and drive 2 miles north on 89. The campground is on the left.

Camp VIP. Within walking distance of Temple Square in downtown Salt Lake City, Camp VIP is open year-round and has 226 full hookups offering 30- and 50-amp electric, an RV wash, and heated spa. Only half an hour from many of the ski areas, this park attracts long-term visitors and big rigs. Reservations: ☎ **800/226-7752** or 801/328-0224; www.campvip.com.

Ten Scenic Side Trips

1. **Kolob Terrace Road to Kolob Reservoir.** Kolob Terrace Road strikes out to the north for 25 miles from the town of Virgin (like the river) on Route 9 west of Zion NP. From farms with lush green grass and trees it climbs up through ranchland terrain set amid rich red rocks, then into groves of aspen and oaks, and finally into the secluded high country. If the dirt road to Lava Rock looks passable, take the short detour out to an overlook down into Zion Canyon. The lightly traveled Kolob Terrace Road, paved for most of its length, is not recommended for long travel trailers and RVs over 32 feet because there are few pullouts and no good turnarounds along the way. Allow 1½ to 2 hours for the round trip.

2. **Kolob Canyons.** The northern end of Zion National Park, Kolob Canyons is only 5 minutes away from I-15 at exit 42, and cannot be reached by vehicle from the rest of the park. The stunningly beautiful 5-mile drive winds its way between the red Navajo sandstone Finger Canyons to a forested overlook among groves of pinon pine and aspen. Several hiking trails set out from the overlook area, including a moderately strenuous 5-mile trek along Taylor Creek and a strenuous 14-mile hike to Kolob Arch, believed to be the world's largest freestanding arch.

3. **Scenic Byway Route 12.** Running between Escalante and Boulder, Scenic Byway Route 12 climbs a narrow hogback ridge near Calf Creek Recreation Area amid breathtaking views and sheer drop-offs on both sides of the road. The Civilian Conservation Corps built the road here in the early 1940s; until then, the mail was delivered by muleback into Boulder. Mountain bikers and four-wheel-drive vehicles can take the original Hell's Backbone dirt road into Dixie National Forest and Box Death Hollow Road, scourge of the mule-riding mailmen. **Petrified**

Forest State Park at Escalante (☎ 520/524-6228) displays colorful specimens of petrified wood, while **Anasazi Indian Village State Park** at Boulder (☎ 435/355-7308) exhibits a reconstructed pueblo where you can try your hand at grinding corn the Indian way. The former also has a campground, but a more attractive spot to overnight, if there's space, is **Calf Creek Recreation Area** (see listing under "Campground Oases in & Around Capitol Reef National Park," above). The 32-mile road between Boulder and Grover, the last of it not paved until 1985, passes through elegant groves of aspen, past several forest service campgrounds, and over a 9,600-foot pass.

4. **Bicentennial Highway.** So-named because it was built in 1976, the Bicentennial Highway opens up one of the most sensational stretches of countryside in the entire West. From Hanksville south on 95 to Blanding in the Four Corners country, the terrain unfolds with one spectacular vista after another. The **Henry Mountains,** snow-capped and framed with red rock buttes and golden fields of hay, stand out against a vast blue sky. Washes are delineated with narrow stripes of cottonwood, leaves bright green in summer and gold in autumn. After a rain, birds flock to the water shining from holes and grooves in the rock. At **Hites Crossing** on Lake Powell, a delicate arched bridge crosses the Colorado River while houseboats bob at anchor all around the nooks and crannies of the lake.

5. **Natural Bridges National Monument.** For RVers in a hurry, there are three natural bridges easily seen from roadside viewpoints along the Route 275 circle loop through the monument; they're accessible by hiking trails for travelers who want to explore. A small visitor center details the differences between natural bridges and arches, in case you were wondering. The campground here, while dotted with trees and very attractive, is too small for any RVs over 21 feet long. Don't even attempt to drive a big rig into it.

6. **The 50-mile loop around Brian Head and Cedar Breaks National Monument.** Beautiful any time of year, but especially in winter when snow sets off the bright red rock formations of the huge natural amphitheater. Many photographers feel it's even more dramatic than Bryce Canyon. The roads are usually clear into Brian Head but might sometimes be closed in winter into Cedar Breaks. Exit 78 at Parowan from I-15 leads to Route 143 and Brian Head; from there, take Route 148 through Cedar Breaks and Route 14 back downhill into Cedar City. Call Cedar Breaks at ☎ 435/586-9451.

7. **Kodachrome Basin State Park.** The aptly named Kodachrome Basin State Park, 7 miles off Highway 12 at Cannonville, makes a short but dramatic detour by paved road into still more stunning rock formations. Hiking trails and horseback riding are available, as well

as a campground with 24 concrete pad sites, tables, grills, piped water, flush toilets, and showers. You'll find a sanitary dump station and camper supply store but no hookups. The National Geographic Society, by the way, is the group that named this colorful basin. ☎ **435/679-8562.**

8. **The Bullfrog Basin loop, Glen Canyon National Recreation Area.** Some 75 miles long, the Bullfrog Basin loop ventures more deeply into Glen Canyon than Route 95. Take the Route 276 cutoff north of Hite Crossing and rejoin Route 95 just before Natural Bridges National Monument. The Bullfrog Marina provides rentals for power- and houseboats, as well as an 86-unit campground and some beach area for swimmers. To complete the loop, you'll have to take the toll ferry called the *John Atlantic Burr* that goes to Halls Crossing; it can handle all sizes of RVs. You could also take a houseboat out for a few days, towing a small powerboat behind, and explore Anasazi caves, discover remote rock arches, and go hiking. Call ARAMARK, the NPs concessionaire, at ☎ **800/528-6154.**

9. **The Riverway (Route 128).** North of Moab, Route 128, also called the Riverway, strikes east along the Colorado River for 45 miles, following a winding scenic drive into Negro Bill Canyon, named for William Granstaff, a mixed-race prospector who ventured through in 1877, some said selling whiskey to the Indians. Along the route you can go camping; river running by raft, kayak, or canoe; mountain biking; hiking; or riding off-road vehicles on designated trails. Big Bend Recreation Site offers attractive non-hookup campsites by the river big enough for RVs and with tables and grills, a good alternative when Arches is full. The Bureau of Land Management suggests wearing a life jacket when swimming or boating in the river. Call them at ☎ **435/259-6111.**

10. **Dead Horse Point State Park.** Dead Horse Point takes your breath away as you peer over the edge of a sheer 2,000-foot cliff into the double gooseneck loops of the muddy Colorado River cutting its way through red earth and green vegetation. Because of exposed cliff edges and a paucity of railings, we heard a young local guide caution his group of chattering Japanese schoolgirls to "Be careful." They chorused back cheerfully in unison, "Be care-full." Wild mustangs were herded and broken here in the old days because a simple brush fence could close the narrow neck to the point. After taking the best of the horses, cowboys would leave the fence open to let the "broomtails" (culls) from the herd pick their way back to the open range. Unfortunately, one group of broomtails got confused and wandered in circles until they died of thirst, ironically while looking down at the waters of the Colorado far below. To get to the park, take 191 to 313 south, which ends at the park. ☎ **435/259-2614.**

Travel Quiz: Location, Location, Location

A lot of movies were shot in Utah, but only one of them is listed here, along with others filmed in other locations. Match the films with the location sites.

1. *Field of Dreams* (1989). "If you build it, they will come" is still true of this baseball field, which is visited by 40,000 people a year.

2. *On Golden Pond* (1981). Henry Fonda and Katharine Hepburn rowed on and fished in this golden pond; the house location by the lake can be visited with local tour operators.

3. *Nell* (1994). Jodie Foster's isolated lakeside cabin was constructed here for the film.

4. *Groundhog Day* (1993). Bill Murray's TV weatherman underwent a constantly recurring day that was supposed to take place in Punxsutawney, Pennsylvania, but another town stood in for it.

5. *Thelma and Louise* (1991). The famous driving-over-the-cliff scene for Susan Sarandon and Geena Davis was supposed to take place in the Grand Canyon, but was shot here instead.

6. *Fried Green Tomatoes* (1991). Life imitates art at the Whistle Stop Cafe, the former general store where the movie was shot, now a cafe serving—what else?—fried green tomatoes.

a. Squam Lake, New Hampshire, north of Laconia near Holderness on Route 25.

b. Woodstock, Illinois, on U.S. 14 about 35 miles west of Waukegan.

c. Dyersville, Iowa, 3 miles northwest of town on U.S. 20.

d. East Juliette, Georgia, exit 60 off I-75 about 75 miles southeast of Atlanta.

e. Fontana Lake, North Carolina, just south of the Great Smoky Mountains National Park.

f. Moab, Utah, on an unpaved road off Route 279 called the Shafer Trail, 19 miles south of town.

ANSWERS: 1 (c); 2 (a); 3 (e); 4 (b); 5 (f); 6 (d)

❼
Driving the Alaska Highway

ALASKA IS WHERE PEOPLE RELISH SPAM AND LINE UP ON HIGHWAY roadkill lists for a chance at the next moose struck down by a car. It's where Warren G. Harding drove a golden spike to mark the completion of the Alaska Railroad in 1923, and where the most powerful earthquake ever to hit the North American continent struck on Good Friday in 1964—a 9.2 on the Richter scale, which lasted an incredible 5 minutes.

It's where you can stand in mud up to your knees and have dust blow in your face, where mosquitoes are as big as hummingbirds, and where you won't be considered a real Alaskan until—to paraphrase the locals in more polite terms—you've wrestled a grizzly, urinated in the Yukon, and had an amorous encounter with a bear.

It's where Arco tapped a $10 billion oil reserve at Prudhoe Bay in 1968 and Exxon spilled 11 million gallons of it off Valdez in 1989, where Russia

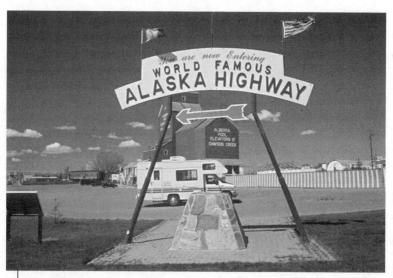

The beginning of the Alaska Highway in Dawson Creek, British Columbia

Alaska Highlights

MILEAGE CHART Approximate driving distances in miles between cities.	Anchorage	Circle	Dawson City	Eagle	Fairbanks	Haines	Homer	Prudhoe Bay	Seattle	Seward	Skagway	Tok	Valdez
Anchorage		520	494	501	358	775	226	847	2234	126	832	328	304
Circle	520		530	541	162	815	746	1972	2271	646	872	368	526
Dawson City	494	530		131	379	548	713	868	1843	619	430	189	428
Eagle	501	541	131		379	620	727	868	1974	627	579	173	427
Fairbanks	358	162	379	379		653	584	489	2121	484	710	206	364
Haines	775	815	548	620	653		1001	1142	1774	901	359	447	701
Homer	226	746	713	727	584	1001		1073	2455	173	1058	554	530
Prudhoe Bay	847	1972	868	868	489	1142	1073		2610	973	1199	695	853
Seattle	2243	2271	1843	1974	2121	1774	2455	2610		1361	1577	1931	2169
Seward	126	646	619	627	484	901	173	973	1361		958	454	430
Skagway	832	872	430	579	710	359	1058	1199	1577	958		504	758
Tok	328	368	189	173	206	447	554	695	1931	454	504		254
Valdez	304	526	428	427	364	701	530	853	2169	430	758	254	

Chukchi Sea

Little Diomede Island

Nome

Norton Sound

Yukon Delta National Wildlife Refuge

Bethel

Yukon Delta National Wildlife Refuge

Bering Sea

Nunivak Island

Pribilof Islands

Bristol Bay

Attu Island

Cape St. Stephen

Rat Islands

A l e u t i a n   I s l a n d s

Adak

Adak Island

Atka Island

Atka

Fort Glen

Dutch Harbor

Unalaska

Unimak Island

Unimak

Cold Bay

Alaska Peninsula

P A C I F I C

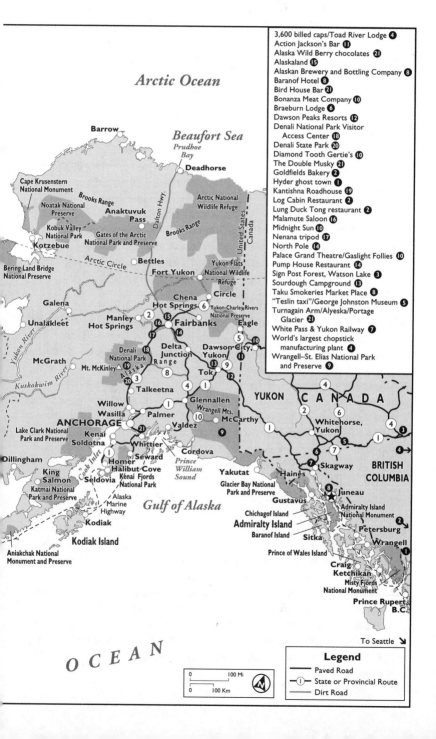

3,600 billed caps/Toad River Lodge ④
Action Jackson's Bar ⑪
Alaska Wild Berry chocolates ㉑
Alaskaland ⑮
Alaskan Brewery and Bottling Company ⑧
Baranof Hotel ⑧
Bird House Bar ㉑
Bonanza Meat Company ⑩
Braeburn Lodge ⑥
Dawson Peaks Resorts ⑫
Denali National Park Visitor
  Access Center ⑱
Denali State Park ⑳
Diamond Tooth Gertie's ⑩
The Double Musky ㉑
Goldfields Bakery ②
Hyder ghost town ①
Kantishna Roadhouse ⑲
Log Cabin Restaurant ②
Lung Duck Tong restaurant ②
Malamute Saloon ⑯
Midnight Sun ⑩
Nenana tripod ⑰
North Pole ⑭
Palace Grand Theatre/Gaslight Follies ⑩
Pump House Restaurant ⑭
Sign Post Forest, Watson Lake ③
Sourdough Campground ⑬
Taku Smokeries Market Place ⑧
"Teslin taxi"/George Johnston Museum ⑤
Turnagain Arm/Alyeska/Portage
  Glacier ㉑
White Pass & Yukon Railway ⑦
World's largest chopstick
  manufacturing plant ④
Wrangell–St. Elias National Park
  and Preserve ⑨

established an outpost in the 19th century, and where a historical marker at a creekside bordello describes the area as a place where the salmon and the fishermen both came upstream to spawn.

It was where wannabe gold miners headed for the Klondike by any means they could, crammed into any boat that could float and some that couldn't, where salesmen brought their inventory, gamblers their cards and dice, women their bodies for sale or their scrub boards and sadirons for labor. And all of them intended to get rich.

> *"They didn't build a city here; they found gold. That's the whole story of Alaska."*
> —Ruth Allman, Alaska pioneer

Last, Alaska is where they keep the Alaska Highway, the road that kept the Japanese from invading the North American mainland during World War II, helped Alaska achieve statehood in 1959, and, more recently, set off a flourishing bumper sticker and T-shirt industry with lurid illustrations around the theme "I Drove the Alaska Highway."

BUILDING THE HIGHWAY

When Japan bombed Pearl Harbor in December 1941, it didn't take long for the U.S. government to look at a map and see that the narrow Bering Strait that separated the westernmost spot in North America—in Alaska—from the easternmost spot in Asia—in Siberia—was only 36 miles across. With the Japanese navy lurking close to North American shores (and even invading the Aleutians) and Russia an ally who desperately needed supplies, the United States decided its Corps of Engineers should construct an inland road to Alaska. Because timing was important, trainloads of U.S. soldiers and equipment began arriving in tiny, remote Dawson Creek before any agreement was signed with Canada. All told, 33,000 men would work on the road that year, 11,000 of them U.S. Army troops, and some 200 would die in the subzero temperatures and hazardous working conditions.

The surveyors were just steps ahead of the bulldozers that winter of 1942, sinking into the mud and the permafrost below it. Not much attention was paid to grades or curves. As the surveyors pointed to what they perceived as the horizon, the bulldozers followed in their footprints. The original 1,422-mile road was built in only 8 months and 12 days.

Canadian construction crews cleaned up and straightened out the roadway for the next several years, but the Japanese threat in Alaskan waters had subsided. By 1949, the road was open to traffic, and paving continued sporadically until the last stretch was more or less covered by macadam in 1992. Drivers today still encounter long rough stretches undergoing construction.

RVing Along the Alaska Highway

While the mighty Alaska Highway still strikes fear into the hearts of travelers, it's tamed down considerably in recent years. The main attraction to the RVer is a combination of end-of-the-world roadways peeling off it at intervals and all the incredible scenery and wildlife waiting to be discovered along the way, from craggy peaks capped with perpetual snow, hanging and calving glaciers, golden midnight sunsets, and swirling acid-green northern lights to grizzly bears, moose, caribou, bald eagles, and sometimes wolves.

The **eastern access route** for the highway goes from Great Falls to Calgary, across Alberta to Edmonton and northwest to Dawson Creek. The **western access route** sets out from Seattle, north on I-5 to the Trans-Canada 1, east to Hope and north via either the fast new Coquihalla Highway or the slower Route 97 to Cache Creek, Quesnel, Prince George, and Dawson Creek.

The first challenge in driving the Alaska Highway is to get to the starting point, the famous **Mile 0,** located in Dawson Creek, British Columbia (BC), 817 miles north of Seattle on the western access route (or 867 miles northwest of Great Falls, Montana, on the eastern access route).

Eighty percent of the Alaska Highway is in Canada, which is why some people still call it by its nickname "the Alcan." While it sounds appropriate, even hip, to citizens of a certain age from the lower 48, the very word "Alcan" makes Alaskans and Canadians of a certain age bristle because it was an acronym for the Alaska-Canada Military Highway, which did not permit civilian travel during the war years.

Rocky Crest Lake, near Muncho Lake on the Alaska Highway

Despite losing their box office billing in the official name, the Canadians got a good deal because in 1946, after the war that created its construction, they bought their share at half what it cost to build.

The precise length of the Alaska Highway keeps changing as engineers straighten out its notorious curves. The original, or historic, mileposts are still used as addresses by the businesses and residents along the highway. Contemporary mileposts reflect the present distances, while in Canada kilometer posts are also in service.

Another point of contention is where the highway actually starts and stops. The milepost for Historic Mile 0 is in **Dawson Creek, British Columbia,** and the true terminus is in Delta Junction, Alaska, because a road connecting Delta Junction and Fairbanks already existed. Most Alaska Highway travelers, however, consider **Fairbanks** the real end of the highway, after which they usually head south via **Denali National Park and Preserve** to **Anchorage.**

HITTING THE HIGHLIGHTS

With only a 2-week vacation, you can still see a lot of Alaska, especially if you fly in (say, to Anchorage) and pick up an RV there (see "To Bring Your Own RV or to Rent?," below for rental information). From Anchorage, take Route 3 north to Fairbanks; Route 2 east to Delta Junction, where you pick up the official Alaska Highway; and continue southeast on Route 2, which becomes Highway 1 when you cross the Canadian border. Through the Yukon, continue southeast on Highway 1 to Whitehorse. From here, you could follow Route 2 north to Dawson or continue along the Alaska Highway, Route 1, to Watson Lake. If time permits, follow the Alaska Highway, now Route 97 in British Columbia, to Dawson Creek, the beginning of the Alaska Highway. If you want to vary your return route, take Route 1 (the Glenn Highway) southwest from Tok to Anchorage.

GOING FOR THE LONG HAUL

If you want to stretch out your Alaska RV adventure for a full summer, follow as many of the 10 side trips listed at the end of this chapter as you can squeeze in and weather permits. In spring and fall, check ahead on weather conditions since there could be a late thaw and some roads still closed by snowpack in spring. We were snowed in one August day in Dawson City when an early storm dumped so much of the white stuff the roads were closed.

Travel Essentials

WHEN TO GO

While the highway is open and maintained year-round, RV visitors will find mid-May to late September best. The "season," according to the locals we met on our mid-May trip, had not yet begun, which meant we could find empty campsites late in the day. On the other hand, a few lodges and service stations along the route had not yet opened for the summer. Try to avoid July and August, when RVs are almost bumper-to-bumper along some stretches of the highway.

TO BRING YOUR OWN RV OR TO RENT?

To take your own RV to Alaska without amassing a lot of overland miles or doubling back over the same territory, consider taking your RV aboard one of the **Alaska state ferries** from Bellingham, WA, to Skagway, which connects by road with Whitehorse or Watson Lake. Call ☎ **800/382-9229** for reservations as soon as possible after January 1 of the year you want to travel—and be patient, since the line is often busy. Or check the Web site: www.akms.com/ferry.

Alternatively, you can rent, starting out from Seattle, Skagway, or Anchorage. To rent an RV in British Columbia or Alaska, reserve as early as possible and determine whether you can pick up at one point and drop off at another. In Alaska, Anchorage is the center of RV rentals, with six reputable companies:

- **ABC Motorhome Rentals,** ☎ **800/421-7456,** www.alaskan.com/abc-motorhomes/
- **Alaska Economy RVs,** ☎ **800/764-4625,** www.goalaska.com
- **Alaska Panorama,** ☎ **800/478-1401,** www.alaskan.com/alaska-panorama
- **Alexander's RV Rental,** ☎ **888/660-5115**
- **Clippership Motorhome Rentals,** ☎ **800/421-3456,** www.custompu.com/commercial/clippership
- **Sweet Retreat Motorhome Rentals,** ☎ **800/759-4861,** www.sweet-retreat.com

Ferries in Alaska carry RVs as well as cars.

Call for prices, making sure to weigh the unlimited mileage rate against per mile fees.

A Seattle-based company called **Alaska Highway Cruises** (☎ **800/ 323-5757**) markets a combination package that includes one of several overland itineraries in a type C motorhome with paid reserved campsites nightly and an Alaska cruise aboard a Holland America Line luxury ship. Its 12-day program lets you fly to Anchorage, pick up an RV, drive to Denali and Fairbanks, take the Alaska Highway to Tok, the Taylor Highway and Top of the World Highway to Dawson City, and then the Klondike Highway to Whitehorse and Skagway. At Skagway you pick up a cruise ship that cruises Glacier Bay, calls in Ketchikan, and returns you to Vancouver for a flight home. The whole package starts around $2,500 per person, double occupancy, plus airfare to Seattle, and includes the cruise with all meals and entertainment, a fully furnished rental RV, campground reservations and fees. You buy the gas and food.

Our 21-foot Fleetwood Jamboree rented from Alaska Highway Cruises averaged 6 to 7 miles per gallon on the Alaska Highway, less than our larger 27-foot Winnebago type-A motorhome usually gets. We drove a total of 3,100 miles, spending approximately $600 on gas and about $500 on food and beverages for two.

WHAT TO TAKE

Binoculars, cameras and plenty of film, a world-class mosquito repellent, sunscreen, and good maps. Fishermen will want to carry fishing gear for lake trout, northern pike, Dolly Varden, arctic grayling, and five species of Pacific salmon. Spin or bait-cast fishing and/or fly-fishing rods and tackle capable of handling fish up to 30 pounds are recommended by the experts.

For the RV, experts suggest spare parts such as fan belt, oil filter, air filter, radiator hose, and heater hose. Mud flaps or "eyelashes" for the back are a good idea to keep gravel and mud from splashing all over the rear window. We took a basic tool kit and an emergency medical kit, neither of which we had to open.

WHAT TO WEAR

Although we took along ski-weight down parkas and heavy-soled hiking boots, we never donned either. Walking or jogging shoes were adequate on the short trails we hiked. But dedicated hikers and climbers should carry specialized equipment. A raincoat and umbrellas are a good idea, since it can rain or even snow, but don't be surprised to find Fairbanks sunny and hot. Dress is casual all over Alaska, so typical RV outfits will pass muster anywhere (except on a cruise ship, if you take the Alaska Highway Cruise package).

TRIMMING COSTS ON THE ROAD

The **type of RV** you choose to drive can make a big difference in expense on the road. The best gas mileage and greatest route flexibility comes from a four-wheel-drive truck camper with a cabover sleeping and cooking unit, but you'll sacrifice some of the comforts a type C or type A motorhome can provide. (This quandary inspired a popular bumper sticker that says, "Sure it gets lousy gas mileage for a car, but it gets great mileage for a house.")

Staying in government campgrounds without facilities is much cheaper than private campgrounds with hookups. Parking by the side of the road is cheapest of all, if you're in an area where you feel safe. However, noting how many RV parks list security as a plus, we don't recommend it. (See "Should You Sleep by the Side of the Road?" in chapter 3, "Where to Sleep: Campgrounds & RV Parks.")

Food is expensive in the north, so **stock up with as many provisions as you can** in the gateway cities to the south.

WHERE TO GET TRAVEL INFORMATION

Contact the **Alaska Division of Tourism,** Dept. 901, P.O. Box 110801, Juneau, AK 99811 (☎ **907/465-2010;** fax 907/536-8399; www.commerce. state.ak.us/tourism), for a free booklet called *Alaska State Vacation Planner.*

Tourism British Columbia, Parliament Buildings, Victoria, BC, Canada V8V 1X4 (☎ **800/663-6000**), provides a lot of free material about the province, including maps, campground guides, and other specialized information.

Tourism Yukon, P.O. Box 2703, Whitehorse, YT, Canada Y1A 2C6 (☎ **867/667-5340**), can also provide material, including maps and camp-ground guides.

Last, don't set out on the Alaska Highway drive without the road bible called ***Milepost,*** $23.95, published annually by Vernon Publications, Bellevue, WA (☎ **800/726-4707**). It includes mile-by-mile logs of all the North Country highways, as well as updated road conditions, best places to spot wildlife, and every hiccup of life along the highway. You can order it from the company or buy it en route in many of the towns or roadside lodges, or at most major bookstores in the United States.

DRIVING & CAMPING TIPS

- **Expect to drive with your headlights on.** In this part of Canada the law requires it, and in times when dust is billowing, you'll be glad the oncoming traffic is visible (and you to it) through the clouds.

- **Don't try to "make time" on the road;** it can make you crazy. We saw too many RVers limping into camp exhausted at 9pm—they'd kept driving because the sun was still high in the sky, either not knowing or ignoring the fact that in summer it almost never sets this far north. Even if you drove your RV hell-for-leather, ignoring loose gravel, buckled roadways, and potholes, you'd miss a lot of the scenery and the wildlife, two of the most important reasons for being there.

- **Always top off your gas tank when you pass an open station.** Sometimes a station ahead may be closed for the day or gone out of business. Our closest call came on the Klondike Highway when we had to drive 269 miles between open stations and finally rolled into Dempster Corner on fumes. Another time, we turned around and drove 20 miles back to buy gas at a station we had passed up because the one we were headed for was closed.

- **Watch for frost heaves.** These are the biggest enemy your vehicle has in Alaska, irregular bumps where the pavement has buckled or sunk because of permafrost melting and refreezing. Spots may be marked with little red flags by the roadside, but sometimes the wind takes them away. If the white center or side lines look squiggly ahead, slow down.

- **Don't drink the water.** We make it a habit never to assume any piped campground water is potable, using it only for the kitchen and bathroom. We drink bottled water and use prepackaged ice, which is available almost everywhere along the route in Alaska and northern Canada, where tap water sometimes comes out in shades of brown. Also, never drink water from a stream or lake, no matter how pristine it looks. The parasite *giardia,* which can cause extreme intestinal upset and is impervious to antibiotics, is present in Northern Canada and Alaska waterways.

- **Come prepared.** Stock up your RV with any esoteric items before you get into the woods. You'll be able to find basic groceries, towing services, RV repairs, and telephones along the road; but if you want to prepare a bouillabaisse with your freshly caught fish, take your saffron and Sauvignon Blanc along with you.

The Best Alaska Highway Sights, Tastes & Experiences

OFF-THE-WALL ATTRACTIONS

The world's largest chopstick manufacturing plant, Fort Nelson, BC. Located at Mile 278.1, it turned out six million pairs of the wooden utensils a day until 1998 when it closed.

A collection of 3,600 billed caps. They're stapled to the ceiling at Toad River Lodge, Mile 422, making an intricately textured soundproofing. ☎ **250/232-5401.**

The Sign Post Forest, Watson Lake. Located at Mile 612, the Sign Post Forest started in 1942 when a homesick GI from Illinois working on the highway put up a road sign to his home town, and has grown to some 42,000 signs from all over the world.

The "Teslin taxi." Photographer George Johnston had a 1928 Chevrolet shipped up to the little Tlingit town of Teslin by barge, despite the fact there were no roads. He built a 3-mile road for summer use, then put chains on the taxi and drove it across the frozen lake in winter. See the restored vehicle in the George Johnston Museum, on the left of the highway as you head north. ☎ **867/390-2550.** Open late May to early September.

Action Jackson's Bar, Boundary. At the Top of the World Highway on the Alaska side of the Alaska/Canada border, Yukon Highway 9, Action Jackson's was one of Alaska's first roadhouses, manned for years by its eponymous owner, who kept six-shooters strapped to each hip. Restless citizens used to drive the 70 miles from Dawson City on a Friday or Saturday night for the action; they were rarely disappointed. Today it has no liquor license, but you can get gas, as a rule.

The Bird House Bar, Indian. Located in Indian, 27 miles southeast of Anchorage on the Seward Highway, the Bird House collapsed during the 1964 earthquake and is half-buried, with a giant blue bird head facing the highway and everything inside on a slant.

Chetwynd, the chainsaw-carving capital of the world. With its distinctive three bears, heroic loggers, and other rustic road sculptures, it sits on BC's Highway 97 at the junction of Route 29.

North Pole. This town, at Mile 349 on the Richardson Highway, 13 miles south of Fairbanks, is where letters to Santa Claus are delivered by the U.S. Post Office. See Mr. and Mrs. Claus at Santa Claus House. ☎ **800/588-4678.**

The big black-and-white tripod in Nenana. It's put out on the Nenana River ice in winter, connected to a clock. When the ice breaks up enough in the river to drag the tripod cable and stop the clock, lottery ticket holders who guessed the closest date and time share a prize that can run up to $180,000. A hint to would-be winners: The ice usually breaks up some time between mid-April and mid-May. Nenana is an hour's drive south of Fairbanks on the Parks Highway. Purchase in person only at Nenana Visitor Center, at the intersection of the highway and A Street. ☎ **907/832-9953.**

Hyder, "the friendliest ghost town in Alaska." Off the Cassier Highway straddling the Canadian border at Stewart, Hyder is where people traditionally pin a dollar to the wall in the Glacier Inn in case they pass through again in the future broke and in need of a drink. The bars here are open 23 hours a day and there's an RV wash called **Wilderness RV Wash,** ☎ **250/636-9276.**

TEN GREAT SPLURGES

1. **Dinner at the elegant Log Cabin Restaurant.** At the Log Cabin, on Tabor Lake near Prince George, BC (☎ **250/963-9515**), host Richard Gunther will show you his astonishing collection of antique stoves and

A CRASH COURSE IN SPEAKING ALASKAN

The Bush: Any place reached by plane instead of road or Alaska ferry.
Cheechako: A newcomer.
Native: Not just anyone born in Alaska, but only those belonging to one of the Native American peoples of Alaska: the Athabaskan, Yup'ik, Cup'ik, Inupiaq, St. Lawrence Island Yupik, Aleut, Alutiiq, Eyak, Tlingit, Haida, or Tsimshian peoples.
Outside: Anywhere that isn't Alaska; generally the lower 48 states.
Permafrost: The permanently frozen subsoil that covers much of the state.
Sourdough: Anyone who's been in Alaska longer than one season, as in "Sour on Alaska without enough dough to get out."

sewing machines, plus Indian artifacts, stuffed and mounted black bears and wolves, and everything else you could imagine. The food is Continental with a German accent (Gunther is from Berlin), and dinner begins with a bottomless tureen of homemade soup.

2. **An evening of gaming at Diamond Tooth Gertie's.** At the corner of Queen Street and 4th Avenue in Dawson City, Gertie's gets especially rambunctious at the end of the season when all the locals are trying to win enough money to head south for the winter. (No one under 19 admitted.) Contact the Klondike Visitors Association for information (☎ 867/993-5575).

3. **An overnight or two at the Kantishna Roadhouse.** The Roadhouse is an appealing if archly rustic place at the end of the road inside Denali National Park. From here, you can go on guided hikes deep in the park. A special permit is necessary to drive in, but there's the park shuttle bus or, if you're in a hurry, a resort airstrip for a Denali air shuttle. Reserve well in advance (☎ 800/942-7420; www.alaskaone.com/krhouse).

4. **A performance of the Gaslight Follies.** Performed in Dawson City's 1899 Palace Grand Theatre, the Follies brings together a surprisingly professional cast; it's far less corny than the similar show in Whitehorse. Nightly except Tuesdays from mid-May to mid-September. Contact the Klondike Visitors Association for information (☎ 867/993-5575).

5. **A 3-hour excursion aboard the White Pass and Yukon Railway.** It takes you along the famous Trail of '98 from Skagway to the White Pass Summit and back. There's also daily afternoon service from Skagway to Whitehorse (via train to Fraser, BC, then motorcoach to Whitehorse) with a morning return. Built in 1899, the narrow-gauge train has one of the steepest railroad grades in North America. Summers only. ☎ 800/343-7373.

6. **A dinner of rare white King salmon at Simon & Seafort's Saloon.** It's all the rage in Anchorage during its very brief season. Start with fresh King crab and follow the salmon with the house's brandy ice, a concoction of vanilla ice cream, brandy, Kahlua, and crème de cacao. 420 L St., ☎ **907/274-3502.**

7. **Shopping for qiviut.** In northern craft shops, look for rare and costly qiviut, the soft underwool of the musk ox, gathered when it's shed each spring and woven into warm, feather-light gloves, scarves, caps, and sweaters. Alternatively, seek carved soapstone pieces, ceremonial wooden masks, or last season's trendy ulus (fan-shaped chopping knives with wood handles).

8. **Flying over Mt. McKinley.** On a clear day you can fly over McKinley and the Susitna Valley, where you might catch glimpses of moose, bear, foxes, and eagles, then land in Talkeetna, the staging area for climbers who tackle the high peaks of the Alaska Range. Call **Talkeetna Air Taxi** (☎ **800/583-2219**), **K2 Aviation** (☎ **800/ 764-2291**), or **Hudson Air Service** (☎ **907/733-2321**) for details.

9. **Dinner at the Pump House Restaurant.** The colorful Pump House, on the banks of the Chena River, 2 miles southwest of Fairbanks on Chena Pump Road, is now a national historic site crammed with gold rush–era artifacts. ☎ **907/479-8452.**

10. **An all-day cruise of Prince William Sound.** The *MV Nunatak* will take you out for the day for $115 per person, including two meals aboard. You'll get close-up views of the vast Columbia Glacier, cliffs with nesting kittiwakes, and marine mammals. Park the RV in Valdez. Call Gray Line Alaska at ☎ **907/835-4282** for details.

TAKE-OUT (OR EAT-IN) FAR NORTH TREATS

Goldfields Bakery, Barkerville. Grab some whole wheat or sourdough bread from Goldfields, in the historic gold rush town of Barkerville, near Quesnel, BC. Call the Barkerville Reception Centre for information, ☎ **604/ 994-3332.**

Lung Duck Tong restaurant, Barkerville. Chinese dim sum in a gold rush town? Why not? Call the Barkerville Reception Centre for information, ☎ **604/994-3332.**

Bonanza Meat Company, Dawson City. At Bonanza Meat you can design your own sandwich. Located on 2nd Avenue in Dawson City. ☎ **867/ 993-6567.**

The Braeburn Lodge. Try the Braeburn's superburgers—one is big enough for two. They also serve something they call "gianormous" cinnamon buns. Big, yes, but not particularly tasty. Mile 55.6, Klondike Highway. Radio Phone **2M-3987,** Fox Channel.

Dawson Peaks Resorts, south of Teslin. Try the grilled Teslin lake trout and rhubarb pie. Seven miles south of Teslin on the lake, Mile 769. Answering service ☎ 867/390-2310. Radio Phone, Mobile **2M-3169,** Teslin Channel.

Alaskan Brewery and Bottling Company. The Juneau-based Alaska Brewing Company has been around only since 1986, but its Alaskan Amber has already been twice voted the most popular brew at the Great American Beer Festival in Colorado. The brewery is at 5429 Shaune Dr., outside Juneau. To get there, turn right from Egan Drive onto Vanderbilt Hill Road, which becomes the Glacier Highway, and then right on Anka Street and right again on Shaune Drive. Tours leave every half hour between 11am and 5pm, Tuesday through Saturday May through September; Thursday through Saturday the rest of the year. ☎ 907/780-5866; www.alaskan-beer.com.

Malamute Saloon, west of Fairbanks. Try the reindeer stew and Alaska crab at the Malamute Saloon, 8 miles west of Fairbanks on Old Nenana Highway, at Ester Gold Camp. At night it includes the price of the Northern Lights Show. ☎ 800/676-6925.

Taku Smokeries Market Place, Juneau. The smoked salmon packaged to go at Taku Smokeries Market Place in Juneau can also be ordered by mail. 230 S. Franklin Ave.; ☎ 800/582-5123; www.alaskasksbest.com/ester.

The Double Musky, Girdwood. Try the Double Musky cake at the restaurant of the same name, with its layers of pecan meringue, brownielike chocolate, chocolate mousse, and cocoa cream frosting. On Crow Creek Road in Girdwood, south of Anchorage near Alyeska. ☎ 907/783-2822.

Alaska Wild Berry chocolates. Get some chocolate and check out the flowing 20-foot chocolate waterfall at the company's new Anchorage outlet. Filling options include wild rosehip, elderberry, salmonberry, high bush cranberry, and lingonberry. On International Airport Road between the Old and New Seward highways. ☎ 907/562-8858.

Sourdough pancakes. You'll find sourdough pancakes almost anywhere up here, but they're especially good in Dawson City's **Midnight Sun,** at Third and Queen Street (☎ 867/993-5495). In Juneau's **Baranof Hotel,** 127 N. Franklin St. (☎ 800/544-0970), they're the size of Frisbees and accompanied by sturdy reindeer sausages, and in Tok you can camp next door to them at the **Sourdough Campground** (see "Campground Oases: Dawson to Fairbanks," below).

WILDLIFE WATCHING

We never got sated with **moose** sightings on our May trip, perhaps because spring is calving time. In early fall, however, plenty of them come down into the lower meadows in Denali. Pulling over to cook breakfast at a rest stop

A caribou crosses a side road off the Alaska Highway.

on the road between Denali and Anchorage, we saw a moose cow browsing at the edge of the trees and managed to snap a couple of shots before she gave us an aggrieved look and ambled back into the woods.

A close sighting of a **porcupine** in the wild, waddling up a bank with his silver-tipped quills aquiver, or a **bald eagle** in the roadway snacking on roadkill, is just as exciting as seeing the big animals. And unless you're unusually quick or patient or the animal very slow, your memory will be clearer than your photograph.

Our first good day of wildlife spotting was on an early morning transit of the Crooked River Nature Corridor south of McLeod Lake in British Columbia, with a wolf, deer, and great blue herons spotted in quick succession. We were too late in the season to catch the trumpeter swans who winter here.

Hummingbird-sized **mosquitoes**—a.k.a. Alaska's state bird—in a campground at Fort Nelson were next, too large, fortunately, to get through the window screens of the RV.

An early morning roadside sighting of a **black bear** a few miles north of Fort Nelson did not net any photographs. He spotted us first, so all we saw was his backside disappearing into the woods.

One of the best places to spot **caribou** is by the side of the road, oddly enough. They stand around morosely by signs and at road junctions as if waiting for a bus. At Stone Mountain Park, there have been great caribou sightings right past a huge sign warning CARIBOU IN THE ROADWAY. **Mountain sheep,** too, like the roadsides. The indigenous stone sheep in Stone Mountain Park, colored cream and brown and bigger than Dall or Rocky Mountain sheep, can be glimpsed looking down from craggy rock cliffs or photographed as they gather by the roadside to lick salt deposits.

<u>INSIDER TIP</u>

One expert says that if you encounter a bear while out on a hike, don't turn and run because he may give chase. Instead, walk backward to get away, facing the bear and continuing to talk in a normal tone ("Nice bear, nice bear"?). Above all, "do not imitate bear sounds or positions, even if they sound funny to you."

On the Road

NORTHERN BRITISH COLUMBIA

Once past Calgary on the eastern access road or Kamloops on the western access road, urbanites need to make an important mental adjustment. There are no more cities until Whitehorse, Yukon Territory, just a series of small towns separated by as much as 8 hours of driving through gorgeous, uninhabited scenery. And while those places with serious names and major crossroads you've been looking at on the map all day might not be what you expect by the time you finally arrive, the inhabitants are generally friendly and helpful.

Dawson Creek is where most of the Alaska Highway drivers stop coming and going to trade war stories, especially at service stations, car washes, RV parks, and the town's major drinking and dining spot, the venerable Alaska Hotel Café & Dew Drop Inn. This is where you photograph your RV in front of the Mile 0 Alaska Highway sign, take a look at one of the three competing pioneer villages, and admire the big red grain elevator that doubles as art gallery and tourist information office.

In **Fort Nelson,** as we were running out of reading and cocktail materials, we found an office supply store that had a treasure-trove of secondhand paperback books sold at half the cover price and a liquor store that had a sparse and pricey inventory. Less exciting was a highly advertised "European deli" with a meager supply of meats and cheese but doing a land-office business in microwaved burritos.

Watson Lake, on the Yukon border, has a unique sign forest (see "Ten Off-the-Wall Attractions") and a modest supermarket. Camp-Ground Services RV park offers 140 sites, full and partial hookups, and a coin-operated car/RV wash to get rid of the top layer of road dust. Don't worry about street addresses—the whole town is laid out in a strip along the highway.

The "lodges" so grandly promoted by highway road signs before you get there usually turn out to be very basic roadside cafes with a straggle of cabins in the back and a gas tank out front, and a cashier/waitress who also sells fishing licenses, pumps gas, makes beds, and does the home cooking in her spare time.

Western Canada Campgrounds

Bigfoot Campgrounds and RV Park ❶
Claybanks RV Park ❷
Dawson Peaks Resort & RV Park ⑫
Downtown RV Park ⑪
Gold Rush Campground ⑮
Guggieville RV Park & Gold Panning ⑮
Husky 5th Wheel RV Park ❽
Kamloops Waterslide & RV Park ❸
Liard River Hot Springs Provincial
Park ⑩
Log House Restaurant and
Campground ❹
MacKenzie's RV Park ⑬
Mile 0 RV Park and Campground ❺
Muncho Lake Provincial Park ❾
Northern Lights RV Park Ltd. ❺
Sasquatch Provincial Park ❶
Sasquatch Springs RV Resort ❶
Sikanni River RV Park ❼
Sourdough Pete's ❻
West End RV Park ❽
Westmark RV Park, Beaver Creek ⑭

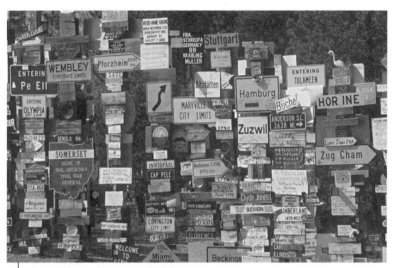

The world-famous Sign Post Forest at Watson Lake, BC, on the Alaska Highway, has some 20,000 signs from all over the world.

Whatever the roadside food lacks in flavor, it more than makes up for in volume. We fussy freewheelers were glad our RV had a kitchen.

Campground Oases: Harrison Hot Springs to Teslin

Bigfoot Campgrounds and RV Park. Harrison Hot Springs makes a good stopover for anyone interested in the legend of Bigfoot, who apparently hangs around this area a great deal. Perhaps it's too obvious to look for him at Bigfoot Campgrounds, where the logo is a silhouette of the 8-foot hairy humanoid. Of the 110 RV sites, all have water and 15- and 30-amp electricity, and 70 provide sewers as well. It's located on Highway 9, also Harrison Hot Springs road, 2 miles north of the junction with Highway 7. For reservations, call ☎ 604/796-9767 or e-mail: bigfoot@uniserve.com.

Sasquatch Springs RV Resort. Sasquatch, the Indian name for Bigfoot, shows up in place names around Harrison Hot Springs, so of course it's in campground names as well. Try Sasquatch Springs, north 4 miles of the junction of Highways 7 and 9 on Harrison Hot Springs Road, where 70 full hookups provide 15- and 30-amp electricity plus cable TV. Call them at ☎ 604/796-2828 or e-mail at jallen@universe.com.

Sasquatch Provincial Park. Located 4 miles north of Harrison Hot Springs on Rockwell Drive, with 177 campsites but no hookups. ☎ 604/869-5853.

Claybanks RV Park. Claybanks is a pleasant, family-run campground at the edge of the historic little town of Merritt and near enough for an easy stroll into town. Take exit 290 from Highway 5 and follow the Sani-Dump signs along Voight Street to the campground, which has 42 full-hookup sites with 15- and 30-amp electricity. Call for reservations at ☎ 250/378-6441.

Kamloops Waterslide & RV Park. Kamloops makes a good major stop for stocking up on groceries and supplies, and a convenient place to overnight. The Kamloops Waterslide & RV Park is 12 miles east of town on Highway 1 and has plenty of holiday diversions for the whole family, including two 18-hole golf courses 5 minutes away. Some 85 sites have water and 30-amp electricity, 73 of which also include sewer connections. Call ☎ **250/ 573-3789** for reservations.

Log House Restaurant and Campground. This place, on Tabor Lake, near Prince George, is a clean, well-run campground with 24 sites, 30-amp electric connections, and water but no sanitary dump available. There's an excellent dinner restaurant on the hill above the RV park, also operated by proprietor Richard Gunther, plus a floatplane base, cottages, and fishing, as well as good bird watching. (We spent much of our stay transfixed by the antics of a pet Canada goose and her wild boyfriend who flies in for the summer, and two pair of horned grebes on the lake.) Reservations accepted (☎ **250/683-2294**).

Mile 0 RV Park and Campground. Dawson Creek marks Mile 0, the beginning of the Alaska Highway, with a half-dozen public and private RV parks and two pioneer villages. We like the public Mile 0 RV Park and Campground, which is actually located at Mile 1½ and has 54 tree-shaded sites, 28 of them with water and 20- and 30-amp electric hookups, rest rooms, showers, a sanitary dump station, laundry, and e-mail service. It's an easy stroll away from the Walter Wright Pioneer Village. Call ☎ **250/ 782-2590** for reservations. You'll need them because it seems as though everyone overnights in Dawson Creek to swap war stories.

Northern Lights RV Park Ltd. Located in Dawson Creek, on 97 south, a mile and a half before Mile 0, Northern Lights offers an almost intimidating list of vehicle preparations available before you set out on the Alaska Highway, with lube and oil changes, windshield repairs, bug screen installation, headlight protectors, tow-car protectors, and do-it-yourself RV wash for $5. Why you'd want to wash your RV on the way north is a mystery, but you'll certainly want to take care of it on the way back. They also have 55 sites with water and 20- and 30-amp electric hookups, 43 with full hookups. ☎ **250/782-9433;** www.pris.bc.ca/rvpark/.

Sourdough Pete's. If everything in Dawson Creek is already spoken for, drive another 43 miles to Sourdough Pete's in Fort St. John, the newest commercial RV park in town. Sixty water and electric (15- and 30-amp) hookups, 48 full hookups, and a sanitary dump station, a modem-friendly office, and an adjacent amusement park with go-karts, miniature golf, batting cages, and driving range. Call ☎ **800/227-8388.**

Sikanni River RV Park. Sikanni River RV Park, in the British Columbia community of Sikanni Chief, offers 26 sites, 22 of them with 20-amp electricity, rest rooms and showers, security, LP gas, and firewood. Call ☎ **250/774-1028.**

Husky 5th Wheel RV Park. Located in Fort Nelson, at Mile 293, Husky 5th Wheel Park provides 55 full hookups with 20- and 30-amp electricity, cable TV, laundry, groceries, RV supplies, LP gas, and a full-service truck stop. Call for reservations at ☎ **250/774-7270.**

West End RV Park. Also in Fort Nelson on the west side of town, the West End RV Park has 110 20- and 30-amp electric sites, 99 of which also have water and 47 of which have sewer connections. ☎ **250/774-2340.**

Muncho Lake Provincial Park. Between Mile 437 and 442 on the Alaska Highway in BC. The lake's icy waters are a gorgeous blue and turquoise from a combination of copper in the rocks and glacial runoff. There are 30 sites, 15 in each location, with piped water, firewood, boat launch, fishing, and hiking. Caribou, moose, and sheep are sometimes seen here, and bears may frequent the area. No hookups, no reservations. ☎ **250/787-3407.**

Liard River Hot Springs Provincial Park. At Mile 496, this is the most popular park along the route, with its 52 sites filling up by noon (no reservations). Besides handsome, tree-shaded spots spaced well apart, the camper will find free firewood and hot springs for soaking away travel aches, but no RV hookups. Playgrounds, heated rest rooms, wheelchair-accessible toilet. Bears sometimes prowl the area. ☎ **250/787-3407.**

Downtown RV Park. By the time you get to Watson Lake in the Yukon Territory, you and your RV will both be ready for a good bath. The Downtown RV Park throws in a free RV wash (they supply the water, you supply the manpower) when you stay overnight in one of the 71 full-hookup sites (20-amp electricity). Call ☎ **867/536-7448.**

Camp-Ground Services. Has 110 water and 20-amp electric hookups, showers, laundry, groceries, LP gas, dump station, adjacent service station, and a free RV wash. Call ☎ **867/536-7448.**

Dawson Peaks Resort & RV Park. South of Teslin at Milepost 769, Dawson Peaks Resort is famous along the route for its grilled Teslin lake trout and rhubarb pie. RVers will find 16 sites with water and 15- and 30-amp electricity. Call ☎ **867/390-2310.**

Campground Oases: Whitehorse

Whitehorse marks a dividing point in the road. From here you'll head north to Dawson City if you want to drive the Klondike Highway, then rejoin the Alaska Highway at Tok, Alaska. If you want to think about it a while, check out:

MacKenzie's RV Park. At Mile 922 of the Alaska Highway. Besides the usual 82 full-hookup sites with 20- and 30-amp electricity, you get cable TV, Laundromat, an RV wash, and free gold panning. Call them at ☎ **867/633-2337.**

THE YUKON

Around Dawson City they joke, "This isn't the end of the world, but you can see it from here."

This is a destination for North Americans with a yen to wander, nagged by an insatiable restlessness to see what lies at the end of the road. It is written in the faces of men wearing rumpled plaid shirts and blue jeans as they climb out of dirty, mud-streaked RVs and 4-by-4s with license plates from Florida, New Brunswick, Texas, California, and Ontario. They have made it to the place where the Yukon and the Klondike rivers meet, to the fabled city of gold and the end of the infamous Trail of '98.

Coming to **Dawson City** is like meeting a childhood idol or your favorite movie star 3 or 4 decades after the fact and being surprised to find the old dear is still alive, let alone lively enough to dance a fandango and tell a couple of salty tales.

Far from being some saccharine gold rush Disneyland or horsehair-stuffed historical monument, Dawson is alive and kicking. Under the aegis of Parks Canada, where "money is always iffy," the town is slowly being renovated. Some buildings—like the splendid Palace Grand Theatre, the old post office, the Arctic Brotherhood Hall (now Diamond Tooth Gertie's Casino), and Madame Tremblay's store—have been restored. Others, sagging and unpainted, lean wearily against each other waiting their turn, looking as though they won't last much longer.

Some of the wilder goings on from earlier years were not in evidence lately. The "Miss Nude Yukon" contest had faded into obscurity and the Eldorado's famous Sour Toe cocktail—a pickled human toe tossed into a beer mug of champagne—has tamed down and moved over to the Keno

Weary buildings in Dawson City await restoration by Parks Canada.

Lounge in the Westmark Inn. But the annual Great International Outhouse Race and Bathroom Wall Limerick Contest is still on the Labor Day weekend agenda.

Today Dawson's biggest gold mine is **Diamond Tooth Gertie's Casino,** the first legal gambling casino in the Yukon.

Campground Oases: Dawson to Fairbanks

Gold Rush Campground. The best bet in downtown Dawson City, although its main appeal is its location, at 5th Avenue and York Street, within easy walking distance of the sights. Some 15- and 30-amp electric connections, a sanitary dump station, and narrow parking lot–type sites are what you'll find; reserve well ahead if you want a spot in midsummer. Call ☎ 867/993-5247.

The Guggieville RV Park & Gold Panning. Located at the south end of Dawson City, Guggieville has 72 sites with water and 15-amp electric hookups, plus gold panning, a gold nugget jewelry shop, and a Laundromat. Call ☎ 867/ 993-5008.

Westmark RV Park, Beaver Creek. Located at AH Mile 1202, the Westmark park has 67 sites with 20- and 30-amp electric and water hookups, and it's adjacent to the Westmark Inn if you want to treat yourself to a meal or two out. Lounge, laundry, gift shop, showers, wildlife display, sanitary dump. To reserve ahead, call ☎ 867/862-7501.

Tok Sourdough Campground and Pancake House. Located in Tok, 2 miles south on the Anchorage Highway, the Tok Pancake House specializes in sourdough pancakes. The RV park adjacent has 48 sites with electric hookups (20- and 30-amp) and water, and 21 with sewer hookups. Sanitary dump station, laundry, showers, flush toilets, cafe, gift shop, walk-through museum of Alaskan artifacts, car wash. To reserve, call ☎ 907/883-5543.

Moon Lake State Recreation Site. On the Alaska Highway at Mile 1332, west of Tok, Moon Lake has 17 campsites amid the trees by a beautiful lake. Toilets, piped water, boat launch. No hookups, no reservations. ☎ 907/451-2695.

FAIRBANKS

In 1902, when the Klondike excitement had quieted down a little, a prospector named Felix Pedro discovered gold in the Tanana Valley near present-day Fairbanks, and a new rush was on. The prospectors and gamblers from Dawson hurried west to the new boom town, rode the crest of the newest wave, then crashed in the depression that followed.

Vestiges of those days can still be seen in **Alaskaland**—located at Airport Way and Peger Road (☎ 907/459-2095) and not as commercial as its name sounds—where the history of the gold mining days is re-created. Original cabins, a replica Indian village, the Crooked Creek & Whiskey

Alaska Campgrounds

Feeding time at the sled dog kennels

Island railroad with its little steam engine, and the stern-wheeler *Nenana,* one-time star of the Yukon riverboats, are all on display. Admission is free.

From Fairbanks, you can take a **paddlewheeler day cruise** along the Chena and Tanana rivers with Alaska Riverways Inc. (☎ **907/479-6673**) or a **motorcoach excursion** along the Dalton Highway following the Trans-Alaska Oil Pipeline farther into Prudhoe Bay than private vehicles can go with Northern Alaska Tour Company (☎ **800/474-1986**).

When in Alaska, do as the tourists do and take in a salmon bake. The **Alaska Salmon Bake** at Alaskaland can also include an after-dinner musical comedy about life in Fairbanks at the Palace Theatre and Saloon across the street. Call ☎ **800/354-7274** for the salmon bake, ☎ **907/456-5960** for the show.

On the other hand, if you've had enough salmon, you can find a Fairbanks branch of every fast-food outlet known to man.

Campground Oases: Fairbanks

Rivers Edge RV Park. Off the Parks Highway in Fairbanks, Rivers Edge has 170 sites with full and partial 20- and 30-amp hookups, a sanitary dump station, laundry, showers, and free shuttle service to attractions such as the stern-wheeler *Discovery* and the Alaska Salmon Bake. On the Chena River, with fishing and boat ramp. For reservations, call ☎ **800/770-3343.**

DENALI NATIONAL PARK

Denali means "the high one" in the language of the local Athabascan people, and is both the current official designation for the former Mount McKinley National Park and the original Native name for 20,320-foot Mount McKinley itself, renamed in 1917 for an assassinated president who never saw it. (The mountain is still called Denali by most Alaskans, Native and non-Native alike, although repeated attempts to change it back officially

Denali National Park

Park Entrance Area

Visitor Center
To Fairbanks
George
Parks Hwy.
Nenana River
Alaska Railroad
To Anchorage
Airport
Railroad Station
Park Rd.
Riley Creek
Horseshoe Lake
To Kantishna
Park Headquarters
Hines Creek

To Fairbanks
Nenana River
Denali Hwy.
Park Entrance (see inset)
Riley Creek
Cantwell
Healy
Sanctuary River
Tokiat River
Toklat River
Teklanika River
McKinley River
Kantishna
Mt. Deception (11,826)
Eldridge Glacier
Muldrow Glacier
Mt. Hunter (14,573)
Ruth Glacier
Tokositna Glacier
Peters Glacier
Mt. McKinley (20,320)
Mt. Foraker (17,400)
Mt. Russell (11,670)
Chedotlothna Glacier
Yentna Glacier
Glacier
Foraker River
Herron River
Yentna River
Lake Minchumina
George Parks Hwy.
Alaska Railroad
Petersville
Petersville Rd.
Talkeetna
To Anchorage

ALASKA
Denali NP

Denali State Park ❼
Eilson Visitor Center ❸
Mt. McKinley ❶
Polchrome Pass ❺
Post Office & Alaska Railroad Station ❽
Riley Creek Campground ❾
Sable Pass ❻
Tokiat Ranger Station ❹
Visitor Access Center ❿
Wonder Lake Ranger Station ❷

DENALI TIP

If you don't have a day or two to wait for space on the free park shuttles, advance-ticket purchases for the Wildlife Tours into Denali National Park can be made by calling Denali Park Resorts at ☎ **800/276-7234**. $64 for adults, $34 for kids.

---

have been unsuccessful in Congress.) The 4-million acre Denali park, slightly bigger than the state of Massachusetts, includes a wilderness area and a national preserve; sport hunting, fishing, and trapping are allowed in the latter by state permit.

Denali State Park is southeast of the national park area, bisected by Parks Highway, which is named for George Parks, a territorial governor in the late 1920s, not for the fact that two major parks lie along it.

With rare exceptions, you cannot drive through Denali, but must park near the visitor center and take one of the shuttle buses run by **ARA-MARK/Denali Park Resorts** (☎ **800/622-7275** or 907/272-7275; fax 907/264-4684; www.denalinationalpark.com), which takes you into the park and allows you to hop on and off at various stops to explore on foot (shuttles come by every half hour or so; you can catch any of them to get back to the park entrance). The park entrance fee is $10 per family, $5 per person, and is good for 7 days. Walk-in reservations for the shuttles begin 2 days out. If it's a busy time of year, desirable shuttle reservations are snapped up early and you may have to wait till the next day to get in. On the other hand, you could get lucky, as the flow of visitors rises and falls unpredictably.

The information desk at the **Denali National Park Visitor Access Center,** Denali Park Road, a half mile from the park entrance (☎ **907/683-2294**; www.nps.gov/dena), is the easiest place to get Park Service information. Stop here for the park map. For advance shuttle reservations, contact **ARAMARK** at the number above.

Campground Oases: Denali to Anchorage

Riley Creek Campground. Riley Creek, at Denali, has 100 well-separated and tree-shaded sites not far from the railway station. Flush toilets, piped water in summer, sanitary dump station, but no hookups. An overnight or two at Denali will allow time to get a spot on the popular park service shuttle bus that goes 66 miles into the wilderness, where private vehicles are not allowed. No reservations; 14-day maximum stay. After mid-June, any empty sites in the campground are usually filled the minute the previous tenant pulls out. ☎ **907/683-2294.**

The Homestead RV Park. In Palmer, Alaska, the Homestead is handily located in the Matanuska Valley near the junction of the Parks Highway between Denali and Anchorage and the Glenn Highway between Tok and Anchorage. With the long hours of summer, you can easily commute to Anchorage for dinner and get home before dark, as well as walk to trout fishing, go hiking, and take in a square dance on Thursday nights. Some 64 sites have water and electric (20- and 30-amp) hookups. Call ☎ **907/ 745-6005.**

ANCHORAGE

In the Bush, they like to say, "The nicest thing about Los Anchorage is that it's only 30 miles from Alaska."

People who don't know Alaska usually visualize Anchorage as an icy out-post in the wilderness populated by moose, grizzly bears, and bush pilots. True, you will find moose and bears—most often in the Anchorage Zoo—and plenty of bush pilots taking off from and landing at Lake Hood. But the first time we arrived there, on a July day, it was warmer and sunnier than Los Angeles and bright with summer flowers. On our most recent May visit, however, it was cold and windy and socked in with fog.

Earthquake Park, on the west end of Northern Lights Boulevard, still shows graphically the results of the 9.2 earthquake on Good Friday in 1964, when two huge chunks of earth fissured and dropped 20 feet in an instant. "It looked like chocolate pudding somebody had been dragging their fingers through," one eyewitness said.

A **statue of Captain James Cook** looks out on Turnagain Arm, so named when the captain told his first mate William Bligh, later to command the *Bounty,* to turn around again when it turned out not to be the Northwest Passage he was seeking.

The fine **Anchorage Museum,** in a stylish building with a frieze of stylized Alaskan designs across the top, displays an excellent collection of contemporary Alaskan and Native arts and crafts. It's located at 121 W. Seventh Ave. (☎ **907/343-4326**).

At night, head for **Fly by Night Club,** on Spenard Road south of Northern Lights Boulevard (☎ **907/279-SPAM**), where the Spam hors d'oeuvres are free if you order a bottle of Dom Perignon champagne, and "The Whale Fat Follies" break up the locals. The house jazz band is called the Spamtones.

___INSIDER TIP___

Don't attempt to drive down to the Kenai Peninsula on a summer weekend; it's bumper-to-bumper traffic heading south from Anchorage on Friday afternoons and heading north back to town on Sunday nights and Monday mornings.

Campground Oases in Anchorage

Anchorage RV Park. At Glenn Highway and Muldoon Road, the Anchorage RV Park has 195 full hookups with city water and 30- and 50-amp electricity, a "welcome back" for big rigs with roof air-conditioning after long days on the road with less amperage. Call ☎ **800/400-PARK** or check the Web site at www.anchrvpark.com.

Ship Creek Landings Downtown RV Park. Close to Anchorage's downtown area at 150 N. Ingra St. at East 1st Avenue, Ship Creek Landing faces the railroad tracks and Ship Creek. The 150 full hookups provide city water and 20- and 30-amp electricity, and you can walk to shopping, fishing, the farmers' market, rail, and boat and bus excursions. For reservations, call ☎ **907/277-0877.**

Seven Rough, Tough Side Trips & Three Easy Ones

TOUGH TRIPS

1. **The Top of the World Highway (Yukon Route 9).** The Top of the World, from Dawson City to Eagle, is 146 miles of unpaved, white-knuckling terror you'll talk about for years, especially if you go early in the season when half the roadway is still covered with ice and snow. There are no guard rails and few markers to let you know whether you're still on the roadway or have ventured off onto a side road that peters out in the tundra. Eagle, where author John McPhee set much of his classic *Coming Into the Country,* is an optional destination at the end of the rough, narrow road. There's been a trading post here for gold miners since the 1880s, and today Eagle is populated by some 150 pioneers, curmudgeons, and refugees from urban life.

2. **The Taylor Highway.** Between Eagle to Tetlin Junction is 161 miles of rough road, with the biggest metropolis en route being the town of Chicken with its population of 37. There's a saloon, a cafe, a gas station, and two gift shops where you can buy T-shirts with slogans like, "I got laid in Chicken, Alaska." The old gold mining town itself is off the main road and closed to visitors except on a daily guided walking tour or gold-panning venture in summer. The original settlers wanted to name it after the ptarmigan, the plump little edible grouse that was a dietary mainstay, but since they couldn't spell it, they called the town Chicken instead.

3. **The Dalton Highway.** This road to Prudhoe Bay takes you across the Arctic Circle, the Brooks Range, and the Continental Divide, but you might have to stop a few miles short of Prudhoe Bay itself; the oil companies sometimes limit access. The 414-mile road was constructed to build and service the Alaska pipeline, and there are very few services

available along it. Before setting out, call the Alaska Department of Transportation (☎ **907/456-7623**) for a recording that will fill you in on road conditions and how far you'll be able to drive. Some years it's open only to Dietrich Camp, about halfway.

4. **Canada's 456-mile Dempster Highway.** The Dempster Highway crosses the Arctic Circle at Mile 252 after striking north from Dawson City and Klondike Highway 2. Final destination is the Northwest Territories' Inuit village of Inuvik, with 57 days of midnight sun beginning May 24 each year. The gravel road, with some slippery clay surface sections, also requires two ferry crossings; the most feasible time to go is between mid-June and the end of August. Black flies and mosquitoes are also a problem, so take plenty of repellent. You may spot wolves, caribou, grizzly bears, moose, eagles, and gyrfalcons. Allow 2 days in each direction to drive this tough tundra route. Government campgrounds are spotted along the road, but few services are available. Stop for gas whenever you see a station open. Experts recommend carrying at least two spare tires. Get a recorded message about road conditions before setting out at ☎ **800/661-0752.**

5. **Atlin Road (Yukon/BC 7).** From Jake's Corner, Mile 836, turn south for a spectacular 58-mile scenic route to Canada's Little Switzerland, with snow-capped mountains, lakes with prime fishing, and a good chance of spotting moose or grizzly bears. The all-weather gravel road is fairly good, although winding and slippery in wet weather. The Atlin Visitors Association (☎ **250/651-7522**) can update road information for you.

6. **The Cassiar Highway (BC 37).** The Cassiar drops south from Mile 726 west of Watson Lake down to the Yellowhead Highway 16. It's also possible to use the Cassiar as an alternative to the Alaska Highway between Prince George and Watson Lake. A lot of adventuresome drivers prefer this route, which they liken to driving the Alaska Highway back in the fifties and sixties. There are some stretches of gravel instead of road, and services are few and far between, but the scenery, from hanging glaciers to snow-capped mountains, is stunning. Just watch out for the logging trucks. Call ☎ **250/771-3000** or 250/771-4511 for road conditions.

7. **Wrangell–St. Elias National Park and Preserve.** Chitina, the gateway to this 13-million-acre park, is reachable by the paved, 33-mile Edgerton Highway, running from the Richardson Highway, the route between Tok and Valdez. Only small RVs or four-wheel-drive vehicles without trailers should attempt the next 58 unpaved, steep, and sometimes slippery miles of the road into McCarthy, but the effort is worth it. The privately owned copper company town of Kennicott, now a ghost town, can be visited by hikers crossing the Kennicott River via

hand-operated cable tram (wear thick gloves). Guided glacier walks, Kennicott tours, backcountry hikes, and horseback riding are available in McCarthy. Ask for road conditions in Chitina at the National Park Service Ranger Station (☎ **907/823-2205**).

EASY TRIPS

1. **Visiting Barkerville, BC.** From Quesnel, BC, take Route 26 over to the Cariboo gold rush town of Barkerville, in its heyday the largest city north of San Francisco and west of Chicago. More than 125 original and restored buildings, many of them occupied by costumed docents, are open, including Lung Duck Ton Chinese restaurant, Eldorado Gold Panning, The Wake-Up-Jake Restaurant, McPherson's Watchmakers Shop, and Cameron & Ames Blacksmith Shop. An historical stage stop called Cottonwood House is also on the route; the round-trip from Highway 97 is 100 miles. The best time to visit is between June 1 and Labor Day. Barkerville Reception Centre, ☎ **604/994-3332.**

2. **Klondike Highway 2.** The Klondike, from Whitehorse 99 miles south to Skagway, via Carcross (short for Caribou Crossing), looks nothing like the precipitous trail, lake, and river route followed by the prospectors of '98, most of them ill-equipped cheechakos who were required by the Northwest Mounted Police to carry a ton of supplies to the gold fields. A few had horses, a few more "sled dogs" that were usually poodles or terriers dognapped from Seattle backyards, but most had to carry the stuff on their backs in relays, caching it along the trail and doubling back for more. Skagway, at the end of the road, is the town where sharpies like gambler Soapy Smith and his cronies fleeced the innocent. The two-lane paved road is asphalt-surfaced and fairly wide.

3. **Turnagain Arm, Alyeska & Portage Glacier.** From Anchorage, drive south along the Arm, keeping an eye out for whales, and stop at Alyeska, Alaska's top ski resort (the lifts take you sightseeing in summer), and the Portage Glacier with its self-guided nature trail to the ice worms. If time permits, you can keep going south to the town of Seward or take the Sterling Highway to Homer and the Kenai Peninsula.

Travel Quiz: Bye, Bye, Mister Eskimo Pie

Alaska has its own unique terminology. See if you can pick out the correct definition for each term from the following choices.

1. "Seward's icebox"
    - (a) The Seward family's back-porch freezer
    - (b) The birthplace of Eskimo pies
    - (c) The Alaska land purchase of 1867
2. The Big Break-Up
    - (a) When Rob Morrow bid Janine Turner goodbye on "Northern Exposure"
    - (b) When the ice in the Nenana River starts thawing and the closest guess to the exact time wins a lottery
    - (c) When Alaska was hit by the largest earthquake ever registered in North America
3. Musher
    - (a) A dogsled driver
    - (b) A toothless prospector
    - (c) A waitress who ladles out hot cereals

4. Cheechako
    - (a) The Inuit comedian formerly teamed with Chong
    - (b) An Inuit village on the North Slope above the Arctic Circle
    - (c) A newcomer or tenderfoot
5. Ice worms
    - (a) Bait used by ice fishermen
    - (b) Nickname for waterpark slides in winter
    - (c) Invertebrates that lay their eggs in glacier ice
6. The Bush
    - (a) Nickname for a popular Anchorage strip club
    - (b) Any place reached by plane rather than road or ferry
    - (c) The last U.S. president acknowledged by conservative former Alaska Gov. Walter J. Hickel

ANSWERS: 1 (c); 2 (b); 3 (a); 4 (c); 5 (c); 6 (a), (b), and (c)

8

The Dakotas: Black Hills & Buffalo Burgers

NORTH DAKOTA IS WHERE TEDDY ROOSEVELT SHOT A BUFFALO, where Peggy Lee learned to sing and Lawrence Welk learned to talk (he spoke only German until he was 21), where Cream of Wheat was invented, and thin Norwegian pancakes called *lefse* are the state dish.

It's where native son Louis L'Amour learned his ABCs and Roger Maris got to first base playing for the Fargo American Legion team as a kid, where Angie Dickinson was born, rodeo great Casey Tibbs first saddled a horse, and Sitting Bull surrendered, where the Space Aliens Grill & Bar is next door to the Kmart in Bismarck and New York–style bagels are explained to the locals as "like bread with an attitude."

North Dakota is where the film *Fargo* didn't take place (you betcha!), and although it's the least-visited state in the union, tourism is its third largest industry.

South Dakota is where Kevin Costner danced with wolves, where the buffalo roam, and where cows outnumber people five to one.

It's where Cheryl Ladd was born, where Wild Bill Hickok was gunned down, and where the Black Hills Motorcycle Classic in Sturgis draws as many as 300,000 bikers every August. The little town of 5,330 also boasts the National Motorcycle Museum and Hall of Fame.

You can tour North America's largest gold mine, watch the world's biggest mountain carving under construction, reminisce at the world's only Amateur Baseball Hall of Fame in Lake Norden, or slurp a soda at a 115-year-old marble fountain in a grocery store where Hickok's killer sought refuge.

Both states cover two time zones. South Dakota hosts the annual Lewis & Clark Cribbage Classic in July, the Sitting Bull Sailboard Regatta in August, and the Jesse James Bicycle Stampede in September; while North Dakota gets a little more down to earth with Irrigation Days in Oakes in June, Coteau Hill's Annual Beef BBQ and Cow Penning in Forbes in July, and Sauerkraut Day in Wishek in October.

North Dakota Highlights

South Dakota Highlights

Akta Lakota Museum **23**
Al's Oasis **30**
Badlands National Park **24**
Barn Restaurant **9**
Black Hills Central Railroad **9**
Black Hills Wild Horse Sanctuary and Mammoth Site **13**
Buffalo Dining Room, Mt. Rushmore **9**
Cedar Pass Lodge **4**
Cheyenne Crossing Café, Lodge & Store **7**
Chinatown Cafe **4**
Corn Palace **27**
Crazy Horse Memorial **10**
Crook County Museum and Art Gallery **3**
Custer State Park **14**
Dakota Sioux Casino **25**
Devil's Gulch **29**
Devil's Tower National Monument **1**
Farm Island State Recreation Area **21**
Firehouse Brewing Company **31**
Gateway 2000 factory outlet **31**
Homestake Gold Mine **5**
Ingalls Family Homestead **26**
Jewel Cave National Monument **2**
Little Bighorn Battlefield National Monument **22**
Lower Brule Sioux reservation **22**
Midnight Star Casino **4**
Minerva's 26th Street Market **30**
Mount Moriah Cemetery (aka Boot Hill) **4**
Mt. Rushmore **9**
Oglala Sioux Reservation **20**
Old Time Saloon Number 10 **4**
Prairie Edge Studios **8**
Prairie Village **28**
Red Cloud Indian Mission School **20**
Sioux Falls Brewing Company **30**
Sioux Pottery and Crafts **8**
Spearfish Canyon Scenic Byway **6**
State Game Lodge **14**
Terry Pea **6**
Trial of Jack McCall **4**
Triple R Dude Ranch **11**
Wall Drug Store **18**
White River visitor center **19**
Wind Cave National Park **15**
World's largest pheasant **22**
Wounded Knee Massacre site **19**

RVing the Dakotas

The West happens suddenly when you arrive at the Missouri River on highways rose-colored from local crushed rock used in the paving. Tumbleweeds roll across the road in front of you, and the grasslands sway in a persistent wind.

If you pull off South Dakota's I-90 at exit 263, you can walk over to a bluff and look down at the river, which, together with the Mississippi, makes up the longest stretch of river on earth. In North Dakota you get a similar sensation on I-94 crossing the Missouri between Bismarck and Mandan.

Lewis and Clark and their 40-man expedition force traveled through these waters in their search for a waterway to the Pacific. They were paid $2,500 for their 8,000-mile, 862-day journey, and spent almost one-third of their time traversing the Dakotas.

HITTING THE HIGHLIGHTS

If you've got 2-weeks-with-pay for your holiday and live on one of the coasts, you might consider flying to the Dakotas and renting an RV there (see chapter 15, "To Rent or Buy?" for a list of nationwide rental outfits). That way, you can take your time sightseeing, hiking, fishing, learning to pan gold, or watching a mountain being carved.

Mt. Rushmore itself doesn't take that long; a tourist in a hurry can drive by, take a snapshot from the parking lot, and move on. But the Black Hills and Badlands deserve more time, especially if you're interested in outdoor activities and seeing wildlife, and the Theodore Roosevelt National Park's two units should be seen.

If you have a carload of kids or your taste is jejune, you'll find more than enough gee-whiz commercial attractions around Rapid City—Bear Country USA, a drive-through wildlife park, Reptile Gardens, Evans Plunge water complex, the Flintstones Bedrock City Theme Park and Campground, the Wild West Wax Museum, Rushmore Water Slide Park, Pioneer Auto Museum, Mountain Music Show, Ghosts of Deadwood Gulch Wax Museum, Cosmos Mystery Area, Wonderland Cave, and Big Thunder Gold Mine.

There's also the 56-year-old Black Hills Passion Play in the town of Spearfish, with a cast of 250 assisted by live camels, Arabian horses, and special-effects sunsets and moon risings. The season runs from early June through August on Sundays, Tuesdays, and Thursdays, and it's a good idea to reserve in advance if you have your heart set on seeing it. Call ☎ **605/642-2646.**

GOING FOR THE LONG HAUL

If you want to spend more time on your Dakotas visit than 2 or 3 weeks, aim for fall and try to avoid the peak summer months. Spring is also a possibility, but the weather can be cold and rainy.

Depending on where you begin, it might take a while just to get to and from the Dakotas. The side trips in this chapter are spread out around both states.

Although there's a tremendous summer demand for campsites in the Black Hills, you might be able to arrange a seasonal stay in a commercial RV park or, barring that, work as a campground volunteer in one of the state or national parks or national forests in the area. (See "How to Become Campground Hosts" in chapter 3, "Where to Sleep: Campgrounds & RV Parks.")

If time and money are no problem, you might consider adding on a trail ride with a packhorse or hiking the 111-mile Centennial Trail. See "Ten Active Adventures" later in this chapter.

Winter camping in the area, while not for everyone, could include plenty of cross-country or downhill skiing. Terry Peak near Lead is South Dakota's leading ski area, while North Dakota's Turtle River State Park is open in winter for sledding and cross-country skiing.

Travel Essentials

WHEN TO GO
The ideal time is late August, September, and early October, when the trees are changing color but the sun still warms the air. Early August is when motorcyclists head for Sturgis, and all summer long the South Dakota campgrounds and attractions are crowded with tourists. On the other hand, North Dakota isn't crowded even on the Fourth of July. Late spring and early summer would be almost as good, but can be cool and rainy.

WHAT TO TAKE
Hiking boots, cameras and film, binoculars, a gold pan if you're planning to camp in the Black Hills National Forest, and fishing tackle for dry-fly trout fishing or lake bass fishing.

WHAT TO WEAR
Summers can be quite hot here, but in spring and fall the temperature is cool in early morning and at night, so layered clothing is best. Nowhere, including Deadwood's casinos, is very dressy, so your camping and RV attire will fit in anywhere.

TRIMMING COSTS ON THE ROAD
Once you get to the admittedly remote Dakotas, you'll find prices modest. And if hearty midwestern home cooking is to your taste, restaurant fare is inexpensive all over both states.

If you can visit the casinos and avoid gambling, meals are especially cheap there. If you're traveling with children, beware the commercial attractions, no matter how "educational" they purport to be, because you'll end up spending more than you'd like.

In heavily touristed Rapid City, skip the big commercial attractions, and instead ask for the city tour brochure where ten family attractions are free. Start at the Rushmore Plaza Civic Center, 444 Mount Rushmore Rd. North (☎ 800/487-3223), where the **Visitor Information Center** has directions on following the city circle tour, marked by buffalo head signs. The **Dahl Fine Arts Center** at 7th and Quincy (☎ 605/394-4101) features work by local Indian artists and a cyclorama of American history with lighted highlights and taped narration. The **Museum of Geology,** on the campus of South Dakota School of Mines at 501 E. Saint Joseph, shows the dinosaurs who once roamed the Badlands; and after the museum, head for the **Dinosaur Park** on Skyline Drive where the kids can climb aboard the outdoor dinosaurs. Adults might enjoy that too, since the park is open until 10 at night and the city lights make a great view. Take Quincy west from its junction with West Boulevard, an extension of I-190. Quincy Street turns into Skyline Drive. The park is about 1 mile west of the intersection of Quincy and West (☎ 605/343-8687).

Staying in campgrounds without hookups when possible always saves money, but in summer they may be hard to find. Check at the local city park in many South Dakota towns, where camping is often free.

WHERE TO GET TRAVEL INFORMATION

The **South Dakota Department of Tourism,** 711 E. Wells Ave., Pierre, SD 57501 (☎ 800/SDAKOTA; www.state.sd.us), will send you a handsome free vacation guide on request, and its nine Welcome Centers at major highway entrances to the state have full stocks of all kinds of information helpful to an RVer.

You can also contact the **Black Hills, Badlands and Lakes Association,** 900 Jackson Blvd., Rapid City, SD 57702 (☎ 605/341-1462), and **North Dakota Tourism,** 604 East Blvd., Bismarck, ND 58505 (☎ 800/HELLO-ND; www.ndtourism.com).

The Rapid City Convention and Visitors Bureau can be contacted at ☎ 800/487-3223, www.rapidcitycvb.com.

DRIVING & CAMPING TIPS

- **Rent a taped narration.** Drivers entering South Dakota can rent an audio cassette about the state from the tourist information offices at the border for $20; $15 is refunded at the other end of the state when you turn it back in, or you can mail it back. In exchange, you get a series of anecdotes, songs, and histories about the state timed for each stretch of the roadway.

- **Watch for low and narrow passes.** The narrow roads and tunnels in the Black Hills might present problems for extra-wide or very long RVs.

Wall Drug Store, one of the most visited sites in South Dakota

The maximum RV size that can safely negotiate Iron Mountain Road, Route 16A, is 12 feet 6 inches high and 8 feet 6 inches wide. On State 87 around Sylvan Lake, anything larger than 10 feet 8 inches high or 8 feet 7 inches wide can't make it through the tunnels; on Needles Highway, the limit is 11 feet 5 inches high and 8 feet 7 inches wide. When checking your width, be sure to include the side mirrors and air-conditioning units on the roof.

The Best Dakotas Sights, Tastes & Experiences

OFF-THE-WALL ATTRACTIONS

Wall Drug Store. Only the most travel-hardened curmudgeon could refuse to turn off I-90 into Wall to see the richly advertised wonders of Wall Drug Store. It started small back in 1931 with road signs promising free ice water for hot, thirsty travelers, and has grown into a monumental Western-themed mall of shops, restaurants, museums, and entertainment that draws 20,000 visitors a day in summer. The ice water is still free, and a cup of coffee costs a nickel. Open daily year-round; ☎ **605/279-2175.**

The Corn Palace, Mitchell. Located at 604 N. Main St. in downtown Mitchell, the Corn Palace is unique in the world, a Taj Mahal of chicken feed, its walls, domes, and turrets covered annually with elaborate murals made of corn, bushel after bushel of red, calico, and white corn, augmented with oats and prairie grass. The decoration is replaced with a new theme every September, when Corn Palace Week carries out the corn motif with concerts by performers like Myron Floren and the Stars of Lawrence Welk and a 3-day polka festival. One version or another of the Corn Palace has been here more than 100 years. ☎ **800/257-2676.** Admission is free

The Corn Palace in Mitchell

except during the Corn Palace festival. Open daily year-round plus evenings in summer.

Crazy Horse Memorial, North of Custer. The world's largest mountain carving is so big that all four heads on Mt. Rushmore would fit inside the chief's head. Begun in 1947 by the late Polish-American sculptor Korczak Ziolkowski in response to a request from Lakota chief Henry Standing Bear, the monument is being carried on by Korczak's wife and large family with donations and private funding. The finished sculpture will be 641 feet long and 563 feet high when completed sometime after the millennium. Open daily year-round in Crazy Horse, north of Custer on U.S. 385. ☎ **605/673-4681;** www.crazyhorse.org.

Mount Moriah Cemetery (a.k.a. Boot Hill), Deadwood. This cemetery is where Calamity Jane Canary and Wild Bill Hickok ended up side by side with matching rock mounds and white granite tombstones. Wild Bill was shot in 1876 by Crooked Nose Jack McCall; Jane died in 1903. Midnight is a popular time to visit the graves. Deadwood Visitors Bureau; ☎ **800/999-1876.**

Old Time Saloon Number 10, Deadwood. Catch a reenactment of the shooting of Wild Bill Hickok, presented several times a day, as Hickok plays out the famous Deadman's Hand at the poker table: a pair of aces, a pair of eights, and the nine of diamonds. ☎ **800/952-9398.**

The Trial of Jack McCall, Deadwood. This 60-year-old audience participation performance recruits onlookers as jury when they depict the capture and trial of the man who shot Wild Bill Hickok. A clue: McCall most often gets off, just as he did at the original trial. It happens nightly except Sundays in the old Town Hall. ☎ **605/578-3583.**

The Buffalo Dining Room at Mt. Rushmore. A cafeteria with a great close-up view of the carved heads and the memory of Cary Grant running amok through the tourists in Alfred Hitchcock's film *North by Northwest*. On the buffet line, the George Washington Breakfast is Continental, Teddy Roosevelt's Rough Rider breakfast consists of biscuits and gravy, Thomas Jefferson's effete fast-breaker is French toast, and Abe Lincoln's is a straight-forward scrambled eggs and toast. ☎ **605/574-2515.**

Devil's Gulch. This is where Jesse James and his horse, hotly pursued after the failed Northfield, Minnesota, bank robbery attempt, jumped across a 20-foot-wide chasm to clear the 50-foot-deep gulch, leaving the dumbfounded posse behind. It's located near Garrotson, 10 miles north of I-90 at the first exit past the Minnesota/South Dakota border. For a guided tour, call ☎ **605/594-3404.**

The world's largest pheasant. Forty feet high and weighing 22 tons, it stands by U.S. 14 in Huron, about 50 miles north of Mitchell. It proclaims Huron as the "Pheasant Capital of the World."

The Crook County Museum and Art Gallery, Sundance, WY. Located in Sundance, Wyoming, the jumping-off town for Devil's Tower, the museum displays the courtroom where Harry Longabaugh was sentenced to 18 months in jail here for stealing horses. His nickname, "Sundance Kid," came from his time in this jail; the town's name came from the summer Sun Dance the Sioux performed on the mountain back of town. ☎ **307/283-3666.**

Giant men and giant animals. In a burst of civic pride, North Dakota offers drivers along the interstates a gee-whiz respite from turnpike tedium—**the world's largest buffalo,** 26 feet high, 46 feet long, and 60 tons, but strangely androgynous when you take a closer look (at exit 258 off I-94 in Jamestown); **the world's largest Holstein cow,** 38 feet high and 50 feet long (at exit 124 off I-94 in Salem); the **world's largest catfish,** the Wahpeton Wahpper (off I-29 at exit 23); and the **world's largest tin family,** the **world's largest grasshopper,** and a **51-foot Teddy Roosevelt** made from livestock watering tanks, sickles, barbed wire, and other discarded scrap metal (at I-94's exit 72 along the Enchanted Highway between Gladstone and Regent).

The National Buffalo Museum. Sitting in the shadow of the world's biggest buffalo (see above), the museum protects the world's most sought-after buffalo, the rare (one birth in a billion) female albino White Cloud. Considered sacred by ancient North American tribes, the white buffalo is thought to be a sign of great things to come. The resident herd, which

The world's largest buffalo

includes White Cloud, can sometimes (but not always) be seen from the museum's deck on the hillside above the pastures. The parking lot is big enough for RVs to turn around in, and admission to the museum is $3. The adjacent Frontier Village (free) has historical buildings moved here along with a general store that sells souvenirs and North Dakota food products and a leather goods store selling locally made hats, belts, and moccasins. Open daily May through September and located at the junction of I-94 and Highway 281, exit 258. For information, call ☎ **800/22-BISON.**

Giant turtles. Turtles, too, are big in North Dakota. **Tommy Turtle** is a 33-foot-high turtle riding a snowmobile on Route 5 near the junction of Route 14 in Bottineau in the north central area, while **W'eel Turtle** is a giant crawling turtle made of 2,000 discarded tire rims at the junction of U.S. 281 and Route 3 in Dunseith. Both towns are in the Turtle Mountains near the International Peace Garden. **Bottineau Chamber of Commerce, ☎ 701/228-3849; Dunseith, ☎ 701/244-5860.**

Prairie Rose Carousel, Wahpeton. This restored 1926 Spillman with 29 handcrafted wooden horses and two chariots is one of only 150 operating carousels in the United States. Located in Chahinkapa Park on Route 13 off I-29 at exit 23 in Wahpeton, North Dakota, in the southeast corner of the state, it's open Memorial Day to Labor Day. Call Wahpeton Visitors Center at ☎ **800/892-6673** for information.

The Lawrence Welk homestead, Strasburg. A pilgrimage site for the musically challenged, although the maestro left here the day he turned 21, carrying his accordion, a train ticket, and $3 in cash. The wood-sided sod house of the Welk family is typical of the Germans from Russia who settled North Dakota around the turn of the 20th century after fleeing first from

Alsace to the Ukraine and then to America. You'll find it off I-94 at exit 182 and south on U.S. 83 to Strasburg, then west on a marked but unpaved road. Open mid-May to mid-September from 10am to 5pm; admission $3. Contact Pioneer Heritage, Inc., Strasburg, ND 58573 (☎ **701/336-7519**).

THE DAKOTAS GAMBLING SCENE
Deadwood, South Dakota

Thanks to its 80 licensed casinos dating from 1989, the long-dormant town of Deadwood looks as bustling as it must have in 1876, when 25,000 miners thronged in looking for gold, and Calamity Jane and Wild Bill Hickok were an item. Today at least that many tourists are still looking for gold, an early lunch, or a tiny T-shirt that reads "My grandma went to Deadwood and all I got was this lousy T-shirt."

The casino was put in place on the premise that the gambling would generate funds to restore the deteriorating town, a National Historic Landmark. (Old-timers have some lively ongoing discussions about what is and isn't historic.) Anyhow, gambling originally went on in Deadwood until 1947, its proponents pointed out, and brothels did discreet business until 1980. Gambling was restored in 1989 and now summer visitors gamble as much as a million dollars a day, which should be enough to gold-plate the historic buildings in a few years. A lot of restoration has already been completed. Day and evening variety shows with cowboys and dance hall girls are plentiful, along with live music for dancing, dinner theater suitable for the whole family, and the nightly reenactment of "The Trial of Jack McCall," about the man who shot Wild Bill Hickok.

The old Western town of Deadwood is alive again with gambling casinos.

RVers will find bright green trolleys to shuttle them from the edge-of-town RV parking lots to the casinos along the main street.

Elsewhere in South Dakota

The **Lower Brule Sioux reservation** offers card games and coin slots, as well as herds of roaming buffalo and elk in the vicinity. Take exit 248 at Reliance and drive north 15 minutes to Lower Brule. For information, call The Alliance of Tribal Tourism Advocates (☎ **605/964-4000**).

The **Dakota Sioux Casino** in Watertown runs blackjack, poker, poker machines, and progressive slots, along with a bar and restaurant. Watertown is 100 miles north of Sioux Falls on I-29 (☎ **800/658-4717**).

North Dakota

North Dakota has five tribal casinos: **Four Bears at New Town,** west of New Town, in northwest North Dakota at the junction of routes 8 and 23 (☎ **800/294-5454**); **Dakota Magic** off I-29, exit 2, south of Hankinson (☎ **800/325-6825**); **Spirit Lake Sioux Tribal Casino,** 6 miles south of Devils Lake on Route 57 (☎ **800/946-8328**); **Turtle Mountain Chippewa Wild Rose Casino,** at U.S. 281 and Route 5 in Belcourt (☎ **800/477-3497**); and **Prairie Knights Casino and Lodge,** 44 miles south of Mandan on Route 1806, (☎ **800/425-8277**). All feature Las Vegas-style gambling and headliner entertainment.

EIGHT SPLURGES IN THE DAKOTAS

1. **Take a helicopter tour around the Mt. Rushmore faces.** You'll get good close-up photos to wow the neighbors back home. The choppers cover only side and distant views; you won't fly into George Washington's nostril. Companies offering tours include **Rushmore Helicopters** (☎ **605/666-4461**) and **Rapid Helicopters** (☎ **605/343-5058**). Rides begin at $20; for $40 per person, the tour goes within a half mile of the faces and flies over them.

2. **Take a couple of days at the Triple R Dude Ranch in Keystone,** especially if you have kids older than 7 who can go with you on trail rides into the Black Elk Wilderness Area. Fishing, swimming, almost effortless game-spotting, and cookouts supplement the daily wilderness and breakfast rides. Call ☎ **605/666-4605** for details.

3. **Hop aboard the 1880 steam-engine Black Hills Central Railroad.** It's a 20-mile chug through the Black Hills along some of the steepest grades in North America. You can get aboard in Hill City or Keystone. Call ☎ **605/574-2222** for times and reservations. Adults, $16; children 4 to 14, $10.

4. **See five states from the top of Terry Peak.** By winter it's South Dakota's major ski area; by summer it's a chairlift ride to a fantastic

view. Rides daily. From I-90, take exit 30 and go southwest on 14A to the marked turnoff 1 mile south of Lead. ☎ **605/584-2165.**

5. **Invest in museum-quality reproductions of Sioux artifacts,** such as the distinctive hand-thrown pottery decorated with western motifs available at **Sioux Pottery and Crafts** (☎ **800/657-4366**) or **Prairie Edge Studios** (☎ **605/342-3086**) in Rapid City, or delicate Black Hills gold jewelry in traditional grape and leaf designs in pale pinks, greens, and yellows.

6. **Hit the factory outlet store for Gateway 2000.** Computer geeks see black-and-white cow spots before their eyes when they see the prices slashed on all sorts of computer equipment, and with a big RV you can take it all back home easily. It's located right by the factory where a good factory outlet should be (instead of in suburban malls). 610 Gateway Drive, North Sioux City, SD 57049, ☎ **888/888-2017.**

7. **Visit Pipestem Creek.** One of our favorite offbeat shops, Pipestem Creek creates beautiful dried floral wreaths and bird feeders from grasses and flowers grown on the family ranch. SunFeeders and SunFlorals are two of the products built around giant dried sunflower heads. Birds love them! On Route 9 south of Carrington in the center of North Dakota; open Monday through Friday from 8:30am to 4:30pm, but production slows down at lunchtime. You can also call to request a catalogue at ☎ **701/652-2623.**

8. **Pick up North Dakota–made products at Pride of Dakota,** from buffalo soap and a General Custer doll to buffalo chips (potato chips dipped in milk chocolate) or chokecherry jelly. The shop is in the Buffalo Mall in Jamestown, but there's also a Pride of Dakota catalogue you can order from Buffalo Mall, Jamestown, ND 58402, ☎ **800/ 447-6564.**

TAKE-OUT (OR EAT-IN) TREATS

Chinatown Cafe, Deadwood. Located in Miss Kitty's Gaming Saloon, 649 Main St., in Deadwood. Funny, we don't remember ever seeing "Gunsmoke's" Amanda Blake dishing up chop suey. Alternatively, you could look for the ever popular Chinese Opium Tunnel Museum on the Chinatown Tour. ☎ **605/578-1811.**

The Firehouse Brewing Company, Rapid City. Firehouse Brewing Co., at 610 Main St., makes boutique beers while you watch, and offers home-made pub food to go with it. ☎ **605/348-1915.**

Cheyenne Crossing Café, Lodge & Store, Cheyenne Crossing. Breakfasts at Cheyenne, at U.S. 85 and the Spearfish Canyon Route 14A, are lavish with sourdough pancakes, homemade sausage and gravy, eggs and buttermilk biscuits, while lunch brings buffalo burgers and Indian tacos. ☎ 800/400-7722.

Barn Restaurant, Huron. For a budget break, try the hamburgers and down-home buffets at the Barn Restaurant in Huron, South Dakota, where Cheryl Ladd once worked as a waitress. It's located on South Highway 37. ☎ 605/352-9238.

Widman's Candy Store, Grand Forks. The Red River flooded disastrously in 1997, and Widman's was one of the first downtown businesses to reopen after the waters receded. This charming candy box of a store is famous for its addictive Widman's Chippers: Red River potatoes cut and cooked into ruffled chips, then hand-dipped in chocolate. Thicker, less salty, and more like a candy bar than the chocolate-dipped Maui potato chips from Hawaii, the Widman's Chippers are cheaper, too, at $8 a pound. Midwestern chocolate humor dictates novelty candies such as Moo Pies, Moose Muffins, and such. The Widman family has other shops in Fargo and in Crookston, Minnesota, across the river from Grand Forks. The Grand Forks store is at 106 S. Third St., and is open Monday through Saturday. ☎ 701/ 775-3480.

The Pitchfork Fondue, Medora. Think of the short-lived 1960s fad for beef fondue, then imagine Grant Wood's painting *American Gothic,* but with rib-eye steaks impaled on the tines of the farmer's pitchfork. That's the general idea of Medora's Pitchfork Fondue, a pre-theater dinner buffet served at the outdoor theater before the Medora Musical in an open-air pavilion with a great view on all sides. Eleven-ounce rib-eye steaks are impaled on each tine and immersed for several minutes in vats of boiling oil. The buffet also includes raw vegetables with dip, fruit salad, coleslaw, rolls, butter, baked potatoes, and baked beans. It's served at 6:30pm sharp; $18 for adults, $12 for schoolchildren, free for preschoolers. It all takes place at the Burning Hills Ampitheatre on the marked drive off the west end of Pacific Avenue in Medora. Advance reservations required: ☎ 701/623-4444.

The Chuckwagon Patio, downtown Medora. The Chuckwagon, at 3rd Avenue near 3rd Street, serves barbecued chicken and ribs of beef brisket between 4:30 and 7:30pm every Saturday for less than $6 to eat inside in the air-conditioning or outside at the open-air picnic tables, then sets up a Sunday brunch buffet in its cafeteria from 8am to 1:30pm. ☎ 701/623-4444.

The Grand Pasta Party, **Grand Forks.** Bring your own fork and join the party on the prairie to salute the fact that North Dakota produces most of the high-quality durum wheat that makes the world's pasta. The annual festival is held in mid-August; in September the same city celebrates **Potato Bowl USA,** with French Fryday, a potato queen, pancake breakfast, and football game. Contact the Grand Forks Convention and Visitors Center (☎ 701/746-0444).

Peacock Alley Bar & Grill, Bismarck. Despite its prestige and romantic 19th-century ambience, Bismarck's Peacock Alley Bar & Grill serves a grand Sunday brunch buffet that may include homemade muffins and sticky caramel buns, French toast, pancakes, sausage, ham, bacon and eggs—and all for a modest price. Located at 422 E. Main St. Adults $5.50, children $3.50. ☎ **701/255-7917.**

The '50s Café, Fargo. The best burgers in Fargo, downtown at 13 S. 8th St. ☎ **701/298-0347.**

BRING ON THE BUFFALO

According to the U.S. Department of Agriculture, buffalo meat is lower in fat, calories, and cholesterol than either beef sirloin or chicken breast, with more protein per gram than beef and no growth hormones, stimulants, or antibiotics. Typical Dakota recipes for buffalo include steaks, roasts, salami, sausage, hamburger, and jerky. Here are some places to sample it or see it running around the prairie, pre-processing:

1. **The Rough Riders Hotel, Medora, ND.** The hotel dining room serves a 9-ounce buffalo rib-eye steak for around $16. Located at 3rd Street and 3rd Avenue. Open 7am to 9pm from May to early September. Call ☎ **701/623-4444** for reservations.

2. **Siouxland Buffalo, Grand Forks, ND.** Chuckwagon buffalo burgers and a gen-u-wine Buffalo Gift Shop at the Earl Buffalo Farm, Route 2 in Grand Forks, North Dakota. ☎ **701/772-1594.**

3. **Al's Oasis, outside Sioux Falls.** Buffalo burgers South Dakota–style are the big seller at Al's, located about halfway between Sioux Falls and the Black Hills, off exit 260 on I-90. Al's is also famous for home-made pie and 5-cent coffee. ☎ **605/734-6054.**

4. **Wall Drug Store, Wall, SD.** Wall stars buffalo burgers at the top of its tourist menu, along with hot beef sandwiches, homemade donuts, pies, cinnamon rolls, 5-cent coffee, and free ice water. Open year-round at exit 109 or 110 from I-90. ☎ **605/279-2175.**

5. **State Game Lodge, Custer State Park, SD.** Spicy buffalo sausage and hot biscuits make a great take-out breakfast or midmorning snack at the lodge's Pleasant Pheasant Dining Room, located on U.S. 16 east of the junction with Route 87 in southwestern South Dakota. ☎ **605/255-4541.**

6. **Cedar Pass Lodge, Interior, SD.** Indian tacos made on Sioux fry bread with buffalo meat are a house special at the Badlands' Cedar Pass Lodge. The 24-cabin lodge is run by the Oglala Sioux tribe and is located in the Badlands in southwestern South Dakota on Route 377, off I-90 at exit 131 south. ☎ **605/433-5460.**

7. **Sioux Falls Brewing Company, Sioux Falls, SD.** Buffalo Stout is brewed on the premises, at 431 N. Phillips Ave. (☎ 605/332-4847). The stout is a primary ingredient in Buffalo Pie, which is a meatless chocolate cheesecake.

8. **Minerva's 26th Street Market, Sioux Falls, SD.** Minerva's sells fresh or frozen buffalo meat at 1716 S. Western Ave., at the intersection of 26th. ☎ 605/334-7491.

9. **Custer State Park buffalo safari, SD.** Take a buffalo safari ride, which leaves from the State Game Lodge to go into the backcountry to see some of the park's 1,400 bison. Located on U.S. 16 east of the junction with Route 87 in southwestern South Dakota. ☎ 605/255-4541.

10. **Custer State Park buffalo roundup, SD.** In late September or early October, the bison are rounded up, branded, vaccinated, and sorted to separate the culls for a November auction. Ask the park for details at ☎ 605/255-4515.

DANCES WITH NATIVE AMERICANS

The worldwide success of Kevin Costner's Oscar-winning film *Dances with Wolves* brought a lot of attention to South Dakota, and visitors ever since have arrived wanting to learn more about the Lakota people and the achingly beautiful film locations. All of the film was shot on location in South Dakota, much of it at a private ranch near Pierre called Roy Houck's Triple U Ranch, home of the world's largest privately owned herd of bison, some 3,500 head. From the Sioux community came 150 extras, along with consultants on the Lakota language and tribal customs. At the end of the shoot, many of the props and costumes were auctioned to local buyers, so if you run across someone claiming original artifacts from the film, you can probably believe them. Props can be seen at the Akta Lakota Museum in Chamberlain (see below). Costumes are on display at the **Midnight Star Casino** in Deadwood.

Guided tours into this area are offered by **Affordable Adventures of Rapid City** (☎ 605/342-7691).

You can go on your own to the winter camp location in Little Spearfish Canyon; ask directions at **Cheyenne Crossing Store,** at the junction of 14A and U.S. 85 (☎ 605/584-3510), or at **Latchstring Village,** on U.S. 14A in Spearfish Canyon (☎ 605/584-3333), 20 minutes from Deadwood or Spearfish and famous for fresh trout, homemade breads, and sourdough pancakes. It's open daily 8am to 8pm, year-round.

The **Akta Lakota Museum** is a fine Lakota Sioux cultural and heritage museum; take the Chamberlain exit 263 off I-90 and drive 2 miles north into town. The museum is free and open daily in summer except Sunday mornings, and weekdays only in winter. Besides arts and artifacts, you'll find

Lakota-made crafts for sale in the gift shop. St. Joseph Indian School in Chamberlain also welcomes visitors. For information, call the Chamberlain Area Chamber of Commerce ☎ 695/734-6541).

Other central and western South Dakota reservations that welcome visitors include the **Cheyenne River Sioux Tribe,** in the center of the state, which celebrates various powwows in the summer, offers tours to its 100-head bison herd, and provides hunting and fishing opportunities. Call toll-free at ☎ 800/831-5975 for more information.

The **Crow Creek Sioux Tribe,** also in the middle of the state, offers walleye fishing and a powwow and fair the third week of August. For information, call the Chamberlain Area Chamber of Commerce (☎ 695/734-6541) or the Alliance of Tribal Tourism Advocates (☎ 605/964-4000).

The reservation for the **Oglala Sioux Tribe** in southwest South Dakota near Pine Ridge is the second largest in the United States and adjoins Badlands National Park. For Sioux tourism, call Tribal Tourism (☎ 605/964-4000). The **White River visitor center** at Badlands is south of the South Unit of Badlands National Park, Route 27, about 20 miles north of Wounded Knee battlegrounds, and sells tribal crafts, and the Cuny Table Cafe sells Indian tacos. The **Red Cloud Indian Mission School** on Route 18 near Pine Ridge offers an art show representing 30 different tribes, plus a gift shop, open on weekdays. The **Oglala Fair, Rodeo and Powwow** is held the first weekend in August. Wounded Knee is also on the reservation.

In North Dakota, where the various Native American tribes are as a group commonly referred to as Sioux, visitors are welcomed to help celebrate powwows throughout the spring and summer. You can join tribal members in dancing when the powwow announcer calls for an "intertribal" dance. One of the biggest is the **United Tribes International Pow Wow** in Bismarck just after Labor Day. For information, call ☎ 701/255-3285. Ask the **North Dakota Tourism Department** (☎ 800/435-5663) for a full list, or contact individual tribal groups for their own special events: **Mandan, Hidatsa, and Arikara,** the Three Affiliated Tribes in New Town (☎ 701/627-4781); **Spirit Lake Sioux Tribe** in Fort Totten (☎ 701/766-4221); **Standing Rock Sioux Tribe** in Fort Yates (☎ 701/854-7201); and **Turtle Mountain Band of Chippewa** in Belcourt (☎ 701/477-6451).

Powwow Protocol

- Take along your folding chairs from the RV to sit on since seats are at a premium.

- Stand for the grand entry, when the flags are brought in; there may be two grand entries a day. Remain standing during the opening prayer. When in doubt, do what the people around you do.

- The program generally begins with a grand entry, then come honor songs, followed by men's traditional dancing in several categories, then women's traditional dancing, then children's dancing. You're not permitted to film some parts of the ceremony; the announcer will tell you when cameras are prohibited. Otherwise, you may photograph the groups of dancers in performance but should ask permission before photographing an individual not in performance.

- It is also a Native American tradition to give money or other gifts when a particular performance has stirred you; you may follow this example if you want, but should not feel compelled to do so.

FIVE ACTIVE ADVENTURES

1. **Fishing the Black Hills.** Head for one of the 14 lakes or 1,300 miles of streams in the Black Hills in pursuit of rainbow, brook, or brown trout. Lake Pactola holds state records with a 22-pound brown trout and a 15-pound lake trout. Deerfield is best for brook trout. Try fly-fishing in Rapid Creek, Spearfish Creek, Castle Creek, and French Creek in Custer State Park. Lakes in the park are stocked, but you may catch some wild trout as well. You can also snag walleyes, bass, bluegills, perch, crappies, and bullheads. Buy a license first.

2. **Dakota golfing.** Golf courses may include hazards like deer grazing on the fairway or beaver dams by the water holes. You'll find 12 courses around the Black Hills with various degrees of difficulty. Meadowbrook Municipal in Rapid City and Boulder Canyon Country Club near Sturgis are considered the toughest. For Rapid City information, call ☎ 800/487-3223; for more information on Sturgis golfing, call ☎ 605/347-2556 for the Sturgis Chamber of Commerce.

North Dakota's Painted Canyon is a favorite of photographers

3. **Horseback riding.** Riders can find more than a dozen outfitters who offer everything from hour-long rides to a 10-day pack trip on the Centennial Trail in the Black Hills. If you bring your own horse along, you'll find "horse camps" with corrals, water wells, feed bunks, picket posts, and stock trailer parking, with room for your RV as well. **JR Bar Ranch Trail Rides** in Custer (☎ **605/673-2199**) can handle beginners on short rides; also in Custer, **Dakota Badland Outfitters** offers four Old West cowboy expeditions into the Badlands (☎ **605/673-5363**). **Gunsel Horse Adventures** in Rapid City (☎ **605/343-7608**) also runs adventurous treks.

4. **Canoeing the Missouri and Sheyenne rivers.** You'll be saying proudly, "I can, canoe" after a beginner's river paddling trip. Rentals and shuttle services for the Missouri River in North Dakota can be arranged at the **Lewis and Clark Café** in Washburn (☎ **701/462-3368**), or at **Cross Ranch State Park,** in nearby Hensler (☎ **701/793-3731**). The shyer Sheyenne can be canoed while you're camped at the **Fort Ransom State Park;** rentals are available at ☎ **701/973-4331.** Always call ahead and ask about river conditions, however. See "Campground Oases in North Dakota," below, for directions to the park.

5. **Fishing for paddlefish.** The prehistoric paddlefish, a 75- to 100-pound freshwater billfish, runs in western North Dakota's Yellowstone and Missouri rivers between early May and late June. Locals promise that once you hook one of these fighting fish, you're hooked forever. Contact the North Dakota Game and Fish Department, 100 N. Bismarck Expressway, Bismarck, ND 58501 (☎ **701/328-6300;** www.state.nd. us/gnf/).

WILDLIFE WATCHING

The Great Plains were once dark with 60 or 70 million buffalo, and while not many remain, you'll still see a surprising number of small herds, particularly in Custer State Park, where they like to graze around the State Game Lodge. Between 400 and 500 bison calves are born each spring in the park.

Also in Custer State Park, you might see bighorn sheep, mountain goats, coyotes, pronghorn antelope, white-tailed deer, mule deer, and, rarely, elk.

Sully's Hill National Game Preserve near North Dakota's Devils Lake was originally set aside by President Theodore Roosevelt in 1904 for a national park, but it was turned into a game reserve to save the endangered American bison. Now, at 2½ square miles, it's the biggest "zoo" in the Midwest, with not only bison and elk but also prairie dogs, white-tailed deer, foxes, swans, ducks, and geese, and sometimes bald and golden eagles. A 4-mile Big Game Auto Tour route is best in early morning and early evening. It's open May 1 to October 31, 12 miles south of Devils Lake on Highway 57. Free admission. ☎ **701/766-4272** for information.

The largest breeding colony of white pelicans in the United States can be seen at **Chase Lake National Wildlife Refuge,** 23 miles northwest of Medina off I-94's exit 230. To see snow geese, visit **Kenmare** on U.S. 52 in northwestern North Dakota, host to hundreds of thousands of migrating snow and blue geese in the fall.

On the Road: South Dakota

SOUTH DAKOTA'S BADLANDS

Geologists and Great Plains aficionados will claim this national park got a bad rap when the first men to record their impressions, French-Canadian trappers, called the area *les mauvaises terres a traverser* ("bad lands to travel across"). But if you stand alone listening to the wind singing a solitary song and imagine yourself tracking your way across it, you'll understand.

Wind and water wreaked this erosion, delivering an endless landscape of folds and crags and gullies, canyons, spires, and pinnacles, the austerity relieved only faintly in spring with a fuzzy green outline of fresh grass, then burned down to the bone again in the summer heat.

This region was once a lush grassland in the Oligocene epoch 35 million years ago, and the fossil-rich plains hold the fossilized bones of prehistoric animals. Then, as the period closed after about 10 million years, volcanoes erupted to the west, in what is now Yellowstone National Park, and covered the rich lands with layers of white ash. Rains lessened and dry winds from the north continued the sculpting. But life forms adapted. In recent years, the bison and Rocky Mountain bighorn sheep were reintroduced.

The Badlands of South Dakota

Dakota prairie dog

If the loneliness begins to get you down, forge ahead on the Badlands Loop Road and take the Creek Rim Road northwest for 5 miles toward **Roberts Prairie Dog Town,** 5 miles beyond the 240 turnoff to Wall. These social, short-tailed rodents seem tremendously busy as they go about their daily chores, ignoring the occasional hungry coyote or badger who stands by waiting to pounce. They pop up from a hole, stand on their hind legs and look around, emitting a sharp barking cry as if to signal their friends below.

LITTLE BIGHORN & WOUNDED KNEE

The **Little Bighorn Battlefield National Monument,** on I-90 286 miles from the Rapid City area at the town of Crow Agency, Wyoming (open June through September only), commemorates the famous battle that lasted less than an hour on a hot June day in 1876, when a force of some 1,500 Sioux and Cheyenne warriors led by Sitting Bull and other great chiefs wiped out Custer's troops while two other battalions of the regiment were on a distant ridge. Custer, underestimating the Plains Indian forces, had rashly decided to divide his 600 troops into thirds to create a pincers action, then attacked without waiting for the others.

The battlefield is a riveting spot, still haunted, still mysterious. From a small visitor center you walk uphill to a fenced cemetery with tombstones naming the soldiers and where each was believed to have fallen, insofar as the names were known. A mass grave under a hilltop monument contains whatever remains were not removed later by relatives. It is debated whether the bones exhumed in 1877 and reburied at West Point are actually those of Custer.

Although eyewitness accounts vary widely, it is thought perhaps 150 braves at the most died in the battle.

Signs on the site caution visitors wandering around the battle sites to watch out for rattlesnakes; one wonders if the snakes were there the day of the battle.

The gravestones at Little Bighorn

The **Wounded Knee Massacre site** is south of the Black Hills on Route 27, a few miles north of the Nebraska border on the Pine Ridge reservation, headquarters for the Oglala Sioux. In 1889, with growing pressure from occupying military forces, rebellious Native Americans, with their traditional Sun Dance banned, began to turn more and more to spiritual movements, including the use of peyote cactus tips to induce visions. The Ghost Dance ritual, introduced by a Paiute mystic named Wovoka, promised that whites would be eliminated in a flood, vanished game and all their dead kin would come back, and Indians would return to the old ways if they just kept on dancing.

Troops were ordered in to stop the dances, and on December 15, 1890, Chief Sitting Bull was shot while troops were attempting to arrest him. Three

THE CUSTER CONNECTION

The last big gold rush in the contiguous United States was set off by the discovery of gold in French Creek by a civilian prospector tagging along with Lt. Colonel George Armstrong Custer in 1874. (A major general during the Civil War, Custer was reappointed a lieutenant colonel after the war.) The flamboyant Custer, dressed in buckskins, rode at the head of a 1,000-man company of soldiers, scientists, newspaper correspondents, and miners, ostensibly surveying for a railroad but actually checking out the possibility of gold in the Black Hills. The area had been designated part of the Great Sioux Reservation only 6 years earlier by the Treaty of Laramie, presumably before rumors of gold in the area had reached Washington.

There was also one woman in the group, Sally Campbell, the cook for sutler John Smith. She stayed in the Black Hills, staking a gold claim and, in her later years, enjoyed telling stories about her adventures. As a non–Native American, she has gone down in history as "the first white woman in South Dakota" despite her African roots.

Little Bighorn Battlefield National Monument

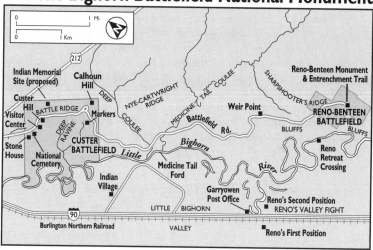

hundred and fifty Sioux under the command of Big Foot were among the last groups to be caught by the 500 cavalrymen; they were led to a military camp at Wounded Knee Creek. A medicine man called for the young warriors to resist being disarmed; fighting broke out and cannon and carbines tore the camp apart. More than 150 of the Sioux, many of them women and children, were killed on the spot, and 44 more did not recover from their wounds.

The battlefield at Wounded Knee was the scene of demonstrations in the 1970s when 200 Indian militants fought off law-enforcement officers and occupied the village for 70 days.

MT. RUSHMORE & THE CRAZY HORSE MONUMENT

The best time to see **Mt. Rushmore** is in early morning, and the best vantage points are the carved rock tunnels that frame the mountain from Alternate U.S. 16 heading north, also called the Iron Mountain Road. The 17-mile route is quite narrow with pigtail bridges and one-way tunnels, some of them a narrow fit for big RVs. If you're early enough, you may glimpse deer, bighorn sheep, raccoons, and some of the herd of 1,400 buffalo on the drive through Custer State Park.

The mountain itself got its name by accident, when a gold miner in a claim litigation was riding past with his recently arrived eastern lawyer, who

GOLD PANNING COURTESY

Don't pan for gold anywhere except in the streams of the Black Hills National Forest or at commercial attractions that promote it. Otherwise, you run the risk of trespassing or claim-jumping— "there's still gold in them thar hills."

SOUTH DAKOTA NIGHTLIFE

If the ruckus in Deadwood doesn't appeal to you, you can go to **Mt. Rushmore** to sing the national anthem and watch the lights come on the presidents' heads (that doesn't take long but it doesn't cost anything), hit a **campfire program** at one of the parks, see the **Lakota Sioux Hoop Dancers** at the Civic Center in Hot Springs (☎ **800/325-6991**), attend a free **Wednesday night band concert** in Rapid City (☎ **800/487-3223**), catch **free movies** in the dark in Hot Springs' Centennial Park, peruse the parading **fife and drum corps** on Mondays in Hill City (☎ **800/888-1798**), or behold the **Black Hills Playhouse** productions of vintage Broadway shows (☎ **605/255-4141**).

was named Rushmore. The lawyer asked the name of that mountain and the miner, as a joke, said, "It's Mt. Rushmore." And so it became.

Sculptor Gutzon Borglum, who started work on Mt. Rushmore in 1927 when he was 60, was a man of boundless energy, a prolific sculptor (175 of his works are in the Cathedral of St. John the Divine in New York City), and a controversial and argumentative character. He charmed President Calvin Coolidge and his wife, who stayed in the State Game Lodge on their 1927 visit to dedicate the sculpture, by hiring a small plane, flying over the lodge, and swooping down to drop a bouquet of wildflowers to Mrs. C.

Borglum wanted to add a Hall of Records on the mountainside so that future archaeologists wouldn't think the Americans of the mid–20th century worshipped giant stone figures. He even persuaded Coolidge to write a text for a Hall of Records dedication, but then sat down and rewrote it to his

Mt. Rushmore is a favorite destination for RVers.

Black Hills

own taste and released it to the newspapers as the president's work, infuriating the taciturn Coolidge.

It was also on his agenda to finish the figures as busts, carved down to the waist, and to remove the stone rubble to build an amphitheater, but shortly after he died in 1941, work ceased on the project.

Korczak Zielkowski, the sculptor of the nearby **Crazy Horse Monument,** worked for a while with Borglum at Rushmore but the two men did not always get along. Korjak began his work in 1947, and since his death in 1982, his wife and 10 children have continued the project, working from private donations and the monies collected by admissions to the site with its museum, shop, and restaurant. It's located on U.S. 385 north of Custer.

CAMPGROUND OASES IN SOUTH DAKOTA

Mt. Rushmore/Hill City KOA. The closest campground to Mt. Rushmore offers free shuttle service to the evening lighting ceremonies at Rushmore and Crazy Horse. Some 235 RV sites have full hookups, flush toilets, showers, fire grates, swimming pool, sanitary dump, restaurant, playground, and pond with trout fishing. Sites are close together in parking-lot style, although some have trees and/or grass. The campground is on Route 244 between

Hill City and the Four Faces, reached from U.S. 16 at State Road 244, then 3 miles east. It's modem-friendly, provides cable TV, and has horses and cars for rent, a waterslide (fee), hayrides, movies, and Indian dances. ☎ **800/KOA-8503** or 605/574-2525.

Mystery Mountain Resort. Next to Bear Country USA on the road to Mt. Rushmore Road at 13752 Highway 16, Mystery Mountain should please families looking for lots to do. A playground, heated 50-foot pool, hot tub, shade trees, and hiking trails are at the resort, plus 35 tree-shaded, full hookup sites (30- and 50-amp electric) and a modem-friendly office. Call ☎ **800/658-CAMP** for reservations or log on to their Web page at www.blackhillsresorts.com.

Lazy J RV Park and Campground. The Lazy J in Rapid City offers view sites and terraced camping, daily bus tours of the region, car rentals available on the premises, and a big new heated pool and spa. Water and 30- and 50-amp electric hookups are available at 110 sites, sewer hookups at 64 of them, and there is plenty of room for big rigs. It's located at 4110 South Highway 16, accessed from exit 57 of Route 90, then driving south 4 miles. For reservations, call ☎ **605/342-2751.**

Cedar Pass Campground. Located near the Ben Rifel Visitor Center in the Badlands on Route 240, Cedar Pass has 100 sites with flush toilets, piped water (in summer), and sewage disposal station. A fee is charged in summer but not in winter when water is off. No hookups, no reservations. ☎ **605/433-5361.**

The Black Hills National Forest Campgrounds. Six campgrounds offer a total of 321 sites suitable for RVs, most with piped water, picnic tables, fire grates, and pit or flush toilets but no hookups or disposal stations. Closest to Mt. Rushmore and most popular is Horsethief Lake with 28 sites. Advance reservations toll-free: ☎ **877/444-6777.** From Rapid City, take Highway 16 south to Hill City. Take 16/385 south to Custer.

Big Pine Campground. Two miles west of Custer on Route 16W, Big Pine has 70 sites with 30-amp electricity and water, 40 with full hookups, pine-shaded, and fairly well spaced. Flush toilets, showers, sanitary dump, laundry, playground, and limited groceries. For reservations, call ☎ **605/673-4054.**

Rafter J Bar Ranch Campground. Located in Hill City, the grounds have 130 sites, most with full hookups, in 80 acres of ponderosa pines. You can choose a campsite near the pool and playground or a more secluded spot back in the trees. Supervised pony rides for kids, flush toilets, showers, sanitary dump, laundry, satellite TV, groceries, and RV supplies. And a trout stream runs through it. Take 16 south to Hill City; go 3 miles and follow the signs. Call ☎ **888/RAFTERV** for reservations or 605/574-2527.

South Dakota Campgrounds

Berry Patch Campground **5**
Big Pine Campground **8**
Black Hills National Forest
   campgrounds **8**
Cedar Pass Campground **11**
Custer Crossing Campground **4**
Custer Mt. Rushmore KOA **8**
Custer State Park campgrounds **9**
Deadwood KOA **1**
Fish 'N Fry Recreational
   Campground **3**
Hidden Valley Campground **3**
Lake Mitchell Campground **12**
Lazy J RV Park and Campground **6**
Mt. Rushmore/Hill City KOA **7**
Mystery Mountain Resort **7**
Rafter J Bar Ranch Campground **7**
Trout Haven Campground **4**
Whistler Gulch RV Park **2**
Wild Bill's Campground **3**
Wind Cave National Park **10**

BEGGING BURROS

A road hazard or an irresistible attraction, depending on your point of view, are the begging burros along Iron Mountain Road who will poke their heads inside your car window looking for something to eat. Originally brought in during the 1950s to carry tourists to the top of Harney Peak, they now roam freely and panhandle. They'll accept and eat almost anything, but bread, cookies, and crackers are their favorites. These are the only animals in the park that visitors are permitted to feed. Don't think you can feed the buffalo!!! They are large, dangerous animals and should not be approached, even in a vehicle.

Custer State Park. Custer Park has some first-come, first-served spaces in each of its seven campgrounds. The areas most accessible to larger RVs are Game Lodge Campground with 65 sites, Legion Lake with 25, and Stockade Lake with 68. Paved camping pads, fire grates, and picnic tables are supplied, and there's a dump station at Game Lodge. None has hookups. The park accepts some campsite reservations: ☎ **605/255-4515.** From Rapid City, take Highway 79 to Highway 36; 36 turns into Route 16A in Custer Park.

Custer Mt. Rushmore KOA. Three miles west of Custer on Route 16, this KOA has 103 sites, most of them shaded by pine trees, all with electricity and water and 32 with sewer. Flush toilets, showers, sanitary dump, laundry, groceries, heated swimming pool, optional chuckwagon breakfasts and barbecue buffalo dinners, and car rental. ☎ **800/KOA-5828.**

Berry Patch Campground. Located in Rapid City at the junction of I-90 and exit 60, Berry Patch has 113 RV sites with water and 30- and 50-amp electricity, of which 64 also have sewers. Flush toilets, showers, sanitary dump, heated pool, laundry, playground. Daily bus tours around the area, free movies, and you can camp every sixth and seventh nights free. Open April through October. ☎ **800/658-4566.**

Wind Cave National Park. Located in Hot Springs, just south of Custer State Park, Wind Cave Park has a year-round campground with no hookups and no reservations. Flush toilets and piped water are available in summer. Hiking, wildlife viewing, and guided tours of the caves are among the appeals here, as well as a popular ranger-led "night prowl" every evening after the campfire programs. Tents and slideouts are not permitted, and there are pet restrictions. ☎ **605/745-4600.** From Rapid City, take Route 79 south to Hot Springs. Take 385 north directly into the park.

Deadwood KOA. The closest campground to the gambling casinos offers a free shuttle bus to town and gold panning in Deadwood Creek, if you want to kill two urges with one stop. But be warned, there's a steep grade at the campground entrance, so if your unit drags at the back, you may want to look at one of the other six campgrounds in the Deadwood area (see below). The KOA has 51 sites with 30-amp electric, 48 of them with water and 26 with sewer, plus a heated pool, playground, grocery, laundry, and dump station. Call ☎ **800/KOA-0846.** From the junction of U.S. 85 and U.S. 14A (in Deadwood), head west 1 mile on 14A. The campground is on the right.

Other Deadwood campgrounds. Other campgrounds in the Deadwood area include Custer Crossing Campground, 15 miles south of Deadwood on U.S. 385 (☎ **605/584-1009**); Fish 'N Fry Recreational Campground, 6 miles south of Deadwood on U.S. 385 (☎ **605/578-2150**); Hidden Valley Campground, 7 miles south on U.S. 385 (☎ **605/578-1342**); Trout Haven Campground, 20 miles south on U.S. 385 (☎ **605/341-4440**); Whistler Gulch RV Park, 3 miles south of the U.S. 85/U.S. 14A junction on U.S. 85 (☎ **605/578-2092**); and Wild Bill's Campground, 5.2 miles south on U.S. 385 (☎ **605/578-2800**).

Lake Mitchell Campground. Located in Mitchell, only a mile or so from the Corn Palace (see "Off-the-Wall Attractions," above), this campground offers 70 shaded sites, some of them pull-throughs, with 20- and 30-amp electric and cable TV. It makes a convenient stopover in the eastern part of South Dakota. Call ☎ **605/995-4057** for reservations. From Rapid City, take I-90 to exit 330. Turn left at the ramp to Highway 37 bypass, then left at Main Street. It's less than a mile to the campground.

On the Road: North Dakota

THEODORE ROOSEVELT NATIONAL PARK

"I have always said I would not have been president if it had not been for my experience in North Dakota," Theodore Roosevelt was to say and write many times afterward.

Remembered as the preserver of our natural resources, a founder of our national parks, and the namesake of the teddy bear, Roosevelt as a young man was dedicated to big-game hunting. He had read of the threatened extinction of the American bison and first came to North Dakota's Badlands in 1883 on a hunting trip, afraid that the last buffalo would be shot by some other hunter before he could get there. He had married 5 years earlier at the age of 20, and took the trip west when his wife Alice was pregnant with their first child.

He and his guide struggled through more than a week of cold, rainy days, not finding any buffalo until the 10th day. Roosevelt killed the buffalo, then thrust a $100 bill into the hands of his astonished guide.

Smitten with the frontier countryside, he invested in a cattle ranching plan with two other partners at the Maltese Cross Ranch in the Badlands, then returned to New York. But on February 14, 1884, both his mother and his wife died within hours of each other, his mother from typhoid, his wife from complications of childbirth. Brokenhearted, he returned to throw himself into his ranch business, buying a second spread, the Elkhorn. He changed almost overnight from a hunter seeking trophy animals to a conservationist protecting the land and wildlife. In 1901, after he was elected president, he established the U.S. Forest Service and proclaimed 18 national monuments. He also got permission from Congress to establish five national parks and 51 wildlife refuges.

The park that honors Roosevelt was dedicated in 1978. One of the most fascinating and least visited, the park is divided into two units, a North Unit 52 miles north of I-94 and a South Unit 70 miles to the south, headquartered at Medora. Both offer scenic loop drives; a mile-by-mile "Road Log Guide" for them is for sale at the visitor centers in the park for $1.50. The Elkhorn Ranch Unit 35 miles north of Medora is also part of the park but difficult to reach without fording streams. The South Unit **visitor center** is in Medora at west end of Pacific Avenue (☎ **701/623-4466**); the North Unit visitor center is on U.S. 85 15 miles south of Watford City (☎ **701/623-4466**).

The **North Unit 30-mile scenic drive** goes past herds of buffalo and longhorns; geologic formations like slump rock, caprock, and lignite coal seams; and steeply eroded canyons in what was once grassland prairie. Less often seen are herds of wild horses, pronghorn, elk, deer, and mountain lions.

On the **South Unit 36-mile loop,** look for the prairie dog town at Milepost 3.3, with adequate RV parking space; petrified tree stumps and

Protected buffalo in Theodore Roosevelt National Park

Theodore Roosevelt National Park

ribbons of lignite coal in the cliffs; the Buck Hill Road overlook with a good view across the Badlands; and, of course, the buffalo, part of a herd of 400.

Don't miss the photogenic Painted Canyon turnout on I-94 and the scenery behind the visitor center. Tourists have been coming here since

1883, and the canyon was a popular tourist rest stop in the 1930s, with curio shops, caged animals on display, and a restaurant and gas station.

For more information, contact the **park headquarters** at P.O. Box 7, Medora, ND 58645 (☎ **701/623-4466**).

MEDORA

In this rustic little town of rough-sawn wood buildings, a young Theodore Roosevelt sipped iced champagne with the town's founder, the Marquis de Mores, a French business tycoon who built a meat-packing plant in 1883 and named the town for his American-born wife. The couple lived in their private railway car while building a lavish 26-room chateau on a hilltop outside town, now owned by the state and open for tours.

The meat plant ran for only 3 years, then de Mores and Medora went back to France, and the plant gradually fell into ruin, until today the site is marked only by one towering brick chimney and some random foundation stones.

The Marquis went on to even grander schemes, trying to build a railway between China and what is now Vietnam, running for French political office, and forging a Franco-Islamic alliance to drive the British from Africa until he was killed by Touareg natives in the Sahara.

History buff Harold Shafer, owner of Gold Seal Floor Wax and Mr. Bubble Bubble Bath, was instrumental in restoring the town in the mid-1960s.

Roosevelt's **Maltese Cross cabin** has been moved into the national park headquarters area here and is open for visitors on a guided tour basis only.

An annual **Cowboy Poetry Gathering** happens in Medora every spring in late May; call ☎ **701/225-9746** for details.

The Medora Musical, running nightly in a 2,900-seat amphitheater from mid-June through Labor Day, salutes Teddy with a rousing song-and-dance revue that climaxes with Roosevelt's Rough Riders at the Battle of San Juan Hill. You'll find signs directing you up the hill to the amphitheater at the west end of Pacific Avenue in Medora. For reservations, call ☎ **800/MEDORA-1.** While you're at it, reserve a spot at the Pitchfork Fondue—see a detailed explanation above in "Take-Out (or Eat-In) Treats"—for dinner before the show.

CAMPGROUND OASES IN NORTH DAKOTA

Fort Ransom State Park. One of the quietest, prettiest spots we camped in North Dakota was at remote Fort Ransom Park in the tiny Norwegian town of Fort Ransom by the Sheyenne River. Canoes are for rent, and you'll find 15 sites with electric hookups, sanitary dump, toilet facilities, and spacious pull-throughs for $11 a night. What you will have trouble finding is the park itself if you want to get there on paved roads. From I-94, take exit 288 and follow Route 1 south to Route 27, turn east for about 5 miles, and follow the Ft. Ransom turnoff north. Call ☎ **701/973-4331** for more information or the cavalry if you get lost.

North Dakota Campgrounds

Cottonwood Campground ❶
Fort Ransom State Park ❼
Four Bears RV Park ❹
Jamestown KOA ❻
Juniper Campground ❸
Medora Campground ❷
Minot KOA ❺
Red Trail Campground ❷
Turtle River State Park ❽

Turtle River State Park. Also $11 a night with hookup, Turtle River is near Grand Forks in Arvilla, 22 miles west of Grand Forks on Highway 2, and has large pull-throughs and 70 20- and 30-amp electric connections. Open year-round for self-contained camping (the utilities are off in winter), sledding, snowshoeing, skating, and cross-country skiing. ☎ **701/594-4445.**

Minot KOA. Our site at the KOA in Minot had its own resident prairie dog, something that delighted us but made our North Dakota neighbors turn up their noses at "that rodent." Some of the 66 sites are shaded and grassy; 49 of them provide 30-amp electric, and the office is modem-friendly. The campground is a little over 2 miles east of Minot at 5261 Highway 52 South; call ☎ **800/KOA-7421** for reservations.

Four Bears RV Park. Located behind the Four Bears Casino in New Town, on Dakota 23 on the Fort Berthold Reservation, the campground is like the prosperous casino itself, operated by the Three Affiliated Tribes: the Mandan, Hidatsu, and Arikara. While the 62 hookup sites with 20- and 30-amp electric are freeform rather than rigidly outlined, you can usually figure out a way to park to best access the connection. Rates are modest at $6 to $12 a night, and you can walk to the tables or to the fishing lake. ☎ **701/627-4018.**

Cottonwood Campground. Located in the south unit of Theodore Roosevelt National Park, at Mile 5.6 on the Little Missouri River (14 miles west of U.S. 85), Cottonwood offers 38 sites accessible for RVs, some of them pull-throughs large enough for big rigs, but with no hookups and no reservations. Call ☎ **701/623-4466** for more information.

Juniper Campground (formerly Squaw Creek Campground). Located in the north unit of Theodore Roosevelt National Park, 4.6 miles off U.S. 85, opposite the Cannonball Concretions pullout, Juniper Campground has 44 paved and shaded sites, none with hookups, plus a dump station and toilets. Sites are available on a first-come, first-served basis. ☎ **701/842-2333.**

Red Trail and Medora campgrounds. The town of Medora offers so many diversions that an interested RVer could spend a week. Unfortunately, neither of the town's two campgrounds with hookups is particularly appealing at peak season when the crowds are there, but each has its pros and cons. Red Trail Campground, where we stayed, offers an easy walk into town and is owned and operated by a friendly family, but the campground is behind a motel and the 93 sites are fairly close together. They offer live entertainment some nights, cable TV, city water, and 30- and 50-amp hookups with a surcharge for cable and 50-amp; call ☎ **800/621-4317** for reservations. Medora Campground is operated by the nonprofit Theodore Roosevelt Medora Foundation, with 185 sites even closer together than those at Red Lodge. It's on the edge of town across from the road to the Medora Musical and Pitchfork Fondue Dinner (but not within walking distance, unless you want to walk uphill ¾ of a mile). Sites provide 20- and 30-amp electricity. Call ☎ **800/MEDORA 1** for reservations; this is also the place to buy tickets for the Pitchfork Fondue Dinner—see "Take-Out (or Eat-In) Treats," above.

Jamestown KOA. This campground cooks up home-style family meals nightly between mid-June and mid-August, a boon for just-arrived travelers who don't want to heat up the galley. The 48 gravel sites are shady, some adequate for big rigs, and 50-amp hookups are available. You'll also find cable TV and a modem-friendly office. It's located on the frontage road south of I-94 at exit 256. Call ☎ **800/KOA-6350** for reservations.

A Dozen Terrific Side Trips in the Dakotas

1. **Visit Devil's Tower National Monument.** Remember Richard Dreyfuss sculpting his mashed potatoes into a fluted, flat-topped mountain in *Close Encounters of the Third Kind?* You can take a detour to that mystical Wyoming mountain, Devil's Tower National Monument, 20 miles west on I-90, then 27 miles north via exit 185 (☎ **307/467-5283**). The 867-foot core of an ancient volcano is surrounded by the pine trees of the Black Hills and has near its base, within the boundary of the national monument, one of the few protected prairie dog towns in the west. There are also 51 campsites here but no hookups. The campground is closed in winter, but the monument is open year-round.

2. **Follow the trail of Lewis and Clark.** Take U.S. 83 north at exit 212 for about 30 miles to visit the Farm Island State Recreation Area (☎ **605/224-5605**), where a monument and interpretive center talks about their expedition. Most of the buffalo in the fields around here were extras in the film *Dances with Wolves.*

3. **Visit Badlands National Park.** Access is from I-90 via exit 131 from the east or 110 at Wall Drug Store from the west. A 40-mile loop on Route 240 lets you travel through a typical section of this eroded but majestic landscape brushed in watercolor pinks, soft grays, and greens—except at sunrise or sunset, when it takes on a warm burnished glow. To visit the prairie dog town, continue on Route 590 along a gravel road for about 5 miles, then turn north again to Wall. ☎ **605/433-5361.**

4. **Drive the Spearfish Canyon National Scenic Byway.** It's a dramatically beautiful 20-mile route any time of year, but especially in early fall when the trees lining the river banks begin to change color. Take U.S. 85 southwest from Deadwood, then U.S. 14A north along the canyon. The views are better if you set out from Lead and drive north.

5. **Drive the Wildlife Loop Road in Custer State Park.** This 18-mile loop offers a chance to see pronghorn antelope, bison, white-tail and mule deer, elk, coyotes, prairie dogs, eagles, and hawks. Try to drive the loop early in the morning or very late in the afternoon for the best sightings. ☎ **605/255-4515.**

6. **Visit the Ingalls Family Homestead.** In tiny DeSmet, northeast of Mitchell on U.S. 14, is the Ingalls Family Homestead, famous as the childhood home of Laura Ingalls Wilder, who grew up to write *Little House on the Prairie*. Her books in turn inspired the long-running TV series. A do-it-yourself tour of 18 sites related to her stories begins at the Surveyors' House at Silver Lake. Be warned, however, that the unpaved road to the homestead site is rough and bumpy. Fans of the show will enjoy a special 3-week pageant that takes place in late June and early July, with wagon rides, home-cooked meals, and an all-volunteer cast in an outdoor stage production. The homestead is marked off U.S. 14 east of town on the south side of the highway and is up an unpaved road. Phone ☎ **605/854-3383** for information.

7. **Visit Wind Cave National Park.** South of Custer State Park via Route 87, Wind Cave has 28,000 acres of wildlife habitat above ground, for buffalo, antelope, elk, deer, and prairie dogs, as well as the 53-mile maze of tunnels underground with its unusual boxwork, frostwork, and popcorn formations. ☎ **605/745-4600.**

8. **Check out the Black Hills Wild Horse Sanctuary and Mammoth Site.** The Hot Springs area south of the Black Hills on U.S. 18/385 has two outstanding attractions, the Black Hills Wild Horse Sanctuary (☎ **800/252-6652**), where hundreds of wild American mustangs are protected, and the Mammoth Site, where the dig goes on to excavate as many as 100 mammoths who died in a sinkhole at the springs 26,000 years ago. Bones are displayed where they were found. Hot Springs Chamber of Commerce (☎ **800/325-6991**).

9. **Visit the Homestake Gold Mine.** If you drive over to Deadwood, add a short detour to Lead (pronounced "leed," which means "lode") to tour the surface workings of the Homestake Gold Mine on one of their daily tours (closed in winter). The largest underground gold mine still operating in the western hemisphere was financed by George Hearst, father of William Randolph Hearst, and two California partners. From Deadwood, take Route 14A and continue on to Lead. Call the visitor's center for information: ☎ **605/584-3110.**

10. **Do a little caving at Jewel Cave National Monument.** Located west of Custer on U.S. 16, Jewel Cave is the fourth largest cave in the world, with 80 miles of passageways already explored and charted. Sparkling calcite crystals and bizarre drapery, balloon, and column formations make this a favorite of cavers, who can take special tours by advance

reservation (☎ **605/673-2288**). Guided tours for the general public are offered on a regular schedule in summer, intermittently the rest of the year. Tours: Adults $6, children 6 to 16 $3, under 6 free.

11. **Visit the Prairie Village.** Located in Madison, South Dakota, Prairie Village offers considerably more than its name suggests, from a rare 1893 steam-driven Hershel-Spillman carousel to an even rarer Barney and Smith railway "chapel car"; Chapel Car Emanuel, equipped with pews, organ, and pulpit, along with a room in the back for the minister to change, was one of seven chapel cars built under the auspices of the Reverend Boston Smith, a Baptist who got the idea of sending the clergy out by rail to serve small frontier settlements without churches. Today it's one of only two cars remaining. The Social Hall, now named the Lawrence Welk Opera House, originally graced the town of Oldham, South Dakota, where Welk used to play in his early days. The old church in the village is still used for Sunday morning services, and some 40 buildings are spread out over a 140-acre area with a sense of a real place and time rather than a museum collection. In August, the village holds a threshing jamboree with steam-driven farm machinery, and three coal-fired steam locomotives are fired up on occasion to offer rail excursions. Two miles west of Madison on Highway 34. ☎ **800/693-3644.**

12. **Take a zigzag route from Minot to Medora.** The drive offers a good overview of North Dakota, from the farm and ranchland along Route 83 south from Minot, then west along Route 23. Both the distinctive Four Bears Bridge across the Missouri and the modern Four Bears Casino were named for a great Mandan chief, while Lake Sakakawea, a few miles to the north, is named for the young Shoshone woman also called Sacajawea who was instrumental in helping Lewis and Clark successfully complete their mission. (You're probably seeing a lot of Sacajawea these days: A coin bearing her likeness is the first being minted by the U.S. in the new millennium.) The Three Affiliated Tribes Museum, operated by the Mandan, Hidatsu, and Arikara people on Route 23 4 miles west of New Town on the Fort Berthold Indian Reservation, is open daily year-round (☎ **701/627-4477**), and tells through the lives of three Mandan of the stressful adjustments Native Americans had to make to reservation life. Continue south along U.S. 85 from Wafford City, detouring to make the loop drives through the North and South Units of Theodore Roosevelt National Park.

Travel Quiz: Way Out West

There are certain unique and historical Western phrases and terms that are almost forgotten today. Can you correctly identify the following?

1. Bonanza Farm
   - (a) Where Adam, Hoss, and Little Joe did exactly what Lorne Greene said.
   - (b) Acres of land that could be turned into single-crop farms; these were paid out to stockholders by the troubled Northern Pacific Railroad after the Panic of 1873.
   - (c) Unproductive tribal farm-land on a reservation that was turned into a casino and parking lot.

2. Ghost Dance
   - (a) A Paiute and Sioux ceremony in which the partici-pants fell into a trance while dancing; they believed the white shirts they wore were impervi-ous to bullets.
   - (b) Whoopi Goldberg, playing a clairvoyant, goes into a trance and performs "Swan Lake."
   - (c) Halloween hijinks in Tombstone's Boot Hill.

3. Boomers
   - (a) People nearing 50 who drive sport utility vehicles.
   - (b) People who carry loud portable radios.
   - (c) People who rushed over the Kansas border in 1889 to force Congress to open Indian Territory to white settlement.

ANSWERS: 1 (b); 2 (a); 3 (c).

The Rio Grande Valley & the Wilds of West Texas

9

ONCE INHABITED BY GIANT FLYING REPTILES WITH 50-FOOT wingspans, Texas has more miles of inland lake and stream water than Minnesota, a million official road signs and markers on its highways, and, as its tourism publications frequently point out, a ranch, a military base, and two counties bigger than certain New England states.

The bottom half of Texas is where rock 'n' roll got sent out all over the universe by Wolfman Jack in the 1950s, broadcasting from a Del Rio radio station's 500,000-watt "pirate" transmitter located across the river in Mexico. The Del Rio station was built in the 1930s by "Doctor" John R. Brinkley to promote his famous goat gland surgery to restore virility.

It's where Pancho Villa and Zsa Zsa Gabor once slept (but not at the same time) in El Paso's Paso del Norte Hotel, where nachos were invented by Ignacio "Nacho" Anaya at the Victory Club restaurant in Piedras Negras, and where fajitas were first served at Ninfa's restaurant in Houston on July 13, 1973.

"The sun has riz, the sun has set, And here we is, in Texas yet!"
— 19th-century doggerel

John Dillinger and his gang vacationed in the sleepy little West Texas town of Balmorhea in 1934, pretending to be "Oklahoma oil men." Locals were mystified by their pastimes, things like jumping on and off the running boards of moving cars, shooting at tin cans tossed in the air, and lobbing an occasional hand grenade. Only after the well-publicized gunning down of Public Enemy Number One outside a Chicago movie house a few months later did the good citizens of Balmorhea realize who their big-spending visitors really were.

Southwest Texas is where camels were trained for combat, where Mexican revolutionary Antonio Zapata was beheaded, and where queenmakers Rex

South Texas Highlights

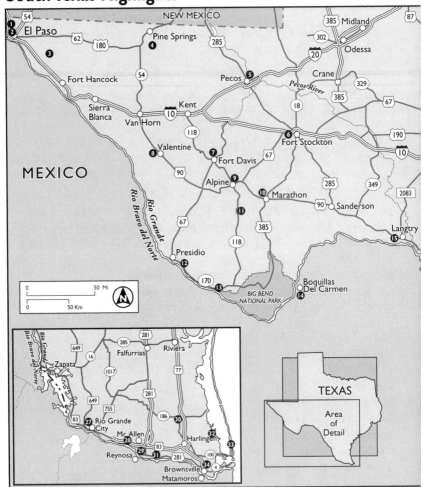

Holt and Richard Guy of GuyRex Associates in El Paso became famous for grooming a string of beauty-contest winners.

RVing Along the Rio Grande

The road that follows the Rio Grande twists and turns 940 miles from the Gulf of Mexico to El Paso, laying out the border between Texas and Mexico.

It was all well and good to use the Rio Grande as the border, except that the river kept changing its course. A 600-acre piece of land called the Chamizal in El Paso/Juarez was wrangled over for 100 years until President John F. Kennedy and Mexico's Adolfo Lopes Mateos worked out a compromise. And one mission church, Nuestra Senora del Socorro, was moved back and forth between Mexico and Texas by flooding a number of times without ever shifting from its foundations.

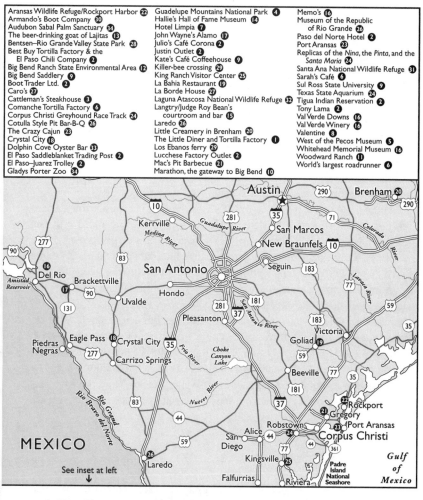

Aransas Wildlife Refuge/Rockport Harbor **22**
Armando's Boot Company **30**
Audubon Sabal Palm Sanctuary **34**
The beer-drinking goat of Lajitas **13**
Bentsen–Rio Grande Valley State Park **28**
Best Buy Tortilla Factory & the
 El Paso Chili Company **2**
Big Bend Ranch State Environmental Area **12**
Big Bend Saddlery **9**
Boot Trader Ltd. **2**
Caro's **7**
Cattleman's Steakhouse **3**
Comanche Tortilla Factory **6**
Corpus Christi Greyhound Race Track **24**
Cotulla Style Pit Bar-B-Q **26**
The Crazy Cajun **23**
Crystal City **18**
Dolphin Cove Oyster Bar **33**
El Paso Saddleblanket Trading Post **2**
El Paso–Juarez Trolley **2**
Gladys Porter Zoo **34**

Guadelupe Mountains National Park **4**
Hallie's Hall of Fame Museum **14**
Hotel Limpia **7**
John Wayne's Alamo **17**
Julio's Café Corona **2**
Justin Outlet **2**
Kate's Café Coffeehouse **9**
Killer-bee crossing **29**
King Ranch Visitor Center **25**
La Bahia Restaurant **19**
La Borde House **27**
Laguna Atascosa National Wildlife Refuge **32**
Langtry/Judge Roy Bean's
 courtroom and bar **15**
Laredo **26**
Little Creamery in Brenham **20**
The Little Diner and Tortilla Factory **1**
Los Ebanos ferry **29**
Lucchese Factory Outlet **2**
Mac's Pit Barbecue **21**
Marathon, the gateway to Big Bend **10**

Memo's **16**
Museum of the Republic
 of Rio Grande **26**
Paso del Norte Hotel **2**
Port Aransas **23**
Replicas of the *Nina*, the *Pinta*, and the
 Santa Maria **24**
Santa Ana National Wildlife Refuge **31**
Sarah's Café **6**
Sul Ross State University **9**
Texas State Aquarium **24**
Tigua Indian Reservation **2**
Tony Lama **2**
Val Verde Downs **16**
Val Verde Winery **16**
Valentine **8**
West of the Pecos Museum **5**
Whitehead Memorial Museum **16**
Woodward Ranch **11**
World's largest roadrunner **6**

In West Texas, you can whiz through more territory in an hour in your RV than stagecoaches and wagon trains could make in 3 days. It's an easy and interesting journey, so long as you avoid the broiling hot days of summer.

Texas is one of those states that likes RVers a lot. Not only do many of their state parks offer hookups, but at the information centers when you drive across the border, you can usually find racks of free booklets with lists of RV campgrounds, state parks, sanitary dump station locations, and places that sell LP gas. The state also puts out a wealth of other free printed materials available at all visitor information centers.

HITTING THE HIGHLIGHTS

Spend 1 night in the Corpus Christi area, visit Padre Island National Seashore but skip South Padre Island, and take the back road, Route 281, through the

Rio Grande Valley, allowing time to visit at least one bird sanctuary if you're there in winter.

If you have kids along, detour up to Bracketville for the Alamo Village theme park, then drive fairly briskly along the border, stopping in Langtry to see Judge Roy Bean's Jersey Lilly Saloon.

Spend as much time as you can spare in Big Bend and the Davis Mountains, then finish up with a day or two in El Paso.

GOING FOR THE LONG HAUL

If you want to spend the winter in the Rio Grande Valley, you'll be welcomed with open arms by the dozens of RV parks, some of them quite lavish, that dot the area between Brownsville and McAllen. The climate is semi-tropical, with a wide range of fresh fruits and vegetables locally grown, and prices are moderate based on the national average.

There's plenty to do, with golf courses, nearby beaches, extraordinary bird watching, shopping in Mexican border towns, and organized activities in every community. Wanna dance? You can learn and practice tap, jazz dancing, square dancing, clog dancing, and line dancing. Some RV parks have their own dance halls and regular square or line dance programs.

Adult education classes on such topics as Spanish language, art, music, and local ecology are offered through colleges in Harlingen, McAllen, and Brownsville. Contact the Harlingen Chamber of Commerce, 311 E. Tyler St. (☎ **800/531-7346**); the Brownsville Visitor Information Center, at the exit to Farm Road 802 from U.S. 77/83 in North Brownsville (☎ **800/626-2639**); and the McAllen Visitors' Information Center, 10 N. Broadway (☎ **800/250-2591**).

Three months is the average stay for "winter Texans," and the RV parks will give discounted rates for long stays. The state parks in the area usually limit your stay to 14 consecutive days.

Travel Essentials

WHEN TO GO

Winter is best, with mild and usually sunny days that cool down to crisp nights. Late fall and early spring are also comfortable. Summer is extremely hot, humid in the east and bone dry in the west, except in the cooler upper reaches of Big Bend, where roads are not suitable for large RVs or trailers, and in the Davis Mountains, where big rigs are able to maneuver.

WHAT TO TAKE

Camera and film, binoculars, strong sunblock and sun hat, insect repellent, stout high-topped hiking boots if you plan to hike the Big Bend and other desert terrain, and an antacid if you intend to follow the chili trail.

WHAT TO WEAR

Casual and comfortable clothing is correct all over Texas except in its biggest eastern-oriented cities, which this tour excludes. If you plan to dine out in one of the splurge restaurants (see "Five Special Splurges," below), you might take along a slightly dressier outfit, but it's not essential.

TRIMMING COSTS ON THE ROAD

Fortunately, this part of Texas is relatively inexpensive for the RV traveler, even if you eat out more often than in. Year-round, roadside produce stands sell regional food products at low prices.

Winter Texans get rates by the month or season in most of the commercial RV parks in the Rio Grande Valley, lowering the per diem cost somewhat.

The state of Texas permits RVers who sleep inside their vehicles to park for **rest periods** of up to 24 hours at any of the more than 1,000 highway roadside rest areas. Pitching a tent is forbidden, however. While we have some personal reservations about overnighting in a roadside rest area (see "Should You Sleep by the Side of the Road?" in chapter 3, "Where to Sleep: Campgrounds & RV Parks"), many RVers don't worry about it. And you would be able to save a lot of campground fees.

Gas is fairly expensive around El Paso but gets cheaper as you travel eastward.

WHERE TO GET INFORMATION

The **Texas Department of Commerce, Tourist Division** (☎ 800/8888-TEX, ext. 728; www.traveltex.com) and the **Texas Travel Information Centers** (☎ 800/452-9292) can provide information. Call the latter for free booklets on public and private RV parks and campgrounds and road conditions.

DRIVING & CAMPING TIPS

- **Stock up on gas.** Particularly in West Texas, where stretches between gas stations may be long, top off your tank whenever convenient. Never let the needle drop below half.

- **Winter in the tropics.** Winter Texans head for the Texas Tropics when the wind starts blowing snow around in the Midwest. For new RVers, wannabe snowbirds, or full-timers who don't know where the Texas Tropics are, look at a map of the Rio Grande Valley between Brownsville and Mission, which is thick with RV parks offering rates by the week, month, or season.

- **Camp in state park campgrounds.** Many Texas state park campgrounds have RV hookups and take advance reservations. Seniors, too, get free park entrance and a price break on camping if they apply for a special state park windshield sticker at any Texas state park.

- **Beware of spring break.** Avoid Padre Island, Corpus Christi, and Port Aransas during "spring break" days in late March and early April unless you like to be inundated with rowdy crowds of party-hearty college students.

- **BYOB?** Each of Texas's 254 counties rules individually on the if, when, what, and how of alcohol sales. Liquor stores are closed on Sundays and holidays throughout the state.

- **Habla Español?** If you drive U.S. 281 along the Rio Grande between Brownsville and Hidalgo, be careful not to cross any bridges unless you want to find yourself in Mexico. You can also walk across. (See "Six Special Side Trips" for some border crossing tips—applicable whether you go on purpose or by accident.)

The Best Sights, Tastes & Experiences of the Rio Grande

OFF-THE-WALL ATTRACTIONS

The beer-drinking goat of Lajitas. At Lajitas Trading Post in Lajitas, a funky combination of authentic old and ersatz new West Texas, you'll find Mayor Clay Henry, Jr., the beer-drinking goat. The original goat, we are sure, has long since succumbed to cirrhosis of the liver, but judging from the dozing goats and empty beer cans we saw in the goat pen, he has worthy successors. Lajitas is 100 miles south of Alpine, Texas. Take Highway 118 to Terlingua, then take Farm Road 170, 17 miles. ☎ **800/944-9907;** www.lajitas.com.

Hallie's Hall of Fame Museum, Boquillas. The late Hallie Stillwell was a genuine pioneer who arrived here at the age of 12, ran a ranch, taught school, and carried a gun. Her family ranch near Boquillas now contains a museum in tribute to her. It's free, and open daily. Located 46 miles southeast of Marathon. Call ahead for directions and museum hours. ☎ **915/376-2244.**

Replicas of the *Nina*, the *Pinta*, and the *Santa Maria*, Corpus Christi. You'll find them moored in town, along with the authentic World War II aircraft carrier *Lexington*, which is now a naval museum. ☎ **512/886-4492** for Columbus ships; ☎ **800/LADY-LEX** for *Lexington*.

The killer-bee crossing, Hidalgo. On the border just west of Brownsville, a frequently photographed $20,000, 20-foot fiberglass and steel bee stands by a fire station on the town's Espersenza Avenue, commemorating the first crossing of the Africanized honeybees into the United States at this point in 1990.

The town of Valentine. Valentine gets very busy every February postmarking heart-shaped cards for romantics everywhere. You can drop off your cards anytime in person at the town's only post office, or mail them in before February 14 to Postmaster, Valentine, TX 79854.

The world's largest roadrunner, Paisano Pete

The world's largest roadrunner, Fort Stockton. It's Paisano Pete, 11 feet tall and 22 feet long. Find him on U.S. 290 at Main Street.

Crystal City, former home of the spinach capital of the U.S. Don't tell any of the Texans they're passé; they still have their Popeye statue in place on the main street. The town is 11 miles north of the U.S. 277 junction with U.S. 83 on U.S. 83. (See "Off-the-Wall Attractions" in chapter 10, "Arkansas, the Ozarks & Branson, Missouri," for the present capital.)

Laredo, capital of the Republic of the Rio Grande. Adding to the usual Six Flags Over Texas (Spain, France, Mexico, the Republic of Texas, the Confederacy, and the United States), Laredo can claim one more: its unique claim as the capital of the short-lived Republic of the Rio Grande. See the flags at the town's Republic of the Rio Grande Museum, 1000 Zaragoza St. (☎ 956/727-3480). And Fredonia didn't start with the Marx Brothers in *Duck Soup;* the Republic of Fredonia was founded in East Texas by disgruntled Anglo settlers in the 1820s.

Val Verde Winery, Del Rio. Val Verde, the oldest licensed winery in Texas, founded by Italian immigrants, offers free tours and tastings. Their tawny port is a local favorite; they also produce a so-so cabernet sauvignon, a Johannisberg Riesling, and a Rio Grande blush. Open Monday through Saturday, 100 Qualia Dr., Del Rio. ☎ 830/775-9714.

The Marfa ghost lights, Marfa. The mysterious lights have been seen almost nightly since the first reporting back in 1883. After it gets dark, drive west of town on Route 90/87 for 8 miles and you'll see the sign for the "official viewing area." Look southwest toward the mountains, and sooner or later you may or may not see a series of shimmering white balls of light in the distance. No one has ever been able to determine what causes them, but our favorite try was the expert who said they are flying bats with

---

DRIFTIN' ALONG WITH THE TUMBLIN' TUMBLEWEED

We used to think tumbleweeds were quintessentially Texan. Turns out they're really Russian and were accidentally imported in 1873 when a few tumbleweed seeds arrived in a shipment of flax seed.

---

radioactive dust on their wings. Marfa is at the junction of U.S. 67 and U.S. 90, northwest of Big Bend. Call the Chamber of Commerce at ☎ **915/729-4942.**

TEN TERRIBLY TEXAS THINGS TO DO

1. **Pick up some fresh shrimp in Aransas Pass.** Aransas Pass is the shrimp capital of Texas. The seafood shacks around the Port Aransas ferry landing sometimes offer 5 pounds for $15 or $20. Another place to buy from the boats is Peoples Street T-Head at the marina in Corpus Christi. Also here: Landry's Seafood, 600 N. Shoreline (☎ **361/882-6666**), sells early-bird special shrimp and oysters with happy hour drinks starting at 4:30pm.

2. **Stare down a shark at the Texas State Aquarium, Corpus Christi.** You'll also see sting rays, barracuda, giant grouper, and tropical fish swimming around an artificial reef created from an oil derrick. Open daily except Christmas. Located at 2710 N. Shoreline. ☎ **800/477-GULF;** www.txstateaaq.com.

3. **Join a jalapeño-eating contest.** Perhaps enter the one at the Brownsville-Matamoros Charro Days celebrations during Mardi Gras, when parades, carnivals, and costume balls highlight the festivities. Alternatively, hit the streets of Laredo, where the jalapeño-downing derby happens every February at George Washington's birthday party celebration. (Don't ask what chiles have to do with George's birthday; the town combined two festivals into one.) The winner is crowned King Chile and may even get a spicy kiss from beauty queen Miss Jalapeño. Brownsville Visitor Information: ☎ **800/626-2639.**

4. **Go fishing.** Dam fishing, for instance, at Amistad Lake near Del Rio, or saltwater sport fishing at Corpus Christi, or join in the big daddy of them all, the Texas International Fishing Tournament (TIFT), in Port Isabel in early August. For details, call ☎ **956/943-8438.**

5. **River raft along the Rio Grande.** Various companies offer 1-day trips into Santa Elena and Colorado Canyons in Big Bend National Park year-round when water flow permits. No previous river experience is necessary, but advance reservations are required. Contact **Far Flung Adventures** in Terlingua (☎ **800/359-4138**) or **Big Bend River Tours** in Lajitas (☎ **915/371-2771**).

6. **See the stars at family "star parties," Fort Davis.** Fort Davis's McDonald Observatory in the Davis Mountains hosts stargazing parties on Tuesday and Saturday nights. The entire family is welcome; no reservations required. Dress warmly and bring binoculars. Free tours are conducted daily at 2pm, and during summer months at 9:30am as well. Located on Route 118 northwest of the town of Fort Davis. Call ☎ **915/426-3640** for information.

7. **Go prospecting outside Alpine.** At Woodward Ranch, 16 miles south of Alpine on Route 118, you can find red plume agate, precious opal, and other minerals and gemstones, and they'll help you identify what you've got (and charge per pound for the rocks you keep). Call the Woodward Ranch (☎ **915/364-2271**) for information.

"I SEE BY YOUR OUTFIT THAT YOU ARE A COWBOY . . ."

Care to do some shopping? Here are a few places to gear up.

Saddles
King Ranch Running W saddles from the ranch's own saddle shop at the Ragland Building, 6th and Kleberg, in Kingsville (☎ **800/282-KING**).

Saddle Blankets
El Paso Saddleblanket Trading Post has handwoven saddle blankets and rugs in traditional southwestern designs. 601 North Oregon, downtown El Paso. ☎ **915/544-1000.**

Boots
When trying on a ready-made Western boot, be sure the heel slips a bit when you walk. When the sole gets more flexible, the slippage will stop. If it doesn't slip, it's too tight and will give you blisters. The instep should be snug, the boot shank long enough to cover your arch fully, and the ball of the foot should fit into the widest part of the boot, not sit forward or back of it.

You can get a good pair of boots in El Paso at the **Justin Outlet,** 7100 Gateway East, I-10 at Hawkins (☎ **915/779-5465**); **Tony Lama,** 7156 Gateway East just off I-10 (☎ **915/772-4327**); **Lucchese Factory Outlet,** 6601 Montana (☎ **915/778-8060**); and **Boot Trader Ltd.,** 10787 Gateway West. Go to **Armando's Boot Company** in Raymondville (on Route 77 near Harlingen), for custom-made boots (☎ **361/689-3521**).

Wrangler Cowboy Cut Jeans
The VF Factory Outlet has branches in Corsicana, Hempstead, Livingston, Mineral Wells, San Marcos, and Sulphur Springs. ☎ **800/772-8336.**

Custom-Crafted, Working-Cowboy Leather Accessories
Bandanas, hats, belts, belt buckles, and everything else for the well turned-out cowboy can be had in Alpine at the Big Bend Saddlery, East Highway 90 ☎ **800/634-4502.**

8. **Catch a game of cowboy polo.** It's sometimes featured at professional rodeos or at arenas in towns with National Cowboy Polo Association member teams. The season runs March through August, and players are required to wear jeans and western shirts and ride western saddle, never English. Headgear is optional; many play in cowboy hats. The cowboy polo field is smaller than in English polo, and the ball is made of rubber rather than wood. The audience is a bit rowdier, too. Top Texas NRA teams include San Angelo in West Texas and San Jacinto, near Houston. Most matches during the season (from Mar through Aug) are held in rodeo arenas. San Angelo's Visitor Information Center (☎ **800/375-1206**) can supply current events information.

9. **Check out the rodeo classes at Sul Ross State University, Alpine.** It's considered the best school for "wannabe" professional saddle bronco riders, ropers, rodeo clowns, barrel racers, and steer wrestlers. Call the school at ☎ **915/837-8059** (www.sulross.edu) for a visit and tour.

10. **Take the trolley to Mexico.** The El Paso-Juarez Trolley makes hourly trips in the daytime year-round from the Convention Center Plaza Terminal on Santa Fe Street; fare is around $10. Call for reservations at ☎ **915/544-0062.** In Juarez, the trolley stops at Pueblito Mexicana, a shopping village for tourists; Sanborn's Department Store; Chihuahua Charlie's Bar & Grill; the colorful city market; and other points of interest.

FIVE SPECIAL SPLURGES

1. **Visit Marathon, the gateway to Big Bend.** Allow some time and/or money for the little town of Marathon, whose antiques shops have cornered the market on Georgia O'Keeffe–type cow skulls, and where the vintage Gage Hotel from 1927 (☎ **800/884-GAGE**) has been gentrified only to the extent it had to be (if you ignore the motel-like annex with pool next door). In early March the town hosts the Texas Cowboy Poetry Gathering. Marathon was named by a retired sea captain who said it reminded him of Marathon, Greece. (Funny, it doesn't remind us of Marathon, Greece.) **Marathon Chamber of Commerce:** ☎ **915/386-4516.**

2. **Drop into the Paso del Norte Hotel for a drink.** The Dome Bar at El Paso's elegant old Paso del Norte Hotel (now the Camino Real) is the original lobby of the hotel, with its Tiffany stained-glass dome ceiling and marble walls and floor. Who knows? You might glimpse Zsa Zsa Gabor. At 101 S. El Paso St. ☎ **800/722-6466.**

3. **Chow down on a steak at Cattleman's Steakhouse at Indian Cliffs Ranch.** Open daily, the restaurant serves huge steaks that *People* magazine called the best in the country, plus side orders from ranch beans to homemade bread. Located 33 miles southwest of El Paso to the I-10

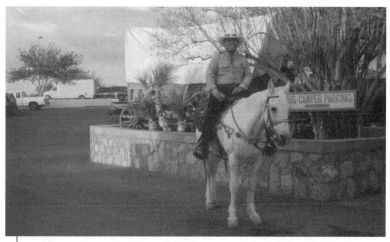

West Texas cowboy at Indian Cliffs ranch

Fabens exit, then north 5 miles on Route 793. Call ☎ **915/544-3200** for a reservation. Open Monday through Saturday 4 to 9pm, Sundays noon to 9pm. Your dinner reservation also gives free admission to the ranch's western-style attractions, which kids particularly enjoy.

4. **Go cowboy.** Grab yourself some cowboy garb, a Stetson, some hand-tooled boots, or a saddle. See "I See by Your Outfit That You Are a Cowboy . . ." for suggested shops and outlets.

5. **Check out the beautifully restored La Borde House in Rio Grande City.** Designed in France and built by a turn-of-the-century French merchant, the New Orleans–style mansion is now a sedate hotel and restaurant with a modern annex at the back. 601 E. Main St., west of McAllen on U.S. 83. Call ☎ **956/487-5101** for reservations.

TAKE-OUT (OR EAT-IN) TREATS

La Bahia Restaurant, Goliad. The historic 1749 Presidio La Bahia in Goliad is still used for church services as well as a museum, but time your visit for lunchtime because next door is La Bahia Restaurant. Family-run for more than 30 years, the big friendly restaurant serves chile con queso on home-made tortillas, wonderful chicken enchiladas with green tomatillo sauce, and beef fajitas in soft tacos. For $16 we got more than we could eat, but since we'd ordered takeout, we refrigerated the leftovers for later. From Highway 59, make a right on Highway 77-S. It is a little over 2 miles on Highway 77. ☎ **361/645-3651.**

The Crazy Cajun, Port Aransas. Try a shrimp and crawfish boil at The Crazy Cajun restaurant in Port Aransas on Mustang Island; take the free 24-hour ferry over from the end of Highway 361 in Aransas Pass. A sort of southern clambake, the boil includes shrimp, crawfish, stone-crab claws, smoked sausage, potatoes, and corn on the cob, served on butcher paper. On Alister Street Square. Closed Mondays. ☎ **512/749-5069.**

Mac's Pit Barbecue, Gregory. In tiny Gregory, north of Corpus Christi on Highway 35 just north of 181, Mac's Pit Barbecue serves old-fashioned Texas barbecue cooked over mesquite wood. Chomp down on beef brisket, beef finger ribs, pork spare ribs, ham, chicken, or Polish sausage. Mac's has been in business for 30 years at his Rockport location at 815 Market St., open daily. The other location, in Gregory, is closed Sundays. ☎ **361/729-9388.**

Grapefruit and onions. The ruby red grapefruit of the Lower Rio Grande Valley is justifiably famous. Hit the late January to early February **Citrus Fiesta** in Mission and buy a bagful, or find an orchard that lets you pick your own. Don't forget the mild Supersweet 1015 onions you can bite into like an apple. Both are on sale at **Bell's Farm to Market** in McAllen at 116 S. Ware Rd. and Business 83. ☎ **800/798-0424.**

Cotulla Style Pit Bar-B-Q, Laredo. In the streets of Laredo, feast on Cotulla pit-style barbecue (very like Mexico's carne asada) and all the side dishes. There's a separate take-out area to the right of the restaurant. We noticed the locals all call their order in ahead of time on weekends, and it's ready to pick up when they get there. Otherwise, lines can be long. You might also want to try two unique Laredo dishes: the mariachi, a fiery local version of a breakfast taco, and panchos, which are nachos with beef layered in alongside the cheese and jalapeños. 4502 McPherson. ☎ **956/724-5747.**

Blue Bell ice cream. Some ice cream aficionados swear by Texas's Blue Bell brand, once not distributed outside the state. *Time* magazine went on record not long ago saying it was the best in the United States. The old-fashioned **"Little Creamery in Brenham"** (on Route 290 about halfway between Austin and Houston) keeps its small-town image and its logo, a girl and a cow, but you can find the brand now in seven southwestern states. Top flavor is vanilla, but strawberry, rocky road, pistachio almond, and chocolate chip also scoop up compliments. If you want to tour the plant, reserve ahead at ☎ **800/317-8135.** You get a free sample at the end of the tour.

Dolphin Cove Oyster Bar, South Padre Island. Dolphin Cove Oyster Bar serves up fresh-shucked oysters and you-peel-'em shrimp from a little grass shack in Isla Blanca Park. Open Tuesday through Sunday noon to 9pm. ☎ **956/761-2850.**

Memo's, Del Rio. Run by the same family for more than 55 years, Memo's serves fajitas, enchiladas, and chalupas on the banks of the San Felipe Creek at 804 E. Losoya. ☎ **956/584-8101.**

Kate's Café Coffeehouse, Alpine. Get your lattes, cappuccinos, and Italian sodas, along with hand-cut sandwiches and homemade desserts, at Kate's Café

Coffeehouse in the historic old Holland Hotel, 209 W. Holland Ave. in Alpine. It's open Monday through Saturday from 11am to 4pm. ☎ **915/837-2001.**

Sarah's Café, Fort Stockton. Just down the street from the restored fort, Sarah's is filled with locals, not tourists, and open for lunch and dinner daily except Sundays and holidays. Chile rellenos with green sauce are a house specialty, but everything is good. Ask the owners to show you old menus from the 1940s when things were really cheap. Even in the 1960s you could buy a Mexican combination plate for around 50¢. Sarah's is located at 106 S. Nelson in Fort Stockton. ☎ **915/336-7700. The Comanche Tortilla Factory** is across the street, open on weekdays only.

Caro's, Rio Grand City. Caro's is a small, traditional Northern Mexico–Tex-Mex Café that's famous around these parts for freshly ground corn tortillas and freshly ground seasonings, as well as their puffed taco, stuffed with cooked ground beef, fresh tomato, and lettuce, and then fried. Their combination plate for hearty eaters includes an enchilada, rice and beans, guacamole, a 4-ounce rib-eye steak, and a grilled chicken breast. For dessert, pick up one of their homemade candies wrapped in plastic and heaped by the cash register. Located at 205 N. Garcia. Opens at 11am every day for lunch and dinner, lunch only on Sundays. ☎ **956/487-2255.**

Tigua Indian Reservation, El Paso. The green chili at El Paso's Tigua Indian Reservation is fiery enough to sear and the red chili is only slightly less incendiary. "White-eyes don't know how to make chili," one of the Tigua told us once. The casual cafeteria is open at lunchtime; the prettier, more formal restaurant, called Wyngs, is open in the evening, and both will dish up take-out portions if you bring your own dishes. Homemade bread baked in an outdoor adobe oven is sold in the cafe and gift shop area as well. Take Avenue of the Americas exit off I-10 south to Ysleta. Wyngs, ☎ **915/859-3916;** Tigua Cultural Center, ☎ **915/859-7913.**

Hotel Limpia, Fort Davis. On the town square in Fort Davis, the doughty pink limestone Hotel Limpia features dishes you would have expected to find in 1912, the year it was built, including homemade buttermilk pies, chicken-fried steak, fried chicken, and fresh catfish. They also serve the only alcohol in town, but you have to join a club to get it. ☎ **800/622-5517.**

The Little Diner and Tortilla Factory, Canutillo. Try the great gorditas—deep-fried masa patties filled with chunks of pork in a red chile sauce, or, as kids and some adults prefer, ground beef with chopped lettuce and tomatoes. They're about a dollar apiece. Homemade thick corn tortillas are 50¢ a dozen and thin corn tortillas, 40¢. For a salad, order avocado tapatia, chopped lettuce, and guacamole on a crisply fried tortilla, and sample the chile rellenos if you're still not full. Canutillo is just north of El Paso. To get there, take exit 6 off I-10 and follow the signs in Canutillo to 7209 7th St., or call ☎ **915/877-2176** for directions.

Julio's Café Corona, El Paso. Julio's originated in Juarez but also has a branch in El Paso at 8050 Gateway East, just off I-10 at the Yarborough exit on the south side. The house specialty is a dish from Zacatecas, Mexico, called *salpicon,* a cold shredded beef brisket with cubes of white cheese and chile chipotle served with sliced tomatoes, chopped lettuce, and sliced avocados—sort of a Mexican version of a Thai beef salad. Hot flour tortillas are served on the side. ☎ **915/591-7676.**

Best Buy Tortilla Factory & the El Paso Chili Company, El Paso. Best Buy is southeast of town, just off I-10 at 1110 Pendale Rd., open daily except Sundays from early morning until 5pm weekdays, 2pm Saturdays (☎ **915/595-6650**). To top them off, stop by the El Paso Chili Company, at 100 Ruhlin Court in downtown El Paso next to the river (☎ **915/544-3434**), for terrific cactus salsa, chile con queso, chile beans, or fajita marinade, all in jars to take away with you.

WILDLIFE WATCHING

Birds are a primary reason to travel the Rio Grande Valley, especially in winter. The **Santa Ana National Wildlife Refuge** near the town of Alamo claims the national record for the most bird sightings in a single day, and famed naturalist Roger Tory Peterson ranks it in the top 12 birding areas in the United States. To date, 390 species have been recorded on the 2,088 acres. Between Thanksgiving and Easter, a tram travels through the refuge on Thursdays through Mondays, making birding easy. You can catch it from the visitor center when you first enter the refuge. For the tram's schedule, call ☎ **956/787-3079.**

Even endangered **wild cats** may be glimpsed by a diligent searcher in the Santa Ana refuge. Four of the only five remaining wild cat species in the United States still live in the valley—cougars, bobcats, ocelots, and jaguarundi. Two other species, the jaguar and the margay cat, have disappeared during the past half century.

Laguna Atascosa National Wildlife Refuge, east of Harlingen on the lagoon inside Padre Island, hosts as many as 394 bird species during the year, notably in fall and winter when Canada geese, snow geese, and sandhill cranes can be seen, along with the great blue heron. On the mammal side, inhabitants include bats, armadillos, coyotes, foxes, mountain lions, ocelots, jaguarundis, bobcats, javalinas, and white-tailed deer. Both driving and walking tours can be taken. For information call ☎ **956/748-3607.**

The rare and distinctive 5-foot-tall **whooping crane** winters at Aransas National Wildlife Refuge north of Corpus Christi, but you may also see roseate spoonbills, ibis, egrets, herons, Canada geese, and diving ducks. We came across dozens of alligators sunning themselves by the edges of the water. Indigenous armadillos and javalinas can also be seen there.

The whole Rio Grande River Valley is dotted with wildlife refuges that celebrate the unique bird, plant, and animal life here. **Bentsen–Rio Grande**

HORSES, DOGS, BULLS & GOATS

Horse racing with pari-mutuel betting can be found at Sunland Park Race Track in El Paso (☎ 505/589-1131), where the season runs from October through May, and at Val Verde Downs, at the County Fairgrounds on 14th Street in Del Rio (call the Del Rio Chamber of Commerce at ☎ 830/775-3551 for current information about its 9-month season). In Nuevo Laredo, across the river from Laredo, off-track betting on live transmissions of horse and greyhound races is available at the Nuevo Laredo Turf Club, 1 block left from the international bridge, at Bravo and Ocampo streets (☎ 956/726-0549).

If you prefer going to the **dogs,** the Corpus Christi Greyhound Race Track, 5302 Leopard Ave. (☎ 800/580-RACE), usually includes discount tickets in a packet of coupons available at area visitor centers.

Bullfights are held seasonally across the river in the border towns of Mexico, particularly in Juarez, Piedras, Negras, and Reynosa. Those in Juarez take place most Sunday afternoons between April and October at the Playa del Toros on Avenida del Charro. Call El Paso Tourism at ☎ 800/351-6024 for information. Piedras Negras, across from Eagle Pass, Texas, occasionally holds bullfights during summer. Call Eagle Pass at ☎ 830/773-3224. Reynosa is across from Hidalgo, Texas. The McAllen Chamber of Commerce (☎ 800/250-2591) has Reynosa information.

If all other entertainment fails, you could head for the goat compound in Lajitas and share a beer with Mayor Clay Henry, Jr. (see "Off-the-Wall Attractions," above). ▤

Valley State Park, 2 miles south of Farm Market Road 2062, near Mission (☎ 956/585-1107), is a good place to see green jays, gold-fronted woodpeckers, white-winged doves, crested caracaras, and the omnipresent chachalacas. At **Audubon Sabal Palm Sanctuary,** 5 miles east of Brownsville (take Farm Market Road 1419; ☎ 956/541-8034), you can walk through the last remaining grove of native Texas palm trees, *Sabal texana*. Take your binoculars (and some insect repellent) on the nature trail walk from the visitor center and maybe you'll glimpse a green jay, black-bellied whistling duck, or hummingbirds.

On the Road

PADRE ISLAND NATIONAL SEASHORE

The only entrance to the paved road to the park is at North Padre Island outside Corpus Christi, and the paving ends in the parking lot of the Malaquite Visitor Center. The vast center of the island is accessible only to hikers and four-wheel-drive vehicles. No driving or camping is permitted on the sand dunes or in the sea grass.

South Padre Island, entered only from Port Isabel in the Brownsville area, has 34 miles of broad sandy beaches, the southernmost 5 miles adjacent to

South Texas Campgrounds

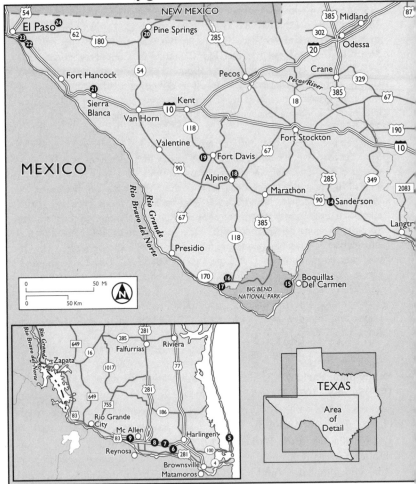

numerous low- and high-rise hotels, condominium towers, and restaurants. The road, Park 100, is paved for 15 miles, but the northern end has remained mostly undeveloped.

South Padre Island also has, according to local legend, some $62,000 worth of 19th-century gold coins and jewelry buried there by John Singer of the sewing machine family when the Civil War broke out. He and his wife, who lived in a driftwood house on the island about 25 miles north of the southern end, buried their valuables in the sand dunes, but when they came back after the war, the dunes had shifted and the gold was never found. In spite of, or perhaps because of, these rumors (and others about gold-laden Spanish ships running aground and sinking off Padre Island), the use of metal detectors or any other treasure-hunting devices is banned.

Today, tenacious wildflowers cling to the dunes, sea grasses blow in the gusty winds from the gulf, and collector-quality seashells sweep in with each tide—along with an unavoidable assortment of litter from Gulf of Mexico shipping.

A standard automobile may be driven 5 miles past the end of the paved road in the park on the beach when conditions allow—don't try this in your motorhome—and only four-wheel-drive vehicles are permitted past the Milepost 5 sign.

RVers without a tow vehicle would be wise to leave the rig in the park's parking lot and set out down the beach on foot. Stories abound of over-ambitious drivers miring down in the sand, and the park's newspaper cautions that "There are no services or means to contact anyone for help should you need it. The park service does not monitor CB radio, nor will it attempt to tow vehicles. Wreckers, when they can be induced to travel down island, cost hundreds of dollars."

Driving a vehicle of any sort is not permitted on the dunes, mud flats, or grasslands.

The seashore has an ongoing program to protect endangered sea turtle species found in the Gulf of Mexico—the Kemp's Ridley, loggerhead, hawksbill, leatherback, and green. If you see a sea turtle alive or dead along the beach, notify a park ranger of its location rather than approaching the turtle yourself.

Bird watching is exceptionally good here, with more than 350 species of seasonal and year-round residents.

Portuguese man-of-war jellyfish sometimes wash up on the beaches here. Give them a wide berth because their sting is extremely painful.

For park information, call ☎ **361/949-8068.**

Campground Oases on Padre Island National Seashore

Padre Island National Seashore's Malaquite Beach Campground. With 50 paved parallel parking or back-in sites along the beach, the campground is ¾ of a mile south of the ranger station visitor center (☎ **361/949-8068**) along the island's one road, and has picnic tables, toilets, cold showers, and a sanitary dump. No hookups, no reservations, and a 14-day maximum stay. Weekend ranger programs and ranger-led beach walks. Call ☎ **361/949-8175** for a recording detailing the island's weather conditions, which may vary from the mainland weather.

South Padre Island's Isla Blanca Park. Operated by Cameron County, the park is located on a 1-mile white-sand beach on the Gulf of Mexico and has 396 full hookup sites (30-amp electric), flush toilets, showers, and laundry, as well as bike trails, a marina, water park, swimming pool, and grocery store. ☎ **956/761-5493.**

Outdoor Resorts. Outdoor Resorts, 900 Garcia St. on South Padre Island, is a lavish, full-service RV resort where some 200 condo spaces (out of 898) are made available by their owners to overnighters. The big rig sites offer landscaping, cable TV, 30- and 50-amp electric, pool, spa, and boating activities. Rates are $25 to $30, about twice what some local parks charge, but in this world, you get what you pay for. Call ☎ **956/943-6449.**

THE TEXAS RIVIERA

The balmy Gulf Coast likes to call itself "the Texas Riviera," but don't expect to find "Lifestyles of the Rich and Famous." There's more Bubba-and-barbecue than Bardot-and-bouillabaisse.

Because of consistent moderate to high winds and expanses of open water, the **Corpus Christi** area has been named one of the world's ten best windsurfing destinations. It's not a bad place to fly a kite, either. And Corpus Christi—locals call it Corpus—has become one of the top snowbird (or "winter Texan") winter resorts.

Jean Lafite and his pirates hung around the area in the early 19th century, and General Zachary Taylor and his troops grouped here to invade Mexico in 1846. The oldest house, built in 1848, is called the Centennial House and has foundations made of shellcrete, a cement made from oyster shells. The city's sculptured 14-foot-high seawall was built after a 1919 hurricane by Gutzon Borglum, who went on to create Mt. Rushmore. The handsome wall is broken up with stairs leading down to the beach and opening up the view of the sea beyond.

If you take the free ferry over to **Port Aransas** on Mustang Island from Route 361 east of Aransas Pass, watch for the bottle-nosed dolphins that usually swim along with the boat.

Brownsville was the site of the last shots fired in the Civil War, a full month after Lee surrendered to Grant at Appomattox. But then the city always had problems. It was taken over briefly in 1859 by Juan Cortina,

TEXAS TALK

Blue norther: A fast-moving cold front in fall or winter that can cause temperatures to drop 50°F in half an hour.

Down island: The roadless part of Padre Island, where two-wheel-drive vehicles, especially RVs, can't go. If they try anyway, no tow trucks will come to pull them out for less than $500 or so.

Dry whiskey: Peyote cactus, also called mescal, which contains a variety of psychoactive alkaloids; it grows wild in Big Bend and is illegal to harvest or possess.

Maverick: An unbranded cow, named for Sam Maverick, who refused to brand his cattle so he could claim any unbranded animal on the range.

Tejas: A group of Indian tribes for whom Texas was named; regarded as friendly by the Spanish invaders until the Spanish wore out their welcome.

Texas ironwood: The mesquite tree, its wood used for barbecuing and smoking meats or making furniture, its long bean pods used for animal feed, flour, beer, or wine.

Texas strawberries: Pickled jalapeño peppers held by the stem and eaten whole in one bite.

Texas turkeys: Armadillos, used for food during hard times like the Depression; also sometimes used in chili, but not legally unless the animal has died from natural causes or been hit by a car.

Tinajas: Rock cavities that trap rainwater, a good place to look for game after a rainstorm in Big Bend.

Whoopers: Short for whooping cranes, the endangered species that winters in Aransas National Wildlife Refuge.

Winter Texans: RVers from colder climates, many of whom spend winter in the Lower Rio Grande Valley.

THE COMANCHE MOON

Old-timers on both sides of the Rio Grande call the first full moon of autumn the Comanche moon because that was when bands of Comanches would go out on raids into northern Mexico. They rode through Big Bend on what came to be called the Comanche War Trail, burning, pillaging, and taking anything they could use or sell, including hostages. After receiving the inadvertent gift of horses from the Spanish, they became perhaps the greatest horsemen the world has ever seen.

The only way the U.S. Army could figure out how to get rid of the Comanches was to decimate the tribe's basic food supply, so they called in the buffalo hunters. One man could kill 1,000 or more buffalo in 3 months. He was paid well for his skills.

either a Mexican bandit or a folk hero, depending on which side you were on, then occupied by the Confederates during the Civil War, after which it was taken by the Union, then the Confederates again.

Campground Oases on the Texas Riviera

Lake Corpus Christi/Mathis KOA Campground. The campground is open year-round by a lake near a 47-acre wildlife reserve, and isn't far from the King Ranch by Texas standards. Ninety-nine of the 137 sites have full hookups with 30- and 50-amp electric and all sorts of fishing and boating activities. To get there, take exit 47 if southbound or exit 40 if northbound from I-37 and follow the signs. It's on Route 3024, which parallels the interstate. For reservations, call ☎ **800/KOA-8601.**

Pioneer RV Resort. Located in Port Aransas, the Pioneer resort is the top-rated campground on the coastal bend, 14 acres of resort-style niceties, from a clubhouse with kitchen to fish-cleaning facilities. The 211 full-hookup sites offer 30- and 50-amp electric, big rig pull-throughs, and easy beach access for fishing and swimming in the Gulf of Mexico. It's south of Port Aransas on Route 361. For reservations, call ☎ **888/480-3246;** log on at www.gocampingamerica.com/pioneerrv.

On the Beach RV Park. Also in Port Aransas, On the Beach is not as highly rated as Pioneer but it is, as the name has it, on the beach south of town at 907 Beach Access Road 1A. Some 53 of the 59 sites are pull-throughs adequate for big rigs and they offer cable TV, 30-amp electrical, and city water. Call ☎ **800/932-6337** for reservations.

SeaWind RV Resort on the Bay. SeaWind is a comfortable resort with 134 wide sites, 30- and 50-amp electric, patio pads, optional telephone hookups, and post office boxes. Unlike most RV resorts with these features, it is a public park located in Kaufer-Hubert Memorial Park on the water at

Riviera Beach, reached off Route 77 at Riviera. They offer daily, weekly, and monthly rates; call them at ☎ **361/297-5738.**

THE LOWER RIO GRANDE RIVER VALLEY

A rich river delta, the 100-mile strip along the river called "the Valley" has a 340-day growing season and a new crop to harvest every month. Citrus was planted more than a century ago, and the area's ruby red grapefruit is cherished by breakfast eaters. Whether it's the grapefruit or the weather that draws 'em, so many visitors have flocked here lately that the valley has had to add a new telephone area code.

The town of **McAllen,** center of the winter Texan activity, was founded by a canny Scot who built a hotel here, then donated land for a railroad depot so the train would stop near his property.

Laredo is where Antonio Zapata, military leader of the self-proclaimed Republic of the Rio Grande, was captured and beheaded after 283 days of revolution against the government of Mexico's General Santa Anna. His head was displayed on a pole, which ended the dissension. Artifacts and history of that period are on display in the town's **Museum of the Republic of Rio Grande,** 10003 Zaragoza St. (☎ **956/727-3480**).

At **Los Ebanos,** near Mission, you'll find the last remaining hand-drawn ferry crossing the Rio Grande.

The town of **Alice** lights up for the entire month of December with more than 280,000 Christmas lights in a 2-block area in the middle of town.

Campground Oases in the Lower Rio Grande River Valley

Bentsen-Rio Grande State Park. This spot, on the river southwest of Mission down Route 2062, offers great camping for birders because of the variety that frequents the campground itself—the loudmouth chachalacas, gorgeous green jays, and black-bellied whistling ducks. Bring your own firewood and insect repellent. There are 77 full-hookup sites with 30- and 50-amp electric and a sanitary dump station, picnic tables, and barbecue pits. The entrance to the park is at the end of Route 2062. ☎ **956/585-1107.**

THE SOUNDS OF THE RIO GRANDE

All along the Rio Grande, listen for the unique local music called variously conjunto, norteno, tejano, or Tex-Mex, an odd mix of eastern European accordion, Mexican 12-string guitar, string bass, and trap drums, with electric bass and guitar, keyboards, and alto saxophone sometimes laid in. The sound is influenced by the polka, Mexican ballads, country/western, and salsa. The border towns between Brownsville and Laredo are good places to hear it.

A little up the Gulf coast, you'll find zydeco alive and well in Corpus Christi, where the Texas Jazz Festival takes place every year in early July.

TRAVEL TIP

If you want to venture into any of the Mexican border towns along the Rio Grande, park your RV on the U.S. side and walk across to go shopping or dining.

La Feria RV Park. Located at 450 E. Frontage Rd. in its namesake town of La Feria, this park is gated and has 152 full hookups with 30-amp electricity and fairly wide sites, plus lots of planned activities. Tents are not permitted. Call them at ☎ 956/797-1043.

Victoria Palms Resort. A really huge RV resort with more than 1,000 sites aimed at retirees and winter Texans. There are usually 500 available with full hookups, 30- and 50-amp electric, wide pull-throughs, city water, and satellite TV. Gilding the lily are an activities director, computer club, dance floor, heated therapy pools, full-service restaurant, post office, beauty and barber shops, free cable TV, card rooms, library, billiards rooms, live dance bands, ceramic shop, exercise room, and card rooms—and even motel suites if you're expecting visitors. Victoria Palms is located at 602 N. Victoria Rd. in Donna. Call them at ☎ 800/551-5303 for reservations.

Llano Grande Lake Park. Adjacent to the Llano Grande Golf Course in Mercedes, the park offers many of the same enticements to retirees as Victoria Palms, but is slightly smaller with only 805 sites, 338 of them with full hookups (30- and 50-amp). Bingo, movies, square and ballroom dancing, a rock shop, exercise and aquacize classes, and photo and art instruction could certainly fill the average day. Located at Mile 2 west in Mercedes. From 83 west, exit at Mile 2 west; turn left at light to entrance. Call ☎ 956/565-2638 for reservations.

Vaquero Village RV Park. Northwest of Laredo at Los Botines, the park has 14 paved pull-through sites with patios and full hookups with 30- and 50-amp electric. The office is modem-friendly. It's located off I-35 at U.S. 83, Exit 18, then north 2½ miles on 83. ☎ 956/417-4141.

Campground Oases on the Road to West Texas

Fort Clark Springs RV Park. A private park near Bracketville's Alamo Village Movie Location and historic old Fort Clark cavalry post, with 84 full hookups, 30- and 50-amp electric, cable TV, flush toilets, showers, and laundry. Just off U.S. 90 at Route 674. ☎ 800/937-1590.

Amistad National Recreation Area. At Amistad, a sprawling 85-mile-long man-made lake jointly owned by the United States and Mexico, two park campgrounds have a total of 36 sites suitable for RVs, with chemical toilets and cooking grills but no piped water or hookups. Year-round fishing; some shotgun and bow-and-arrow hunting are permitted, and there's scuba diving in the lake, with the best visibility in winter and early spring. It's located west of Del Rio on U.S. 90. ☎ **830/775-7491.**

Seminole Canyon State Historic Park. The home of ancient Indian pictographs and paintings on canyon walls. Those in Fate Bell Shelter are believed to have been painted 5,000 years ago; visitors can enter the area only with a ranger. Guided tours are offered year-round Wednesdays through Sundays at 10am and 3pm. The hike is moderately strenuous. Some 27 campsites with water and electric hookups (20- and 30-amp) and sanitary dumps on the premises are available, as well as hiking and mountain bike trails. Reservations are advised, especially during March through June. Call ☎ **915/292-4451** at least 4 weeks in advance. It's near Comstock, 30 miles northwest of Del Rio on U.S. 90, 8.6 miles west of the junction with 163.

Canyons RV Park. Canyons is the only game in town in Sanderson, Texas, so if you're looking for an overnight hookup between the Del Rio area and Big Bend, this is pretty much it. It offers full hookups with cable TV, long pull-throughs, and a beauty shop (just the thing after a long dusty day in West Texas). It's right on Highway 90, 1½ miles east of the junction with Route 285, so you can't miss it. (Anytime anyone tells us that, we miss it.) Call ☎ **915/345-2916** for reservations or in case you miss it.

BIG BEND NATIONAL PARK

A huge but lightly visited park because of its relatively inaccessible location, Big Bend sprawls over 1,250 miles of wildly varied terrain, with mountains, desert, river flood plains, and narrow, rocky canyons bisected by a sometimes turbulent Rio Grande.

The local Indians say this is where the Great Spirit put all the leftover rocks after he created the earth. The Big Bend pterodactyl, with its 51-foot wingspan, the largest flying creature known, lived here 65 million years ago.

While the park is home to 1,100 plant species, 75 mammal species, 6 amphibians and reptiles, and 400 species of birds, you'll see mostly roadrunners and jackrabbits, creosote bush, and ocotillo if you don't take a hike or spend some time searching them out. We photographed some exquisite beavertail cactus in vivid fuchsia bloom on a December visit. The daggertipped lechaguilla is a unique local plant you'll see frequently; it's a favored food for the javalina, or collared peccary, a wild pig found throughout the park. Endangered peregrine falcons are still found as well, protected during nesting season, when rafting through the canyons is forbidden.

Watch out for scorpions and centipedes, both nocturnal, that might be waiting inside your shoes if you leave them outside overnight. Rattlesnakes

Big Bend National Park

To Marathon

▲	Campground
🐾	Picnic area
= =	Primitive road (4-wheel drive only)
🏠	Ranger Station
- -	Unpaved road

and copperheads also inhabit the area, so wear high boots when hiking off the usual tourist trails. While mountain lions are rarely seen, there have been two attacks on people in recent years. If you encounter one, park rangers advise you to stay where you are, waving your arms, shouting, and throwing rocks. Never run.

There are two unusual industries that used to be in Big Bend—the second-largest cinnebar mine in the world, which produced liquid mercury until the veins ran out before World War II, and the unique candlelilla plant, whose wax was used for candles, chewing gum, and phonograph records until 1950. It's now illegal to gather it in the park.

RVers headed for Big Bend National Park should fill up their gas tanks before leaving U.S. 90 at Marathon or Marfa. There is a service station in the park, but hours of operation are limited.

A breathtaking drive that should not be missed by travelers with smaller RVs is the route through the **Big Bend Ranch State Environmental Area** along Route 170 between Presidio and Study (pronounced "stewdy") Butte. Some guidebooks discourage RVers from this route because of a 1-mile-long 15% grade between Lajitas and Redford, although we had no problem

Teepees are roadside picnic spots in West Texas.

driving it in our 27-foot motorhome. Roadside rests along the way sport individual teepee shelters housing picnic tables and grills.

Primitive hiking and backpacking, rafting, and canoeing are available in the environmental area. For information on them, plus the occasional 10-hour bus tours offered through the park's outback, visit the **Warnock Environmental Education Center,** located 1 mile before Lajitas on FM 170 (☎ **915/424-3327**).

Campground Oases Around Big Bend National Park

Rio Grande Village Campground. In Big Bend National Park, 20 miles southeast of the park's Panther Junction headquarters on the river. Adjacent to the 100 tree-shaded sites without hookups is a general store and a large parking lot with 25 hookups (30-amp) that is called **Rio Grande Village Trailer Park.** Stay here if hookups are essential. Otherwise, the campground is a much nicer place, with sites laid out in a circle like pioneer wagons under siege. Hiking trails set out from here, and there are flush toilets, pay showers, and a sanitary dump station. ☎ **915/477-2291** for the park concessionaire; ☎ 915/477-2251 for the park rangers. The campgrounds are on Route 118, 20 miles east of Panther Junction.

CAMPGROUND TIP

While the **Rio Grande Village Trailer Park** in Big Bend has 25 paved, full-hookup spaces that are booked on a first-come, first-served basis inside the adjacent village store, it is basically a parking lot with electricity and plumbing. If you can go self-contained for a couple of days, consider staying instead at the nearby **Rio Grande Village Campground** (see text above).

> ### INSIDER TIP
>
> In Big Bend National Park, the 7-mile, dead-end **Green Gulch Road** to Chisos Basin is limited to RVs under 24 feet or 20-foot travel trailers pulled by trucks or autos. The same recommendation is made for the **Ross Maxwell drive** between the Sotol Overlook and Castolon. If you have questions about which area roads may be inaccessible for your RV, ask the rangers at the Panther Junction Visitor Center, in the park at the junction of U.S. 385 and 118 (☎ **915/477-2251**). A road guide booklet sold at the center is also helpful.

Lajitas on the Rio Grande RV Park. Part of the old western town complex that includes a resort and golf course, as well as a beer-drinking goat (see "Off-the-Wall Attractions," above), Lajitas on the Rio Grande has 78 full hookups with 30-amps, flush toilets, showers, and laundry. ☎ **915/ 424-3469.** It's on Route 170, east of Terlingua and Big Bend.

Big Bend Motor Inn and RV Campground. This Terlingua campground offers a big dollop of civilization among the back roads of West Texas, with 126 full hookups, 30- and 50-amp electricity, satellite RV, laundry, groceries, food service, motel units, horseback riding, river rafting, and bird watching. Located at the junction of 118 and Farm Road 170. Reserve well ahead for the chili cook-off weekend in early November by calling ☎ **800/848-BEND.**

THE WILDS OF WEST TEXAS

"Not a stone, not a bit of rising ground, not a tree, not a shrub, nor anything to go by," Coronado is said to have sighed as he passed through West Texas en route to the seven cities of Cíbola, where he expected to find gold. He didn't realize what wonders he was missing en route.

One of our favorite West Texas towns is **Marfa,** site of the famous "Marfa ghost lights" (see "Off-the-Wall Attractions," above). It was also the primary location for the 1956 blockbuster film *Giant.* The El Paisano Hotel, listed on the National Register of Historic Places, has a photo display in the lobby with photographs of stars James Dean, Elizabeth Taylor, and Rock Hudson. The town was also the setting for the play and film *Come Back to the Five and Dime, Jimmy Dean, Jimmy Dean,* about the effect the filming of *Giant* had on the town. To complete the trio of trivia lore, Marfa also boasts the highest golf course in Texas, at a 4,882-foot elevation.

Another of our favorites is **Langtry,** perhaps the most famous of all the windblown, tumbleweed-tossed, one-horse Texas towns. Here Judge Roy Bean ruled as "the law west of the Pecos" and indulged in his admiration of voluptuous British actress Lillie Langtry by naming his combination saloon

FIVE WAYS TO ENTER TERLINGUA'S INTERNATIONAL CHILI COOK-OFF

Terlingua, west of Big Bend National Park on Route 170, claims fame as the birthplace of the chili cook-off competition, founded in 1967 by humorists Wick Fowler and H. Allen Smith. A later rivalry split the ranks of chili-heads, and now there are two annual cook-offs in Terlingua, on the first Saturday of each November, attracting more than 5,000 people. Here's a few ways to enter:

1. Enter a sanctioned CASI (Chili Appreciation Society International) cook-off and win one of the top three prizes. Call Vickie Childers at ☎ 806/352-8783 for details or log on to www.bigbend.com/casi/.

2. Accumulate 12 points at these cook-offs during the chili year (October 1 to September 30) for placing among the top 12 at each.

3. Show up in Terlingua on the first Sunday in November and see if one of the competing qualifying teams needs an extra helper at the CASI cook-off.

4. Cook your chili anyhow. While the judges will ignore you, you might get some attention from the chili-heads. Remember, no beans are allowed!

5. Look for the rival Terlingua cook-off, labeled the Original and held the same weekend behind Arturo White's store on Highway 170. It claims to be the original version and has less rigid rules. Call ☎ 903/874-5601 for a nitty-gritty rundown.

In early February, Terlingua holds a Cookie Chill-off—a competition for no-bake desserts—to raise funds for the Terlingua Foundation.

and courtroom The Jersey Lilly [sic] and claiming he had also named the town for her. Railroad records of the time show it was actually named for a construction foreman named Langtry, so the wily Bean probably cashed in on the coincidence.

Although often invited to visit by the judge, who knew her only from photographs in the popular press, the actress never got to Langtry until a few months after the judge's death in 1904, when she was welcomed effusively by his son and other locals. A nicely restored version of his Jersey Lilly saloon, where a defendant after a trial would be ordered to buy a round of drinks for the judge and jury, tells the whole story. Also here are a museum with dioramas and recorded tales of the judge, a visitor center, and a short nature trail through a cactus garden with area trees and plants labeled.

There are two replicas of the Jersey Lilly in south Texas, one in the **Whitehead Memorial Museum,** 1301 S. Main St., Del Rio (☎ 830/774-7568), where the judge and his son are buried on the museum grounds, the other in Pecos in the **West of the Pecos Museum,** 120 E. First St., (☎ 915/445-5076).

The interior of Judge Roy Bean's combination courtroom and bar in Langtry

Cary Grant slept in **Van Horn,** they say, at the old El Capitan Hotel, now the Van Horn State Bank. **Shafter,** a ghost of a town on U.S. 67 between Presidio and Marfa, was once the silver mining capital of Texas.

Presidio's original town name was Nuevo Real Presidio de Nuestra Senora de Betlena y Santiago de Las Amarillas de La Junta de Los Rios Norte y Conchos. It is also known as "The Hottest Town in Texas" and "The Onion Capital of the World."

Camels were trained for combat at **Fort Davis** in the Davis Mountains after an idea introduced in the pre–Civil War days by Jefferson Davis, then Secretary of War, whom the fort was named for. The camels worked out much better than mules in the desert terrain, except for an unfortunate tendency for the males to bite each other in the legs if left untended. When the Civil War started, the fort was abandoned, then taken over by the Confederates briefly before it was burned by the Mescalero Apaches. Although the U.S. Army rebuilt the fort after the war, they never followed up on the combat camel idea because Davis, having served as president of the Confederacy during the war, was considered a traitor.

Campground Oases in West Texas

The Lost Alaskan RV Resort. Mush, you Huskies! The Lost Alaskan is in the West Texas town of Alpine, about 4,000 miles south of Alaska but with plenty of year-round sunshine. With 71 full-hookup sites (30- and 50-amps), lots of shade trees, cable TV, bird watching, and a modem-friendly office, it offers almost everything the average Alaska RV park might except fishing. It's north of town just past the junction of 223. Call them at ☎ **800/ 837-3604.**

Davis Mountains State Park. Located on Route 118 west of the town of Fort Davis, the park has 27 full hookups, 61 with electricity (30- and 50-amps), and 88 with water. Spacious and well laid out, most are shaded by oak trees. There are flush toilets, showers, a sanitary dump station, and a playground. You may be visited in late afternoon by a family of mule deer or see a resident longhorn herd. When you camp here, imagine the families in covered wagons that used to stay here, an oasis in the middle of vast expanses of desert. The weather is comfortable for camping year-round. Reservations: ☎ **915/426-3337.** The Fort Davis National Historic Site nearby has been beautifully restored and offers a living history program in summer.

High Country RV Park. Located in Sierra Blanca at I-10's Exit 107 off Business Loop 10, High Country RV Park has 35 full-hookup sites with 30- and 50-amp electric, cable TV, modem access at your site and in the office, food service, and laundry. For reservations, call ☎ **915/369-2212.**

GUADELUPE MOUNTAINS NATIONAL PARK

One of our least-known national parks, this dramatic mountain range contains Guadelupe Peak, at 8,749 feet the highest mountain in Texas. The surrounding countryside is so wild that many of the peaks in the range are still unnamed.

Camping here is at **Pine Springs Campground** (see below), where the area is divided into tent camping sites in natural terrain with space for a tent and car parking and RV camping sites in a paved area like a parking lot with double-sized sites marked off and numbered. Some sites have a little dirt beside them and a chained-down picnic table, others are just wide parking sites. Hikers are cautioned not to park in the numbered RV sites. There are no hookups and camping is $7 a night, half-price for seniors with national park passes.

From the camping areas, some 80 miles of trails set out into the backcountry, but the rugged terrain should not be attempted by anyone except experienced backpackers. Permits are required for overnight trips; they can be obtained at the headquarter's visitor center, 4200 Smith School Rd., Austin (☎ **830/438-2656**). There is also a short, dramatic slide show about the park and its geologic and human history. The ruins of a **Butterfield Stage Station** and a museum of man's encroachment into this area at the **Frijoles Ranch and Museum** are other sights in the park.

A Campground Oasis at Guadelupe Mountains National Park

Pine Springs Campground. Located in Guadelupe Mountains National Park, 110 miles east of El Paso on Route 62/180 and up the hill into the park. There are paved, pull-through sites in the parking-lot style with rest rooms and hiking trails, but no hookups. They do not accept reservations, and pets are not permitted. For information, call ☎ **915/828-3251.**

EL PASO

Originally named El Paso del Norte by Juan de Oñate, the rich grandson-in-law of Cortes, the pass here was the main route between Mexico and the missions in San Antonio and East Texas.

The local Tigua Indians, many of them Christianized by the Spanish in the 17th century, settled at Ysleta when a mission was established there in 1680. Today the town, completely surrounded by El Paso, is the oldest continuously occupied settlement in Texas.

El Paso del Norte was eventually divided into the two border towns that are today called Juarez and El Paso.

Together in one compact area you'll find the handsome 1910 **Paso del Norte Hotel,** now the Camino Real, with its Tiffany stained-glass dome on Mills and El Paso; the **Plaza Theater** on West Mills Avenue, built in 1930, with a ceiling full of twinkling stars and a cloud machine; and the site of the old **Acme Saloon** on San Antonio, where outlaw John Wesley Hardin, considered the fastest gun in the west, was shot in the head (some say in the back of the head) in 1895. Both Hardin and his killer, lawman John Selman, are buried in the city's **Concordia Cemetery,** just north of I-10 at the U.S. 54 interchange on Yandel Drive. Hardin's grave is in the Boot Hill section of the graveyard near the gate to the walled Chinese section. He claimed to have shot 40 men. A newspaper of the time reported, "except for being dead, Hardin looked remarkably well."

The city's wild and woolly gun-slinging era ran from around 1880 to 1916, with everyone from trigger-happy Texas Rangers to Mexican revolutionaries engaging in daily brawls and shootouts. Neither of its most famous marshals, Bat Masterson and Wyatt Earp, were able to tame El Paso. One marshal, Dallas Stoudenmire, saw four men gunned down in 5 seconds (he killed three of them) only a block away from the spot where he would be shot dead a year later.

The **San Jacinto Plaza** in downtown El Paso was donated to the city in 1873 by a city parks commissioner who stocked a small pond in it with alligators; some of these reptiles continued to live there until the 1960s.

The **El Paso Museum of History** at 12901 Gateway West (☎ **915/ 858-1928**), is a good place to get filled in on local history with exhibits and dioramas. The museum is located in an easily accessible area just off I-10 with a parking area big enough for RVs.

The distinctive architecture of the **University of Texas at El Paso** was inspired by a National Geographic magazine photograph of a Bhutan lamasery because the Himalayas in the background reminded the first dean's wife of El Paso's mountains.

Fort Bliss, we are reminded, is bigger than the state of Rhode Island. It has three different military-related museums, The Museum of the Non-commissioned Officer, in Building 11331 at Barksdale and 5th streets in Biggs Army Airfield; The Air Defense Artillery Museum, in Building 5000 on Pleasanton Road near Robert E. Lee Road; and the Fort Bliss Museum, on Pleasanton Road and Sheridan Drive. All are free; call ☎ **915/568-5412** or 915/568-4518 for more information.

El Paso is also home to a classic Spanish drama festival, an international rodeo, a balloon festival, and a holiday tour of lights. Call the **El Paso Convention and Visitors' Bureau** (☎ **800/351-6024**) for details.

Campground Oases Around El Paso

Hueco Tanks State Historical Park. Located 32 miles east of El Paso on Road 2775 just north of U.S. 62/180, the park has 17 campsites with water and electric hookups and a sanitary dump station on the premises, as well as flush toilets, showers, a pond, and a playground. The *huecos,* or natural rock basins to trap water, have aided travelers in this arid terrain for centuries, and many, from prehistoric hunters and gatherers to '49-ers on their way to the California Gold Rush, repaid the hospitality with primitive rock drawings and initials. Ruins from a stage stop from the old Butterfield Overland Mail stagecoach have also been moved here. Rock climbing is a major activity except during summer, when the rocks are too hot to handle. Advance reservations: ☎ **915/857-1135.**

Mission RV Park. We'd like to be enthusiastic about Mission RV Park in El Paso since it is usually our first choice when we overnight there. We've tried all the other local campgrounds—great in winter, hot in summer, and dust-blown on windy days—and Mission gets the nod for location if you want easy access to downtown, the Tigua Reservation, or Juarez. It's at I-10 exit 34 on the north side next door to the El Paso Museum of History and offers 188 full hookups with 30- and 50-amp electricity, city water, cable TV, and a modem-friendly office. Call ☎ **800/447-3795** for reservations.

Cotton Valley RV Park. If you're in El Paso to enjoy the great steak dinners at Cattleman's Steakhouse (listed under "Five Special Splurges," above), you'd do well to choose this place, only 10 minutes away in Clint at I-10, Exit 42. It offers 30- and 50-amp electricity, and paved interior roads make it a good choice for big rigs. ☎ **915/851-2137.**

INSIDER TIP

Sign in on the **King Ranch Visitor Center** guest register and you too may get a Christmas card in the mail that reads, "The grass is short, the range is dry/Good prospects ain't a half inch high/The cows ain't fat, this verse ain't clever/But Merry Christmas, same as ever."

Six Special Side Trips

1. **Stop in at the King Ranch, Kingsville.** Located southwest of Corpus Christi, the King Ranch covers more than 825,000 acres and is three times bigger than the state of Rhode Island. It developed the Santa Gertrudis cattle breed. The Visitor Center, on the western edge of Kingsville off West Highway 141, showcases a small museum and conducts bus tours around the ranch daily. Open between 9am and 4pm Monday through Saturday, noon to 5pm on Sunday. ☎ **361/592-8055.**

2. **See the rare whooping cranes at Aransas Wildlife Refuge.** The flock of endangered 5-foot-tall cranes that winters here has grown from only 18 in 1937, when the refuge was established, to some 140 today. Local boats take you out from Rockport Harbor to see them, weather permitting. The season runs from December through March. Call ☎ **800/782-BIRD** for daily boat tours in season; adults, $25, children, $17. Other tour operators are at ☎ **800/338-4551** and 800/245-9324. Call for reservations for boat tours at various prices.

3. **Visit the no-bars Gladys Porter Zoo in Brownsville.** Endangered species from all over the world make up the exotic population. Ranked as one of the top ten American zoos, it's located at Ringgold and Sixth streets and is open daily from 9am to 5pm and accessible by wheelchair. Call ☎ **956/546-2177.**

4. **Visit John Wayne's Alamo.** Why fight traffic to get to San Antonio's Alamo when you could visit John Wayne's Alamo, the one built near Bracketville for his 1960 movie of the same name? The kids will like the imitation better because there are daily shootouts staged during summer. The village has 28 buildings, including a John Wayne Museum and a working ranch. Parts of the TV miniseries "Lonesome Dove" were also shot here. You'll find it 7 miles north of town on Route 674. Open daily except Christmas week. ☎ **830/563-2580.**

5. **Head 'em off at the canyon like the cavalry tried with the Apaches.** Fort Davis National Historic Site is an excellent re-creation of a 19th-century fort in a spectacular box canyon setting. It was home of the U.S. Ninth Cavalry "Buffalo Soldiers," African-American troops

nicknamed that by the Apaches for their courage and their dark curly hair. The fort presents a living history program in summer with costumed inhabitants, as well as Black History events in February. Most evocative of all if you're standing on the empty parade ground is the recording they play at regular intervals of bugle calls and the sound of calvary troops with jingling spurs and hoofbeats. Open daily, 8am to 5pm except national holidays, the fort has a museum and gift shop on the premises. In the Davis Mountains south of I-10 on Route 17. The Fort Davis Chamber of Commerce (☎ **800/524-3015**) can answer questions about the area.

6. **Hop the border into Mexico.** Bridges off U.S. 281 along the Rio Grande between Brownsville and Hidalgo will take you into Mexico. Here are some border crossing tips courtesy of the *Big Bend Area Travel Guide*:

- North Americans usually don't need a passport to go 15 miles or less into Mexico, but you will need proof of citizenship (such as an original birth certificate), plus a bit of traveler's Spanish.

- If you drive across an international bridge, your driver insurance from home is good for only 15 miles into Mexico.

- Time zones in Mexican border cities do not always match those across the Rio Grande in Texas.

- Never, ever, under any circumstances, carry a gun into Mexico no matter where you hide it in your vehicle; it is against Mexican law and you will be jailed immediately with no questions asked.

- If you have any questions about what you can legally bring back from Mexico, call U.S. Customs at ☎ **915/229-3349.**

WALKING TO MEXICO

Even if you decide to walk across one of the bridges into a Mexican border town for a few hours, you'll still need to have proof of citizenship with you—a birth certificate or passport. A driver's license is not considered adequate proof of citizenship.

Not Quite a Travel Quiz: The Horror, the Horror

Each of the trivia details listed below relates to a famous horror film below—
see if you can match them up.

1. James Arness, later to achieve fame and fortune as Marshall Dillon on TV's long-running series "Gunsmoke," appeared in the title role of what horror film?

2. In 1974, future TV star John Larroquette got no respect—and no billing—as narrator of what horror classic?

3. For what horror film did the star win an Academy Award, the only one ever given to an actor in this genre?

4. Sam Goldwyn's immortal line "A rock's a rock, a tree's a tree, shoot it in Griffith Park" might have been said to the producers of this horror classic, since the picture's climax was shot in Griffith Park's Bronson Canyon caverns.

5. Horror film buffs should recognize the Dunsmuir House and Gardens in Oakland, California, which appeared prominently in a James Bond flick (*A View to A Kill*) and several horror films, two of which are listed here.

6. A car driving across the Golden Gate Bridge is the setting for a climactic and emotionally—not to mention physically—draining scene in which scary film?

7. The sedate Washington, D.C., suburb of Georgetown is featured prominently in which horror film?

a. The Texas Chainsaw Massacre
b. Dr. Jekyll and Mr. Hyde
c. Burnt Offerings
d. The Thing
e. The Exorcist
f. Invasion of the Body Snatchers
g. So I Married an Axe Murderer
h. Interview with a Vampire

ANSWERS: 1 (d); 2 (a); 3 (b); 4 (f); 5 (c) and (g); 6 (h); 7 (e)

10

Arkansas, the Ozarks &
Branson, Missouri

ARKANSAS IS WHERE HERNANDO DE SOTO LOOKED FOR THE
Fountain of Youth, Jesse James held up stagecoaches, Al Capone got in hot
water, and saloon-basher Carry Nation buried her hatchet.

General Douglas MacArthur was born here, as was the fictional Lorelei
Lee from *Gentlemen Prefer Blondes* (remember Carol Channing in the show
or Marilyn Monroe in the film singing "I'm Just a Little Girl from Little Rock"?).
It's where Wal-Mart's Sam Walton started putting his fortune together in
Bentonville, where Don Tyson's chickens came home to roost in Springdale,
and where, once upon a more innocent time, every American boy's dream
toy, a Daisy air rifle (a.k.a. BB gun) was manufactured in Rogers.

Genial but corny radio comedians of the 1930s and 1940s like Lum and
Abner, who ran the Jot 'Em Down Store in fictional Pine Ridge, and bucolic Bob Burns perpetuated the hillbilly image of the Ozark dweller for the
rest of the nation. Less friendly and folksy was the image of then-Governor
Orval E. Faubus calling up the national guard to keep nine black students
from attending Little Rock's Central High School in 1957. (After his death,
Faubus's dramatic hilltop summer house in Huntsville was turned into a
bed-and-breakfast.)

Another Arkansan, Bill Clinton, went from governor of Arkansas to president of the United States and during two media-maddened terms was
instrumental in contributing new words and phrases like "Monicagate" and
"I feel your pain" to our lexicon.

Missouri, on the other hand, contributed Harry S Truman, Jesse James,
the Pony Express, JCPenney, Mark Twain, Belle Starr, General John J.
Pershing, kewpie dolls, the strongest earthquake in the lower 48 states, and
the world's tallest woman, 8-foot, 4-inch Ella Ewing. Walt Disney spent his
boyhood in Marceline, Missouri, and modeled Disneyland's Mainstreet USA
after his memories of it.

RVing the Ozarks

Highways throughout the Ozarks are slow and scenic. You can't count on making much time in an RV on the roads in the Ozarks, but you could use I-40 or I-30 to cover extra ground.

HITTING THE HIGHLIGHTS

A loop roughly 700 miles from Hot Springs would go to Fort Smith, Eureka Springs, and Berryville, then jog up to Branson, Missouri, back down to Harrison, Mountain Home, Batesville, Stuttgart, Pine Bluff, and Little Rock. That covers the main points of interest.

Because the area around the Ozarks is fairly compact, despite the many scenic highways you could manage to cover most everything in 8 or 9 days, leaving 3 days to get to and from this centrally located area. I-40 is the east-west interstate through Little Rock, while I-55 cuts into the eastern edge of Arkansas on its north-south route. I-30 runs diagonally across much of the state, through Little Rock to Texarkana on the Texas border.

GOING FOR THE LONG HAUL

The Ozarks are an appealing destination to spend more than 2 weeks exploring. You could settle into a luxurious campground like **DeGray Lake Resort State Park** (see "Campground Oases Around Hot Springs," below) and stay for the 14-day limit, then move on for a while and come back in a second 30-day period, with another 14-day stay permitted.

You could sign up for **crafts and music classes** at the Ozark Folk Center, take a weeklong **canoe trip** along the Buffalo National River, or hike some or all the 165 miles of the **Ozark Highlands National Recreation Trail.** You might even want to learn mountain biking or fly-tying.

Woman spinning at Ozarks Folk Center

Arkansas/Ozarks Highlights

Adult farm home of Laura Ingalls Wilder ❸
America's flea market ㉔
Bass Outdoor World ❷
Beaver Lake area ❾
Birthplace of the Bowie knife ㉜
Buckstaff Bathhouse ㉙
Bull Shoals Lake ⓴
Catfish 'N' ⑯
Coursey's Smokehouse ⑱
Crater of Diamonds State Park ㉛
Crescent Dragonwagon's Dairy Hollow House ⑪
Dardanelle Lake ⑮
DeGray Lake Resort State Park ㉚
Dick's Oldtime 5 & 10-cent Store ❻
Doe's Eat Place ㉟
Evening Shade, Arkansas ㉕
Feltner's Whatta-Burger Drive Inn ⑰
George Washington Carver National Monument ❶
Greers Ferry Lake ㉓
Hillbilly Smoke House ❽
Hollywood Wax Museum ❻
Lake Ouchita ㉘

Lambert's ❷
McClard's ㉙
Miss Laura's Bordello ⑫
Mount Ida,
    "Quartz Crystal Capital of the World" ㉗
Mount Magazine ⑭
Norfork Lake ㉑
Ozark Folk Center ㉒
Palace Hotel and Bath House ⑪
Pasquale's Tamales ㉞
Pea Ridge National Military Park ❼
Pearls Unique ㉖
Sam and Mary Walton's
    first five-and-10-cent store ❹
Serenity Farm ⑲
Silver Dollar City ❻
Stubby's Bar-B-Q ㉙
Stuttgart Agricultural Museum ㉝
Table Rock Lake ❺
War Eagle Bean Palace ⑩
World's largest Popeye ⑬

Take the scenic drives and side trips suggested in this chapter, and take time to chat with the people you encounter. Most people in the Ozarks seem to have both the time and inclination to converse as long you want. You may make lasting friendships—or maybe even stay longer than you'd intended. If you're a full-timer who likes to settle down for a month or two on a temporary job, we noticed a lot of HELP WANTED signs around Branson in shops, hotels, and restaurants. For even longer stays, Arkansas actively encourages retirees to consider settling in the state, citing its four-season climate and warm hospitality, plus "a quality of life fast disappearing in some other areas."

Travel Essentials

WHEN TO GO

Summer can get awfully hot in Arkansas, even in the mountains. Springtime from March through May is ideal, when the dogwoods, redbud, and wildflowers are in bloom. The hills come alive with autumn foliage in September, with good weather likely through October.

WHAT TO TAKE

Hiking boots, fishing tackle, binoculars, camera and film, rain gear, jacket, and a sun hat.

WHAT TO WEAR

The Ozarks are casual, even at the shows in Branson, to judge by the garb we saw being worn. In spring or fall, you'll want to layer your clothes as the day warms up or cools down. "Clean and decent" is the only dress code around here, along with random instances of "No shoes, no shirt, no service."

TRIMMING COSTS ON THE ROAD

Penny-pinchers will be delighted with the Ozarks, because prices, especially restaurant meals, are generally much lower than in most other areas. What you have to watch out for on this itinerary is to not get carried away buying tickets for too many country music shows in Branson or spending too long with the kids at Silver Dollar City.

Speaking of kids, you'll find big, **family-style meals,** often "all you can eat," at places like the Old Apple Mill Restaurant on the strip in Branson, and The Mine and Molly's Mill Restaurant in Silver Dollar City. The food is usually of the predictable buffet variety, but it's bounteous.

The other place you'll have to show restraint is shopping, because the handmade crafts are so pretty and appealing.

Plan to catch your own fish for dinner at least part of the time. Then go diamond-digging. Who knows? Maybe you'll strike pay dirt.

WHERE TO GET TRAVEL INFORMATION

Arkansas maintains 14 tourist information centers located at all the primary interstate and highway accesses to the state. You can contact the **Arkansas Department of Parks and Tourism** (☎ **800/NATURAL** or 501/682-7777; www.arkansas.com), for a copy of the Vacation Planning Kit. Campground guides and state park guides are also available.

For information about Branson, contact the **Branson/Lakes Area Chamber of Commerce,** P.O. Box 1897, Branson, MO 65615 (☎ **417/ 334-4136**). An information packet can be ordered by dialing ☎ **900/ 884-2726,** for a total charge of around $5, or log on at www.branson.com.

To get a free **Missouri Vacation Packet,** call ☎ **800/887-1234,** or access www.missouritourism.org.

DRIVING & CAMPING TIPS

- **Get a fishing license.** To get an out-of-state fishing license for Arkansas, call ☎ **800/364-GAME** or check www.agfc.state.ar.us. Children 15 and under do not need a license.

- **Reserve campsites ahead.** All state park campgrounds in Arkansas have water and electrical hookups for RVs, and each park sets aside a limited number of sites available by advance reservation. Call each park individually to reserve. Pick up state park brochures at the Welcome Center when you enter the state or check www.arkansas.com.

- **BYOB.** Parts of both Arkansas and Missouri are "dry," meaning they have restricted sales or no sales at all of alcoholic beverages, and even in communities where sales are legal, Sundays may be completely dry. Some communities that do permit limited alcohol sales may operate on a "private club" basis, whereby you pay to become a "member" and then can access the bar.

The Best Ozarks Sights, Tastes & Experiences

OFF-THE-WALL ATTRACTIONS

The bigger-than-life statue of Popeye, Alma, AR. In downtown Alma, Arkansas, a couple of freeway exits east of Fort Smith, a giant Popeye salutes "the Spinach Capital of the World," while a giant spinach can keep watch north on Highway 71. Alma's Allen Canning Company produces 56% of all the canned spinach in the United States. SEE the giant Popeye! SEE the world's largest spinach can! ☎ **800/NATURAL;** www.arkansas.com.

Crater of Diamonds State Park. A shovel and a bucket are all you need to dig for diamonds, but if you forget them, the park rangers will lend you equipment. The fee for digging is $4 a day for adults, $1.50 for kids 6 to 12.

Since the park opened in 1972, lots of diggers have struck pay dirt, including one who unearthed a 16-carat stone. Bear in mind that dirt doesn't stick to diamonds, so look for clean shiny little pebbles. Any you find, you can take home. There's also a 60-unit campground with hookups. Near Murfreesboro, the park is about 55 miles south of Hot Springs. From Hot Springs, take 70 west to Glenwood. Near Kirby, the road becomes Route 27. Take 27 to the center of Murfreesboro, drive around the courthouse, and pick up 301. The park is 2 miles south. ☎ **870/285-3113.**

Bass Outdoor World, Springfield, MO. Bass Pro Shops (or Bass Outdoor World) is one of the biggest tourist attractions in the state of Missouri, a vast sporting goods store and museum that carries everything you could imagine, from hunting and fishing licenses to fly-tying demonstrations to deer processing books like *Field Dressing and Skinning.* Four-story waterfalls flow inside the store, surrounded by craggy rock cliffs and mounted goats and bears that are masterpieces of taxidermy. There's an indoor shooting range where you can test your new rifle, a museum of the outdoors ($5.50 adults, $2.50 children, $4.50 seniors; open Mon to Sat 8am to 8pm and Sun 9am to 5pm) on the second floor, a barbershop, and a macho all-day eatery called Hemingway's with a 30,000-gallon aquarium stocked with sharks. They even stock boats and RVs under their own Tracker label. Open Monday through Saturday from 7am to 10pm, and Sunday from 9am to 6pm. Look for it at 1935 S. Campbell at the intersection of Sunshine, which is also U.S. 60 and Missouri Route 13 in Springfield. ☎ **417/887-7334.**

Birthplace of the Bowie knife, Washington, AR. The blacksmith shop where smithy James Black made the first Bowie knife is located at Washington Historic State Park in Washington, Arkansas, where guides in 19th-century garb will show you around. The knife, nicknamed the "Arkansas Toothpick" by Mark Twain, was made for Jim Bowie and patented by his brother Rezin. An example of Bowie's last such knife, believed to have been found on the Alamo battlefield, is on display at the Arkansas Territorial Restoration in Little Rock. The courthouse here was the Arkansas Confederate Capital during Civil War days. Washington State Park is on 278, 9 miles north of Hope, Bill Clinton's birthplace. ☎ **870/983-2684.**

The green duck-feather coat in the Stuttgart Agricultural Museum. Stuttgart proclaims itself the "Rice and Duck Capital of the World," and as evidence we offer this coat, made from the feathers of 450 mallards by the late Ruby Abel, a champion duck plucker who stumped the panels on TV's "What's My Line?" and "I've Got A Secret." Located on the Mississippi Flyway, Stuttgart's town slogan is "The duck stops here." Located at 911 E. 4th St., about 5 blocks from downtown. Open 10am to 4pm Tuesday to Saturday, 1:30 to 4:30pm Sunday. Closed Monday. Free admission. ☎ **870/673-7001.**

The Hollywood Wax Museum, Branson, MO. The Hollywood Wax Museum in Branson has something for everyone, from a tableau of the birth of Jesus to the boys from "Bonanza." They recently melted down Roger Maris to make a new Mark McGwire. Located at 3030 West Highway 76. ☎ **417/33 STARS** or 800/720-4110.

Dick's Oldtime 5 & 10-cent Store, Branson, MO. Also in Branson, Dick's is as genuine as the wax museum is ersatz, dating from 1929 and looking as though it hasn't changed since then. Its wood floors creak and its shelves are still stocked with Evening in Paris perfume, yard goods, popcorn, and bubble gum. Located at 103 W. Main St. in downtown Branson. ☎ **417/334-2410.**

Mount Ida, "Quartz Crystal Capital of the World." Dig for crystals by going through mine tailings with a pick and shovel, or do it the easy way— buy a crystal from one of the stores along U.S. 270. Maybe you can use it to contact Shirley MacLaine. Mount Ida is about 35 miles west of Hot Springs. A number of area locations offer a chance to dig for your own quartz crystals for a fee. Call the local tourist office at ☎ **870/867-2723** for specific locations. The town also celebrates an annual Charley Weaver Day in June. ☎ **870/867-2723;** www.mtidachamber.com.

Fort Smith's Belgrove Historic District. See the courtroom where "Hanging Judge" Isaac C. Parker sentenced 151 outlaws to death during the 21 years between 1875 and 1896; 79 of them were hanged, many on a unique gallows that could handle six men at the same time and sometimes did. In fairness to Parker, 69 of his deputy marshals were murdered during the same period, which gives a clearer picture of the times. Parker was considered incorruptible and scrupulously fair. The museum, under reconstruction at this writing, is on Rogers Avenue between 2nd and 3rd streets. The

The courthouse in Fort Smith's Belgrove Historic District

gallows is a reproduction, suggesting that the original might have worn out. ☎ 800/637-1477; www.fortsmith.org.

Miss Laura's Bordello, Fort Smith, AR. While you're in Fort Smith, visit Miss Laura's at 2 N. B St., the only bordello listed on the National Register of Historic Places. Today a visitor center is located in the famous turn-of-the-century establishment; it was under reconstruction at press time. ☎ 800/637-1477; www.fortsmith.org.

Evening Shade, Arkansas. Although the real town of Evening Shade (pop. 397) doesn't look like the fictional one in the Burt Reynolds TV series, it does have a new gym named for the actor, and some footage of the turn-of-the-century Victorian area found its way into the series here and there. Look for it on Route 167 about halfway between Ash Flat and Batesville in the north central part of the state. Visitors Center, ☎ 870/66-3833.

Sam and Mary Walton's first 5-and-10-cent store, Bentonville, AR. Opened in 1945, this modest store was the beginnings of the Wal-Mart empire and is now a museum and visitor center filled with 1950s and 1960s merchandise as well as 35 electronic displays. It's located in Bentonville, on the square on Main Street. Bentonville is in the northwest corner of Arkansas on U.S. 71. Wal-Mart Visitors Center, ☎ 501/273-1329.

Elephant trekking in Arkansas. Ozark Elephant Treks offers an elephantine educational opportunity with its 3-day elephant ride safaris through an Ozarks landscape. You get to feed, bathe, and care for your own Asian or African elephant. Call them at ☎ 501/589-3291 for details and reservations, or visit their Web site at www.hendrix.edu/other/elephant.

SIX SPECIAL SPLURGES

1. **Have a six-course dinner at Crescent Dragonwagon's Dairy Hollow House in Eureka Springs.** Crescent Dragonwagon's offers perhaps the best food in Arkansas—but bring your own bottle of wine. Local rainbow trout is usually on the menu of "Nouveau'Zarks cuisine." And as it says in some ads, "Not high-falutin', you'll see." Make reservations at ☎ 800/562-8650.

2. **Book a soak and massage at the classic Buckstaff Bathhouse.** The place dates from 1912 and is one of the few still open to the public on Hot Springs's bathhouse row. The usual treatment begins with a relaxing soak in a private whirlpool bath, then a choice of a needle shower or steam cabinet session, a cool-down in cold mineral water, and finally a rubdown. It's at 509 Central Ave. (☎ 501/623-2308).

3. **Visit America's flea market.** In the hamlet of Batesville, any weekend year-round starting on Friday afternoons, you'll find 142 booths

under one roof and plenty of free parking. 310 W. Main St. Batesville is on U.S. 167 northeast of Little Rock. ☎ **870/793-7508.**

4. **Splurge on a hickory-smoked, salt-cured country-cured ham.** Hillbilly Smoke House, open daily except Sundays till mid-afternoon at 1801 S. 8th St. in Rogers, on Route 71B in the northwesternmost corner of Arkansas, also sells sugar-cured, hickory-smoked bacon and smoked turkey. The ham lasts for months in a cool, dark place, so you can store it in the RV and take it home. ☎ **800/759-9439.**

5. **Spring for "the works" at the Palace Hotel and Bath House in Eureka Springs.** The Palace opened in 1901 and has been restored to its original style. "The works" includes whirlpool mineral bath, eucalyptus steam treatment, clay mask, and half-hour massage, for around $50. Open daily except 2 weeks at Christmas, 135 Spring St. ☎ **501/ 253-8400** for an appointment; www.eureka-springs-usa.com/lodging/ palace.atm/.

6. **Invest in unique Arkansas natural pearl.** Most of the stock at Pearls Unique, 102-D McLain St., Pratt Square in Newport, dates back to the 1920s. The freeform pearls come in shades of pink, peach, apricot, lavender, bronze, silver, cream, white, or gold and can be purchased loose or set into a piece of jewelry. Elizabeth Taylor and Richard Burton were customers, as well as the monarchs who don the Royal Crown of England. Call ahead for an appointment if you're a serious shopper. ☎ **800/637-3233** or 870/523-3638.

GREAT TAKE-OUT (OR EAT-IN) TREATS

McClard's, Hot Springs, AR. The pit barbecue at McClard's has been called the best in the United States, but McClard's itself simply claims "best in the state since '28." Locals say it's Bill Clinton's favorite. There's a "secret sauce" that was given to the family in 1928 to settle a $10 debt by a lodger in their motor court. The recipe is still used today and still kept in the family. Try the chopped pork, ribs, fantastic beans, homemade tamales, and tangy

SPEAKING OZARK

Granny woman: Nature-savvy herbal healer
Greening-up time: When the first wild greens can be harvested in early spring
A mess of sallat: These same greens cooked together in a pot with bacon fat
Vittles: Victuals
Yarbs: Herbs
Jokes you'll hear more than once: "Arkansas strawberries" are beans, "Arkansas wedding cake" is cornbread, and "Arkansas asphalt" is a dirt road.

coleslaw. Decor and table setting is paper and plastic. The house pièce de résistance, favored by most locals and ex-residents (including Bill Clinton), are the tamale spreads, a tasty, sloppy banquet of one (half-spread) or two (whole spread) tamales topped with corn chips, beans, chopped beef, cheese, and onions. 530 Albert Pike in Hot Springs. Call ahead for take-out at ☎ **501/624-9586.** They're closed Sundays and Mondays and don't take credit cards.

Catfish 'N', Dardanelle, AR. Catfish 'N' dishes up award-winning fried catfish fillets and hushpuppies along with French fries, coleslaw, pickled peppers, and tartar sauce. On our to-go orders, one plate had four catfish fillets, the other five, plus at least half a dozen hushpuppies apiece. If you go, skip the so-so French fries in favor of still more hushpuppies. You can also get fried or boiled shrimp and hot fruit cobblers for dessert. It's near the Arkansas River bridge on Route 7. Closed Mondays. ☎ **501/229-3321.**

The War Eagle Bean Palace, near Eureka Springs, AR. At a working, water-powered grist mill off Highway 12 on the War Eagle River, the War Eagle Bean Palace serves stone-ground grits with sausage, buckwheat waffles with sorghum, sausage gravy and biscuits at breakfast, old-fashioned pork and beans with slabs of cornbread at lunch. In the adjacent general store, you can buy the grits, cornmeal, sorghum molasses, hushpuppy mix, and buckwheat pancake mix turned out by the mill's rollers and packaged in pretty cloth bags. A statewide favorite is War Eagle Mill Fish Fry Coating Mix, first developed by radio/TV's "The Sportsman's Friend," Harold Ensley. The mill is open daily until 5pm, the restaurant till 4pm from March through December, and on weekends in January and February. It's on Highway 98 south of 12E between Eureka Springs and Rogers; from Eureka Springs, take Highway 23 south to 12E, then south on 98. ☎ **501/789-5343;** www.wareaglemill.com.

Pasquale's Tamales, Helena, AR. Pasquale's Tamales (what a name!) is a serious vendor of excellent Delta-style hot tamales hand-rolled in corn shucks with no preservatives or fillers. The first Pasquale came from Italy before the turn of the 19th century and swapped recipes with Mexican farm workers in the Delta. Helena is on the Mississippi south of Memphis, and Pasquale's is at 211 Missouri St. ☎ **800/ 390-3992.** They promise free samples to tourists. They're open weekdays from 11am to 5pm.

Doe's Eat Place, Greenville, MS. Doe's is a great, albeit funky, down-home steakhouse run by the Dominic Signa family. For us, it's worth the 100-mile detour from Helena south along the Mississippi to Greenville. Thick T-bones are cooked to perfection in old-fashioned wood-burning stoves, French fries are sizzled in cast-iron skillets, and iceberg lettuce becomes something delicious with the house lemon and oil dressing. Take your own wine (and corkscrew and glasses) and reserve your dinner spot in advance by calling

Doe's Eat Place, our choice for one of the best steakhouses in the United States

☎ **601/334-3315.** Don't expect a bargain just because the place has no decor. Doe's delta tamales are delectable too, just skinnier than Pasquale's and wrapped in parchment instead of shucks. Located at 502 Nelson St. in downtown Greenville.

Lambert's, Springfield, MO. Lambert's is "the home of the throwed roll," and if you think that involves a new kind of kneading, think again. It's about tossing food around the room. This highly popular restaurant touts all you can eat, and throws some of it (the fluffy, slightly sweet dinner rolls, for instance) at you. The rest is heaped on or around your paper place mat, such as the sorghum and butter that come with the rolls, the fried okra—well, you get the idea. Ham and white beans makes a good main dish, as does Lambert's crunchy fried chicken. Expect huge portions; we usually get one order to take out for the two of us. It's at 1800 West Highway J, off U.S. 65. ☎ **417/581-7655.**

Stubby's Bar-B-Q, Hot Springs, AR. We sampled the pickings at Stubby's, at 310 Park Ave. in Hot Springs, partly out of guilt, because we'd parked our motorhome in the vacant lot adjacent to the restaurant. But the smoky baked potatoes cooked in the pit, the meaty ribs baked along with a rich dark barbecue sauce, and the piquant coleslaw were quite tasty. ☎ **501/624-2484.** Stubby's II is at 3024 Central Ave.

Serenity Farm Bread, Leslie, AR. In downtown Leslie, 1 block east of U.S. 65, south of Harrison, Serenity Farm turns out sourdough bread made in the European style without artificial yeast or sugar, then baked in wood-fired ovens. Besides the French, whole wheat, and rye loaves, there are pizza shells, focaccia, and fruit-filled breakfast loaves. Baker David Lower uses only freshly milled flour from organically grown, stone-ground wheat, unrefined sea salt, and filtered water. These are tasty loaves to treasure! ☎ **870/447-2211.**

Coursey's Smokehouse, north of Leslie, AR. North of Leslie and outside St. Joe on Route 65, Coursey's still smokes meats the old-fashioned way; the family's original smokehouse sits in front of the modern one. Besides smoked bacon, sliced smoked ham, peppered beef, and smoked turkey, they sell homemade relishes, like a pepper chow-chow, and jams, such as wild blackberry. If you want, they'll make sandwiches for you. ☎ **870/ 439-2503.**

Feltner's Whatta-Burger Drive Inn, Russellville, AR. Feltner's cooks up the most famous hamburger in Arkansas, an award-winner for more than a decade. If you're hungry, order a double-double, which means double meat and double cheese. Whatta-Burger is at 1410 N. Arkansas St. ☎ **501/ 968-1410.**

WILDLIFE WATCHING
White-tailed deer are plentiful in the Ozarks, and you might even glimpse **wild turkeys,** especially around Yellville during the October National Wild Turkey Calling Contest.

In Hot Springs National Park, daytime visitors are limited to sightings of **squirrels** and **chipmunks,** with an occasional rabbit early or late in the day. However, at night the park is frequented by **raccoons, possums, skunks,** and nine-banded **armadillos.** Drivers may see gray foxes or an occasional white-tailed deer along the roadways. Also resident in the Ozarks but rarely seen are **black bears, cougars,** and **bobcats.**

On the Road

For all their remoteness and crags, the Ozarks, among North America's oldest mountains, are only about 2,300 feet high. "Our mountains ain't too high, but our valleys sure are deep," the saying goes. Made of limestone and heavily forested, they were named by French trappers, who called them "Aux Arcs" for a local Indian tribe (called variously Quapaw, Oo-gaq-pa, or O-ka-na-sa), which also gave its name to the state. Needless to say, every explorer spelled it differently, but the spelling that was adopted when Arkansas was admitted as a state in 1836 was from a French explorer named LaHarpe. By 1881, the pronunciation "Ark-an-saw" was dictated by the legislature.

Despite the vast number of authentic craftsmen and musicians that populate Arkansas these days—more than any other state, we would guess— there are still pockets of what one writer calls "painfully quaint" contrived roadside attractions. The natural beauty of the Ozarks, fortunately, even makes these diminish, except in the tackiest of strip mall mayhem.

Perhaps the blessing for latter day visitors is that Arkansas has been so poor all these years. During the Depression, many of the hill people gravitated to the cities to make a living, leaving parts of the Ozarks to revert to wilderness. In the 1950s, when everyone else was tearing down their beautiful Victorian and art deco buildings to put up characterless "modern" facades, lovely but declining old towns like Hot Springs and Eureka Springs made do with what they had because they couldn't afford not to. Beginning in the 1940s and continuing into the early 1970s, Arkansas was the playground for the U.S. Corps of Engineers, as more and more rivers were dammed, creating 600,000 acres of water area to attract recreational tourism. The sports-fishing season never closes.

The nation's first federally protected river park, the Buffalo National River Park, so named in 1972, was rescued after a decade of struggle by local and national environmentalists from threatened dam development by the U.S. Corps of Engineers. Today it's a major destination for canoers, kayakers, and family float trips.

HOT SPRINGS

Famous nowadays as the town where Bill Clinton grew up, Hot Springs was once the most fashionable watering hole in the Midwest, where the notorious (and peripatetic) Al Capone always booked the entire fourth floor in the Arlington Hotel, built in 1925, when he came to take the waters. The ever-restless Hernando de Soto is believed to have ventured here in his search for a fountain of youth.

The eponymous hot springs recycle rainwater that seeps into the ground, makes its way down to heated rock near the center of the earth, then reap-

One of the historic bathhouses in Hot Springs

pears some 4,000 years later naturally sterile at a temperature of 143°F, gushing out at a rate of 850,000 gallons a day. In 1921, the 47-springs area became **Hot Springs National Park,** the only national park within a city.

A few intrepid souls had been venturing over the rugged mountain trails to soak in the healing waters ever since Jefferson was president. As early as 1832, President Andrew Johnson set aside parcels of land around the springs as a federal reservation, which could be considered the beginning of the federal park system. By 1851, a town grew up around the springs, and local entrepreneurs filed claims and counterclaims around the springs, setting up crude canvas bath shelters and rickety wooden sheds around their springs and reservoirs.

After the Civil War, tourists began arriving by stagecoaches that were sometimes held up en route by Frank and Jesse James or the Younger brothers.

Town growth took off in 1874 when the railroad came in, and soon lavish hotels were being constructed for prestigious visitors, which came to include Theodore Roosevelt, Franklin Delano Roosevelt, Babe Ruth, Andrew Carnegie, Jay Gould, and Harry Truman.

Hot Springs Creek, which ran along the middle of the bath shelters, was channeled and roofed over in 1884, and a road, now Central Avenue, was laid down on top of it. By now the government was exerting some influence over the town and springs, although elaborate private bathhouses were allowed to be built. It wasn't until 1921 that Hot Springs became the 18th national park.

But when the gambling, always illegal but tolerated until the late 1960s, was closed down, Hot Springs settled into a quieter, gentler resort without the high rollers. The only action these days is at **Oaklawn Park,** when the racetrack season runs from late January to mid-April; the track is open year-round for off-track betting.

Bathhouse Row is a splendid parade of bathhouses and hotels along the city's Central Avenue. Most dramatic of all is Fordyce Bathhouse at 401 Central Ave., with a statue of an Indian maiden offering a bowl of spring water to de Soto and, above her, an 8,000-piece stained-glass skylight. Today it serves as the visitor center for the national park. Take a peek into the gymnasium, the 1915 version of a fitness center, with its punching bags, vaulting horses, and rings.

The Arlington Hotel is still open, with its own bathhouse reserved for guests. The 16-story art deco Medical Arts Building at 236 Central Ave. was for many years the tallest building in Arkansas. We liked the well-preserved old downtown stores with faded signs like UNEEDA BISCUIT 5 CENTS painted on brick side walls. The classic revival Mountain Valley Spring Water building won a National Preservation award from the National Historic Trust.

Hot Springs is also famous for its amphibious **ducks:** World War II landing craft converted to tourist transportation. Downtown at the "Duckport" you can board one to bop around Lake Hamilton over land and water.

Arkansas/Ozarks Campgrounds

Branson City RV Park ❷
Branson KOA ❸
Branson Stagecoach RV Park ❸
Branson's Musicland Kampground ❷
Cooper Creek Campground ❸
Crater of Diamonds State Park ⓮
DeGray Lake Resort State Park ⓭
Gulpha Gorge ⓬
Hot Springs KOA ⓬
Jacksonport ❼

Kettle Campgrounds ❺
Lake Dardenelle State Park ❾
Petit Jean State Park ❿
Queen Wilhelmina State Park ⓫
Rogers/Pea Ridge KOA ❹
Silver Dollar City Campground ❷
Springfield Missouri KOA ❶
Wanderlust RV Park ❺
Withrow Springs State Park ❻
Woolly Hollow State Park ❽

HOT SPRINGS RV WARNING

If you're in a motorhome with no tow vehicle, you'll find parking space very limited in the downtown historic district, Bathhouse Row, and the park visitor center. We found space on a weekend afternoon in the 200 block of Park Avenue at a large dirt lot behind Stubby's Barbecue and across from the Ramada Hotel. Note, too, that the park's Hot Springs Mountain Drive is restricted to vehicles less than 30 feet long.

Besides the ducks, visitors ride around in horse-drawn carriages and a free, wheelchair-accessible trolley that makes the rounds of the downtown area.

For folks who get restive confronted by a lot of hot springs and art deco architecture, there are more jejune pursuits, from a magic show, house of reptiles, and alligator farm to a passion play, a bathhouse musical advertised as "good clean fun," and a Josephine Tussaud Wax Museum with Bill and Hillary Rodham Clinton portrayed in wax.

Campground Oases Around Hot Springs

Lake Dardanelle State Park. A handsome hilltop park by a lake with ducks and swans. The 83 campsites are divided into three different locations; all have water hookups and all but four have electric hookups as well. Seniors get half-price rates. Shade trees, picnic tables, flush toilets, hot showers, fishing, water-skiing, and sanitary dump station. It's located near Russellville off I-40 at Exit 81, then west 4 miles on Arkansas 326. You can access it also from Dardanelle; drive 4 miles west on Arkansas 22. Call ☎ **501/967-5516.**

Petit Jean State Park. Near Morrilton between the Ozarks and the Ouchita mountains, Petit Jean State Park has 127 sites with water and 20- and 30-amp electrical hookups and a sanitary dump station, with 24 sites available by advance reservation. The park is named for a legendary French girl who disguised herself as a boy to follow her sailor sweetheart to America. The 95-foot Cedar Falls, a lake with pedal boating, fishing, hiking trails, and a rustic lodge are in the park. Also nearby, the Museum of Automobiles, founded by Winthrop Rockefeller, displays various cars in its collection in an ever-changing exhibit. President Clinton's 1967 Mustang convertible is sometimes on display. Call ☎ **501/727-5441** for reservations. The visitor's center is on Highway 154. From Morrilton, take Route 9 south to 154. From Russellville, take Route 7 south to Centerville and pick up 154.

Woolly Hollow State Park. Fifty miles north of Little Rock on Highway 285 near Greenbrier, Woolly Hollow offers 20 campsites near the lake among the trees with water and electrical hookups, grills, picnic tables, lake swimming, pedal boats, hiking trails, and the restored 19th-century log homestead of the Woolly family. From Little Rock, take I-40 north to Conway, then north on 65 to Greenbrier to Highway 285 East. Some reservations are available at ☎ **501/679-2098.**

Gulpha Gorge. Gulpha Gorge is the Hot Springs National Park Campground off Highway 70B east of town, with 43 paved, narrow sites, most of them shaded. The park has toilets but no showers and no water or electric hookups. There is a sanitary dump station. Campsites with tables and fireplaces are available on a first-come, first-served basis for a maximum of 14 days at a fee of $8 a night. For more information, call ☎ **501/ 624-3383.**

The Hot Springs KOA. The highest-rated RV park in the area, with 112 sites, mostly shaded, some suitable for big rigs. While sites are not wide, they are terraced with trees and landscaping, which gives a sense of privacy. Hookups include 30- and 50-amp electric, city water, and cable TV. It's modem-friendly and offers weekend pancake breakfasts. Located on Highway 70 east, about 3 miles out of town. Call ☎ **800/KOA-5903** for reservations.

DeGray Lake Resort State Park. South of Hot Springs near Bismarck, DeGray Lake is a huge watersports and fishing resort with lodge, campgrounds, golf, tennis, and marina. Its 113 sites have water and electrical hookups, flush toilets, hot showers, picnic tables and grills, and sanitary dump stations. Some sites offer scenic views. Boat rentals, including canoes and catamarans, 18-hole championship public golf course, pro shop with rentals, ranger programs, bicycle rentals, tennis courts, and restaurant. Each January, bald eagles migrate to the lake. Located on Highway 7. From Hot Springs, take Highway 7 south for 21 miles. Open year-round. Campsite reservations: ☎ **501/865-2801.**

Crater of Diamonds State Park. In Murfreesboro, Crater of Diamonds Park has 60 campsites with water and electrical hookups, laundry, snack bar, gift shop, and hiking trails. Here you can dig for diamonds, amethyst, garnet, jasper, agate, and quartz and take home whatever you find. The 35-acre field, the eroded surface of an ancient, diamond-bearing pipe, is plowed regularly to keep moving the stones to the surface. Digging tools are for rent at the park, and the rangers help you with identification. The park is located on Highway 301, 2 miles west of Murfreesboro. From Hot Springs, take Highway 70 south (becomes Route 27 in Kirby) to the center of Murfreesboro; go to the right of the courthouse and onto 301. Some advance reservations are accepted: ☎ **870/285-3113.**

Queen Wilhelmina State Park. Located on the border of Arkansas and Oklahoma at the top of the Talimena Scenic Drive (a.k.a. Highway 88 West) between Mena, Arkansas, and Talihina, Oklahoma. Besides the 35 campsites with water and 20- and 30-amp electrical hookups, there's a splendid contemporary lodge with dining room and 38 guest rooms, a mini-railroad, miniature golf course, and petting zoo. Why was this Arkansas park named for a Dutch queen? Because Dutch banks had financed the area's Kansas City, Pittsburg and Gulf Railroad, and local officials hoped the young queen would come to visit. She didn't, and the lodge shut down and fell into ruin a few years later. It was reconstructed in 1963 after the state park was developed, then burned in 1973 and was rebuilt in the present design. Call ☎ 800/264-2477 for reservations only; otherwise, call ☎ 501/394-2863.

OZARK FOLK CENTER: REAL MOUNTAIN MUSIC

"We don't allow counterfeit cornpone around here," folk musician Jimmy Driftwood is reported to have said when asked the difference between the folk music you hear at Mountain View's Ozark Folk Center and the hillbilly and country music shows staged elsewhere.

The Ozark Folk Center State Park, the first folk cultural center in the United States, was established in 1973 to preserve the cultural traditions of the mountain region, its music, dancing, handicrafts, and folkways. Open from May through October, the center is located near the town of Mountain View in northcentral Arkansas, in a beautifully wooded mountain area on a curved mountain road that is not difficult for RVs to negotiate. (To get there, take Highway 59/14 North-South or Route 66 East-West.) You park in a spacious parking lot at the base and take a free tram ride up a steep hill into the park itself.

Two dozen individual **craftsmen** are at work in the rustic cabins and outdoor areas, and they spend as much time answering questions and

At the Ozark Folk Center, local craftsmen, like this blacksmith, explain their craft.

explaining what they're doing as any visitor could wish. Items made are for sale in the individual cabins and in the center gift shop. There's a second country store with some crafts in the parking area as well.

The primitive furniture shop promises, "We measure our chairs to fit our customers." There's a lithographer and photographer, an old-fashioned print shop, candle maker, basket weaver, a chatty lady who makes dolls from cornhusks and dried apples, plus potters, spinners, weavers, and quilters. There's also a weathered schoolhouse and a splendid Heritage Herb Garden dedicated in 1986 by then Arkansas First Lady Hillary Rodham Clinton. You can sign up for classes from the craftsmen, make special orders, or buy crafts directly from them.

Music is presented at scheduled intervals throughout the day, with local musicians and clog dancers, many of them elderly, bantering among themselves before, during, and after each tune. In the evenings, musicians gather on the steps and lawn of the Stone County courthouse in the simple little town of Mountain View and play for their own pleasure and that of their listeners. Many of them come home from work, eat supper, wash up, and come on down for some picking and singing. No musicians performing at the center or gathering in the town square are permitted to use electronic amplification, and all musical selections must predate 1937. You may encounter musicians playing mountain dulcimer, autoharp, five-string banjo, fiddle, mandolin, or even spoons. Special gospel music concerts are offered on Sunday evenings.

In the center's restaurant, **traditional down-home dishes** like fried chicken, catfish, country ham, and cornbread are dished out family-style, and there's also a snack bar serving barbecue and smoked meat sandwiches, and hot fried apple or peach pies. A **60-room lodge** on the premises is open year-round,; call ☎ **800/264-FOLK** for information and reservations.

For **information** about the center, call ☎ **870/269-3851** or write to The Ozark Folk Center, P.O. Box 500, Mountain View, AR 72560. Closed in winter.

A Campground Oasis Near the Ozark Folk Center

Jacksonport. We recently discovered this charming historic state park in northeastern Arkansas and definitely plan to revisit in 2000 when the renovations on the stern-wheeler *Mary Woods #2* and the 1872 courthouse are completed. Both date from the days when Jacksonport was a busy county seat and steamboat port. When the railroad came into the area, the city fathers and the steamboat operators refused to give it right-of-way, so first the railway and then the county seat moved north to Newport and the steamboat port gradually faded away. The park is northwest of Newport, a half mile down Spur Road off Highway 69, and the 20 sites are on or near the White River, with water and 30-amp electric hookups. It's spacious and grassy, with plenty of mature shade trees. For information on hours and fees, call ☎ **870/523-2143.**

EUREKA SPRINGS

These long-lost Indian curative springs are believed to have been rediscovered in the 1860s by a doctor out hunting with his son. The boy's chronic eye infection healed when he washed his face in the water, and his father touted the springs as healing waters, selling "Dr. Jackson's Magic Eye Water" from "Indian Healing Spring."

In the days before antibiotics, this was hot news, and a community grew up quickly around the 63 springs, erecting boardinghouses to bed and feed health-seeking visitors. After the railroad arrived in 1883, construction really took off; more than 50 plush hotels were built in the next 3 decades.

Famed temperance crusader **Carry Nation** arrived in 1908 to settle down in retirement, naming her home Hatchet Hall after her favorite saloon-smashing tool. She died here 3 years later.

Today the entire downtown area is listed in the National Register of Historic Places. Streets are steep and narrow, and none of the 230-plus thoroughfares intersect at right angles. **Victorian houses** painted in lush colors and trims, many of them turned into bed-and-breakfast establishments, perch on the sides of hills, either leaning against a rocky backdrop or staring down into a canyon. A house might appear to be one-story from the front but have as many as five stories in back.

Crafts shops, art galleries, and superb inns and restaurants make Eureka Springs a romantic getaway for urban honeymooners, and the town has the largest and most upscale collection of **bed-and-breakfasts** in the state.

The town also has a long association with fundamentalism and **the religious right,** represented today by the long-running show *The Great Passion Play,* performed nightly in summer except Mondays and Thursdays, and by

Eureka Springs, Arkansas, has dozens of historic Victorians, many of them turned into bed-and-breakfast establishments.

<u>RV TRAVEL TIP: EUREKA SPRINGS</u>

Driving a large RV on the steep, narrow, one-way streets in Eureka Springs is not a good idea, especially in summer, except very early in the morning when there's little traffic. Hills are so steep that one church is entered through its bell tower. It's best to park and walk around. Some streets are restricted to vehicles under 30 feet.

a trio of attractions developed by the late Gerald L. K. Smith, a minister nicknamed "the old hatesmith" for his anti-Semitic publication *The Cross and the Flag* back in the 1920s—the 70-foot concrete statue of Christ that can be seen over the treetops, a Bible museum, and the Christ Only Art Gallery (now called the Sacred Arts Center), also on the premises with some 500 portraits of Christ. ☎ **501/253-8559.**

Campground Oases Near Eureka Springs

The Rogers/Pea Ridge KOA. West of Eureka Springs, this KOA is on U.S. 62, 10 miles north of Rogers, only a mile south of the Pea Ridge National Military Park, a major destination for Civil War buffs. The March 1862 Civil War battle here included two regiments of Cherokee Indians on the Confederate side under the command of Brigadier General Albert Pike; after 2 days of fierce fighting, they were forced to surrender for lack of ammunition, a loss that secured Missouri for the Union. The campground has 50 well-shaded sites with 30- and 50-amp electric. Call ☎ **800/KOA-6572** for reservations.

Withrow Springs State Park. Twenty miles from Eureka Springs on Highway 23 south, Withrow Springs park offers 25 campsites, 17 with water and electrical hookups. Located in a wilderness area along the bluffs of the War Eagle River, the park has a swimming pool, tennis, snack bar, bathhouse, and sanitary dump station. For reservations, call ☎ **501/559-2593.**

Kettle Campgrounds. At the north edge of Eureka Springs, on Highway 62 east less than a mile east from Passion Play Road, Kettle Campgrounds is an attractive, family-run private campground with 50 full- and partial-hookup sites shaded by pine trees, flush toilets, showers, sanitary dump, and laundry. They also promise a schedule of pig roasts, barbecue rib events, catfish fries, and Sloppy Joe nights. The campground can book tickets for the *Passion Play,* performed nearby, as well as other theaters in town. Ask when you call for camping reservations at ☎ **800/899-CAMP.**

Wanderlust RV Park. Located in Eureka Springs, Wanderlust is modem-friendly, has a trolley and bus stop on the premises, and, located at 468 Passion Play Rd., it's the closest RV park to the play. The 82 sites have 30- and 50-amp electric hookups, 40 pull-throughs, and some big rig sites. For reservations, call ☎ **800/253-7385** or log on to www.eureka-net.com/wanderlust.

BRANSON, MISSOURI

In 1913, this was a little town by a dam site when the White River was turned into Lake Taneycomo by the Powersite Dam. In the late 1950s, a second dam created Table Rock Lake above Lake Taneycomo, turning the latter into a cold-water lake, ideal for trout.

Today, this town of 3,706 that nobody ever heard of a few years ago is the second most-visited tourist area in the United States (after Orlando), claiming to attract more visitors annually than the Grand Canyon, Yellowstone, or Washington, D.C., and proclaiming itself "country music capital of the universe," just in case a few banjo-strumming Martians try to get into the act.

Branson has some 35 **live-music theaters** that play daily matinee and evening shows for the five million tourists who show up in season, from April through the end of October. Don't expect a late night, however, since the last show starts at 8pm.

After years on the road in one-night stands, country music stars like letting their fans come to them for a change, and are willing to invest a bundle in glitzy theaters in exchange for being able to stay home for a while.

Live country music shows actually began in Branson back in 1960 with the Baldknobbers Hillbilly Jamboree, but after Roy Clark, longtime host of TV's "Hee Haw," opened his own theater in 1983, followed in 1987 by Boxcar Willie, a down-home comic who whistled train noises while dressed as a hobo, things really took off.

Now traffic is usually backed up bumper-to-bumper all day every day along Route 76, moving along so slowly that you have plenty of time to see who's playing where through your RV windshield. Locals tell of wives who hop out of the car, go shopping, and return to the vehicle a block or two farther along.

Headliners who've performed in Branson read like a Grammy Award show, not only in country music but also in pop—Roy Clark, Johnny Cash, Loretta Lynn, Shoji Tabuchi, Glen Campbell, Wayne Newton, Mel Tillis, Andy Williams, the Smothers Brothers, the Osmonds, Bobby Vinton, Tony Orlando, Boxcar Willie, Micky Gilley, the Oak Ridge Boys, Louise Mandrell, and more. Many have their own eponymous theaters, including Tabuchi, the Osmonds, Yakov Smirnoff, Moe Bandy, Vinton, Williams, Newton, Tillis, and Gilley, and a breakfast or morning show is almost as common as a matinee.

WHERE TO GET AUTOGRAPHS IN BRANSON

If getting a country music star's autograph heads your want list for Branson, book a bus tour to the show instead of going in on your own. Many performers will climb on tour buses after the show to sign autographs.

Branson

MISSOURI

Branson

LEGEND
ⓘ Information
Congested route

Shepherd of the Hills Expressway

248

65

James F Epps Rd.

ⓘ ■ **Chamber of Commerce**

76

65B

Shepherd of the Hills Expressway

Roark Valley Rd.

Roark Valley Rd.

Downtown Branson ⓘ

265

The Strip

Mutton Hollow Pkwy.

Gretna Rd.

Wildwood Dr.

St.

Forsythe

Truman Dr.

76

76

ⓘ **The Strip**

Rosalee St.

Francis St.

ⓘ

76 ②

Frank Rea Blvd.

The Strip

⑤

The Strip

Green Mountain Dr.

Wildwood Dr.

Fall Creek Rd.

Lake Taneycomo

College of the Ozarks ■

Hollister ○

Safari Rd.

Fall Creek Rd.

③

Lake Taneycomo

④

65

Table Rock Lake

■ **Corps of Engineers Visitors Center**

165

165

265

Branson City RV Park	⑤
Branson KOA	③
Branson Stagecoach RV Park	③
Branson's Musicland Kampground	②
Cooper Creek Campground	④
Dick's Oldtime 5 & 10-cent Store	⑦
Hollywood Wax Museum	⑥
Sheperd of the Hills park	ⓘ
Silver Dollar City Campground	ⓘ
Silver Dollar City	ⓘ

I-1229

The 1890s **Silver Dollar City** (☎ 800/831-4386) is a 90-acre amusement park themed to look like an old mining town. (We're just not sure which old mining town.) It began as a traditional crafts village where some 100 costumed craftspeople blow glass, make brooms, weave baskets, grind corn, spin yarn, stitch quilts, and throw pots, but has accelerated these days with big-time amusement park rides, from high-speed roller coasters to wilderness toboggans, a train, carousels, Ferris wheels, and balloon rides, all of which seem designed more to coax money out of family pockets than celebrate the traditions of the mountains. Additionally, there are seven music venues, a dozen restaurants, street vendors, and 45 shops. Marvel Cave, the original attraction back in the 1960s when the park was built, is all but overshadowed. (Of course, those 500 steep steps down into the cave might have something to do with its waning popularity as well.) Singer Kenny ("The Gambler") Rogers is one of the owners of the park. From Branson, take Highway 76 west and turn left onto Indian Point Road.

The Shepherd of the Hills, an affectionate novel about the Ozarks written in mountain dialect in 1907 by Harold Bell Wright, has been turned into a summer-long pageant that's been running for more than 30 years with a cast of 75 plus horse-drawn wagons and a burning cabin. It's performed in a park just outside Branson. Call the Chamber of Commerce for information (☎ 417/334-4136).

Campground Oases in the Branson Area

Branson's Musicland Kampground. At 116 N. Gretna Rd., it's within walking distance of 18 shows and many restaurants and attractions. The 107 sites are mostly narrow but shaded, with gravel bed and 30- and 50- amp hookups. For reservations, call ☎ 888/248-9080.

Branson City RV Park. On the banks of the lake in downtown Branson at 300 S. Boxcar Willie Dr., it's within walking distance of the shopping areas and some music shows. The 350 hookup sites are divided between gravel and grass, with 20- and 30-amp electric. No reservations; the park accommodates visitors on a first-come, first-served basis. For more information, call ☎ 417/334-2915.

The Springfield Missouri KOA. One of the highest-rated KOAs in the United States is just west of town on Interstate 44, convenient to I-40 but far enough away you don't hear the traffic noises. The 78 sites with 30- and 50-amp electric are wide and most of them shaded with young trees. The office offers modem connections, and the adjacent 18-hole golf course provides senior discounts. Call them at ☎ 800/KOA-1228.

Cooper Creek Campground. If trout fishing is what lures you to Branson, check out this campground and resort on Upper Lake Taneycomo, which has boat rentals and lighted fishing docks. There are 91 mostly shaded sites with full hookups, flush toilets, showers, laundry, a store, and swimming pool. Located at 471 Fall Creek Rd. off Highway 76. Call ☎ 417/334-5250 for reservations.

Silver Dollar City Campground. Adjacent to the amusement park on Highway 265, with 134 sites with full or partial hookups. There are flush toilets, showers, sanitary dump, laundry, groceries, swimming pool, playground, and waterslide. From Branson, take Highway 76 west to 265. Call ☎ 417/338-8189 for reservations.

The Branson KOA. Also at Lake Taneycomo, the Branson KOA has trout fishing and boat rentals, is handily located 5 miles west of Route 65 on Route 165, quieter and less traffic-clogged than Route 76, the main Branson Loop road. While you can't walk to any in-town attractions, they do provide free shuttle transportation to selected shops and shows in season, but with a limited number of seats. Most of the 165 sites are full-hookup pull-throughs with 30- and 50-amp electric, and the office is modem-friendly. Open year-round, the park offers a free pancake breakfast daily. For reservations, call ☎ 800/KOA-7028.

RV TRAVEL TIPS: BRANSON

The heaviest traffic on Route 76 is around noontime, from 6:30 to 8pm, and again when the evening shows let out between 10 and 11pm. The center lane in the three-lane road is for turning only. You could also leave your RV at one of the campgrounds along the strip and ride the local trolley.

Branson Stagecoach RV Park. Five miles west of Route 65 on Highway 165, the Branson Stagecoach is out of town near the Showboat Branson Belle and Table Rock Dam. Many of the 41 sites can accommodate big rigs with 50-amp electric and sites 60 to 70 feet long. Call them at ☎ **417/335-8185** or visit their Web site at www.gocampingamerica.com/stagecoachstop/.

Ten Scenic Ozarks Side Trips

1. **Highway 7 through parts of the Ouchita and Ozark National Forests.** From Arkadelphia, south of Hot Springs, north to the Route 65 connection to Branson, Missouri, this route cuts a swath through some 200 miles of the most scenic parts of the Ozarks. Roadside shopping opportunities run from sincere arts and crafts to ersatz "silly hillbilly" items suitable only for friends who collect ugly souvenirs. National forest campgrounds without hookups and private campgrounds with full hookups are plentiful along the route. You go through Hot Springs, past Jessieville's crystal mine, Lake Dardanelle, Russellville, Pelsor with its 1922 general store, rustic Jasper and the beginning of the Ozark Highlands National Recreation Trail, and Pruitt with its "old swimming hole" and canoe launch on the Buffalo River.

2. **Sylamore Scenic Byway of the Ozark National Forest.** Between Mountain View and Mountain Home on Route 5, this is a short, lightly traveled, and beautiful route between the Ozark Folk Center and the Bull Shoals Dam area. Drive past small family farms, lushly wooded areas, villages like Calico Rock, and Lake Norfork's crystal-clear waters.

3. **The I-40 small town and Arkansas footnotes route.** I-40 (or its parallel, U.S. 64) between Conway and Fort Smith covers some fascinating towns and Arkansas footnotes, such as the historic Potts Tavern Inn in Pottsville (now a hat museum), Clarksville and its famous peaches, and Altus and the Arkansas wine country (don't expect the Napa Valley!). Morrilton is the gateway to Petit Jean State Park (see "Campground Oases Around Hot Springs," above) and its Automobile Museum, which sometimes displays Bill Clinton's 1967 Mustang

convertible. Atkins is "The Pickle Capital of Arkansas," with fried dill pickles and an annual spring Picklefest. Mount Nebo State Park has a campground with RV hookups and takes advance reservations (☎ **501/229-3655**).

4. **Ozark Highlands Scenic Byway.** Thirty-five miles along Route 21 from Clarksville north to Ponca, this route goes through the Ozark National Forest and over Boston Mountain, especially lovely in its fall foliage or spring dogwood bloom. There's an eight-site National Forest campground without hookups at Ozone, a trailhead for the Upper Buffalo Wilderness Area, and a canoe and kayak put-in for the Buffalo National River at Ponca.

5. **Mount Magazine.** The relatively modest 2,753-foot Mount Magazine is nevertheless Arkansas's highest point. There's a state park in development and some national forest campgrounds without hookups along 25-mile Route 309 between Havana and Paris. The vistas are great.

6. **Van Buren to Springdale by train.** Take a scenic journey by train aboard the Arkansas and Missouri Railroad Company in turn-of-the-century rail cars between Van Buren, on Route 71 on the Oklahoma border north of Fort Smith, and Springdale, on Route 71B north of Fayetteville. The train operates between early April and mid-November. ☎ **800/687-8600** for information.

7. **Arkansas Scenic Highway 74.** Famous for its Ozark vistas, Highway 74 meanders along some 35 miles from Kingston at the intersection with Highway 21 (also designated a scenic highway) to Fayetteville. There are numerous picnic areas along the way, and the route crosses War Eagle Creek.

8. **Civil War reenactments, etc.** A 50-mile loop out of Eureka Springs follows Route 62 to the historic Pea Ridge National Military Park, where costumed Confederate and Yankee troops re-create the pivotal Civil War battle every March. A detour into Rogers brings you to the first Wal-Mart store, founded back in 1945 and now a visitor center (see "Off-the-Wall Attractions," above). Out Route 12, head 13 miles east to War Eagle Mill, where grains are still ground by water-powered buhrstones for local farmers and sold to visitors, and the Bean Palace Restaurant serves up great breakfasts and lunches. Head past Beaver Lake State Park and back into Eureka Springs via Route 23 north.

9. **The George Washington Carver National Monument.** South of Joplin, Missouri, southwest of Diamond on County Highway V off Route 71A, the monument preserves the birthplace of the noted agronomist who promoted peanut butter; it's now a museum. From Joplin, go south on 71 and then 4 miles on V.

10. **The adult farm home of Laura Ingalls Wilder.** It was here, in the little town of Mansfield, Missouri, off U.S. 60 some 40 miles east of Springfield, that Laura Ingalls Wilder wrote the *Little House on the Prairie* series of books based on her childhood experiences in DeSmet, South Dakota. The books inspired the popular TV series. Adjacent is a museum on the city square. From Highway 60, there are signs as you near Mansfield. Take Highway A to the square. Open daily from March through mid-November. ☎ **417/924-3626.**

Trivia Quiz: High on the Hog

As all ham, bacon, and barbecue aficionados know, the humble hog, *suidae artiodactyla,* has entered our language in various ways, many of them distinctly non-culinary. See if you can root out the answers.

1. Porkopolis is the nickname of which American city famous for its pig production?

   (a) Peoria
   (b) Chicago
   (c) Cincinnati
   (d) Dayton

2. Speed aficionados fondly call their road-eating vehicles "hogs." Which types of vehicles are officially accorded the term in most dictionaries? (Select two.)

   (a) Big heavy motorcycles
   (b) Big heavy cars
   (c) Big heavy trucks
   (d) Big heavy RVs

3. Pork barrels are legendary troughs that benefit what type of American?

   (a) Barbecue fans
   (b) Hog farmers
   (c) Policitians
   (d) Diet pill producers

4. What famous American is most closely associated with the porkpie hat?

   (a) Comic strip hero Jughead
   (b) Porky the Pig
   (c) Pogo the Possum
   (d) Buster Keaton

5. What notable New York City landmark began as a 17th century pigpen that farmers built to keep their animals from straying?

   (a) Wall Street
   (b) The Bowery
   (c) Washington Square
   (d) Gramercy Park

6. Which classic sports accessory is made from pigskin?

   (a) A catcher's mitt
   (b) A football
   (c) O. J. Simpson's Isotoner gloves
   (d) None of the above

The Florida Keys (with Side Trips to the Everglades & Orlando)

KEY WEST IS "THE LAST RESORT," THE T-SHIRT CAPITAL OF THE world, the place Tennessee Williams called Cocalooney Key. A sign at the end of the dock says 90 MILES TO CUBA, and a local mayor once water-skied the distance to emphasize how close it is.

It's where fashion icon Calvin Klein bought a million-dollar Bird Cage, where "tea dancing" doesn't call for white gloves, and where Presidents Truman, Kennedy, Nixon, and Bush all lodged at the same upscale fishing lodge, Cheeca Lodge, although not at the same time.

The Keys are where the famous 1948 film noir *Key Largo* with Humphrey Bogart and Lauren Bacall was not filmed, although the Key Largo tourist office implies it was, but where the 1955 movie *The Rose Tattoo* with Burt Lancaster and Anna Magnani *was* filmed, much of it in author Tennessee Williams's own house at 1431 Duncan St., a fact hardly (if ever) mentioned in Key West.

It's where buccaneers swashbuckled and pirates pirated, where Harry Truman played poker, where ice from the frozen lakes of Maine was delivered by ship until well into the 20th century, where Anna Pavlova danced with the Russian Ballet, and Truman Capote danced with Tennessee Williams.

RVing the Keys

The first overland transportation to Key West was an extension of Henry M. Flagler's railroad, called "Flagler's Folly" or "the railroad that went to sea," which covered 25 miles of the distance on land, 75 miles over water.

The aging tycoon's railway began in 1896 when Flagler, content in north Florida's St. Augustine until the freeze of 1894–95 destroyed all the citrus and vegetables north of Palm Beach, decided to move south to get warm. The indomitable Julia Tuttle, a dowager hell-bent on bringing some attention to south Florida, sent a bouquet of fresh orange blossoms to Flagler from her farm, along with an offer to share the land the Tuttles and their neighbors, the Brickells, owned, in exchange for Flagler extending his railway down to their obscure village on the banks of the Miami River. He did, she did, and the rest is history.

From 1905 to 1912, Flagler took his rail line even farther south along the Florida Keys despite the naysayers, running 150 miles of track that connected the Florida mainland with the southern islands. He died shortly after it was finished, secure that his single biggest accomplishment, the famous **Seven Mile Bridge,** would also be his lasting monument. Although many of the railroad tracks were uprooted by a hurricane in 1935, the bridge remained.

Road engineers were able to use the old railroad pilings to support the 43 bridges of the **Overseas Highway,** which opened in 1938. While the original bridges and road have been widened or replaced, you can still see some of them, including the first Seven Mile Bridge, as you drive south. In April, the annual Seven Mile Bridge run sets out from Marathon with runners from all over the world.

For RVers, even those towing 40-foot travel trailers, these long, flat, over-water roads are good, free of curves and hills.

The drive from Miami to Key West is 3 to 4 hours each way if you don't stop—but if you don't stop, you have little reason to drive down.

HITTING THE HIGHLIGHTS

For most RVers, it's an easy matter to drive the Keys from Miami and back in 1 day, but that would defeat the best reasons for coming—a little sightseeing, a little fishing, a little beach camping, and fresh seafood (maybe some you caught yourself) for dinner.

Allow a half day for snorkeling at one of the national or state parks. Take a detour into Everglades National Park via Route 9336 from Homestead and walk the boardwalk trails with binoculars to catch sight of herons, egrets, white ibis, and alligators (see "Two Great Side Trips," below). Bicycle around Key West for a day and catch the highlights.

Who knows? You still might have time left over to take the kids to Disney World on the way back home (see "Two Great Side Trips," below).

GOING FOR THE LONG HAUL

If you wanted to hang around Key West for the season—and a lot of people do—you could spend some time creatively by signing up for adult courses in Spanish, bird watching, or swamp ecology at the **Florida Keys Community College** in Key West (☎ **305/296-9081**; satellite campuses located in Key Largo ☎ 305/852-8007, and Marathon ☎ 305/743-2133). Other classes offered sometimes include quilting, watercolors, or puppet theater.

Florida Keys Highlights

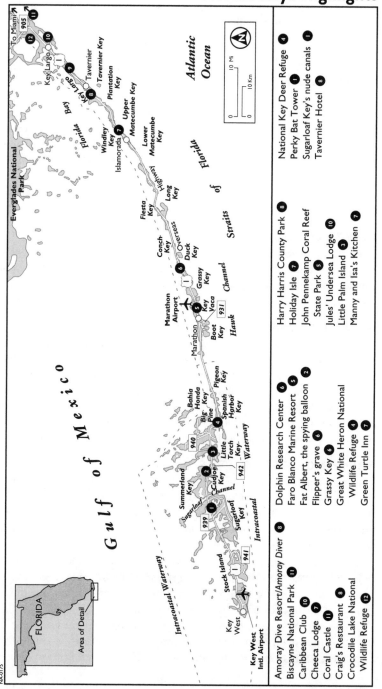

Amoray Dive Resort/Amoray Diver 8
Biscayne National Park 11
Caribbean Club 10
Cheeca Lodge 7
Coral Castle 11
Craig's Restaurant 8
Crocodile Lake National
Wildlife Refuge 12

Dolphin Research Center 6
Faro Blanco Marine Resort 5
Fat Albert, the spying balloon 2
Flipper's grave 6
Grassy Key 6
Great White Heron National
Wildlife Refuge 4
Green Turtle Inn 7

Harry Harris County Park 8
Holiday Isle 7
John Pennekamp Coral Reef
State Park 5
Jules' Undersea Lodge 10
Little Palm Island 3
Manny and Isa's Kitchen 7

National Key Deer Refuge 4
Perky Bat Tower 1
Sugarloaf Key's nude canals 1
Tavernier Hotel 8

NA-0175

Or you could extend your RV trip into a full Florida tour, spending the winter covering the state (although you should bear in mind that from Orlando north it can be chilly in midwinter).

Travel Essentials

WHEN TO GO

The weather is warm year-round, but the winter months have the most comfortable temperatures for bicycling around Key West. Late spring brings bright bloom to Key West's streets—bougainvillea, jacaranda, and oleander. Summer's muggy temperatures often combine with ferocious but brief thunderstorms; more actual rainfall comes down during fall and winter but rarely enough to bother your sightseeing. Hurricane season is early fall. Spring break can fill the streets of Key West with party-hearty college students—consider yourself forewarned.

WHAT TO TAKE

Binoculars, camera and film, powerful insect repellent to combat champion mosquitoes, a sun hat, and a good strong sunblock. If you've forgotten your sunblock or are running low, pick up some of the excellent locally produced Key West Aloe Sunblock at their shop/factory on Front Street.

WHAT TO WEAR

Shorts, flip-flops, and a tank top or T-shirt is the most common outfit on the streets of Key West on a hot day, but something a little more conservative is appreciated in upscale restaurants and hotels. If you splurge on a meal or overnight at Little Palm Island (see "Ten Special Splurges," below), take some casually elegant resort-type sportswear. Carry a sweater or jacket for rainy days or cool evenings in winter. If you forget anything, you can find plenty of well-made, moderately priced sportswear manufactured locally.

TRIMMING COSTS ON THE ROAD

The most expensive item for freewheeling RVers in the Florida Keys is a hookup site at a private campground, so if money is tight, head instead for the state parks and Everglades National Park for an overnight or two, easiest to get a site if you arrive early in the day on a weekday when public schools are in session.

Restaurant portions are very generous all over south Florida, so if you're not starving, plan to split some servings, especially the main dish. This is easiest to do tactfully as take-out. Or pick up a walk-around lunch or snack from the Cuban sandwich or conch-fritter vendors.

While Key West has a number of entertaining options, we find some of the attractions overpriced. The Hemingway House is almost as interesting from the outside as it is inside, and considerably cheaper. Unless you're a real Hemingway fan or a six-toed cat freak, we suggest you stop, take a picture, then walk on by.

The Conch Train and Trolley tours are cute, and ideal for day-trippers that come off the cruise ships, but you can cover the same territory by bicycle (rentals are easy to find if you're not carrying your own on the RV) or even on foot with some free walking-tour brochures from the tourist information office in Mallory Square. Since the open-air trolleys use amplified narration, you could tag along behind one on your bike and hear the same information the cruisers pay $18 for.

We've detailed some under-$10 attractions in Key West: See "Five Things to Do in Key West for $10 or Less," later in this chapter.

WHERE TO GET TRAVEL INFORMATION

Call ☎ **800/771-KEYS** within the Florida Keys area to be hooked up with a live multilingual operator who offers problem-solving assistance. The number is manned 24 hours a day, 7 days a week. Call **Florida Keys Information** (☎ **800/FLA-KEYS** in the U.S., or 800/GO-TO-KEYS; www.fla-keys.com) to get a $9.95 video and brochure. Call **Florida State Parks** (☎ **850/488-9872**) for a free state parks guidebook. **Florida RV Parks and Campgrounds** (☎ **850/562-7151**) supplies Florida campground info and will, upon request, send a camping directory of over 300 Florida listings with maps and 30 campground brochures.

DRIVING & CAMPING TIPS

- **"MM" means mile marker.** The letters MM, which you'll see throughout this chapter as well as on much printed material about the Keys, stand for Mile Marker, the most commonly used address. The markers are green-and-white signs posted on the right shoulder of the roadway. Miles are measured from Key West (MM 0) to the mainland (MM 126).

- **Don't mess with the coral.** The pieces of coral and the tacky coral souvenirs you'll see for sale in the Keys come from the Philippines. The taking of any Florida coral is illegal, and snorkelers and divers who harm it or the other protected marine species are subject to fines and punishment.

- **Don't mess with the manchineel tree, either.** The pretty little manchineel tree growing on the beach with its green and yellow leaves makes an inviting canopy in a rain shower. But watch out—it literally drips a burning, acid-like poison from its leaves as the rain runs down them. Never touch its tiny apple-like fruit, its thick milky sap, or its smooth gray trunk. Everything about it is poisonous.

- **Keep on your toes to get a campsite.** Privately owned RV parks in the Keys, particularly those that are so-called condo parks (meaning they sell memberships or time-share spaces), can be very pricey, especially at high season. Expect to be charged $30 or more for an overnight hookup. Even the state parks are expensive compared to their peers in other states. They make half their sites available for advance booking, but only within 60 days of your anticipated arrival. For first-come, first-served sites in the state parks, go in the morning and get your name on a waiting list if the park is full and come back in mid-afternoon to see if you've scored a space.

- **Call ahead about pets.** Many Florida recreation areas and state parks, as well as some private RV parks, have a "no pets" rule. Be sure to call ahead if you're traveling with furry friends.

The Best Sights, Tastes & Experiences of the Keys

OFF-THE-WALL ATTRACTIONS

Sunset at Key West's Mallory Square. A nightly happening in the sixties sense, with wandering fire-eaters, jugglers, mimes, contortionists, T-shirt sellers, fortune-tellers, and a bicycling woman selling brownies with the call, "Here come the fudge!"

Goofy graves, Key West. At the Key West Cemetery, seek out especially the stones of B. P. Roberts, 1929–79, engraved "I Told You I Was Sick" (at the end of Seventh Street); another that says, "A Devoted Fan of Singer Julio Iglesias"; the grave of Joseph "Sloppy Joe" Russell, Hemingway's favorite bartender, who died on a 1941 fishing trip with the author; and the famous "bound woman" on the grave of Archibald John Sheldon Yates (at the intersection of Angela and Grinnell). Most are stone vaults raised above the impenetrable coral base and the high water table. It's open dawn to dusk.

Lots of people, lots of beer, lots of fish. If you like to hang out in crowds with people who swap fishing stories and drink a lot of beer, Holiday Isle at MM 84 on appropriately named Windley Key is mobbed on winter weekends. If you don't, consider yourself warned. ☎ **800/327-7070** or 305/664-2321.

Duval Street, Key West. Key West conchs claim that Duval is the longest street in the world because it stretches from the Gulf of Mexico to the Atlantic Ocean, a distance of about a mile and a half. Late at night the pub-lined street is also the setting for "the Duval crawl."

Coral Castle, in Homestead. Located on U.S. 1 Southwest 286 Street on your way to the Keys, Coral Castle is a living testimony to "the magic and power of love." It seems a heartsick Latvian named Ed Leedskalnin was jilted by the 16-year-old girl he loved and so made his way to south Florida, where he spent the next 25 years carving 1,100 tons of coral into pieces of furniture and other unwieldy artifacts, including a table shaped like the state of Florida, all in memory of her. What he did for love, or rather how he did it, is still a mystery, since he weighed only 97 pounds and did not use any heavy machinery to move the blocks of coral. (One lunatic-fringe tome suggests he had the help of aliens from flying saucers.) When the neighbors came around to look, he stopped working until they left. He died of starvation, it's said, in 1951, with thousands of dollars hidden around the coral house. There's a Psychic Fair held on the grounds on the fourth Saturday of every month. ☎ **305/248-6344.**

Theatre des Seances, Key West. Take in some table-rapping or a message from your late great-aunt Tess in Key West's Theatre des Seances. A 19th-century parlor at Porter Mansion at 429 Caroline St. at Duvall Street is the location for Victorian-era "love and romance spirit seances." Reservations are required, at least from the world of the living, and one or more seances is scheduled each evening at 8pm. Call ☎ **305/292-2040** for details.

Flipper's grave, Grassy Key. Yes, that Flipper, whose real name was Mitzi. A 30-foot high monument to a mother and baby dolphin is also on the site, on U.S. 1 at MM 59 on Grassy Key, as is the **Dolphin Research Center** (see "Ten Watery Wonders," below). ☎ **305/289-1121.**

Fat Albert, the spying balloon, Cudjoe Key. Fat Albert bobs around 2,000 feet above Cudjoe Key (when he isn't blown off his tether) watching for drug dealers in small planes and boats heading across the Florida straits. His avoirdupois is made up of millions of bucks of electronic surveillance gear.

The Perky Bat Tower, Sugarloaf Key. Not a celebration of energetic nocturnal flying mammals, but rather an earnest effort to lure same to devour the mosquitoes that were the scourge of the area. Built on Sugarloaf Key in 1929 by an eager real estate promoter named R. C. Perky, the tower was supposed to bring in bats so Perky's resort would be bug-free. Perky, his casino, cabins, and fishing resort are long-gone, but the bat tower still stands. And the mosquitoes are still flying. Located on U.S. 1 near MM 17 on the Gulf side.

Tupperware World Headquarters and Gatorland, Kissimmee. We're usually torn between the two, both located near each other on Route 441 between Orlando and Kissimmee. Since Tupperware no longer gives tours of their headquarters, though, we now head for Gatorland with its alligators and crocodiles. You walk into the gaping jaws of a plaster alligator, then watch live alligators leap out of the water to snag a mouthful of chicken dangling overhead in the Gator Jumparoo show. Old-time gator wrestling, an alligator breeding march, even a smokehouse offering tidbits of smoked gator ribs and deep-fried gator nuggets are highlights of one of the few old Florida roadside attractions remaining amid the Disney/Universal virtual world. Gatorland is at 14501 South Orange Blossom Trail, open daily 9am to 6pm. Call ☎ **800/393-JAWS** for details.

TALKIN' CONCH: A KEYS GLOSSARY

Conch (konk): A native of the Keys; named for a chewy gastropod that inhabits local waters

Eyebrow house: A dwelling where the second-story roof overhangs the windows

Fretsaw: Gingerbread trim on houses, much of it applied by ship's carpenters from termite-resistant hardwood

Hardwood hammock: Not a bed slung between two posts, but a dense grove of small hardwood trees growing on a limestone reef in a marshy area at a slightly higher elevation so they form humps

Mangrove: Small, broadleaf, evergreen tropical trees growing in marshes or tidal shores with much of their root systems exposed

Shotgun house: A long hall you could shoot a bullet through that runs from front to back through a house

Square grouper: What local fishermen call bundled bales of marijuana bobbing in the water, thrown overboard by drug smugglers when the Coast Guard is near

Stranger: Everybody on the Keys who's not a conch

Tourist tree: The gumbo-limbo, whose peeling red-orange bark looks like the results of a bad sunburn

TEN SPECIAL SPLURGES

1. **Book a stay on Little Palm Island.** Book a day or two at the most laid-back and romantic, not to mention the most expensive, resort in the Keys, reached by launch from Little Torch Key at MM 28.5 by guests whose reservations are in the computer. Snorkeling, bonefishing, sunset sailing, and fine dining are some of the popular activities. At night you snuggle down in one of 30 South Pacific–style ersatz grass huts that miraculously conceal a Jacuzzi tub, minibar, and queen-sized bed. Non-resident guests may reserve for lunch or dinner. ☎ 800/343-8567.

2. **Have lunch at Louie's Backyard.** In Key West's varied dining scene, most visitors regard Louie's Backyard as the obligatory dinner out, but we like lunch better, sitting at outdoor tables with a grand view of sailboats gliding past. A warm fried-chicken salad (spears of chicken atop greens) is a house special, and fresh grilled fish are accompanied by Cuban black beans, fried plantains, and lime wedges. Reserve well ahead at this popular spot, located at 700 Waddell Ave. (☎ 305/294-1061). Musician Jimmy Buffet used to eat here when he lived in the big white house next door.

3. **Shell out for a lazy open-air tour of Key West.** The colorful Conch Train and the Old Town Trolley both leave from Mallory Square and offer 90 minutes of corny, good-natured jokes aimed at the over-50

cruise ship day-trippers. You'll get good views of 60 or so must-see spots around town. Tickets for each are $18 adults, $9 children 4 to 12.

4. **Expand your imagination with a Ghost Tour of Key West.** It leaves nightly from Noah's Ark, 416 Fleming St. (☎ **305/294-9255** or 305/293-8009). You'll be led on a lantern evening stroll down Key West's shadowy lanes and discover the ghosts, ghouls, and legends of this haunted island paradise. Tours go out year-round, but space is limited and reservations are required. Tickets are $18 adults, $10 children under 12.

5. **Take a cat to see the coral.** The *Amoray Diver,* a motorized catamaran from Key Largo's Amoray Dive Resort, can take 49 snorkelers or 34 scuba divers out to the Key Largo National Marine Sanctuary for some coral reef viewing. Cost is $54.50 per person and includes tank and weights. Reservations are requested. ☎ **305/451-3595.**

6. **Take a snuba tour.** A combination of diving and snorkeling in which the air source is in a surface raft and the diver goes only 20 feet down, snuba tours offer underwater sightseeing at John Pennecamp Coral Reef State Park and Key Largo National Marine Sanctuary. No dive certification is necessary. Tours ($35 to $70) are 45 minutes to a half day. Call them in Key Largo at ☎ **305/451-6391.**

7. **Head out into international waters for a little gaming.** The 150-passenger casino boat *Pair-a-Dice* sails from Key Largo's Holiday Harbor Marina on 4-hour midday sailings (11am to 3pm for early birds; night owls can book a 6:30 to 11pm cruise). The midday sailings are $12 a head plus a $12 port tax and include lunch; evening cruises go for $20 a person plus $12 port tax and include dinner. Both feature live entertainment in addition to the ship's slot machines and blackjack, craps, and poker tables. In deference to the boat's 92-foot length, there are also mini-roulette wheels and mini-baccarat tables. ☎ **305/451-9665.**

8. **Take a night off from the RV to sleep in a lighthouse or aboard a houseboat.** The kids will love it. Faro Blanco Marine Resort in Marathon, built in the 1940s, offers both options. Call ☎ **800/759-3276** for information.

9. **Drop by Cheeca Lodge for seafood.** If you want to splurge on a politically correct seafood meal, this Islamorada hotel restaurant is your kind of place. The ever-eco-aware lodge took all conch dishes off its menu several years ago because taking the mollusks in U.S. waters is illegal; therefore, all conch is imported from the Bahamas and is "neither indigenous nor fresh," says Chef Dawn Seiber, a native of the Keys. She serves Jamaican seafood soup instead of conch chowder and buys much of her fish and shellfish from seafood farms. Polish off a

Fort Jefferson from the air

piece of passion-fruit pie for dessert. Located on U.S. 1 at MM 82. Call for a reservation at ☎ **800/327-2888.**

10. **Take a seaplane down to Fort Jefferson.** Head to the Dry Tortugas, 68 miles west of Key West, to see the remains of the 19th-century brick fort that was the Civil War prison for Dr. Samuel Mudd, who reset John Wilkes Booth's leg, broken on his jump to the stage of Fords Theater after he assassinated Abraham Lincoln. Mudd was accused of conspiring in the crime, although it is generally believed he was innocent of any knowledge of it. He was released in 1867 after a heroic stint taking care of 270 men who came down with yellow fever in an epidemic at the isolated fort. While the visit itself is free, getting there costs around $159 a person for a half-day trip. Call **Key West Air Service** (☎ **888/FLY-FORT**) or **Seaplanes of Key West** at ☎ **305/294-0709.** You can look down into the clear water from the plane and see numerous shipwrecks below, as well as swimming sharks and rays. The fort itself is as eerie and haunted a place as you'll ever see under a hard blue sky and dazzling sunlight.

GREAT TAKE-OUT (OR EAT-IN) TREATS

The cheeseburgers at Jimmy Buffet's Margaritaville, Key West. Those at Jimmy's restaurant are almost as famous as the song of the same name; most customers order margaritas as well. 500 Duval St. ☎ **305/292-1435.**

The Key lime pie at Manny and Isa's Kitchen, Islamorada. You can buy by the slice or the pie to eat in or take out. They grow the Key limes out back. If it's mealtime, sample their Cuban black bean soup or conch fritters too. Located at MM 81.6. ☎ **305/664-5019.**

Seafood at the Half-Shell Raw Bar. A longtime local favorite, with paper plates, plastic forks, and a big turnover of tables around mealtime. They sell shrimp from the local fleet, as well as clams and oysters on the half-shell and a tasty conch chowder. The cracked conch—breaded and fried conch steak—is yummy. It's on Margaret Street in Key West. ☎ **305/294-7496.**

The Sloppy Joes at Sloppy Joe's, Key West. The sandwich may or may not have originated here, but it's a good story. They serve the Original Sloppy Joe as well as the Sloppy Joe Quesadilla, if you're really curious. The bar is hard to miss; just follow the cruise ship day trippers to 201 Duval St. ☎ **305/294-5717.**

Weekly Thanksgiving dinner at Pepe's, Key West. Pepe's is a resoundingly local Key West eatery, there since 1909 and noted for huge breakfasts and haphazard decor that includes everything from Christmas lights to nude paintings. Every Thursday night a Thanksgiving dinner is served, along with oysters from Apalachicola Bay (safest to eat them cooked). It's at 806 Caroline St. ☎ **305/294-7192.**

Cuban sandwiches at the Five Brothers Grocery, Key West. Get them to take out. Alternatively, try the hot, deep-fried cornmeal bollitos with a *buchi,* a Cuban coffee similar to espresso. At the corner of Southard and Grinnell. ☎ **305/296-5205.**

Street food, Key West. Key West street vendors proffer conch fritters, Cuban coffee, hot dogs, piña coladas, and dolphin sandwiches (no, not Flipper, but the fish Hawaiians call mahi-mahi).

Turtle steak, etc. at the Green Turtle Inn, Islamorada. Years ago, the Green Turtle Inn was the first (and last) place we ever knowingly ate alligator, and, yes, it does taste sort of like chicken. These days they serve farm-raised turtle steaks and chowders, as well as their own canned conch chowder, politically correct turtle soup (they use North Florida river turtles), and Key lime pie filling to go if you want to stock up the RV. It's old-fashioned, good-natured, eclectic, and eccentric, as well as usually crowded, with only a faint whiff of tourist trap. At MM 81. ☎ **305/664-9031.**

"The world's best fish sandwiches" at Craig's Restaurant, Tavernier. At least that's what they promise. It's good if you're looking for a quick and casual lunch. At MM 90.5. ☎ **305/852-9424.**

The fresh grilled seafood at Kelly's, Key West. The full name of the place is Kelly's Caribbean Bar, Grill and Brewery. It's on Whitehead and Caroline, just off Duval, and the grilled seafood is topped off with a boutique brew. ☎ **305/293-7897.**

Traditional Native American dishes at The Miccosukee Restaurant, near Shark Valley. Located on Tamiami Trail (U.S. 41) near Shark Valley, Miccosukee serves traditional Indian dishes like fried catfish, pumpkin bread, and Indian fry bread (crunchy deep-fried bread dough), which can be topped with cooked ground beef and garnishes to make an Indian taco. ☎ 305/223-8380.

Fresh seafood at Disney's Boardwalk resort. The Flying Fish Café makes an evening out special with fresh seafood that's beautifully prepared and served. It's not cheap, and reservations should be made well ahead of time, but the food is so much better than the other Disney venues, perhaps because it's operated by a chef from outside the Mouseworks. Before or after, stroll along the boardwalk and pretend you're in Atlantic City. 1800 Epcot Resorts Blvd., Buena Vista, FL. ☎ 407/939-5100.

TEN WATERY WONDERS

1. **John Pennekamp Coral Reef State Park.** Near Key Largo and part of the Florida Keys National Marine Sanctuary, this is a 78-square-mile underwater park made up of reefs like those that formed the keys. The living coral colonies are endlessly fascinating for divers and snorkelers; there are underwater observation rooms and glass-bottomed boats for those who want to keep their heads above water. The reef has more than 50 forms of coral and 500 species of tropical fish, and is the only living coral reef in the continental United States. It's at Mile 102.5. ☎ 305/451-1202.

2. **Islamorada.** Located on Upper Matecumbe Key, Islamorada is a popular fishing resort area, with the Theater of the Sea offering dolphin and sea lion shows plus a shark pool and aquarium; Lignumvitae Key State Botanical Site (☎ 305/664-2540), displaying rare lignum vitae trees, an extremely dense wood that can outlast steel; and Indian Key, a formerly settled key where John James Audubon visited in 1832. The latter two are uninhabited islands that can be toured with park rangers, but you have to get there by local boat service. Robbie's (☎ 305/664-9814) charges $20 for adults, $15 for kids. Boat departures are timed to coincide with tour times.

3. **Grassy Key.** Located near Marathon Shores, Grassy Key is the location of the Dolphin Research Center at MM 59, where visitors can call on the first day of each month for a reservation to swim with dolphins later that same month. The swim cost is $110 per person, but if you just want to visit the center, without the swim (and without an appointment), the admission price is $15. ☎ 305/289-1121 for reservations.

4. **Harry Harris County Park.** A wide expanse of sandy beach with palm trees and picnic tables facing the Atlantic, in Key Largo at MM 92.

If you have your pet along, he'll have to stay in the RV. ☎ **305/852-7161.**

5. **Crocodile Lake National Wildlife Refuge.** This is where they keep the largest collection of crocodiles in the United States, up to 500. Located on Key Largo, the refuge represents a victory of environmentalists over real estate developers. While visitors are not encouraged at this time, Route 905 north of its junction with U.S. 1 on Key Largo goes through the edge of the refuge, with three dead-end roads—Madeira Drive, Tamarind Drive, and Poinciana Drive—going a short distance into the area. (See "Miracle of the Keys," below.) ☎ **305/451-4223.**

6. **Jules' Undersea Lodge.** Ever want to spend the night underwater? Then make a reservation at Jules' Undersea Lodge, the world's first underwater hotel, with two bedrooms below the surface and a price starting around $200 a night per person for a party of four. Beginning divers and snorkelers are welcome, they say. It's located at 51 Shoreland Dr., MM 103.2, in Key Largo. Call ☎ **305/451-2353** for information. No alcohol is permitted unless you're on your honeymoon, in which case champagne is permissible. What we wonder is how can they tell if you're really on your honeymoon?

7. **Biscayne National Park.** Biscayne National Park is an aquatic park with 181,500 acres of islands and reefs. Several concessionaires offer boat tours from the park itself. Two shallow-draft, glass-bottomed Reef Rovers set out from the park's Convoy Point headquarters daily and skim lightly over the reefs. Afternoon snorkel and scuba trips (with rental equipment available) last 4 hours, departing at 1:30pm, while morning reef sightseeing tours start at 10am. Reservations required: ☎ **305/230-7275.** Headquarters are 9 miles east of Homestead at 9700 SW 328th St.

8. **July Underwater Music Festival, Big Pine Key.** Divers listen to an underwater symphony at Looe Key National Marine Sanctuary. For details, call ☎ **800/USA-ESCA.**

9. **Bahia Honda State Park, Bahia Honda Key.** The park has one of the best sandy beaches in the Keys, allowing you the luxury of wading out into the water on sand instead of—ouch—coral. 12 miles south of Marathon. ☎ **305/872-2353.**

10. **Dog Beach, Key West.** Dog Beach, near Louie's Backyard, is the only beach in Key West where owners and dogs can swim together, while the so-called **nude canals** in an abandoned real estate development on Sugarloaf Key's Sugarloaf Boulevard are where clothing-optional sunbathers gather to catch some rays between dips.

WILDLIFE WATCHING

There are several wildlife refuges in the Keys, each named for the species that inhabits it. For example, the new **Crocodile Lake National Wildlife Refuge** on North Key Largo has the single largest population of **alligators** in the United States, with as many as 500 in residence. Alligators are the most obvious reptiles, and the one a casual visitor is most likely to see, if he/she is patient enough to watch a floating log in a murky pond to see if that bump on it has an eyeball.

Less frequently seen are the state's numerous nonpoisonous snakes, and the three poisonous ones. Most deadly is the dainty, pretty orange-and-black-banded **coral snake,** but as an old swamper told us once, "He's gonna have to chew on you a long time before you die." Keep your eye out for cottonmouth moccasins sunning on a stretch of boardwalk in a swampy area, or diamondback rattlesnakes in a palmetto patch or hammock.

The shyest of Florida's indigenous fauna is the **manatee,** a 1-ton, plant-eating sea mammal that is also called a "sea cow." Legend has it early sailors thought these were mermaids, but anybody who made a mistake like that must have been away from women a long, long time. The biggest threat to the dwindling manatee population is the south Florida boater with his whirring propellers that tear into the mammal's tender flesh.

The best place to see the manatee up close is at **Homosassa Springs State Wildlife Park,** where a number of them are in residence, either lazily floating around in the water or scarfing down lettuce from their underwater "salad bar." You'll also see Florida alligators and crocodiles and learn the difference between the two during one of the park's excellent Animal Encounters programs. The park is about 90 miles west of Orlando on the Gulf of Mexico off U.S. 19 (☎ **352/628-5343**).

The reclusive and extraordinarily beautiful **roseate spoonbill,** although rarely seen, nests in spring. They were once virtually extinct because feather collectors killed them and sold their wings for hats and fans, not realizing the brilliant orange and rose feathers gradually fade when the bird dies. Audubon didn't realize this either, apparently, as he depicted the bird's foliage as pink. He commented that they were hard to kill and their flesh was oily and bad-tasting.

Especially in spring, you'll have easier sightings of **osprey,** who usually nest atop utility poles (their nests are big and klutzy looking), and **white egrets,** who stalk haughtily in marshes and ponds. We spotted several from the wooden walkways in **Everglades National Park.** Check in at the Royal Palm Visitor Center, 3 miles past the park entrance; a campground without hookups is nearby. A number of walking trails, most of them over boardwalk, take you into the swamp.

At Big Pine Key, delicate little 30-inch **Key deer,** like miniature white-tailed deer, roam in the **National Key Deer Refuge;** go early in the morning or just before dusk for the best chance of sighting them. There are fewer than 300 left in existence. Stop off at the rangers' office at Pine Key Shopping Center (with the Winn-Dixie), near MM 30.5 off U.S. 1. They'll give you a brochure and map of the area (**☎ 305/872-2239**).

Also on this key is the **Great White Heron National Wildlife Refuge.** These big, graceful birds are among the most beautiful of all seabirds. Freshwater ponds on the key have led some geologists to suggest it may once have been part of the Appalachian Mountain range. The refuge is located at MM 28–31. For information, call the National Key Deer Refuge (see above).

On the Road

KEY LARGO

Key Largo, the classic 1948 Humphrey Bogart and Lauren Bacall film, was shot almost entirely on a Hollywood soundstage, but that didn't stop the town of Rock Harbor from taking the name Key Largo after clearing it with the U.S. Postal Service in 1952, then building a cottage industry around the film's stars, none of whom were in town during the filming. The boat used in *The African Queen,* for instance, is proudly on display at the Holiday Inn Key Largo, and, according to local tourist handouts, is "a nostalgic addition to Key Largo's unique old film atmosphere." More recently, the owner added the *Thayer IV* from *On Golden Pond,* which was shot in New Hampshire.

Ironically, the only location in town where some second-unit footage for *Key Largo* was actually shot was the funky Caribbean Club Bar at MM 104.

The old **Tavernier Hotel** in the downtown district claims to be the first hotel in the Keys, and managed to survive the great, unnamed Labor Day hurricane of 1935. Back then, weathermen didn't do cute stand-ups in front of cameras, so tropical storms didn't need names.

The African Queen in Key Largo

Old hands say the upper Keys have the best fishing, especially around Marathon and Islamorada, the latter usually billed as Sportfishing Capital of the World, but visitors with visions of Hemingway dancing in their heads keep driving south to Key West before booking a boat.

Bonefish and permit are in shallow waters of mangrove islets on the Gulf of Mexico side (but not as easy to catch as they look), while marlin and sailfish are deep-water dwellers that require a captain and crew to take you out into the Atlantic. Charter boats and guides can be found at Garrison Bight Marina on Palm Avenue in Key West or at one of the charter fishing fleet companies on U.S. 1 just south on Palm Avenue.

KEY WEST
Part One: Cayo Hueso Becomes Key West

The 8-square-mile coral island used to be called Cayo Hueso (which means "bone key"), the name deriving from piles of human bones found by early visitors. No one is quite sure where the bones came from, but they were already in place when the first non-Indians, a bunch of bloodthirsty buccaneers, hit town. Ponce de León had probably discovered the Keys in 1513 as he worked his way north looking for the Fountain of Youth, which he found in St. Augustine.

In 1815, Cayo Hueso belonged to Juan Pablo Salas of St. Augustine under a Spanish land grant, but when Florida became part of the United States in 1821, he sold it to John Simonton, an American businessman, for $2,000. Simonton called in the U.S. Navy's Anti-Pirate Squadron, drove out the pirates, and put the place under military control. From that day forward until 1974, there was always a Navy base on Key West.

Old houses of Key West

Florida Keys Campgrounds

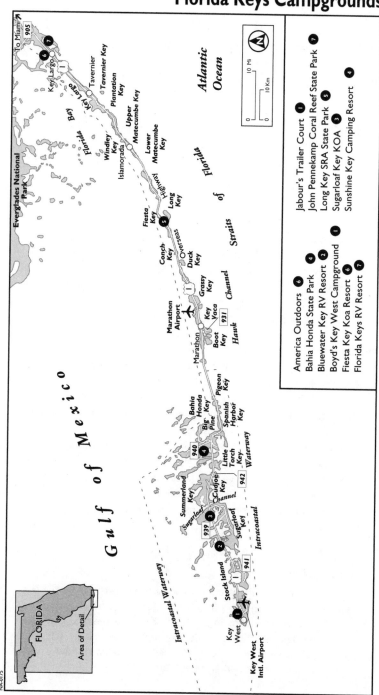

Jabour's Trailer Court ❶
John Pennekamp Coral Reef State Park ❼
Long Key SRA State Park ❺
Sugarloaf Key KOA ❸
Sunshine Key Camping Resort ❹

America Outdoors ❻
Bahia Honda State Park ❹
Bluewater Key RV Resort ❷
Boyd's Key West Campground ❶
Fiesta Key Koa Resort ❻
Florida Keys RV Resort ❼

NA-0175

By the 1830s, the island, now anglicized into Key West, was inhabited primarily by "wreckers" who made their livelihood from what was euphemistically known in the early 1800s as the "wrecking trade," salvaging sunken ships for a good living—even perhaps, as some historians suggest, luring those same ships to wreck onto the shoals and then salvaging them. In a good season, there would be more than a ship a week run aground. The best wreckers, it's said, lived aboard their ships so they could get to a wreck even more quickly.

Most were Cockneys coming from the Bahamas, along with Loyalists to the British Crown after the Americans won the Revolutionary War, plus a polyglot assortment of Cubans, seafarers from New England, and, later, émigrés from the Civil War.

But both the buccaneers and the wreckers missed the greatest haul of loot ever recovered by American salvage hunters: **Mel Fisher's treasure trove** from the sunken Spanish galleons *Atocha* and *Santa Margarita,* millions of dollars worth of gold bars, silver coins, and emeralds. The ships sank off Key West in 1622 on their way back to Spain, laden with the riches of the New World. Some key pieces of the indescribably valuable find are on display in Fisher's museum at Whitehead and Greene streets. (On our first visit there more than a decade ago, Fisher's mother sold us the tickets and showed us around with visible maternal pride.)

At the turn of this century, the city, already the richest settlement in Florida, was the cigar-producing capital of the world. Many of the 6,000 cigar makers were Cubans who flocked here to find work.

The wrecking industry bottomed out in 1921—"The Navy put channel markers and buoys to warn the ships about the reef," locals said— and the cigar industry burned out when investors in Ybor City, near Tampa, lured the cigar manufacturers away with promises of fewer labor problems.

By the late 1920s, Key West had become a backwater and one of the poorest places in the United States. In 1934, with 80% of the population unemployed, the desperate city declared bankruptcy, and the federal government sent in a New Deal administrator called Julius Stone who decided to turn the island into a tropical tourist paradise. He put people to painting and cleaning up the town and the beaches, training young women to be

KEY LIME PIE

Key limes, which in this country grow only in the Florida Keys, are not green, but yellow fruits the size of a golf ball, with green speckles. Ergo, the filling in a genuine Key lime pie is also yellow, not green. The first Key lime pie is thought to have been whipped up in the kitchen of the Curry Mansion in Key West, now a popular Caroline Street bed-and-breakfast.

Key West Highlights & Campgrounds

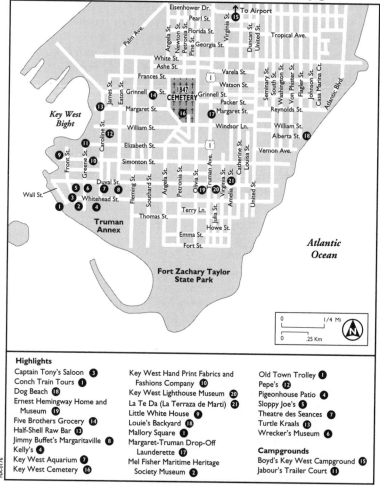

Highlights

Captain Tony's Saloon **3**
Conch Train Tours **1**
Dog Beach **18**
Ernest Hemingway Home and Museum **19**
Five Brothers Grocery **14**
Half-Shell Raw Bar **13**
Jimmy Buffet's Margaritaville **8**
Kelly's **4**
Key West Aquarium **7**
Key West Cemetery **16**

Key West Hand Print Fabrics and Fashions Company **10**
Key West Lighthouse Museum **20**
La Te Da (La Terraza de Marti) **21**
Little White House **9**
Louie's Backyard **18**
Mallory Square **1**
Margaret-Truman Drop-Off Launderette **17**
Mel Fisher Maritime Heritage Society Museum **2**

Old Town Trolley **1**
Pepe's **12**
Pigeonhouse Patio **4**
Sloppy Joe's **5**
Theatre des Seances **7**
Turtle Kraals **13**
Wrecker's Museum **6**

Campgrounds

Boyd's Key West Campground **15**
Jabour's Trailer Court **11**

---

hotel maids, even suggesting that all the local men wear shorts to appear picturesque.

The plan was a huge success in the winter of 1934–35, but the Labor Day hurricane of 1935 swept away the railway tracks and with them all the hopes and dreams. Tourism increased again after World War II, spurred by sailors who had been stationed here.

Part Two: A Bird in the Bush

Writers and artists have always been fascinated with Key West. One of the first artistic visitors was **John James Audubon,** who arrived in 1832 aboard the cutter *Marion.* A crack shot, the Haitian-born painter, natural- ist, and egoist had worked his way through the American south as a tutor

HEMINGWAY'S CATS

The six-toed cats who run all over the grounds of the Hemingway House are said to be descended from Hemingway's own six-toed cat. While far short of the 70 the author kept at his Cuban farm, the Key West team numbered 42 at our last visit and cost $700 a month to feed.

and dancing master, often biting the hand that fed him. His modus operandi was to kill as many birds from a species as he could because he enjoyed shooting, then mount one or two of them and arrange them in a habitat, often tree branches. While Audubon usually drew the birds himself, a young assistant—one or another always traveled with him—filled in the backgrounds. In Key West, Audubon produced two bird drawings, one of them a white-crowned pigeon perched on a branch of an orange-blossomed Geiger tree.

This type of tree was introduced from the West Indies by a Captain John Geiger, who also built the house now called the Audubon House, although Audubon's connection with it is tenuous. However, there is a Geiger tree in the yard of the Whitehead Street property. The tree, by the way, was not named for the captain, and the house in its present incarnation was not at this location in 1832. The island has a long tradition of inhabitants moving buildings from one spot to another.

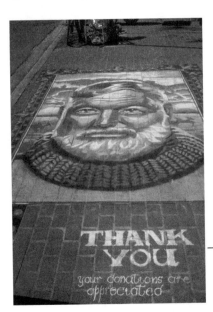

A sidewalk chalk drawing of one of Key West's most famous citizens

Part Three: The Further Adventures of Key Weird

Key West may sometimes be referred to as "Key Weird" by its detractors, but it's certainly a town that knows how to party.

April's **Conch Republic Days** celebrate the time not long ago (April 1982) when the Border Patrol put up road blocks on Route 1 to look for drugs and illegal aliens. Tourists took one look and turned back, and the town's income fell off considerably. So, perhaps remembering when they declared bankruptcy back in 1934, Key West proclaimed itself the Conch Republic and seceded from the United States, then applied for foreign aid. This weeklong celebration usually involves silliness such as a bed race and a lot of drinking.

Tennessee Williams' birthday, March 25, is often an occasion for celebrating, as is the weekly **Doris Day Night** at a local gay bar, and, of course, every day at **sunset,** when there's a lot of drinking.

We're fond of the Laundromat at the corner of Margaret and Truman streets in Key West, named, logically enough, the **Margaret-Truman Drop-off Launderette.**

The big brick building down by the dock was designed in 1890 as a government office building (or so a Conch tour guide told us), and the engineer had almost completed it when he died. A second engineer was sent in from up north and made them start all over again, digging a huge basement for oil-fired heating equipment, adding chimneys, and making the roofs steep enough "so the snow could slide off."

Designer-icon Calvin Klein is said to have paid a million dollars for a house locals call the **Bird Cage** or Octagon House at 712 Eaton St., only one of a group of turn-of-the-century Bahamian-style wooden mansions on that street. Ship's carpenters were often the builders, and salvaged wood from wrecked ships was sometimes worked into the structures.

A restaurant called **Pigeonhouse Patio,** on Caroline Street in the 400 block, near Whitehead Street, recalls the original use of its building, to raise homing pigeons that could be sent out with boats so if the crew got into trouble at sea, the captain could release the bird and help could be sent.

The city's sizeable gay population has done more than anyone in restoring the old Conch houses, setting up a flourishing bed-and-breakfast community, and generally glamorizing the mainstream in this laid-back, live-and-let-live community.

But some of the high hilarity of the 1980s has softened somewhat in the 1990s, in some cases to the detriment of the lounge scene. The outrageous **La Te Da** (local nickname of the La Terraza de Marti, 1125 Duval St., ☎ **305/ 296-6707**) and its Sunday afternoon tea dances have toned down the campiness, with no more owner-and-dog look-alike contests like the one described by Joy Williams in her excellent guidebook *The Florida Keys.* "The Look-Alike trophy went to Frank Cicalese and his Chihuahua Sam. They appeared as identical, perfectly pink Easter bunnies in identical bunny suits, slippers, and hats, carrying matching Easter baskets. Both wore sunglasses."

THE PRE-SUNSET EVACUATION

Cruise ships that call at Key West, an increasingly popular port, are encouraged to sail away at least 45 minutes before sunset so their bulky lines don't block the view from Mallory Pier.

Getting Around Key West

Rent a **bicycle** or **moped** from one of the shops along Truman Avenue, especially if you're traveling in a motorhome without a tow vehicle (that way you can leave the rig plugged in). If you don't want to do the pedaling yourself, hail a **pedicab** and let a well-tanned and shapely young thing pedal you around.

Alternatively, you can hop aboard an **Old Town Trolley** or **Conch Tour Train** (the tickets are sold in Mallory Square or aboard the vehicles). These open-air trams zigzag back and forth across town for 90 minutes while a friendly, folksy driver fills you in with yarns, anecdotes, and an overgenerous collection of corny jokes.

Three Key West Sights

The Little White House. Where Harry and Bess Truman vacationed in winter 11 times during his presidency, beginning in 1946. Recently restored to the 1940s period with original furniture, the museum offers a guided tour and video. Open daily. 111 Front St. ☎ **305/294-9911.**

The Ernest Hemingway Home and Museum. Where the author lived with his second wife, Pauline, from 1931 to 1940, is a National Historic Landmark. Self-guided or escorted tours are available through the house and the gardens, where a number of feral six-toed cats wander at will. Open daily. 907 Whitehead St. ☎ **305/294-1136.**

The Key West Aquarium. You can hand-feed sharks, pet a barracuda, or reach into a touch tank to feel sea creatures. The ticket is good for several days if you want to return. Open daily. ☎ **305/296-2051.**

Five Things to Do in Key West for $10 or Less

1. **Visit the Mel Fisher Maritime Heritage Society Museum.** Heft a solid gold bar and see silver bars, emeralds, and golden chalices from 17th-century Spanish galleons discovered by the late treasure hunter Mel Fisher. Open daily 9:30am to 5:30pm year-round, 200 Greene St. ☎ **305/294-2633.** Admission: adults $6.50, children $2.

2. **Touch turtles at the old Turtle Kraals.** *Kraals* is a South African term for corrals. These particular kraals once processed turtle steaks and canned turtle soup, but are now the home of the Florida Marine Conservancy. Sick and injured sea turtles and birds are tended here, and there's a touch tank for kids. Free. Open daily from 11am to 1am.

Land's End Village at Land's End Marina at the Turtle Kraals Restaurant & Bar. ☎ **305/294-2640.**

3. **Visit the Wrecker's Museum.** Also called the Oldest House, it's where a sea captain and his nine daughters once lived. The 1829 house displays memorabilia of the wrecking business; there's also an elaborately furnished period dollhouse. Open daily year-round, 322 Duval St. ☎ **305/294-9502.**

4. **Take a free guided tour of the Key West Hand Print Fabrics and Fashions Company.** Go backstage in a former 19th-century tobacco warehouse to watch hand-printed fabrics being designed and sewn into tropical sportswear, fabric toys, bedding, place mats, and napkins. Open daily 9am to 6pm year-round, 201 Simonton St. ☎ **305/294-9535.**

5. **Climb the stairs at the Key West Lighthouse Museum.** A spiral staircase inside leads up to a spectacular panoramic view of the island from this 1847 lighthouse, which was the recipient of an award-winning restoration in 1987. Exhibits tell the history of the town and the Keys. Open daily except Christmas Day, 938 Whitehead St. ☎ **305/294-0012.**

Key West at Night

The Keys' theme song is about wasting away in **Margaritaville,** easy enough to do at singer Jimmy Buffet's popular eatery and nightspot of the same name (500 Duval St.; ☎ **305/292-1435**), where you'll hear you-know-what played frequently if not incessantly. If you want something more down

---

"AND THEN I WROTE . . ."

Key West claims eight Pulitzer Prize winners among its residents, and, according to a knowledgeable local, more than 100 published authors live there at present.

Writer John dos Passos passed through here in the 1920s, looked around, and recommended it to fellow writer Ernest Hemingway, who arrived in 1928, finished off *A Farewell to Arms* in a rented house on Summer Street in 1929, then bought a fine house on Whitehead Street in 1931.

To Have and Have Not, published in 1937, is what Hemingway called his Key West novel. One of the "have-nots" was Harry Morgan, a local fishing charter-boat operator reduced to rum-running and smuggling Chinese immigrants into the United States. The author, however, was clearly one of the "haves," with a wealthy wife, a limestone mansion, the first swimming pool in Key West, and a 40-foot boat named *Pilar.*

Somewhere in the mid-1930s, while still married to his second wife, Pauline, Hemingway spotted journalist Martha Gelhorn sitting on a barstool at Sloppy Joe's. She would become his third wife in a short and tumultuous marriage after he divorced Pauline in 1940 and left Key West for good.

"You'll like Key West," Papa is reported to have written to a friend 2 decades later. "It's the St.-Tropez of the poor."

to earth, check out the **Caribbean Club** at MM 104.5 in Key Largo (☎ **305/451-4466**), the only local location that was actually shot for the eponymous movie. But don't expect yuppies and Bogart/Bacall types; it's more of a redneck-and-biker bar.

Hemingway's favorite bar in Key West, as everybody knows, was called **Sloppy Joe's,** and you can't miss the large bar with neon signs screaming the name at 201 Duval St. (☎ **305/294-5717**). When Hemingway drank there, however, Sloppy Joe's was down the street at the present site of **Captain Tony's Saloon,** 428 Greene St. (☎ **305/294-1838**), which used to be owned by Tony Tarracino, a former Key West mayoral candidate. Late one night back in 1937, Sloppy Joe Russell and his barflies moved the bar furniture from the old building over to the new building to protest a $1 raise in the rent on the former.

Then there's the famous **"Duval crawl,"** an evening spent prowling mile-long Duval Street, checking out the bars and restaurants, the attire of the natives, and the general wackiness. Once upon a time, six different taverns along this street were named Bucket of Blood.

Listen for the unique Key West style of jazz called Conchtown rhythm, a blend of New Orleans jazz and calypso.

CAMPGROUND OASES IN THE KEYS

John Pennekamp Coral Reef State Park. Located at MM 102, this park has 47 gravel sites with water and 30- and 50-amp electrical hookups, shade, flush toilets, showers, sanitary dump, swimming, fishing, and boat rentals. The reef lies several miles offshore, so you can just jump out of the RV and dive in. No pets. Reservations: ☎ **305/451-1202.**

America Outdoors. Right on the Gulf of Mexico between MM 97 and 98, America Outdoors has swimming, saltwater fishing, boating, a marina, and boat rentals. Rates are $35 to $50. The 154 sites provide water and 20- and

One of Florida's many giant oranges

MIRACLE OF THE KEYS

Where Card Sound Road runs into Route 905 at North Key Largo, you'll find the Crocodile Lake National Wildlife Refuge, some 12,000 acres of hammock and mangrove wetlands that is home to six endangered species, including the alligator, the wood rat, and the cotton mouse.

It could also be called the modern-day miracle of the Keys when it replaced a proposed 2,800-unit "faux Mediterranean" housing development called Port Bougainville, which would have featured man-made lakes and canals and drive-in boat garages. Despite a series of articles in the *Miami Herald* showing a pattern of political chicanery and conflicts of interest by Monroe County officials, the project continued to plow ahead.

The proposed site was atop the most fragile ecosystem in south Florida, and the resulting "big pollution dump," as ardent environmentalist Captain Ed Davidson called it, would have ruined the living coral reefs in Everglades National Park, John Pennekamp Coral Reef State Park, and Biscayne National Underwater Park (See "Ten Watery Wonders," earlier in this chapter.)

It would be nice to say the miracle happened solely because of the relentless battles of Captain Davidson, who operated the sightseeing boats at Biscayne National Park. But even his determined fight, which included a lawsuit he filed as president of the Florida Keys Audubon Society under the Endangered Species Act, only caused nuisance and delays. The project buckled under its own weight, due partly to the delays, and the developers went bankrupt. The property was ultimately purchased by the state of Florida, the Nature Conservancy, and the U.S. Fish and Wildlife Service.

30-amp electricity, but only 41 have sewers. There is a dump station as well, plus mobile sewer service. Call ☎ **305/852-8054** for reservations.

Florida Keys RV Resort. At MM 106 in Key Largo, 22 miles south of Homestead, this place has 139 sites, some of them shaded and all with water and 15- and 30-amp electricity. The office is modem-friendly and rates are $25 to $28, including cable TV. Call ☎ **305/451-6090** for reservations.

Fiesta Key KOA Resort. Located at MM 70 on Long Key, the campground has 288 sites with full or partial hookups, 20- and 30-amp electric, flush toilets, showers, sanitary dump, laundry, groceries, heated pool and spa, adult recreation room, boat ramp, and a dock. Boat rentals available to registered campers. Pets are permitted, but rates are high—$60 to $75 a night. ☎ **800/562-7730.**

Long Key SRA State Park. At MM 67, Long Key SRA has 60 sites with water and electrical hookups, flush toilets, showers, ocean front, fishing, and boat rentals. Most are shaded. There's a well-labeled nature walk and some good bird watching on the flats. No pets. ☎ **305/664-4815.**

Bahia Honda State Park. At MM 37, Bahia Honda has a 48-site campground with water and 20- and 30-amp electrical hookups, flush toilets and showers, some shade, sanitary dump, fishing, swimming, boating, and a marina. The beach is good, and there are wading birds and a small nature trail. No pets and no slideouts. For advance reservations, call ☎ **305/872-2353.**

Sunshine Key Camping Resort. At MM 39, Sunshine Key has 405 sites with water and 30- and 50-amp electric, 302 with full hookups. The park permits pets, but they have to abide by a long list of rules. There's also a private beach, marina, clubhouse, pool, and a number of waterfront sites, as well as nature trails and a bird sanctuary on an undeveloped side of the island. Rates are $22 to $56 a night, depending on season and site location. For reservations, call ☎ **800/852-0348.**

Sugarloaf Key KOA. A private RV park located north of Key West at MM 20, with 206 sites, half of them grass and half gravel. Full hookups in most with 20- and 30-amp electricity, cable TV, flush toilets, showers, laundry, groceries, fishing, and swimming pool. Some sites are shaded. Pricey at $33 to $63, they do allow pets and take reservations at ☎ **800/KOA-7731** or 305/745-3549.

Bluewater Key RV Resort. On the ocean side at MM 14.5 in Saddlebunch Keys, the resort offers 80 sites, 71 with full hookups, including 30- and 50-amp electricity as well as tiki huts, ocean swimming, heated pool, modem and phone hookups, dog walk, cable TV, and city water. Rates range from $40 to $65. Call ☎ **800/237-2266** for reservations.

Jabour's Trailer Court. If camping in downtown Key West appeals to you, Jabour's Trailer Court at 223 Elizabeth St. has 74 sites with full hookups and cable TV. Don't expect spacious or woodsy spots surrounded by nature, but at least you'll be able to leave the rig hooked up and walk wherever you want to go. Slideouts are not permitted. Flush toilets, showers, sanitary dump; from $40 to $60 a night. ☎ **305/294-5723** for reservations.

Boyd's Key West Campground. Boyd's promises 24-hour security and local bus service at their 6401 Maloney Ave. location. They offer 165 full hookups with 20- and 30-amp electricity, city water, cable TV, ocean swimming, and saltwater fishing, and it's modem-friendly. Some sites are on the water, and the swimming pool here is resort-sized with plenty of lounging space around it. Expect to pay from $30 to $50 a night, and there are some pet restrictions. Call them at ☎ **305/294-1465** for details or reservations, or see www.gocampingamerica.com/boydskeywest/.

Two Great Side Trips

EVERGLADES NATIONAL PARK

Everglades National Park is not only the world's largest freshwater marsh but also the third largest national park in the lower 48 states, exceeded in size only by Yellowstone, the second-largest, and Death Valley, the largest.

It is also, unfortunately, our most endangered national park because of encroaching housing developments, agricultural runoff, and several disastrous fires during the past 3 or 4 years.

Everglades National Park

Campgrounds

Boardwalk RV Resort ❷   Long Pine Key Campground ❹   Southern Comfort RV
Flamingo Campground ❺   Miami Everglades KOA ❶   Resort ❸

The Everglades has had a human population for some 3,000 to 5,000 years. The Calusa Indians, hunters and gatherers who sometimes grew to 7 feet tall and lived off shellfish, left behind huge 20-foot mounds of shells, the tallest landmarks in the Everglades. Then came the Spanish with their weapons and European diseases, followed by the Creeks from Georgia and Alabama who fled south. They were called Seminoles by non–Native Americans, and were ordered to relocate to Oklahoma at the same time the Cherokees from North Carolina and Tennessee marched on their Trail of Tears.

But the Seminoles declared war on the United States Army and fought sporadically from the early 1830s to 1859. Today's Native Americans in the Everglades are descendants of the survivors and call themselves Miccosukee.

For decades, politicians fought legislation attempting to protect the Everglades and its fauna, calling it "the alligator and snake swamp bill." But in 1947, President Harry S Truman dedicated the Everglades National Park.

Today's visitor can go sportfishing in Florida Bay, where no commercial fishing is allowed; hike and walk on trails and on boardwalks above the marsh; rent boats, canoes, and bicycles; or take boat cruises into Florida Bay from the Flamingo Marina Store. The park's entrance is south of Homestead off the Florida Turnpike, also known as Route 1 or the Dixie Highway. Turn off onto Route 9336. The turns to the park are well marked. In the 38 miles from the entrance to the **Flamingo Visitor Center** at the southern end of the park, you pass through six different ecosystems, but the changes are so subtle you'll have to watch for them.

A second visitor center is at Shark Valley on the Tamiami Trail, U.S. 41, with wildlife tram tours into the sawgrass prairie. For information about the park, call ☎ **305/242-7700.**

Campground Oases in the Everglades

Long Pine Key Campground. In Everglades National Park, 10 miles south of the junction of U.S. 1 and Route 9336, the campground has 108 paved sites, toilets, a sanitary dump, and bass fishing on Long Pine Key Lake; no hookups, no reservations. Some sites are shaded. Wooden overlooks and boardwalks in the park allow good bird watching. Call Everglades National Park, ☎ **941/695-3101** or 800/771-KEYS.

Flamingo Campground. Also in Everglades National Park, 38 miles southwest of the park entrance on the park road, a continuation of Route 9336, Flamingo Campground has 234 paved back-in sites with no hookups and no reservations. ☎ **305/242-7700.**

Southern Comfort RV Resort. Located in Florida City, Southern Comfort is adjacent to the entrance to the Everglades National Park at 345 East Palm Dr. (also 344th Street), with 350 full hookups, 30- and 50-amp electricity, optional phone hookups, planned activities (including exercise classes), special dinners, tournament shuffleboard courts, and 24-hour security. Rates of $18 to $25 are refreshingly lower that in the Keys, but there are pet restrictions. For reservations, call ☎ **888/477-6909.**

Boardwalk RV Resort. This new park at 100 NE 6th Ave. in Homestead boasts a designer clubhouse, nearby championship golf courses, a 24-hour security gate, dance floor, air-conditioned exercise facility, and 170 full-hookup sites with 30- and 50-amp electricity. Rates are $25 to $30. Call ☎ **888/233-WALK** for reservations.

Miami Everglades KOA. Six miles west of the junction of U.S. 1 and SW 186th Street near Monkey Jungle and the Miccosukee Indian Casino, the park has a security gate, satellite TV, shade from fruit trees, and wide pull-through sites. Some 258 sites offer water and 20- and 30-amp electricity; there is a surcharge for 50-amp electricity. Rates are $28 to $40. For reservations, call ☎ **800/KOA-7732.**

Buglewood Resort. A good choice if you're hitting Ft. Lauderdale before or after your Everglades visit, Buglewood is off I-95 at Exit 31, 5 miles from the beach but only 3 miles from the world's largest flea market. Only 19 of the 172 paved sites are pull-throughs; the rest are back-ins with only 22 feet of width. Electricity is 30- and 50-amps, and an air-conditioned room for adults only offers a big-screen cable TV set. Your pets are welcome. Expect to pay $25 to $32 a night, less by the week. Call ☎ **954/485-1150** for reservations.

ORLANDO

The greater Orlando area offers a dizzying array of diverting, tacky, educa-tional, glitzy, environmentally sensitive, and generally expensive attractions, which you'll be able to find on your own. In fact, given the high-pitched pitches and inescapable billboards, you can't miss them. So we offer our perspective from the point of view of a vacationer traveling by recreation vehicle.

Summer is the busiest season in Orlando, with more than 100,000 admis-sions a day, but with some of the worst weather, stiflingly hot and muggy much of the time. If you can possibly visit during any other season, do so.

If not, start out as early in the morning as possible—some attractions are open at 7am—and budget midday time to come back to the RV and its air-conditioning or hit the water parks with a splash.

Entertainment venues are spread out all over the greater Orlando area, including the **Walt Disney World** complex over at Lake Buena Vista and **Universal Studios** between Bay Hill and the turnpike. The colorful **Church Street Station,** in downtown Orlando at 129 W. Church St. (☎ **407/ 422-2434**), is a fanciful collection of shops, restaurants, and music halls cre-ated from Orlando's railway station and filled with antiques and oddments. One admission ticket gives you access to the shows, but no tickets are need-ed to visit the shops and restaurants. **Kissimmee,** the world headquarters for Tupperware, is where most of the RV parks are located. It's also where you'll find **Gatorland** (☎ **407/855-5496**), open daily 9am to 6pm and locat-ed on U.S. 441 next to the Tupperware plant; the **Medieval Times Dinner Tournament,** 4510 U.S. 92 (☎ **407/396-1518**), nightly at 8pm (tickets $38.95); and **Xanadu,** the home of the future, located ¼ mile east of the junction of U.S. 192 and State Road 535 (☎ **407/396-1992**).

If you're traveling by motorhome, you'll find it easier to have a tow car along or to rent a car in the area. Prices are low and car rental offices abound, some of them on the premises at larger RV parks.

Campground Oases in Orlando

Fort Wilderness Resort. Disney's own campground at the Disney complex

Orlando/Disney Area

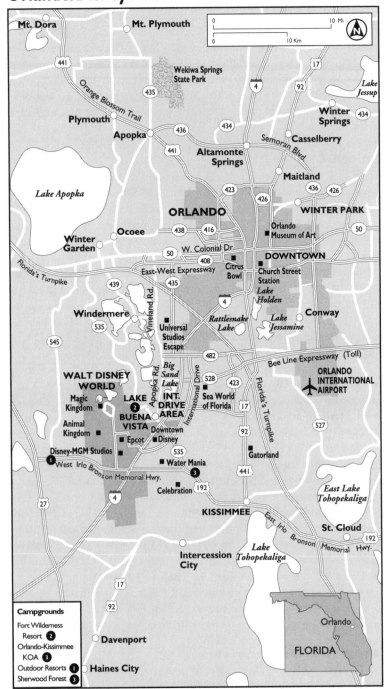

(drive ¾ mile from Exit 25B off I-4 to the marked entrance) combines Walt Disney World attractions with RV camping—and you don't even need an RV to do it, since they have rental RVs on the premises. There's a free shuttle to all the Disney attractions (although in summer at peak hours, it can be jam-packed and standing room only) and a full restaurant and lounge on the premises. Some 695 of the 784 paved sites are full hookups with 20-, 30-, and 50-amp electricity, city water, cable TV, and a modem-friendly office. Rates range from $35 to $65. Call ☎ **407/934-7639** for reservations.

Orlando-Kissimmee KOA. Located at 4471 Irlo Bronson Highway, this KOA is within reasonable driving distance of the major Orlando attractions, and also provides free transportation to certain attractions, on-site car rental, and discount ticket sales. Most of the 340 sites are paved, some are shaded, and all are 30 feet wide. Rates are from $28 to $40 a night. Call them at ☎ **800/562-7791** or log on to www.orlando-koa.com.

Sherwood Forest. Located at 5300 Irlo Bronson, Sherwood Forest is just down the road from the KOA, with 362 grassy sites, most of them wide pull-throughs with 30- and 50-amp electricity. Rates are around $29. They even have park models (a sort of mobile home) for rent if you don't have an RV or have friends coming to visit. Call ☎ **800/548-9981.**

Outdoor Resorts. This excellent condo park chain offers both RV sites and RVs for rent, so it's a good place for wannabe RV owners to try out different models. Expect to pay around $30 a night for a site, more for a rental. About 100 of the 980 sites are made available for overnighters and all have full hookups, including 30- and 50-amp electricity. Stay 6 nights and get the 7th free. It's located 5 minutes west of Walt Disney World on U.S. 192. Call ☎ **800/531-3033** or log on at www.outdoorresorts.com.

Travel Quiz: Monster Mash

Creepy movies about monsters and aliens are standard box office and TV fodder, and states like Florida supply the down-to-earth locations. Can you match the movie with its location?

1. Where did the Creature from the Black Lagoon (1954) make his home?

2. Where is the real summer camp where those spooky kids in *Addams Family Values* (1993) spent their painful vacation?

3. Where can you find the small town that served as the location for the original *Invasion of the Body Snatchers* (1956)?

4. What location was used as Hannibal Lecter's prison cell in *The Silence of the Lambs* (1990)?

5. *Texas Chainsaw Massacre* (1974), a cult classic, was filmed where?

6. In *Interview with a Vampire* (1994), where is Brad Pitt's family home located?

a. Sierra Madre, California, northeast of Pasadena off I-210

b. The Soldiers and Sailors Museum, 4141 Fifth Ave. in Pittsburgh, Pennsylvania

c. Wakulla Springs State Park in Florida, south of Tallahassee off Route 61

d. Sequoia Lake, Fresno County, California

e. Oak Alley Plantation near Vacherie, Louisiana

f. Round Rock, Texas, near Austin off I-35

ANSWERS: 1 (c); 2 (d); 3 (a); 4 (b); 5 (f); 6 (e)

The Blue Ridge Parkway & Skyline Drive

VIRGINIA IS WHERE EIGHT U.S. PRESIDENTS WERE BORN, WHERE 60% of the Civil War's battles were fought, and where "Taps" was composed, *Dirty Dancing* was filmed, and Chap Stick invented. It's where George Marshall wrote his Plan, where Jerry Falwell launched the Moral Majority, and where Disney lost the Third Battle of Manassas when they proposed to build a Civil War theme park adjacent to the battlefield and raised such a storm of protest that they had to back off.

Country singing legend Patsy Cline, who died in a plane crash at the age of 30, was born and buried in Winchester, the Statler Brothers were born and continue to live in Staunton, and Bela Bartok dropped by Hot Springs long enough to compose his *Piano Concerto No. 3.*

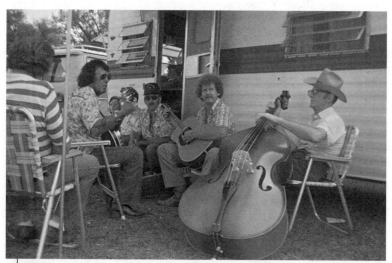

At the Old Fiddlers Convention in Galax, VA, some RVing musicians get together.

It's where John-Boy said goodnight to the rest of the Walton family, where Cyrus McCormick invented the first mechanical reaping machine, where a local doctor named Charles Kenneth Pepper gave his name to a soft drink, and where Rudolph Valentino's 1925 Rolls-Royce came to rest in the Historic Car and Carriage Caravan at Luray Caverns.

Ronald Reagan filmed *Brother Rat* in the cadet barracks at **Virginia Military Institute (VMI),** the same school where Stonewall Jackson's horse Little Sorrel was stuffed for the VMI Museum. Despite being somewhat moth-eaten, Little Sorrel is their most popular exhibit. The horse fared better than the general, who was accidentally shot by his own troops at Chancellorsville in 1863 and died a week later after having his arm amputated. The raincoat he was wearing with the bullet hole in evidence is in the same museum. He himself is buried in two places, his arm in Wilderness Battlefield and the rest of him in Stonewall Jackson Memorial Cemetery in Lexington.

Germany's General Erwin Rommel, "the Desert Fox," came to VMI to study the military tactics of Stonewall Jackson, which he later used in his North Africa campaign against the Allies during World War II.

Western Virginia is where Henry Ford couldn't cash a check—he was on one of his famous camping trips with Thomas Edison and Harvey Firestone (see "Public History: The Tin Can Tourists" in chapter 1, "Life on the Road: A Personal & Public History of RVing"); where John D. Rockefeller used to throw dimes into the pool by the first tee at the Homestead's Cascades golf course to watch the caddies scramble for them; and where the late multi-millionaire treasure-hunter Mel Fisher came up from Key West to search for the mysterious **Beale Treasure,** now worth about $23 million (see "Off-the-Wall Attractions").

Typical Blue Ridge farmhouses are restored along the Blue Ridge Parkway.

Virginia Highlights

Appomattox Court House
  National Historical Park **16**
Awful Arthur's **19**
Battle of New Market
  re-enactment **4**
Bedford Treasure file at the
  Bedford City/County
  Museum **17**
Bedrooms of America
  Museum and Pottery **4**
Belle Boyd cottage museum **3**
Blue Ridge Farm Museum **15**
Boar's Head Inn hot air
  balloon rides **10**
Booker T. Washington
  National Monument **17**
Buck Mountain Grille **17**
C&O railway station ice cream
  parlor **9**
Carl's Frozen Custard **6**
Explore museum **15**
Floyd County General Store **15**
George Washington's French
  and Indian War office **1**
Hardware Store Restaurant **9**
Haunted caves of Natural
  Bridge Caverns **12**
Homestead Resort **12**

Humming llamas/Virginia Highland
  Llamas **23**
Huyard's Country Kitchen **8**
Luray Caverns **4**
Mabry Mill **22**
Michie Tavern **15**
Miniature Graceland **15**
Montano's **15**
Monticello **10**
Mountain Lake Hotel **20**
Museum of American Frontier
  Culture **9**
Pest House Medical Museum and
  Confederate Cemetery **17**
Pig 'N Steak **7**
Rowe's Family Restaurant **9**
Shenandoah National Park **5**
Skyland Lodge **5**
Southern Kitchen **4**
Strasburg Antique Emporium **2**
Toliver House Restaurant **11**
Tuttle & Spice General Store
  and Museum **4**
Virginia's state theater **24**
Waltons Mountain Museum **13**
World's largest man-made
  illuminated star **15**

I-0946

And it's where—we cannot tell a lie—a young George Washington carved his initials in one of the seven wonders of the natural world, Virginia's **Natural Bridge.**

In the Blue Ridge Mountains of North Carolina, Tom Dula (better known as Tom Dooley of "Hang Down Your Head" ballad fame) was imprisoned in Wilkes County Jail in Wilkesboro after killing his sweetheart, and Frankie Silver, heroine of an even bigger ballad, became the first woman to be hanged in the state when she was tried and put to death in Morganton for murdering her two-timing lover Johnny, who "done her wrong."

RVing the Blue Ridge Parkway & Skyline Drive

The combined mileage of the Blue Ridge Parkway and Skyline Drive is 575 miles, plus any side trips you'll want to add along the route.

If you're going from north to south, Skyline Drive begins at Front Royal, Virginia, and the two-lane road snakes its way 105 miles through Shenandoah National Park, then joins up with the Blue Ridge Parkway at Rockfish Gap near Waynesboro, Virginia. The mileposts are numbered from 0.6 at Front Royal's fee entrance station to 105 at Rockfish Gap and the entrance to the Blue Ridge Parkway, which starts again at Milepost 0. While there are frequent turnouts, not all of them are long enough for a big rig.

The maximum speed limit along the parkway is 45 m.p.h., but don't expect to maintain that, what with the curving road and sightseeing traffic.

HITTING THE HIGHLIGHTS

If you diligently drive the route from the Washington, D.C., area to the Great Smoky Mountains, you could spend less than a week covering it by cutting down on the side trips.

While the ridge routes along Skyline Drive and the Blue Ridge Parkway are beautiful drives, do plan to drop down into parallel routes through country towns and farm communities from time to time to get a better sense of the people who live there.

Plan ahead selectively to cover some but not all the many battlefields, living history exhibits, and historical homes throughout the Appalachians.

GOING FOR THE LONG HAUL

If you're a craftsman or collector of antiques, you could happily and perhaps profitably spend a season or two ensconced in the Appalachians, where people are friendly and prices are modest. There are crafts courses open to the public and countless antiques shops and rural flea markets. One of the biggest and most famous is the **Hillsville Flea Market** every Labor Day weekend with more than 2,000 vendors on hand. It's about 8 miles north of the Blue Ridge Parkway, near Mile 200, via old Route 52 or I-77.

If you're a **Civil War** buff, Virginia will be endlessly fascinating, since 60% of the war's battles were fought there and battlefields and museums take the subject seriously.

Blue Ridge Highlights & Campgrounds

Highlights

Applewood Farm's Apple Barn **4**
Blowing Rock **22**
Brown Mountain Lights **17**
Carl Sandburg farm **5**
Dollywood **5**
Folk Art Center of the Southern Highland Handicraft Guild **18**
George Vanderbilt mansion **16**
Grove Park Inn **16**
Mast General Store **21**
Museum of Appalachia **1**
Museum of the Cherokee Indian **11**
Oconaluftee Indian Village **11**
Thomas Wolfe's Old Kentucky Home **18**

Julian Price Memorial Park **20**
Knoxville East KOA **2**
Look Rock **6**
Mt. Pisgah **14**
Newport KOA **3**
Outdoor Resorts **5**
Pigeon Forge/Gatlinburg KOA **5**
Smokemont **11**

Campgrounds

Abrams Creek **6**
Balsam Mountain **12**
Big Creek **14**
Cade's Cove **7**
Cataloochee **13**
Cosby Campground **15**
Deep Creek **9**
Doughton Park **22**
Elkmont **8**

Travel Essentials

WHEN TO GO

Early spring through late fall is best. Dogwood and wildflowers begin to bloom in April. Peak time for the showiest blooms comes mid-May to mid-June for flame azalea and mountain laurel, with June the best month for the thickets of vivid purple Catawba rhododendron. Craggy Gardens around Mile 365 is a particularly good place to see the latter. Autumn foliage creates another peak season as the trees turn color and begin to drop their leaves. Expect sometimes long and slow-moving lines of traffic in spring blossom, late summer, and autumn foliage seasons. Many of the facilities along the route are closed in winter. Plan early-morning starts, when the air is usually clearest, then stop in early afternoon to camp.

WHAT TO TAKE

Binoculars, cameras and film, hiking boots, sunscreen, mosquito repellent, detailed area maps, and fishing tackle if you want to go trout fishing. Carry a sweater or jacket even in midsummer because evenings are cool.

WHAT TO WEAR

Casual but smart sportswear is best if you plan to visit resorts or restaurants, especially in fashionable northern Virginia. Along the Blue Ridge Parkway and in North Carolina, things are a bit more casual, so your usual RV garb will pass muster almost everywhere.

TRIMMING COSTS ON THE ROAD

Shop at local fruit stands for fresh produce; you'll find fresh-from-the-farm seasonal fruits and vegetables at prices far below what supermarkets charge.

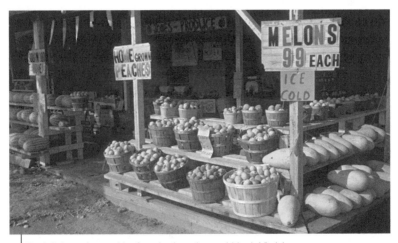

Fresh fruits and vegetables for sale along the roadsides in Virginia

Steer clear of commercial theme parks and heavily touted roadside attractions such as Natural Bridge and Luray Caverns. Besides admission fees, they are surrounded by other attractions that seem particularly alluring to children. Instead, take a free hike to a nearby waterfall or scenic overlook.

You'll save money too, if you can **stay self-contained** with overnight stops rather than hooking up at a private campground adjacent to the Parkway. By driving every day, you'll keep the battery charged and can top off water storage and empty holding tanks in many of the public campgrounds.

WHERE TO GET TRAVEL INFORMATION

For a packet of **Virginia information,** call ☎ 800/VISIT-VA. They deliver it more promptly than any other state in our experience. Their Web site is www.virginia.org.

For **Shenandoah National Park information,** write Route 4, Box 348, Luray, VA 22835, or call ☎ 540/999-2243.

For information about the **Blue Ridge Parkway,** write 400 BB&T Building, One Pack Square, Asheville, NC 28801, or call ☎ 704/271-4779.

To get more information about **private campgrounds,** contact **Virginia Campground Association,** 2101 Libbie Ave., Richmond, VA 23230 (☎ 804/288-3065).

For details about state parks, contact **Virginia State Parks Department of Conservation and Recreation,** 203 Governor St., Suite 302, Richmond, VA 23219 (☎ 804/786-1712; www.state.va.us/~scr/).

For **reservations** in a state park campground, call ☎ 800/933-PARK.

North Carolina Tourism is at 430 N. Salisbury St., Raleigh, NC 27611 (☎ 800/VISIT-NC; www.visitnc.com).

Tennessee Tourism is at 320 6th Avenue N, #500, Nashville, TN 37243 (☎ 800/TENN-200; www.state,tn.us/tourdev/).

For **Great Smoky Mountain National Park,** contact ☎ 423/436-1200, www.nps.gov.

DRIVING TIPS

- **Check the weather.** Winter is often mild, but periods of fog or rain may make driving larger RVs along the ridge route difficult. In summer, unfortunately, increased pollution and haze along Skyline Drive have reduced visibility tremendously. You can check out the day's clarity with park rangers by calling ☎ 703/999-3644 or 703/999-2243.

- **Don't be a roadhog.** Because the two-lane roadways are heavily traveled, RVers should remember to pull out into the frequent overlooks and turnouts to let traffic behind them go past.

- **BYOB.** Southern states have local liquor-control laws governed by the city, county, or community. If you are accustomed to having wine with dinner, it's a good idea to inquire about the restaurant's policy before you go. Some permit diners to bring their own.

The Best Blue Ridge Sights, Tastes & Experiences

TEN TERRIFIC SPOTS WHERE HISTORY COMES ALIVE

1. **Museum of American Frontier Culture, Staunton, VA.** Shows us where many of our 18th- and 19th-century settlers came from—neat, small farms in England, Northern Ireland, and the German Rhineland—and a typical Shenandoah Valley farm that reflects the influence of all three. Costumed interpreters carry out daily and seasonal tasks from plowing to planting, spinning to gardening. From I-81, take exit 222, and then follow the signs on 250 west. It's open daily 9am to 5pm in summer, 10am to 4pm in winter. Adults $8, seniors $7.50, students $7. ☎ **540/332-7850;** www.frontiermuseum.org.

2. **Appomattox Court House National Historical Park, outside Lynchburg, VA.** Twenty miles east of Lynchburg via Route 460 to Route 24, the Appomattox Court House has re-created the entire village as it was when Lee surrendered to Grant here. Living history exhibits in summer animate Meeks Store, Woodson Law Office, and Clover Hill Tavern, and there's a museum as well. The park is open daily except major holidays February through November, 9am to 5pm. ☎ **804/352-8987.**

3. **Explore Museum, near Roanoke, VA.** A new living history museum near Roanoke, VA, Explore interprets the pre–Civil War period with its Blue Ridge Settlement depicting life on the Virginia frontier in the early 1800s. Historic buildings have been reassembled on-site, including the Hofauger Farmstead, where costumed interpreters cook at the hearth, weave, spin, garden, and tend livestock. Gardens are planted in heirloom seeds, orchards grow traditional varieties of fruit, and farm animals represent now rare breeds that were typical of the time. Open Saturdays and Sundays in April and daily through October. A gift shop on site sells candleholders made by the local blacksmith and other crafts from the project. Admission adults $8, seniors $6, students $4.50. From the Parkway's Milepost 115, follow the signs to 3900 Rutrough Rd., in a residential area. ☎ **800/842-9163;** www.explorepark.com.

4. **Battle of New Market re-enactment, New Market, VA.** A re-enactment of the 1864 Battle of New Market takes place every May 15, recalling when 247 young cadets, the entire student body of Virginia Military Institute, fought alongside veteran Confederate soldiers against the Union Army. Ten cadets died, including a descendent of Thomas Jefferson, and 47 others lay wounded. The Hall of Valor in the New Market Battlefield Park poignantly commemorates the battle. For information, contact the New Market Chamber of Commerce (☎ **540/740-3212;** www.svta.org/New-Market/). New Market is located in the Shenandoah County of Virginia, near the intersection of I-81 and Route 211.

Mabry Mill on the Blue Ridge Parkway

5. **The Blue Ridge Farm Museum, Ferrum, VA.** The Farm Museum displays an 1800 German-American farm and the daily life of settlers who came here, with heirloom vegetables, vintage livestock breeds, and costumed interpreters. From Roanoke, take U.S. 220 south to Route 40. Ferrum is about 12 miles southwest off Route 40 west. Call for hours (☎ **540/365-4416**).

6. **Mabry Mill, near Meadows of Dan, VA.** At Mile 176 of the Blue Ridge Parkway, Mabry Mill is animated with working craftsmen and musicians during the peak summer and fall season. Besides the water-powered gristmill and a shop selling its stone-ground flours and meal, there's also a coffee shop serving pancakes and country ham all day long. Open May 1 to October 31. ☎ **540/952-2947.**

7. **Booker T. Washington National Monument.** Located where the great educator and inventor was born in 1856, the monument features demonstrations of 19th-century farming methods. The house where Washington, his mother, and two other children slept on a bare dirt floor has been reconstructed on the site. It's in Hardy, VA, 20 miles southeast of Roanoke via routes 116 south, then 122 north, near Smith Mountain Lake. Open daily. ☎ **540/721-2094.**

8. **The Mast General Store, near Boone, NC.** The Mast General Store was built in 1883 and is a living example of a 19th-century country store with its potbellied stove and old advertising posters. With merchandise "from cradles to caskets" and the family's 1812 log cabin and 1885 farmhouse (now an inn) nearby, it is a good one-stop example of a mountain farm complex. It's also great fun just to browse through the stacked and packed shelves of this rambling store, now listed on

the National Registry of Historic Places. In Valle Crucis, 7 miles south of Boone on Route 194. ☎ **828/963-6511.**

9. **The Museum of Appalachia, Norris, TN.** A bit off the basic driving route, but for anyone going or coming from the Midwest or West, it could be on the way. Located 16 miles north of Knoxville at exit 122 from I-75, this living village is open daily year-round and preserves the lifestyle of the southern Appalachians as its costumed interpreters split shingles, plow the fields, play fiddles, and cook meals in dirt-floored cabins. A museum displays 250,000 regional artifacts, including a Roy Acuff fiddle and Sergeant Alvin York's World War I leather Army jacket. ☎ **423/494-0514.**

10. **Oconaluftee Indian Village, Cherokee, NC.** A re-created Cherokee village from 225 years ago, before many of the tribe were taken to Oklahoma on a forced relocation still remembered as the Trail of Tears. One-fourth of them died along the 1,000-mile journey. Descendents of the 1,200 tribal members who escaped and fled into the nearby Great Smoky Mountains in 1838 make up an 8,000-member reservation here today. Costumed animators produce pottery, weave baskets, sew beadwork, and build canoes in traditional fashion. The nearby **Museum of the Cherokee Indian** on Route 441 (follow signs from the highway) is a remarkable exhibit of Cherokee history. The museum is open daily year-round except for major holidays; the village is open mid-May to late October. ☎ **800/438-1601;** www.cherokee-nc.com.

OFF-THE-WALL ATTRACTIONS

Tuttle & Spice General Store and Museum, New Market, VA. Four miles north of New Market off I-81, exit 269, Tuttle & Spice houses spice boxes and tobacco boxes, corsets and cruets, as well as a reproduction of a small-town main street, circa 1900. Everything jammed into the museum's nine period replica shops is a museum item not for sale, but a large gift shop on the premises takes care of any acquisitive stirrings you may feel. The store/museum is free and open daily year-round. ☎ **800/296-4545.**

Bedrooms of America Museum and Pottery, New Market, VA. At the traffic light on Congress Street (a.k.a. U.S. 11), only 2 blocks from I-81, exit 264 in New Market, is a period house crammed full of antiques, collectibles, and junk, and includes 11 bedrooms, each filled with vintage furniture and furbelows depicting a different specific period between 1650 and 1930. ☎ **540/740-3512.**

The Brown Mountain Lights, Morganton, NC. Mysterious ghost lights called the Brown Mountain Lights can sometimes be seen near Morganton, the area where Indians first noted them. In the 1950s, locals attributed the phenomenon to UFOs. A good spotting place is from Beacon Heights off the Blue Ridge Parkway near Grandfather Mountain, and the best time is a clear fall night. Call Burke Country and Tourism for information (☎ **828/ 433-6793**).

Miniature Graceland, Roanoke, VA. Built by the truly dedicated Donald and Kim Epperly in their front yard on Riverland Boulevard in Roanoke, Miniature Graceland is a tribute to Elvis that includes an Elvis doll singing Elvis songs to a throng of Barbies, plus replicas of Graceland, Elvis's birthplace in Tupelo, and some of the theaters he performed in. Kim Epperly is also editor of an Elvis newsletter. There are no set tour schedules; visitors leave donations. ☎ **540/427-4254.**

The world's largest man-made illuminated star, Roanoke, VA. A full 88½ feet high, the star shines nightly until midnight from a mountain above Roanoke. Like a fluorescent tube, the 50-year-old-plus monument usually glows in a ghostly blue-white and hums to itself, but turns red, white, and blue on patriotic holidays and turns just plain red when there's a traffic fatality in the area. Newscaster Lowell Thomas and actor John Payne, Roanoke-born, dedicated it in 1949.

The haunted caves of Natural Bridge Caverns. A moaning female ghost lives somewhere inside the limestone formations and pipes up periodically, scaring the wits out of guides and tourists alike. The sound has been going on for more than a century at the caverns, located on U.S. 11 near the Natural Bridge. If the ghost disappoints you, there's a wax museum on the premises as well. ☎ **540/291-2121.**

The Whitetop Mountain Ramp Festival, Whitetop, VA. Not dedicated to freeway entrances, but to a particularly strong-smelling wild onion that goes by the same name. At the annual festival in mid-May you get the chance to sample ramps cooked with bear meat, with trout, in soups, and in salads. It's held at Mount Rogers Fire Hall in Whitetop, southwestern Virginia (off U.S. 58 near the VA/TN/NC borders), with bluegrass music, a crafts fair, and a quilting display. ☎ **540/388-3257** or 540/388-3480.

The Pest House Medical Museum and Confederate Cemetery, Lynchburg, VA. The museum with the irresistible name attracts the morbid and medical-minded to Lynchburg's Old City Cemetery at 4th and Taylor streets. In the 19th century, patients ill with smallpox or measles were quarantined in the Pest House, then, when they almost inevitably died, were buried in the cemetery next door. The museum, at 401 Taylor St., shows curiosities such as an 1860s hypodermic needle and an early chloroform mask. Open daily dawn to dusk. ☎ **804/847-1465;** www.lynchburgbiz.com/occ.

The Belle Boyd cottage museum, Front Royal, VA. The former residence of a pretty teen-aged girl who doubled as a Confederate spy, gathering information on a Union Army plan by eavesdropping, then hopping on a horse and riding 15 miles in the middle of the night to take the information to Stonewall Jackson and the Confederates so they could defeat the Yankees at the Battle of Front Royal in 1862. The cottage, at 101 Chester St., is open variable hours, so call ahead (☎ **540/636-1446**).

The mysterious Beale Treasure, Bedford, VA. The legend of the Beale Treasure is based on three pages of cryptically coded information in a strong-box left for safekeeping with a Lynchburg hotel owner in 1822. Only one of the pages has been decoded; it claims there are 2,981 pounds of gold and 5,092 pounds of silver buried in the Bedford area, worth approximately $23 million today. A group of 100 computer experts are presently working to unravel the multiple substitution ciphers. The late Key West treasure hunter Mel Fisher also took a crack at it without any luck. The Bedford City/County Museum houses the file, and is located at 201 E. Main St. and open Tuesday through Saturday 10am to 5pm, except January and February. ☎ **540/586-452.**

Blowing Rock, NC. A strong updraft at a rock ledge hanging over the Johns River Gorge usually returns items tossed over the edge. An old Indian legend says a maiden prayed to the God of the Winds for return of her warrior, who had fallen over; the wind came up and blew him back. About 50 miles south, as the crow flies, Dr. Elisha Mitchell, a college professor making measurements on a mountain later named for him, had no such luck. He fell to his death over a ledge by a waterfall in 1857. On Route 321, South Blowing Rock. Call the Blowing Rock Chamber of Commerce at ☎ **828/295-7851.**

TEN SPECIAL SPLURGES

1. **Visit the Grove Park Inn.** Plan a meal or even an overnight in Asheville's splendidly baronial Grove Park Inn, built in 1913 by a patent-medicine tycoon from Tennessee. Author F. Scott Fitzgerald frequently stayed here when visiting his wife Zelda, who spent the latter part of her life in a local mental hospital. He usually stayed in Room 441, which is still decorated as it was during his visits. Do check out those elevators by the huge, walk-in stone fireplaces; they actually run up the chimney shafts. To get there from Greenville, NC, take 25 north about 55 miles. To get there from Winston-Salem, NC, take 40 west about 140 miles. ☎ **800/438-5800** or 828/252-2711.

2. **Go shopping for authentic mountain handicrafts.** With an RV, you can probably find space to stow some split-willow baskets, a hand-made broomcorn broom, finely polished wooden toys, or even a hand-stitched heirloom quilt, all for sale at the Folk Art Center of the Southern Highland Handicraft Guild on the North Carolina end of the parkway at Mile 382, in Asheville. Open daily 9am to 5pm except major holidays. ☎ **828/298-7928.**

3. **Have tea or a meal at the Homestead Resort.** Don your smartest outfits and hit the Homestead Resort at mealtime (call ahead for reservations, ☎ **800/838-1766**) for a sumptuous lunch or dinner in the grand old American resort tradition. Teatime with violins is also a classic pleasure here in this red brick, Colonial-style building dating from 1892. A hotel has been on the site for 230 years because of the healing springs on the premises. At one time, the waters promised to cure such exotic maladies as gum-boot poisoning, clergyman's throat, and a surfeit of freckles. There's a lot large enough for RV parking halfway down the hill to the hotel, but the doorman may eye your rig nervously if you drive right down to the porte-cochère. It's in Hot Springs, VA, on U.S. 220 near the West Virginia border.

4. **Visit America's largest private home.** The 250-room George Vanderbilt mansion on the Biltmore Estate in Asheville (see "Asheville," below) is open daily except Thanksgiving and Christmas from 8:30am to 5pm. Admission is $29.95 for adults, $22.50 for youths 10 and over, and free for children 9 and under when accompanied by a paying adult. There's also a raft of other money-making ventures on the property, from gift shops to a winery, as well as special seasonal and evening events of all sorts. ☎ **800/543-2961** is an automated information number with numerous options, and the estate's Web site is www.biltmore.com. From the Blue Ridge Parkway, Biltmore is about 4 miles from the Highway 25 north exit. From Interstate 40 West, the entrance is north of exit 50B on Highway 25. From Interstate 40 East, the entrance is north of exit 50 on Highway 25.

5. **Go antiques-hunting in the 100-shop Strasburg Antique Emporium.** Located at 160 N. Massanutten St. in the northern Virginia town of Strasburg (near Front Royal and the beginning of Skyline Drive), the emporium has 60,000 square feet of display space, with dealers offering everything from Civil War–era buttons to Jetson lunchboxes. ☎ **540/465-3711;** www.waysideofva.com.

6. **Sing along with a humming llama.** Hit the hiking trail near Wytheville, VA, with some humming llamas from Virginia Highland Llamas (☎ **540/688-4464**) for an all-day picnic hike on the Big Walker Mountain section of the Appalachian trail. You walk while the llamas carry lunch, each humming a different tone. Why do they hum? "Because they don't know the words," says their owner.

7. **Cash in a chicken or ham for theater tickets at Virginia's state theater in Abingdon.** During the Depression, area farmers paid for their tickets to the classic Barter Theater with produce. (These days you have to pay with cash or credit card—sorry.) Gregory Peck, Patricia Neal, Hume Cronyn, and George C. Scott all worked here early

in their careers. The theater once paid royalties to famous Irish play-wright and noted vegetarian George Bernard Shaw by sending him a country ham, which he returned with a note requesting spinach instead. From Highway 81, take exit 17. Follow signs to the theater, which is on Main Street. ☎ **800/435-3440;** www.abington.com/tourism.

8. **Visit the Buck Mountain Grille.** If you're in the Roanoke area and looking for some trendy vegetarian dishes, or even a steak, along with a glass of wine, try this place, open daily lunch and dinner except Monday and Saturday lunch. It's at Blue Ridge Parkway, exit 121, on Route 220 south. ☎ **540/776-1830** for reservations.

9. **Take a hot-air balloon ride.** Float over some of the Shenandoah Valley's outstanding landmarks from the lavish grounds of the Boar's Head Inn, 220 Ednam Dr. in Charlottesville (☎ **800/476-1988;** www.boarsheadinn.com). It's also a top-seeded tennis resort, ranking among *Tennis Magazine*'s top 50, and scene of a predictable Merrie Olde England Christmas banquet starring a you-know-what on a silver platter.

10. **Find a secluded mountain lodge that takes you back 30 years.** At least that's what the producers of the film *Dirty Dancing* thought when they used Mountain Lake Hotel to stand in for a Poconos resort in the sixties. To find it, leave I-81 at exit 118 and follow Route 460 west, bypassing Blacksburg, to road 700, then drive 7 miles farther up a winding road to Mountain Lake. Open May through October. Call them at ☎ **800/828-0490.**

GREAT TAKE-OUT (OR EAT-IN) TREATS

Carl's Frozen Custard, Fredericksburg, VA. Carl's turns out 120 gallons of this classic dessert (in vanilla, chocolate, and strawberry) daily in a 1940s ice cream machine. Look for the stand at the corner of Princess Anne and Hunter streets; there's no phone.

C&O railway station ice cream parlor, Staunton, VA. An authentic Victorian-era ice cream parlor on Middlebrook Avenue in the center of Staunton dishes up sodas and sundaes in the restored C&O railway station. (For more railway comestibles, try the crab croquettes at Charlottesville's **C&O Restaurant,** 515 E. Water St., across from the train station. Lunch, weekdays; dinner, nightly. ☎ **804/971-7044**).

Toliver House Restaurant, Gordonsville, VA. Toliver House serves up old-fashioned fried chicken. It's at the junction of U.S. 15, 33, and State Road 231 in the little town of Gordonville, northeast of Charlottesville. ☎ **540/832-3485.**

Huyard's Country Kitchen, Dayton, VA. Run by a former Mennonite missionary, Huyard's Country Kitchen is set inside the Dayton Farmer's Market south of Harrisonburg on Route 42. From I-81, use exit 240, Bridgewater, or exit 245, James Madison University. The moderately priced buffet of home cooking includes ham, chicken, beef, and vegetables. You may see horse-drawn buggies tied up outside, traditional transportation for the Old Order Mennonites who live in the area. ☎ **540/879-2613.**

Mabry Mill, near Meadows of Dan, VA. Located right on the Blue Ridge Parkway at Mile 176, Mabry Mill serves up corn and buckwheat pancakes made from grains stone-ground by the mill, along with trout, country ham, and biscuits, all available all day long. You can also buy the pancake mix and cornmeal to take home. The restaurant is open from late April through October between 8am and 6pm; be prepared for a queue. ☎ **540/365-4416.**

The Southern Kitchen, New Market, VA. This non-fancy place on U.S. 11 is famous for peanut soup (which we've always been fond of), along with a dish called Lloyd's Fried Chicken. ☎ **540/740-3514.**

The Hardware Store Restaurant, Charlottesville, VA. Stop in at East Main and Water streets for great gourmet sandwiches made to go amid the authentic furnishings of a turn-of-the-century hardware store. Park your RV on the Water Street side. ☎ **804/977-4344.**

Rowe's Family Restaurant, Staunton, VA. Rowe's, on Route 250 in Staunton, is a longtime sanctuary for real Virginia home cooking—and coincidentally where the Statler Brothers often eat. Have the fried

> *"The South is that part of America where no soft drink is ever called a soda."*
> —Reynolds Price

chicken, real mashed potatoes, hot biscuits, and hot homemade rolls, and for dessert, traditional banana pudding. Exit 222 off I-81. ☎ **540/886-1833.**

The Pig 'N Steak, Madison, VA. The Pig 'N Steak is one of Virginia's top barbecue places, but also where the fictional Jason Walton from the TV series used to play the piano at the "Dew Drop Inn." Hickory pit–smoked ribs are the draw here. The restaurant is north of Charlottesville on Washington Street in Madison at the stoplight. ☎ **540/948-3130.**

Applewood Farm's Apple Barn, Sevierville, TN. The hot fried apple pies at Applewood are prepared while you watch through a glass window. Look for Dolly Parton chocolate lollipops in the candy shop at the farm's complex of food preparation centers. 230 Apple Valley Rd. ☎ **800/421-4606.**

Delicacies at Applewood Farm

EVERYTHING YOU EVER WANTED TO KNOW ABOUT COUNTRY HAM

Yankees may invest fortunes in mail-order Smithfield hams, but the fine cured ham you'll encounter in restaurants and roadside stands throughout this drive is correctly called "country ham."

The **Smithfield ham** began in the 17th century when local farmers let their hogs run loose in the peanut fields after harvest to eat up the leftovers. They soon found they had an excellent-tasting ham with yellow fat that kept the meat from drying out, an export in great demand back in England. These hams are smoked and coated with black pepper. Only hams produced by peanut-fed hogs in the peanut belt and processed in Smithfield, a small town in Tidewater Virginia near Norfolk, can be called Smithfield hams.

Country ham, on the other hand, is a product of the Appalachians that can be either smoked or dry-cured without smoke. The fresh ham is rubbed down with a dry mix of salt, sugar, and perhaps saltpeter, then covered for 4 to 6 weeks in a bed of salt. After this, it is washed and trimmed, then usually hung by the hock in a smokehouse where it sweats in hickory smoke through the summer. A total of 9 to 12 months is the minimum curing period. Some processors skip the smoking stage, saying the smoke makes little flavor difference. And some processors label their hams "sugar cured," although the sugar has no part in the curing.

The finished ham is a salty, densely textured, and intensely flavored meat that can be sliced raw and fried for breakfast or boiled whole and then baked. If you buy a country ham to take home, rest assured it will keep for a long time, up to a year, if stored in a cool, dark place. A cooked ham also keeps well under refrigeration, and a small bit of it sliced or diced can add flavor to any number of dishes.

To prepare a country ham, you need to soak it for 24 hours in a pot of cold water, then drain it, scrub off the spices and any mold from the surface, and put it in a fresh kettle of cold water to cover. Cook it at a simmer for 20 minutes per pound or until the flat bone at the butt end is loose enough to move back and forth, usually from 4 to 5 hours. Let it cool enough to handle, cut off the skin and excess fat, but leave a half-inch layer of fat to cover. Remove the loose, flat bone. Put liquid in the pan (water, wine, ginger ale, or sherry) to cover it by an inch and bake in a slow oven for an hour, covered with foil. Then remove the foil, score the fat, and cover it with any paste or glaze you wish (a mix of brown sugar, cornmeal, and a little prepared or dry mustard is good). Return it to the oven for another half hour, basting frequently. Then let it cool and slice it in very, very thin slices to serve. It's delectable with hot biscuits.

The word *ham*, to denote a bad actor, comes from **"hamfatter,"** a word 19th-century audiences applied to second-rate actors such as minstrel show performers, who had to use ham fat to take off their makeup because they couldn't afford cold cream.

OUTDOOR ACTIVITIES

Hikers will find plenty of trails, from 10-minute leg-stretchers to much longer and more demanding walks along the way. In **Shenandoah National Park,** more than 500 miles of side trails set out from the ridge road.

One of the most famous walking trails in America, the **Appalachian Trail,** stretches from Maine to Georgia across the crest of the mountains. Some of the prettiest of the trail's 500 miles in Virginia are those in Shenandoah National Park between Front Royal and Rockfish Gap. The trail also parallels the Blue Ridge Parkway for 103 miles between Rockfish Gap and Mile 103.

Canoe trips along the Shenandoah River for novices or experienced canoeists can be booked with **Downriver Canoe Company** in Bentonville,

SOUTHERN ACCENTS: A GLOSSARY

Bald: A treeless area at about 4,000 feet in elevation covered with shrubs or grass, perhaps part of earlier Indian agricultural clearing or the product of lightning fires

Holler: A yell of communication between farms in the days before telephones; also, a valley

Moonshining: Making illegal corn liquor in "dry" areas of the south; most rural areas have a few moonshiners, but you're not likely to encounter any unless you know the locals very well

Pop: A soft drink

Put up: To can or preserve foods for winter

Virginia, between early April and late October (☎ 800/338-1963). If you want to paddle your own canoe, they can provide a shuttle service for you. **Front Royal Canoe Company** in Front Royal (☎ 800/270-8088 or 540/635-5440; www.frontroyalcanoe.com) can also take you canoeing along the Shenandoah between mid-March and mid-November. **Shenandoah River Outfitters** in Luray (☎ 800/6CANOE2; www.shenandoahriver.com) is open year-round for rentals, overnight trips, and all-you-can-eat steak dinners on the trail.

Horseback riding along mountain trails is particularly popular in the fall, and a good alternative to driving when traffic on the roadways may be bumper-to-bumper. Guided trail rides from **Skyland Lodge** in Shenandoah National Park leave several times a day; call them at ☎ 540/999-2210 or visit www.visitshenandoah.com for times and details.

Or you can spend the time doing nothing more urgent than watching a robin search for worms or marvel at the opening of a bud or the unfolding of a leaf.

WILDLIFE WATCHING

The Blue Ridge Mountains are the stomping ground for all manner of birds and mammals, from plentiful **white-tail deer** and **black bears,** on display at the privately owned Grandfather Mountain Park, to **wild turkeys,** which we've glimpsed several times from the roadway. Seldom seen but indisputably present are **bobcats,** sometimes glimpsed at night. Most commonly sighted along the roadways are woodchucks (groundhogs), chipmunks, and squirrels in the daytime; skunks, raccoons, opossums, and foxes at night. More than 100 bird species may be seen during spring migrations.

Some 300 or more **wild ponies** wander in Grayson Highlands State Park, off U.S. 58 near the point where Virginia, North Carolina, and Tennessee meet; a few of them are rounded up each fall to be auctioned off during the last week of September in the park.

On the Road

THE SHENANDOAH VALLEY

Nobody knows for sure what *Shenandoah* means. It has been translated variously as "sprucy stream," "land of the big mountains," even "daughter of the stars." One etymologist says it is the Iroquois word for "deer," animals that are still plentiful in the valley.

The fragrance of apples perfumes the valley, from the pink-and-white blossoms in spring through the harvest of the fruit in autumn, to the sweet-sour tang of apple cider in winter in the apple sheds.

History is deeply etched in the towns along the Shenandoah River, once America's western frontier. During the Civil War, the northern Virginia town of **Winchester** changed hands 72 times—and 13 times on one particularly

Virginia Campgrounds

Beartree Campground **13**
Big Meadows Campground **3**
Claytor Lake State Park **9**
Douthat State Park **5**
Fairy Stone State Park **10**
Fox Trail Family Campground **11**
Front Royal KOA **2**
Grayson Highlands State Park **14**
Hungry Mother State Park **12**
Lake Fairfax Park **1**
Lewis Mountain Campground **3**
Loft Mountain **3**
Matthews Arm **3**
Natural Bridge/Lexington KOA **6**
Peaks of Otter **7**
Roanoke Mountain **8**
Walnut Hills Campground **4**

I-0946

Re-created farm in Virginia's Museum of American Frontier Culture

memorable day alone. Pick up a walking tour map at the city's welcome center (1360 S. Pleasant Rd.) and set out to see the modest log-and-limestone cabin on Braddock Street that was George Washington's office during the French and Indian War. (It's now a museum; call ☎ **540/662-4412.**) A brick house down the street was Stonewall Jackson's headquarters during the Civil War. Don't be startled to see a picture of TV star Mary Tyler Moore at the headquarters; her great-grandfather owned the house at the time and invited the general to use it. Call the Winchester Chamber of Commerce (☎ **540/662-4118**) for other information.

Virginia's **Museum of American Frontier Culture** in Staunton is a recently re-created village of cottages, barns, and small farms that show both the farmsteads the settlers left in the Old World and the way they reinterpreted them in the New World. (See "Ten Terrific Spots Where History Comes Alive," above.)

Thomas Jefferson is still very much alive in the countryside around Charlottesville, where people speak often of "Mr. Jefferson" as they would any respected neighbor and friend. **Monticello,** the dream home he designed and built himself, is magnificent but not overwhelming because it is built on a human scale. The moose and deer antlers on display in the entry hall were brought back to Jefferson by Meriwether Lewis and William Clark from their explorations in the West. Monticello is located in the Virginia Piedmont about 2 miles southeast of Charlottesville. To get there, take Interstate 64, exit 121 (if traveling westbound) or exit 121A (if traveling eastbound), make a right at the first light for the **Monticello Visitor Center** (☎ **804/984-9822;** www.monticello.org) or make a left at the first light for Monticello itself.

Jefferson was always generous and hospitable to guests, spending freely to entertain them even though he died with debts of $100,000, the equivalent of a million today. Dinner began at 4pm and often continued until dark, with the fine wines the president had shipped from France accompanying the fresh vegetables from his gardens. Dishes were prepared by one of Jefferson's servants, who had trained in Paris.

Jefferson tried to establish a vineyard at Monticello, so he'd be pleased to note that today the Charlottesville area is the wine capital of Virginia, with 10 local wineries producing table vintages. Oakencraft Vineyard and Winery, Simeon Vineyards, Montdomaine Cellars, and Totier Creek Vineyard usually offer tours and tastings except in winter. Get a free wine country guide from the **Virginia Wine Marketing Program,** VDACS, Division of Marketing, P.O. Box 1163, Richmond, VA 23219 (☎ **800/828-4637**).

Campground Oases in the Shenandoah Valley

Lake Fairfax Park. A Corps of Engineer Public Park in Reston, Virginia, Lake Fairfax Park is about 50 miles east of Front Royal (not in the Shenandoah Valley at all, but we had to fit it in somewhere) and within commuting distance of Washington. It provides 74 sites, 48 of them with 15- and 30-amp electric hookups. Toilets, showers, and a sanitary dump are provided, and there is a 7-day camping limit during the park season, which runs from March to early December. From the junction of I-495 and Route 7, head west 6.5 miles on Route 7 to Route 606, then south 0.1 miles to Lake Fairfax Dr. Turn left into the entrance. ☎ **703/471-5415.**

The Front Royal KOA. Open from mid-March to late November, the Front Royal KOA has a big swimming pool and 350-foot waterslide (there's a fee for the latter), hot tub, miniature golf, and stocked fishing pond. The 135 sites, while not large, are terraced and landscaped, some of them paved and some of them gravel, and the hilltop locations offer some cooling breezes in summer. Best of all for sightseers who don't want to drive their RVs in Washington, D.C., the park offers a daily shuttle tour by advance reservation. Located just outside Front Royal. Take Route 81 to Route 66 east; take exit 6 onto Route 340 South. Drive through town past Shenandoah National Park on the left. The entrance is 4.5 miles past the national park, also on the left. Call ☎ **800/KOA-9114.**

Matthews Arm. The Matthews Arm in Shenandoah National Park, on Skyline Drive at Mile 22.2 (which indicates the area is 22.2 miles south of the Front Royal Park entrance), is usually open late May through October, and offers several tree-shaded loops with 180 gravel back-in sites, not all of them large enough for big RVs. There is a sewage disposal dump and toilets, but no hookups, showers, or laundry. Ranger campfire programs are presented several times a day on summer weekends, less often during the week. Camping is on a first-come, first-served basis and costs $14 a night. Designated campsites for the disabled are available. ☎ 540/999-3500.

Big Meadows Campground. At Mile 51 on Skyline Drive, also in Shenandoah NP, Big Meadows provides 227 RV sites in a designated area separate from tent campsites. Hot showers are available for a small fee, and there's a sanitary dump station, laundry, and firewood for sale, but no hookups. Most sites are paved and can be reserved in advance by calling ☎ 800/365-CAMP or visiting www.reservations.nps.gov. Fees are $17 a night and ranger campfire programs are scheduled daily in summer. ☎ 540/999-3500.

Lewis Mountain Campground. Right off Skyline Drive at Mile 57.6 in Shenandoah NP, Lewis Mountain Campground has 31 sites, half of them tent sites and three of them pull-throughs, which in this park means a sort of curved driveway off the main road. There are no hookups and no sanitary dump, and sites are available on a first-come, first-served basis at $14 a night. ☎ 540/999-3231.

Loft Mountain. Lake Mountain is our favorite of the four sites in Shenandoah NP. Located off Skyline Drive at Mile 79.5, it has 221 paved sites, most of them shaded and more than half of them pull-throughs, some long enough for big rigs. Sites are available on a first-come, first-served basis at $14 a night, and there is a sanitary dump but no hookups. Ranger campfire programs are provided daily except Wednesdays in summer. ☎ 540/999-3500.

THE BLUE RIDGE PARKWAY

Construction began in 1935, and the final leg of the 469-mile road was finally completed in 1987 with the spectacularly engineered Linn Cove Viaduct,

---

NIGHTLIFE ALONG THE ROAD

Things are better than they used to be. We remember visiting in North Carolina a few years ago when someone suggested going out for a drink. "Where's the nearest bar?" we asked. "Washington, D.C.," our host answered dryly.

The best places in Virginia to look for life after dark are college towns like Charlottesville or rapidly gentrifying cities like Roanoke, where **Awful Arthur's**, at 108 Campbell Ave. downtown (☎ 540/344-2997), promises live entertainment Thursday nights and weekends, and **Montano's**, at 3733 Franklin Rd. SW (☎ 540/344-8960), offers jazz and a good wine list. Frankly, though, we prefer **Floyd County General Store** at 206 S. Locust St. in the town of Floyd (6 miles off the Blue Ridge Parkway at Mile 165.2) for its Friday Night Jamboree with live country music and clog dancing. ☎ 540/745-4563. 🚐

which seems to float lightly around venerable Grandfather Mountain as though suspended in midair.

Skyline Drive and the Blue Ridge Parkway were among President Franklin D. Roosevelt's make-work projects for the CCC (Civilian Conservation Corps) during the 1930s Depression. The intention was to provide drivers with a variety of untrammeled rural scenes, with the road following the landscape for optimum scenery rather than speed, which is limited to 45 m.p.h. The park area along the two roads averages about 1,000 feet wide, including the roadbed.

Split-rail fences, small log cabins, water-operated mills, barns, and farm fields may be glimpsed along the roadsides, as well as brilliant pink and lavender stands of wild rhododendron and mountain laurel and vivid orange splashes of flame azaleas in late spring and early summer. Arched stone bridges ornament the roads that cross over or under the parkway.

Nine visitor centers and 11 campgrounds, none with hookups but all accessible to any but the largest RV, are along the route, which passes through four national forests and the Cherokee Indian Reservation at its southern end, where it connects with Newfound Gap Road and the Great Smoky Mountains National Park.

The Appalachian Mountains were once the western frontier of America, and the isolated homesteads that remain—such as the **Puckett Cabin** at Mile 189, where "Aunt Orlean" Puckett gave birth to 24 children, none of whom lived past infancy, and the **Brinegar Cabin** at Mile 238, where weavers show how mountain women made their own fabrics—give a clearer picture than any history book of the hard and often lonely life of these fiercely independent people.

Our own favorite stop along the parkway is **Mabry Mill,** where volunteer musicians and craftspeople may hold an impromptu dulcimer concert or tell tall tales to a group of wide-eyed children. Someone's usually weaving split-willow baskets or whittling or blacksmithing. And the miller is almost always there, turning out white stone-ground cornmeal for sale by the bag. You can sample cornmeal and buckwheat pancakes at the little restaurant next door, along with slabs of country ham and hot homemade biscuits. (See "Ten Terrific Spots Where History Comes Alive," above.)

Animal life along the parkway is fairly sparse, except around campgrounds and at road crossings in early morning and late afternoon. White-tailed deer, opossums, raccoons, and skunks are the most common, along with chipmunks, squirrels, and woodchucks, also called groundhogs.

NINE BLUE RIDGE THINGS TO DO

1. **Head down into Luray Caverns.** Luray is the biggest among a number of cave complexes that lie like honeycombs beneath the Shenandoah Valley. It's big enough for claustrophobes to go inside to

LITERARY LIGHTS

Poet and Lincoln biographer **Carl Sandburg,** whose name is linked forever with Chicago, spent the last 22 years of his life on his farm at Flat Rock, near Hendersonville, NC. Now a National Historic Site, the farm Sandburg called Connemara is where the two-time Pulitzer Prize winner wrote a novel, poems, a screenplay (for *The Greatest Story Ever Told*), and his autobiography, in between playing his guitar and singing folk songs. His wife Paula Steichen, sister of photographer Edward Steichen, raised prize goats; there's still a herd of them around. The farm is on Little River Road off Route 25, 3 miles south of Hendersonville, and is open daily from 9am to 5pm. ☎ **828/693-4178.**

Old Kentucky Home, the boardinghouse at 48 Spruce St. in Asheville where author **Thomas Wolfe** spent his childhood and which he immortalized as Dixieland in his autobiographical novel *Look Homeward, Angel,* has served in recent years as the Thomas Wolfe Memorial State Historical Site, but was damaged by fire not long ago and at press time was undergoing reconstruction. While the interiors are not open to the public, exterior tours of the house and adjacent visitor center at 52 North Market St. are offered. Call ☎ **828/253-8304** for information. The angel of the book title, a funeral monument sold by Wolfe's father, can be seen in Hendersonville's Oakdale Cemetery ornamenting the grave of Margaret E. Johnson. 🚐

see and hear the world's only "stalacpipe" organ: tuned stalactites that are tapped with rubber-tipped hammers to make music. (How do you tune a stalactite? By grinding it down slightly.) Trivia lovers will like discovering the petrified fried eggs on one canyon wall and the blind albino shrimp that live in the underground river. But check out the times for the frequent carillon concerts, played out of the bell tower near the entrance. You don't want to be standing too near. ☎ **540/743-6551.**

2. **Visit Thomas Jefferson's vegetable gardens at Monticello.** The gardens are a re-creation of his original plantings in the late 18th century, which he painstakingly documented in 1807. Some rare and exotic vegetables no longer produced anywhere else share space with familiar favorites such as asparagus and artichokes, as well as 15 different varieties of English peas. Jefferson is the gardener who introduced eggplant to the United States. Open daily 8am to 5pm. ☎ **804/984-9822.**

3. **Drink a Dr. Pepper in rustic Rural Retreat, VA.** At exit 60 from I-81, tilt a cool one back in memory of the soda's inventor, a lovesick pharmacist's assistant who fell head over heels for his boss's daughter, was forbidden to woo her, and finally moved to Waco, Texas, where he patented and bottled his soft drink, named for his former boss and sweetheart's father, Dr. Charles Pepper.

4. **Check out far-out Floyd, VA.** Six miles off the Blue Ridge Parkway near Mile 165, Floyd is where New Age/neo-hippie handicrafts gallery New Mountain Mercantile co-exists with a 75-year-old general store that holds free hoedowns every Friday night. Just down the road a piece is Blue Ridge Restaurant, with home cooking and real mashed potatoes (☎ **540/745-2147**). Next door to the country store is Country Records, featuring the biggest collection of bluegrass music in the world, they say. Finally, just when you think you're getting a fix on Floyd, you run into Chateau Morrisette Winery with its jazz concerts, wine tastings, and French restaurant. At Mile 165, take State Route 8 north 5 miles into Floyd. Contact the Floyd County Chamber of Commerce for more information. ☎ **540/745-4407.**

5. **Lunch at Charlottesville's historic Michie Tavern.** Pronounced "Mickey," the Michie Tavern serves traditional southern dishes, from fried chicken and biscuits to black-eyed peas, stewed tomatoes, and cornbread plus local Virginia wines. This and more is served daily 11:30am to 3pm year-round for well under $10. Located at 683 Thomas Jefferson Parkway on Route 53 southeast of the city. ☎ **804/977-1234.**

6. **Follow the sound of fiddles to Bristol, VA.** The birthplace of country music has a mural commemorating Mother Maybelle Carter, matriarch of the legendary Carter Family, on State Street at Volunteer Parkway (on the side of the Lark Amusement Building, facing east). Every Saturday night at 7:30pm there's a live bluegrass show ($4 admission fee) at the Carter Family Fold in Hiltons, Virginia, off U.S. 58, five miles east of Kingsport, Tennessee (take Rte. 58—off exit 1 from Rte. 81—about 20 miles into Hilton; signs will show the directions to the house). Arrive early so you can browse through the displays of 78-rpm recordings, photographs, and musical instruments in the A. P. Carter Museum, open only on Saturdays from 6 to 7:30pm. ☎ **540/386-9480.**

7. **Head for the Galax Moose Lodge #733 Old Fiddlers' Convention in Galax, VA.** Located just off the Blue Ridge Parkway via Route 97 west, Galax hosts the world's oldest and largest old-time fiddlers contest over several days during the second week in August, drawing musicians who play as much for their own pleasure and each other as for the audience of thousands who congregate to this 60-year-old tradition. Many of the musicians arrive and stay in their own RVs, so other RVers should feel right at home here. ☎ **540/236-8541** or 540/238-8130.

8. **Visit the annual Natural Chimneys Jousting Contest.** The oldest continuously operated sporting event in the country is set against a backdrop of castlelike rock towers. The tournament, scheduled in

Musician at the Old Fiddlers' Convention in Galax, VA

August, has been going on since 1821 at this site near Mount Solon, southwest of Harrisonburg on Route 607. Natural Chimneys Regional Park and its 120 RV hookup sites is nearby. ☎ **540/350-2510** for jousting information or RV reservations.

9. **Run over and say "hidy" to John-Boy and his family.** The Waltons Mountain Museum in Schuyler, VA, on Route 617, commemorates the home town of Earl Hamner, Jr., creator of the popular TV series, and includes video interviews and episodes from the show, as well as recreations of the Hollywood sets for the series. (The "real" Waltons Mountain can be found at Frazier Park near Gorman in southern California, where location filming for the series often took place; one of this book's authors appeared occasionally on the show.) The museum is right on 617 at the top of a hill; open daily 10am to 4pm from early March until the end of November except for major holidays. ☎ **804/831-2000.**

Campground Oases Along the Blue Ridge Parkway
Walnut Hills Campground. Near Staunton, Virginia, Walnut Hills is a good base for visiting the notable Civil War sites in the area as well as the Frontier Culture Museum. Take exit 217 from I-81 and drive west on 654 to Route 11, then south to Route 655 and follow the signs. Most of the 125 modem-friendly sites are wide and shaded, with 30- and 50-amp electric hookups and satellite TV. It's open March 1 through mid-November. For reservations, call ☎ **800/699-2568** or use their e-mail, jpeter@cfw.com.

Natural Bridge/Lexington KOA. Open year-round off I-81, Exit 180, with some full hookups and pull-throughs for most of its 87 sites. Flush toilets, showers, a sanitary dump, laundry, groceries, LP gas, and dinner available nightly. ☎ **800/KOA-8514.**

Peaks of Otter. Peaks of Otter, on the Blue Ridge Parkway at Milepost 86 near Bedford, VA, has 59 paved sites, some with shade, 25 pull-throughs, flush toilets, piped water, and a sanitary dump. No hookups. Each site has a table and fireplace. Closed November through April. No reservations. ☎ **540/586-4357.**

Douthat State Park. Listed on the National Register of Historic Places for the role it played in the development of parks around the United States, Douthat State Park has been a family tradition in Virginia for more than half a century. The campground has 38 gravel sites with 30-amp electric hookups, toilets, showers, and a sanitary dump station, but the area also offers lodges, cabins, a restaurant, bathhouses, boating, and fishing in a lake stocked with trout. Take exit 27 off I-64 to Route 629, then turn north for 7 miles. ☎ **800/933-PARK** for reservations or 540/862-8100; www.state.va.us/~dcr.

Roanoke Mountain. Roanoke Mountain, near Vinton at Mile 120 of the Blue Ridge Parkway, has 105 campsites, some shaded, all paved, with flush toilets, piped water, and sanitary dump station. No hookups, no reservations, 14-day camping limit. Towed vehicles are not permitted on the Roanoke Mountain scenic loop drive. To get to the campground from Vinton, go east 2 miles on State Road 24 to Blue Ridge Parkway, then south 8 miles on the right. ☎ **540/982-9242.**

Claytor Lake State Park. Claytor Lake park, near Dublin, VA, has 139 sites, with water and 30-amp electric hookups, bass fishing, swimming, fishing, boating, and boat docks at the lake. Some shaded sites, some pull-throughs. Closed in winter. Located on State Road 660 two miles south of I-81 at Exit 101. The historic Howe House in the park features exhibits about the life of the early settlers in this region. ☎ **800/933-PARK;** www.state.va.us/~dcr.

Fairy Stone State Park. Fairy Stone State Park, on Route 57 between Stuart and Bassett, VA, is named for the little brown cross-shaped stones found in the area that legend says are the tears shed by elves and fairies when Christ was crucified. While hunting for them is permitted, don't worry if you can't find one on the ground; the gift shops in the area will be glad to sell you one. 51 sites with water and electrical hookups (20-amps), flush toilets, showers, sanitary dump station, bass fishing, swimming, boat ramp, and rentals. Closed in fall and winter. ☎ **540/930-1136.**

Fox Trail Family Campground. Just a quarter-mile down Route 683 off the Blue Ridge Parkway in Fancy Gap, Virginia, at Mile 199.5, Fox Trail campground is open year-round. Some of the 96 sites are shaded and there are 19 pull-throughs; 80 are full hookup with 30-amp electric. Contact them at ☎ **540/728-7776** or via e-mail at rwhite@tcia.net.

Hungry Mother State Park. Located near Marion, Virginia, Hungry Mother has 32 sites with electric (15- and 30-amp) and water hookups and a sanitary dump. Since some of the sites are quite narrow, they do not permit slideouts, but a lake offers freshwater fishing, swimming, and boating. Rates are $15 to $18 a night. Take I-81's exit 47 and follow Route 11 to State Road 16, then drive north 4 miles. ☎ **800/933-PARK** for reservations; www. state.va.us/~dcr.

Beartree Campground. Mt. Rogers National Recreation Area, near Marion, is tucked into the corner of southwestern Virginia not far from where its border touches both North Carolina and Tennessee. Beartree Campground has 91 gravel sites with flush toilets and showers, sanitary dump station, trout fishing, and swimming. No hookups, no slideouts. Closed in winter. Seven miles east of Damascus on U.S. 58. ☎ **540/783-5196.**

Grayson Highlands State Park. Located near Mouth of Wilson, VA, Grayson Highlands Park has 73 sites with electrical hookups and sanitary dump station. The town name comes from its position at the head of Wilson Creek, famous regionally for its trout fishing, and the campground provides good fishing access to the stream. From I-81, take exit 45 and go south on State Road 16 to Route 58, then west 8 miles. ☎ **800/933-PARK** for reservations, or 540/579-7092; www.state.va.us/~dcr.

Doughton Park. On the Blue Ridge Parkway at Mile 238.5, Doughton Park has 20 grass sites open May 1 to November 1. Flush toilets, sanitary dump, planned activities schedule. No hookups, no reservations. This is an especially good place to spot deer at dawn and dusk. ☎ **828/298-0398.**

Julian Price Memorial Park. On the Blue Ridge Parkway near Mile 297, Julian Price park has 68 paved sites, flush toilets, sanitary dump, fishing, and boating. No hookups, no reservations. Most sites shaded, some pull-throughs, 14-day maximum stay. Open May to November. ☎ **828/ 298-0398.**

ASHEVILLE

The pretty mountain city of Asheville will be forever mingled with the memory of native son Thomas Wolfe for many readers. His thinly fictionalized story of "Altamont" and Eliza Gant's "Dixieland" boardinghouse in his epic first novel *Look Homeward, Angel* apparently embarrassed everyone in town, including his mother, the model for the boardinghouse keeper. His books were banned by the local public library until 1935, when F. Scott Fitzgerald, shocked that the local author was not represented, bought two copies of *Look Homeward, Angel* and donated them to the library.

Later, after Wolfe's death (he died before his 38th birthday), all was forgiven, and **Old Kentucky Home,** that boardinghouse at 48 Spruce St., is today the Thomas Wolfe Memorial State Historic Site.

Another Blue Ridge author, Greensboro-born short story writer **O. Henry,** is buried in Asheville's Riverside Cemetery, on Birch Street, not far from Thomas Wolfe's grave.

In years past, a lot of wealthy Americans liked the city's cool summer climate and clear mountain air enough to set up seasonal residence, including Henry Ford, Thomas Edison, John D. Rockefeller, Grover Cleveland, and Theodore Roosevelt. In the 1890s, George Washington Vanderbilt, grandson of the fabulously wealthy Commodore Vanderbilt, constructed **Biltmore House,** a 250-room French Renaissance mansion at the edge of Asheville. It's open daily for fairly pricey house tours ($29.95 for adults, $22.50 for youths 10 and over), as well as rose garden tours and wine-tasting from the Vanderbilt vineyard. If the mansion looks familiar, you're remembering it as the location for the Peter Sellers film *Being There,* a classic forerunner to *Forrest Gump,* as well as the home of Macaulay Culkin's Richie Rich in the film of the same name. From the Blue Ridge Parkway, Biltmore is about 4 miles from the Highway 25 north exit. From Interstate 40 West, the entrance is north of exit 50B on Highway 25. From Interstate 40 East, the entrance is north of exit 50 on Highway 25. Call ☎ **800/543-2961.**

Besides its evocative turn-of-the-century resort buildings (see Grove Park Inn under "Ten Special Splurges," above), Asheville also is a treasure trove of art deco architecture, with a city hall and First Baptist Church (5 Oak St.) from the late 1920s, as well as the handsome S&W Cafeteria on Patton Avenue.

Campground Oases Near Asheville

Mt. Pisgah. On the Blue Ridge Parkway near Mile 408, Mt. Pisgah has 70 paved campsites available with patios, some shade. Flush toilets, sanitary dump station, groceries. No hookups or reservations. Open May to November; 14-day camping limit. ☎ **828/298-0398.**

GREAT SMOKY MOUNTAINS NATIONAL PARK

The most visited national park in the system, Great Smoky Mountains gets some eight million people a year passing through its rather garish portals, the commercial strip in **Cherokee** on the east side with its "Indian chiefs" standing by Plains Indian teepees, holding tom-toms and wearing feathered war bonnets Cherokees never used, and gaudy **Gatlinburg,** which has turned shopping, sleeping, and eating into big business.

The only place tackier than either is nearby Pigeon Forge with its flashy **Dollywood** theme park and bumper-to-bumper traffic inching its way past wall-to-wall motels and fast-food joints. Country singer/movie star Dolly

Dolly Parton invites visitors to Dollywood in Pigeon Forge, TN.

Parton, keeping abreast of the trend, has turned this formerly bucolic pottery-making village near her birthplace into a tawdry tourist town gripped with gridlock. If we didn't know better, we'd think she built it to get even with some brats who snubbed her in grammar school.

But you can get away if you try. Pay heed to any of the "Quiet Walkways" signs within the National Park to take an easy and enchanting streamside or woodland stroll. Exploring the side roads leads to special pleasures. A detour to Clingmans Dome winds past the **Indian Gap Trailhead** with its ruts well worn from the countless horse-drawn vehicles that labored along this former toll road in the 19th century. **Hiking trails,** except in the most popular months of June, July, and October, are often uncrowded, since many of the visitors are making a beeline for Gatlinburg or Pigeon Forge.

The park is an international Biosphere Reserve and a World Heritage Site, and bear sightings are still fairly common, with some 850 of the furry fellows in residence. Both peregrine falcons and river otters have also been seen there lately.

Campground Oases in Great Smoky Mountains National Park

There are ten developed campgrounds in the park, none with showers or hookups. The summer camping limit is 7 days, with 14 days permitted at those that are open in winter.

Advance reservations for summer and fall camping may be made at Cades Cove, Elkmont, and Smokemont campgrounds by calling ☎ **800/365-CAMP** or contacting their Web site at reservations.nps.gov. Except during the winter months, there are sewage dump stations available at Smokemont, Cades Cove, Deep Creek, and Cosby campgrounds and across from the Sugarlands Visitor Center at the Gatlinburg entrance. These campgrounds are on a first-come, first-served basis. Contact the rangers office (☎ **423/436 1200**) for information.

Great Smoky Mountains National Park

NORTH CAROLINA

Area of Detail

Legend

♦ Lookout tower
▲ Peak
■ Point of interest

Campgrounds

Abrams Creek **2**
Balsam Mountain **7**
Big Creek **9**
Cade's Cove **3**
Cataloochee **8**
Cosby Campground **10**
Deep Creek **5**
Elkmont **4**
Look Rock **1**
Smokemont **6**

GREAT SMOKIES RV SAFETY TIPS

A traffic sign just inside the park from the Gatlinburg entrance to Great Smoky Mountains National Park cautions that tunnels ahead on the highway have a clearance of only 12 feet 2 inches, a close call for many modern basement-model motorhomes with roof air conditioners, TV antennae, and satellite dishes.

"I wish they had consulted with me before they put that up," said a ranger on duty at Sugarlands Visitor Center. "The 12 foot measurement is on the extreme sides of an arched tunnel that measures 17 feet in the center and almost all the RVs get through without scraping."

When in doubt, inch toward the center when entering the tunnel and you should clear it without a problem.

The same ranger cautioned that motorhomes and vehicles pulling trailers should avoid traveling the dirt and gravel scenic drives in the park, but that the popular Cades Cove Loop is accessible to all.

About the campground limits specified in the park newspaper and listed above, he said RVs slightly larger than the limit may be able to access some sites in the campgrounds if the driver is adept.

A valuable **Auto Touring Map** ($1) is available at the park visitor centers, mapping in detail most of the 270 miles of roadway in the Smokies. Check at Sugarlands Visitor Center at the Gatlinburg, TN, entrance; Oconaluftee Visitor Center at the Cherokee, NC, entrance; and Cades Cove Visitor Center inside the park on Cades Cove Road, 2 miles south of Townsend, TN. In addition, a knowledgeable ranger can easily recommend which routes to take and which to avoid, depending on your RV's dimensions.

Abrams Creek. Reached by Happy Valley Road from Chilhowee, Tennessee, at the extreme western end of the park (and not accessible to any other park areas), Abrams Creek has 16 sites. No RVs over 12 feet. Open mid-March to early November. $10.

Balsam Mountain. Balsam Mountain is accessed by the Blue Ridge Parkway from Mile 458.2 and 12 miles along the Heintooga Ridge Road spur, which is paved but very narrow, steep, and winding. Do not attempt to drive beyond the campground along the one-way gravel Balsam Mountain Road because motorhomes and vehicles pulling trailers are prohibited. 46 sites, accommodating RVs up to 30 feet. Open late May to late September. $10.

Cades Cove. Reached by the loop road from Sugarlands Visitor Center outside Gatlinburg or from the Townsend Visitor Center entrance on Tennessee's Route 73, Cades Cove has 161 sites and allows RVs up to 35 feet. Open year-round. $12 to $15.

Cataloochee. Reached from I-40 at exit 20 along Cove Creek Road (much of it unpaved), Cataloochee has 27 sites, accommodating RVs up to 31 feet. Open mid-March to early November. $10.

Cosby Campground. Outside the bustling little town of Cosby, Tennessee, on Route 32 off U.S. 321 (or via the Foothills Parkway turnoff, Exit 443 from I-40), the Cosby Campground has 175 sites accommodating RVs up to 25 feet. Open mid-March to early November. $12.

Deep Creek. On Deep Creek Road, just inside the park boundary from Bryson City, NC, Deep Creek has 108 sites that take RVs up to 26 feet. Open early April to early November. $12.

Elkmont. Just off Cades Cove Road not far from Sugarlands Visitor Center at Gatlinburg, Elkmont has 220 sites accommodating RVs up to 32 feet. Open mid-March to late November. $12 to $15.

Look Rock. At the edge of the park's northwest boundaries off Foothill Parkway 10 miles northeast of Chilhowee, Look Rock offers 92 sites, taking RVs up to 35 feet. Open late May until early November. $12.

Smokemont. Located along Newfound Gap Road a few miles north of Oconaluftee Visitor Center on the North Carolina side of the park, Smokemont has 140 sites accommodating RVs up to 27 feet. Open year-round. $12 to $15.

Campground Oases on the Tennessee Side of the Smokies

Pigeon Forge/Gatlinburg KOA. A great location for families who want to visit Dollywood and revel in the gaudy tourist traps of Pigeon Forge—it's only a few blocks off the main street and has city trolley shuttle service to town and to the Dollywood park. The 181 hookup sites (30-amp) are comfortably spacious, mostly gravel surface with some paved or grass. Cable TV, shuffleboard, heated pool, and hot tub are on the premises when the lure of Pigeon Forge and Gatlinburg wears off. From the junction of U.S. 411 and Wears Valley Road (U.S. 321-S), go south 2.1 miles on U.S. 411 to Dollywood Lane, east 0.3 miles to Cedar Top Lane, north 1,000 feet, then follow the signs. Call ☎ 800/KOA-7703 for reservations; call well in advance for summer and fall stays. If Pigeon Forge KOA is fully booked, try **Knoxville East KOA,** only 12 miles away off I-40 at exit 407 (☎ **800/KOA-8693**), or **Newport KOA** (☎ **800/KOA-9016**) on Route 27W-70, 1.6 miles west of I-40, exit 432B, half an hour from the Great Smokies NP entrance, Pigeon Forge, Dollywood, or Gatlinburg.

Outdoor Resorts. Like its sister resorts in Palm Springs, Outdoor Resorts, in Gatlinburg's Cobbly Nob resort area, is a "condo park," meaning the sites are owned and occupied except for 26 (in this park) that are made available for transient visitors. These spacious, sparkling clean, beautifully landscaped parks are a cut above most private RV parks, and, if you're fussy about your surroundings, worth the higher price. Here, it's $26 to $30, about $10 a night higher than some neighboring parks. Located on 321 north out of Gatlinburg. Call ☎ **423/436-5861** for reservations.

Travel Quiz: Hello, Dolly!

In honor of a pair of Dollys associated with Virginia and Tennessee, each of the following Dollys, real or fictional, is identified with a specific geographic location. See if you can match them up.

1. Dolly Parton

2. Dolly Levi

3. Dolly Madison

4. Dolly Sinatra

5. The Dolly Sisters

6. Salvador Dalí

7. The Dalai Lama

a. Descending the grand staircase of Delmonico's Restaurant, New York City

b. Hanging in an eponymous museum in Tampa, Florida

c. Running a tavern in Hoboken, New Jersey

d. Hanging out with actor Richard Gere in Hollywood

e. Headlining at the Palace in New York City

f. Keeping abreast of an amusement park in Pigeon Forge, Tennessee

g. Hosting an ice cream social in Washington, D.C., or Montpelier, Virginia

ANSWERS: 1 (f); 2 (a); 3 (g); 4 (c); 5 (e); 6 (b); 7 (d)

⑬ The Lobster Coast: New England & the Canadian Maritimes

AS THE MAN WHO LED A LOBSTER ON A LEASH THROUGH THE gardens of the Palais Royal in Paris explained, "I have a liking for lobsters. They are peaceful, serious creatures. They know the secrets of the sea, they don't bark, and they don't gnaw on one's monadic privacy like dogs do."

Lobsters were served at the first Thanksgiving dinner, and were so plentiful that until this century they were used for fertilizer, fish bait, and jail food. The largest lobster ever recorded was 48 pounds with a length of 3½ feet. They are nocturnal and generally eat fish and shellfish. And, as the man said, they don't bark.

Our Lobster Land drive covers New England and Canada's Maritime provinces of New Brunswick, Prince Edward Island, and Nova Scotia.

It was along this North Atlantic coast that Alexander Graham Bell invented the telephone and Guglielmo Marconi sent out the first wireless message across the Atlantic, where Ruth Wakefield baked the first Toll House cookies, and where Sicily-born Benedetto Capalbo floated the first submarine sandwich. So popular were they during World War II that he supplied 500 a day to the local submarine base in New London, Connecticut—which is how the sandwich he called a "grinder" got its new name.

New England is the birthplace of the graham cracker and the Parker House roll, where Lydia Pinkham's Vegetable Compound "for periodic female weakness" was produced and the birth control pill invented, where Lizzie Borden took an ax and the Brink's burglars took a powder, where the burglar alarm was invented, Earl Tupper sealed up Tupperware, Clarence Birdseye flash-froze food, and the first snowmobile cranked up back in 1913.

The first Frisbees came from fun-loving Bridgeport, Connecticut, where Robert Mitchum was born and P. T. Barnum lived, only they were originally spelled "Frisbies"—pie tins from a local bakery with the name stamped on the bottom that Yale students in the twenties tossed as a fad.

Newport, Rhode Island, boasts the first traffic ordinance (1687) and the first automobile arrest—for speeding at 15 m.p.h. (1904).

Saint John, New Brunswick, is where Donald Sutherland was born, MGM's Louis B. Mayer grew up, Captain Kidd raped and pillaged, and the King of Siam's Anna Leonowens retired to found an arts academy. Benedict Arnold was burned in effigy and driven out of town—not for being a traitor (he was a hero to the Loyalists) but for nefarious business dealings.

RVing in New England & the Maritimes

The Lobster Coast route heads north along the edge of Connecticut and Rhode Island, jogs over to Cape Cod, then back up the shore to Boston, Salem, and Gloucester, the 18-mile coastline of New Hampshire, and the 3,500-mile coastline of Maine. (You'll know you're in Maine when the license plates have bright red lobsters on them.) After that, it carries on through New Brunswick's Loyalist and Acadian country to Nova Scotia. Prince Edward Island, which also has very fine lobsters, was once reached only by plane or ferry, inconvenient but not impossible for RVers, but now has a bridge from New Brunswick. The whole route one-way is approximately 1,200 miles, more if you dip into all Maine's picturesque coves and make a loop around Nova Scotia, and explore inland.

Canada's Maritimes offer good driving in most areas for freewheelers, but maneuvering an RV through New England is not always easy. Roads are narrow and often crowded with traffic, especially in summer around Cape Cod or Kennebunkport, and there are not a lot of pullover spots spacious enough for a big rig. The best way to explore most of the towns and villages along the Lobster Coast is to park your RV and set out on foot.

HITTING THE HIGHLIGHTS

If 2 weeks is the maximum time you have for a Lobster Land vacation, you'll still be able to make the coastal drive to Nova Scotia and back from a New York or Connecticut starting point, as well as the journey around Cape Cod, but you might have to miss the day trips to Nantucket and Martha's Vineyard. Allow 1 week for New England, the second week for Canada's Maritimes. June is less crowded than July and August and the autumn, but some of the campgrounds and attractions may not be open for the season.

GOING FOR THE LONG HAUL

If you want to spend more than 2 or 3 weeks on the Lobster Coast, you'd better make your plans and arrangements well in advance for July and August. And don't expect to get reduced rates for a long stay in a private campground during the summer; one New Hampshire operator charged us double for the Fourth of July weekend, even though we were in residence for a month, because that's his peak season. As a Cape Cod friend reminded us, they have to make their profits for the whole year in only a few short months.

Highlights of the New England Coast

Acadia National Park ❷
Arnold's Lobster & Clam Bar ㉕
Baxter State Park ❶
Boothbay Harbor/*Islander* cruises ❼
Cape Cod Potato Chip Factory ㉖
Cape Cod Scenic Railroad ㉖
Cappy's Chowder House ❹
Clam Box ⓲
Claremont Hotel ❸
Durgin-Park ㉑
Farnham's ⓲
Foxwoods Casino ㉘
Frank Pepe Pizzeria Napoletana ㉙
Harlow's Bread & Cracker Company ⓭
Harraseeket Lunch & Lobster ❾
Jared Coffin House ㉗
John F. Kennedy Library and Museum ㉑
Jordan Pond Lodge ❷
Juventino's Portuguese Bakery ㉔
Kitchen Little ㉘
L.L. Bean Showroom ❾
Louis' Lunch ㉙
Moxie shop ❽
Museum of Family Camping ⓮
Mystic Seaport ㉘
New England Carousel Museum, Bristol ㉚
New England Carousel Museum, Mystic ㉘
New England Maple Museum ⓱
Old Sturbridge Village ㉛
Owls Head Transportation
   Museum ❺
Peabody Essex Museum ⓴
Plimouth Plantation ㉓
Portland Public Market ❿
Salem Witch Museum ⓴
Sally's Apizza ㉙
Strawberry Banke ⓬
Vermont Country Store, Rockingham ⓯
Vermont Country Store, Weston ⓰
Wauwinet Inn ㉗
Wedding Cake House ⓫
White Cap ⓲
Wiscasset's antique shops ❻
Wonder Bread/Hostess Bakery ㉒
Woodmans clam stand ⓲

Top Lobster Spots
Abbott's Lobster
   in the Rough ㉘
Beal's Lobster Pier ❸
Clam Shack ⓫
Fisherman's Landing ❷
Gloucester House ⓳
Harraseeket Lunch
   & Lobster Company ❾
Lobster Pot ㉔
Lobster Shack ❿
Lobsterman's Co-op ❼
Mabel's Lobster Claw ⓫
Nunan's Lobster Hut ⓫

The only time more popular in New England than July and August are the autumn foliage months when the "leaf peepers" arrive by the carload and busload. Still, it's the prettiest time of the year, so try to take refuge in some off-the-beaten-track towns and villages or head north to Canada to wait out the invasion. New Brunswick is filled with great discoveries and is uncrowded the year-round; you could easily spend a month exploring there.

Travel Essentials

WHEN TO GO
Summer and fall is prime lobster season, and also when the weather is best. Unfortunately, that's also when everyone else goes. If you go too early in June, you'll encounter the mosquitoes, black flies, and no see'ums. Autumn is crowded with leaf peepers, who go for the fall foliage. They travel in groups, often by tour bus.

WHAT TO TAKE
Binoculars, film and camera, rain gear, hiking boots, sun hat, sunscreen, and insect repellent. To enter Canada, you should have proof of citizenship, such as a passport, birth certificate, or voter registration card because a driver's license is no longer acceptable. (Some Canadian border guards let people through with only a license, but it's not technically legal. Better safe than sorry.)

WHAT TO WEAR
If you want to mingle at the posher purlieus of New England like Bar Harbor, Nantucket, and Martha's Vineyard, wear anything from the L.L. Bean, J. Crew, or Land's End catalogues, topsiders without socks, plaid or khaki Bermuda shorts, Oxford cloth shirts, and pastel sweaters tied casually around your neck. Otherwise, don your usual RV garb and you'll fit in almost everywhere.

Always have a sweater or jacket handy. The Maine coastal weather on a nice summer day is described by author Frances FitzGerald as Baked Alaska, a simultaneous sensation of hot sun and cool breeze. And 18th-century Nova Scotia residents were nicknamed "Bluenoses" for bearing up under the cold winters.

TRIMMING COSTS ON THE ROAD
First of all, never eat your lobster in a restaurant. You can pick it up at a lobster pound live or cooked. Take a live lobster back to the RV and cook it or refrigerate it until later (see "Looking for Lobster in All the Right Places," below). A hot cooked lobster can be brought back to the RV or eaten on the spot at a picnic table thoughtfully provided by the pound or the town. At many pounds, you'll be able to pick up side dishes and beverages, even beer or wine, to go with your steaming crustacean.

Canadian Maritimes Highlights

Acadian Historic Village ⓫
Alexander Graham Bell National
  Historic Park, Museum & yacht ❺
Algonquin Resort ⓭
Anne Murray Centre ❿
Cooperative Artisanale ❷
Fortress Louisbourg National
  Historic Park ❼
Ganong's Chocolate Factory ⓬
Glendora Falls Distillery ❻
Highland Village ❸

Keltic Lodge ❶
Kings Landing ⓬
Maritime Museum of the Atlantic ❽
Moosehead Brewery ⓮
Old City Market, Saint John, NB ⓮
Reversing Falls Rapids ⓮
Roots Cape Breton genealogical
  research center ❻
Salmon Museum ❸
Shelburne, Nova Scotia ❾

I-0367

Even though the Canadian dollar is considerably lower in value than the U.S. dollar at this writing, don't let it go to your head.

Make the most of admission to living history parks by planning to spend the day, either taking a lunch in with you or buying one (prices are reasonable) in the on-site restaurants. If you have children along, they'll experience new dishes and utensils so interesting they'll forget they never liked such-and-so.

Plan your beach visits for state parks or national parks like Cape Cod or Acadia; many of the beaches in the northeast are private.

WHERE TO GET TRAVEL INFORMATION

It's easy to find out what's going on in New England and the Maritimes. Stop at any tourist information spot, particularly those on main highways at the entrance to a state or province, and you can pick up campground information, times and prices for attractions, maps, and leaflets on everything from local farmer's markets to self-guided drives or walks—all of it free. If you want to get information and maps ahead of time, contact the following regional tourism offices.

- **Connecticut Department of Economic Development,** Tourism Division, 865 Brook St., Rocky Hill, CT 06067 (☎ **800/CT-BOUND;** www.ctbound.org).

- **Maine Office of Tourism,** 189 State St., State House Station 59, Augusta, ME 04333 (☎ **800/533-9595;** www.visitmaine.com).

- **Massachusetts Office of Travel & Tourism,** 100 Cambridge St., 13th floor, Boston, MA 02202 (☎ **800/447-6277;** www.mass-vacation.com).

- **New Hampshire Office of Travel and Tourism,** Box 856, Concord, NH 03302 (☎ **800/FUN-IN-NH,** ext. 7963, or 603/271-2666; www.visitnh.gov).

- **New Brunswick Tourism,** Dept. 243, P.O. Box 12345, Woodstock, NB, Canada E7M 6C3 (☎ **800/561-0123** for the U.S. and Canada outside New Brunswick; www.gov.nb.ca.tourism), publishes a New Brunswick Travel Guide.

- **Nova Scotia Tourism,** P.O. Box 519, Halifax, NS, Canada B3J 2M7 (☎ **800/565-0000;** www.explore.gov.ns.ca/virtualns). Can also arrange reservations at hotels or campgrounds.

- **Rhode Island Tourism Division,** 7 Jackson Walkway, Providence, RI 02903 (☎ **800/556-2484;** www.visitrhodeisland.com).

- **Tourism Prince Edward Island,** Marketing Council Visitor Services, P.O. Box 940, Charlottetown, PEI, Canada C1A 7M5 (☎ **888/PEI-PLAY;** www.peiplay.com/emily).

DRIVING & CAMPING TIPS

- **Watch for low and narrow passes.** On New England and Canada's old side roads, be a stickler for reading underpass and tunnel clearance signs, gauging overhead branches, and eyeballing narrow roads before you start your turn.

- **Beware of small-scale campgrounds.** Many of the RV parks and campgrounds in this region were built a couple of decades ago, even earlier, to accommodate mostly tent campers and small trailers or folding camping trailers. Today's large motorhomes with extra-wide bodies and slideouts—as well as basement storage that means more height on top, satellite dishes, and rooftop air conditioners—may face a tight squeeze in some New England campgrounds.

- **Check ahead about power requirements.** Many older campgrounds have not added 50-amp electricity although most (not all) have 30-amp. In places, particularly New England and Canadian state and provincial parks, the hookups may offer 15- or 20-amp electricity only. We found it a good idea to phone ahead and emphasize our size and amperage requirements, then reiterate it when we check in.

- **Expect fog.** You'll probably encounter some foggy or misty patches of road along the coast, especially in the mornings, with drizzle that might go on all day.

Best Sights, Tastes & Experiences of the Lobster Coast

OFF-THE-WALL ATTRACTIONS

The New England Carousel Museum, Bristol & Mystic, CT. Everything you need to know about carousels and carved wooden horses (for example, they're not carved from one block of wood, but assembled from more than 50 separate pieces of wood). You can watch antique wooden horses being reconstructed, learn the distinctive characteristics of the different types, and see some of the band organs that cranked out the music for the carousels. There are two locations: the main museum in Bristol, 95 Riverside Ave., Route 72, 06010 (☎ 860/585-5411), and a branch in Mystic at 193 Greenmanville Ave., Route 27 (☎ 860/536-7862), just off Exit 90 from I-95. Admission is $4 for adults, $2 for children.

The New England Maple Museum, Pittsford, VT. You'll meet an animatronic New England maple syrup maker, peek into some dioramas that show sugaring in the early 1900s, admire some maple-syrup-inspired folk art, and take a maple syrup tasting (don't knock it if you haven't tried it) that shows the subtle flavor differences between the different grades. An extensively stocked gift shop sells everything maple syrupy you can imagine and then some. The museum is north of Pittsford, on Route 7, and is open daily 8am to 5:30pm between late May and October, as well as November 1 through December 23 and late March to late May, 10am to 4pm. ☎ **802/483-9414.**

Vermont Country Store, Rockingham & Weston. Want to pick up some cow udder balm to keep your hands soft or supple, some almost-forgotten candies like Walnettos or Valomilk bars, or some soft, all-cotton Buster Brown socks? Head for the Vermont Country Store. It has two locations, but we like the Rockingham branch with its bargain attic, really a ground-level side building full of steeply discounted items so weird they might not move even at 75% off. You can also taste and buy Vermont farmhouse cheeses, including a wonderful Crowley Colby-type cheese "made just down the road," along with Vermont common crackers baked on the premises. The Rockingham store is off I-91's Exit 6 on Route 103 and is open daily (☎ **802/824-3184**). The main store is a few miles northwest in Weston, on Route 100 (☎ **802/463-2224**). Mail order: ☎ **802/362-8440.**

Cape Cod Potato Chip Factory, near Hyannis, MA. Watch the chips being kettle-cooked one batch at a time at Breed's Hill Road in Independence Park near Hyannis, where they turn out 200,000 bags of the crunchy little darlings every day. They'll give you a bag free as you leave. Self-guided tours year-round on weekdays only between 9am and 5pm. From Route 6, turn onto Route 132; on Route 132, take a left at the fourth traffic light onto Independence Drive, go to the second stop sign, and take a right onto Breed's Hill Road. The chip factory is on the left. ☎ **508/ 775-7253.**

The Salem Witch Museum. Located in a former church by Salem Common, the museum re-creates the hysteria of the 17th-century witch hunts with satanic symbols, taped music, mimed hangings in silhouette, and other spooky silliness performed with more enthusiasm than expertise. The audience loves it. It's in downtown Salem, on Route 1A diagonally across from the commons. ☎ **978/744-1692;** www.salemwitchmuseum.com.

Peabody Essex Museum, Salem, MA. Also in Salem, this classy museum on East India Square displays an astonishing collection of the curiosities local sea captains brought back home from the exotic East—shrunken heads, stuffed penguins, giant sea clams, ship models, Chinese export porcelain, Polynesian barkcloth, Japanese warrior costumes, and a huge moon bed carved from a single piece of teak. Open year-round. Adults $8.50, children $5. ☎ **800/745-4054;** www.pem.org.

Alexander Graham Bell's Yacht, Baddeck, NS. Learn to sail aboard Alexander Graham Bell's classic 59-foot yacht *Elsie,* which has been cruising the Bras d'Or from Baddeck, Nova Scotia, for 80 years. You can book

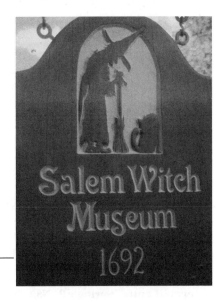

The Salem Witch Museum

lessons aboard, as well as day cruises, overnights, and longer cruises of up to 2 weeks between mid-June and the end of October. Call ☎ **800/ 565-5660** or visit www.elsie@morandan.com

The Wedding Cake House, Kennebunk, ME. Located on Summer Street, Route 35, Kennebunk, this is a gorgeously ornamental 19th-century house built, it is said, by a sea captain for his new bride after he went to sea without even having a taste of his own wedding cake. It's a drive-by site not open to the public.

Owls Head Transportation Museum, Owls Head, ME. Watch the Red Baron's Fokker triplane from World War I soar into the sky or listen to the hiss of a Stanley Steamer. On summer weekends you not only see antique motorcycles, biplanes, automobiles, and farm machinery but hear them and smell them—these antique machines are all in working order and cranked up regularly. Visitors may even be offered a ride in a Model T Ford. Call ahead to see which machines are running and when. The museum is 2 miles south of Rockland on Route 73. ☎ **207/594-4418;** www.ohtm.org.

Claremont Hotel, Southwest Harbor, ME. The nine-wicket croquet tournaments at the Claremont Hotel, located on the Claremont Road in Southwest Harbor, draw international attention from the croquet circuit; you can watch the action from the big front porch. Call for dates: ☎ **207/ 244-5036;** www.acadia.net/claremont. Take the Maine Turnpike to Augusta, and exit to Route 3. Take Route 3 through Ellsworth to the Trenton Bridge and Mount Desert Island. Once over the bridge, take Route 102 to Southwest Harbor and follow the signs to Claremont.

The Reversing Falls Rapids, Saint John, NB. The reversing rapids are produced by a phenomenon called a *tidal bore*. It happens twice a day when high tides in the Bay of Fundy cause the Saint John River to turn back on itself and flow upstream until the bay again drops below the river level and the river reverses itself again. Since the tides here are the highest in the world and the river bed has an underwater ledge, the boiling and surging of the water is dramatic. Best way to watch is from Fallsview Park, near the Reversing Falls Information Center (15 Market Square, St. Johns, NB). The highest tides are when the moon is full. Sea kayaking in the bay is the latest thrill around Saint John. Call Saint John Visitors and Convention Bureau at ☎ 506/658-2990.

Glendora Falls Distillery, Cape Breton Island, NS. For a real Scottish moment, head for this distillery on Highway 19 between Mabou and Inverness, where the only single-malt Scotch whiskey in North America is produced. The place is still new and the whiskey still aging, but you can take a tour. ☎ 902/258-2662.

Anne Murray Centre, Springhill, NS. This is the most popular tourist attraction in town dedicated to the town's top pop singer, whose recording of "Snowbird" might well be the theme song for all winter-escaping RVers. You should be able to find a copy in the gift shop, if you want to spring for the admission fee. 36 Main St., Springhill, Nova Scotia. ☎ 902/597-8614.

Wonder Bread/Hostess Bakery, Natick, MA. If you ever wondered how that sweet creamy glop gets inside a Hostess Twinkie, take a detour in the Boston area to the Wonder Bread/Hostess Bakery in Natick, Massachusetts, where free tours take you along the assembly line where Twinkies, Wonder Bread, and Hostess cupcakes are made. Free samples, too. A tip: The floors are slippery, so wear rubber-soled shoes. Call ☎ 508/655-2150 for the four daily tour times and a reservation. Tours are offered on non-holiday Mondays, Wednesdays, and Fridays between September and May. Natick is off I-90 west of Boston at Exit 13. Take Route 30 east and turn right on Speen Street to the bakery parking lot.

THREE THOUGHT-PROVOKING PLACES

The John F. Kennedy Library and Museum, Dorchester, MA. Exhibits, films, tapes, and slides trace JFK's career and that of his brother Robert F. Kennedy. A half-hour biographical film runs regularly. The striking building design is by I. M. Pei. Located by the sea (follow directional signs from I-93) and open daily 9am to 5pm except major holidays. ☎ 617/929-9523.

Baxter State Park. Maine's 200,000-acre Baxter State Park is rugged, primitive, and guaranteed to stay pristine forever. Back in the 1920s, Governor Percival Proctor Baxter suggested the legislature acquire Mount Katahdin and its surroundings to be preserved as a park, but the legislators balked at the expense. So Baxter spent the next 30 years buying up parcels of land himself and donating them as a park "to be maintained primarily as Wilderness . . . [and] be Forever Wild." Roads are gravel or dirt and usually narrow and winding. Self-contained RVs, motorcycles, and pets are not permitted inside the park; all overnight camping is by reservation only. Backpackers and hikers will find 175 miles of wilderness trails. Even if you take a 4×4 and drive through the park, you'll have to get out and walk down a trail to see the most spectacular scenery; it's designed that way. The park can be found northwest of Millinocket off Route 11/157 via a paved private road to the park entrance or via 163 east from Adesque Isle to Ashland, then by private unpaved road into the park. Both access roads require a permit and fee. Call ☎ **207/ 723-5140** for reservation forms that can be made only by mail.

The Maritime Museum of the Atlantic, Halifax, NS. A deck chair and other wood artifacts from the *Titanic* are among the displays in this museum. As the closest port to the disaster, Halifax hosted hundreds of funerals for more than 10 days. Today the unclaimed bodies of some 150 victims are still buried in three different Halifax cemeteries. Only 5 years later, the city faced its own disaster, the Halifax Explosion, when two ships, one of them carrying a half-million pounds of TNT plus other explosives, collided in the harbor, killing 2,000 people instantly and destroying much of the city. Located at 1675 Lower Water St. in Halifax, NS. Open daily 9:30am to 5:30pm and some evenings. Admission: Adults $4.50, seniors $3.50, children 5 and under are free. ☎ **902/424-7490.**

LIVING HISTORY SITES

New England and Canada's Maritimes have a plethora of "animated" villages that re-create life in an earlier time. Costumed actors, also called interpreters or animators, usually portray a real person who lived in the village at a chosen time. Some villages are fixed permanently in a given year, and day-to-day life goes on exactly as it would have then. No one seems to mind if you come into their kitchens while they prepare a meal, poke your head in the barn, or talk to someone tending a garden or feeding the farm animals. They are happy to pose for pictures as well.

Mystic Seaport. Connecticut's Mystic Seaport, at Exit 90 off I-95, is a restored 19th-century village with whaling ships you can go aboard, costumed craftsmen to chat with, and maritime artifacts to see. The construction of a replica of the *Amistad,* the early-19th-century schooner depicted in Steven Spielberg's film of the same name, is expected to be completed in the spring of 2000 to travel the waterways of America as an educational "floating classroom." Plan to spend a full day at this engrossing place, which is open daily from 9am to 5pm between April and October. Admission is $16 for adults, $8 for youths 6 to 12, and free for those under 6. ☎ **888/9SEAPORT** or 860/572-5315; www.mysticseaport.org.

Plimoth Plantation. At Plimoth Plantation, near Plymouth, MA, you can talk with Pilgrims who are still living in the year 1627, tending their crops and remembering in detail their long, cramped sea journey on the *Mayflower.* You'll hear 17 different dialects in the village, reflecting the different places the Pilgrims came from. Even the livestock is authentic, "back-bred" to re-create the Pilgrims' stock. Handcrafted items you can watch being made are for sale in the gift shop. It's open daily 9am to 5pm between April and November. Accessible only from southbound Route 3. Take Exit 4 to the Plimoth Plantation highway and follow the signs. ☎ **508/746-1622.**

Old Sturbridge Village. Located on Route 20 in Sturbridge, MA, at the intersections of Interstates 84 and 90 (about an hour inland from Boston), Old Sturbridge Village has re-created rural New England life as it existed in 1830, with costumed interpreters, craftsmen, farm animals, and the beginnings of industry with shoemakers, coopers, tinners, and blacksmiths. Open daily year-round except Mondays in winter. ☎ **508/347-3362.**

Strawberry Banke. This 10-acre historic community has 42 buildings, seven that illustrate different time periods in the area's history, plus 17th-century herb and vegetable gardens, furnished houses, and crafts shops that include weavers, coopers, cabinetmakers, potters, and boatbuilders. Entrance tickets are good for 2 days; you may need that to see it all. Closed November to April. Located in Portsmouth, along New Hampshire's 18 miles of coastline; take 95 to Exit 7, and follow signs from the Exit to a 10-acre site near the waterfront. ☎ **603/433-1100;** www.strawberrybank.org.

Shelburne, Nova Scotia. Once the fourth largest city in North America, Shelburne—located on the southeast tip of Nova Scotia on Route 103 some 60 miles southwest of Liverpool—is today a sleepy little town with a magical historical complex, but in 1783 some 10,000 Loyalists from the United States, protesting the American Revolution and remaining loyal to the British Crown, arrived in ships from New York City. The restored historic district has re-created the oldest store in America, a dory-making shop that still produces the working boats in traditional fashion, and the only remaining privately owned cooperage (barrel-making shop) in North America. The Shelburne waterfront along Dock Street was also the location for the Demi Moore and Robert Duvall 1994 film *The Scarlet Letter.* ☎ **902/875-4453.**

Fortress Louisbourg National Historic Park. One of North America's largest historical reconstructions, Fortress Louisbourg, near Sydney, Nova Scotia, is for us the most realistic and engrossing of all. It is always the summer of 1744 and the fortress is staffed with scruffy, unruly soldiers (who were to mutiny 6 months later) and French aristocrats in exquisite houses. Inns with pewter mugs and earthenware dishes serve 18th-century food to visitors. "A moment in time" is portrayed in remarkable detail by a cast of

Officer's wife at Fortress Louisbourg demonstrates lace-making.

more than 100 in and around the 50 or so buildings. Spend at least half a day; try to arrive first thing in the morning. Buy a loaf of soldiers' bread from the bakery and some farm cheese from the Destouches House to take along on the road (but bring your own plastic bags to take them back to the RV— there was no plastic in 1744). And bring a jacket and an umbrella, as the weather can change suddenly along this coast. Open 9am to 7pm; admission adults $11, seniors $8.25, children $5.50, and under 6 free. Located south of Sydney, NS, on Route 22 just beyond the modern town of Louisbourg. Take Exit 8 near Sydney. ☎ **902/733-2280.**

Kings Landing. This re-creation of a Loyalist settlement of the early 1800s has more than 100 costumed animators and 60 buildings—farmhouses, mills, churches, and inns. You may see Scottish dancing or caber tossing between June and mid-October, when the park is open daily 10am to 5pm. Located on the Trans-Canada Highway near Fredericton, NB, about 60 miles north of Saint John. ☎ **506/363-4999.**

Acadian Historic Village. You'll have a window into the lives of Acadians between 1780 and 1890 as you walk through time here, watching costumed residents from fur trappers to blacksmiths at work. A cafeteria and restaurant in the village serve traditional Acadian dishes, which bear no resemblance whatsoever to the food their Cajun cousins cook in Louisiana. West of Caraquet on Route 11 near Chaleur Bay on the banks of the Riviere-du-Nord, about 160 miles north of Moncton. Open daily in summer between June and late September. ☎ **506/726-2600.**

Highland Village. Scottish Americans looking for their roots should visit the Highland Village on Route 223 in Iona, on the south shore of Cape Breton

Island, Nova Scotia, which commemorates the settlement of the area by the Highland Scots. Open daily in season, the village contains 10 historic structures dating from 1810 through the early 20th century and moved here to be staffed with costumed interpreters following traditional crafts and farming methods. Also on the premises is **Roots Cape Breton,** a computerized genealogical research center with data collected from census, cemetery, birth, death, and marriage records. It's in Iona by the Bras d'Or Lake in the heart of Cape Breton Island and open early June to mid-October. Call ☎ **902/725-2272** or log on to www.highlandvillage.ns.ca.

TEN SPLURGES

1. **Spend a weekend at the Wauwinet, on Nantucket.** Wauwinet is an elegantly understated, gray-shingled, and white-trimmed seaside inn that sprawls on a remote, sandy neck of land between Nantucket Harbor and the Atlantic. The whole place looks as though it were decorated by Ralph Lauren with Martha Stewart arranging the flowers, and has sailboats, clay tennis courts, bicycles, and a 21-foot launch that's available for picnics and bay cruises. Nantucket is accessible by ferry from Hyannis, MA. ☎ **800/426-8718;** www.wauwinet.com.

2. **Go shopping in Nantucket.** Pick up a classic Nantucket Lightship Basket purse, considered an heirloom that increases in value; prices start at around $350. Or you could choose some delectable chocolate almond buttercreams in pretty hand-painted tins at Sweet Inspirations on India Street. For some of us, that's a splurge.

3. **Take a scenic cruise aboard the *Islander.*** From Boothbay Harbor the boat takes you to a Clambake at Cabbage Island in Boothbay Harbor, ME, where each feaster gets fish chowder, two lobsters, steamed clams, corn on the cob, Maine potatoes, and blueberry cake. There's also a full service bar. Call for information and reservations for the clambake (☎ **207/633-7200**) mid-May to mid-September; $37.50 per person.

4. **Check out the treasures in Wiscasset's antiques shops.** There are more than 20 shops within easy walking distance of each other, featuring everything from early American furniture to 19th-century paintings. Call Wiscasset Regional Business Association at ☎ **207/882-4600** for information. Wiscasset is about 15 miles east of Bath on U.S. 1.

5. **Take a summer whale-watching cruise.** Boats leave from Hyannis, Provincetown on Cape Cod, and Gloucester. Take cameras, binoculars, a jacket, a securely fitting or tie-down sun hat, and sunscreen. **From Provincetown:** Whale Watch Inc., aboard the *Ranger V,* three trips a day (☎ **800/992-9333**); Dolphin Fleet (☎ **800/826-9300**); and Portuguese Princess Whale Watch (☎ **800/442-3188**). **From Hyannis:** Hyannis Whale Watcher Cruises (☎ **800/287-0374**). **From**

Gloucester: Seven Seas Whale Watch (☎ 800/238-1776); Yankee Whale Watch (☎ **800/WHALING;** www.yankeefleet.com); and Cape Ann Whale Watch (☎ **800/877-5110;** www.caww.com). The last leaves from Rose's Wharf, Gloucester, from Exit 10 off 128, and promises plenty of parking—RVs are welcome.

6. **Have a 17th-century meal at Massachusetts' Plimoth Plantation.** Every Friday and Saturday evening a period dinner is served at the Visitor Center. Vegetables come from the plantation gardens, and you eat with your fingers and a knife (forks were not in general usage at the time) while listening to madrigal singers. The museum is located in Plymouth, MA, and is accessible only from southbound Route 3. Take Exit 4 to the Plimoth Plantation highway and follow the signs. For reservations, call ☎ **508/746-1622.**

7. **Book a dinner train ride on the vintage Cape Cod Scenic Railroad.** Enjoy a five-course meal on a 3-hour twilight ride through 42 miles of the cape. There is also a morning trip. Located at 252 Main St., Hyannisport, MA. ☎ **508/771-3800.**

8. **Go antiques shopping along Old King's Highway on Cape Cod.** Also known as Route 6A, Old King's Highway is lined with countless antiques shops. Glass collectors must not miss the Sandwich Glass Museum in Sandwich, showcasing glassware made here between 1825 and 1888 with sand imported from New Jersey (Cape Cod sand has iron oxides that discolor the glass).

9. **Take a day sail aboard a Maine windjammer out of Camden.** The *Appledore,* a windjammer that's sailed around the world, will take you out among the rocky islands of Penobscot Bay where seals sun themselves on the rocks and porpoises play in the water. Come to the dock at Bayview Landing by the Town Landing and sign up or call ahead at ☎ **207/236-8353.**

10. **Stop off for lunch or tea at a 19th-century resort.** Relive the golden days of summer-long vacations in stylish, old-fashioned resort hotels by visiting the half-timbered 1899 **Algonquin,** 184 Adolphus St., St. Andrews-by-the-Sea, NB (☎ **506/529-8823**), surrounded by manicured lawns, lush flower gardens, and a century-old golf course; or at **Keltic Lodge** (built in 1940 but looking much older) near Ingonish Beach on Nova Scotia's Cape Breton Island. ☎ **800/565-0444.**

LOOKING FOR LOBSTER IN ALL THE RIGHT PLACES
Where to Find 'Em

A single-minded lobster lover along the Maine coast can cheerfully overlook Bar Harbor day trippers and T-shirt vendors, fudge fairs, and ye olde gift shoppes to search out a lobster pound or an "early-bird lobster dinner."

Before 5:30 or 6pm, you can dine on a whole fresh lobster weighing around 1¼ pounds for the price of the day. You might even hit a two-for-one lobster special, two 1-pounders on the same plate and enough for two. This is best done as a takeout, since the thrifty New England proprietors usually won't allow two to share. With a little concentration, you can hit a couple of these spots before prices go up for the evening and it's time to get ready for dinner.

How to Eat 'Em
The peerless *Homarus Americanus Northern,* or American lobster, has meaty front claws that his warm-water cousins lack. We think he is also a great deal more succulent.

Only when driven to desperation (or boredom) should you order lobster prepared any way other than steamed or boiled, except on a cold day, when a lobster stew goes down well, and perhaps at lunchtime, when a lobster roll fills the bill nicely. For the uninitiated, a lobster roll is a top-sliced hot dog bun filled with chunks of cold lobster moistened with mayonnaise or melted butter or both, and sometimes a crunch of chopped celery.

Buying 'Em Live
When buying a live lobster, look for the liveliest, with a good greenish-brown color. Avoid any that have turned blue. Look for one with long antennae and pick a feisty one just as you would a puppy at the dog pound. That means he's been there less time than the ones with short antennae, which get bitten off by their fellow lobsters. Lobsters can last up to 2 days out of seawater if you refrigerate them in your RV in a heavy brown paper bag with a few strands of seaweed or several layers of newspapers. Never close a lobster up in a plastic bag, where it will suffocate, or store it in a pot of cold tap water, where it will drown.

How to Cook 'Em
To cook a lobster, put several inches of water—preferably seawater—in a pot, bring it to a boil, and drop the lobster in, holding him by the underside of the body to keep him from splattering the water, then cover the pot quickly. Listen for the water to boil again, then reduce the heat to keep it from boiling over. The lobster is cooked when all of its shell has turned red,

LOBSTER-EATING CHAMP
Back in the 1970s, a New Hampshire native named Tom Shovan (who later moved to California) claimed the all-time lobster-eating record by devouring 61 of the tasty crustaceans at Custy's Restaurant in North Kingstown, Rhode Island.

Lobster pots off Boothbay Harbor, Maine

usually in as little as 10 minutes for a small lobster to a maximum of 20 for a large one. The happy medium seems to be 13 or 14 minutes for a 1¼ pounder, adding 3 minutes for each additional quarter pound. Softshell lobsters, if you're lucky enough to find some, take less time than hardshell. Another expert suggests that when the lobster turns bright red and floats, cook for 3 or 4 minutes longer.

The British Society for the Prevention of Cruelty to Animals suggests the most humane way to cook a lobster is to lower it into the pot head first, starting with cold water, which will put the lobster to sleep as it gradually warms.

TOP LOBSTER SPOTS

Nunan's Lobster Hut, Cape Porpoise, ME. At Nunan's, the crustaceans are steamed to order in a little water rather than boiled in a lot. A bag of potato chips and a hard roll with butter fill out the lobster dinner tray. Finish off with a slice of homemade apple or blueberry pie. It's located at 11 Mills Rd. and is open evenings from 5pm. ☎ **207/967-4362.**

Beal's Lobster Pier, Southwest Harbor, ME. Beal's serves soft-shelled lobster, steamer clams, corn on the cob, and onion rings. You sit at picnic tables at the end of the pier and feast, after fetching drinks and condiments from a side annex. Located at the end of Clark Point Road. ☎ **207/244-7178.**

Fisherman's Landing, Bar Harbor, ME. At Bar Harbor's waterfront, you'll find live or cooked lobster by the pound to take out, along with wonderful lobster rolls, fried clams, and crab rolls. Of course, you don't have to take them any farther than the picnic tables outside the restaurant. Open 11:30am to 8pm daily. ☎ **207/288-4632.**

LOBSTER TRIVIA QUIZ

The Maine Lobster Promotion Council put out a trivia quiz to test your lobster IQ. Here are some of the questions. You'll find the answers following the quiz. To learn more about lobsters, log on to www.lobster.um.maine.edu/lobster.

1. The lobster's nervous system most closely resembles the nervous system of what insect?

2. How long have lobsters been harvested in Maine?

3. What do lobsters eat?

4. What is the tomalley, the light green substance found inside the lobster's carapace?

5. Why do lobsters turn red when they are cooked?

6. How fast can a lobster swim?

ANSWERS: (1) The grasshopper. (2) The first report of caught lobsters was in 1605 when early explorers caught them in a net. Commercial lobstering began in the mid-1800s. (3) Crabs, clams, mussels, starfish, sea urchins, and other lobsters. (4) The liver and pancreas of the lobster, which can contain contaminants; consumers are urged not to eat the tomalley, although some lobster aficionados relish it. The red coral eggs found inside the female lobster, on the other hand, are treasured by gourmets and used in sauces or cooking. (5) The lobster shell carries different color pigment chromatophores; when cooked, all but the background red pigment called astaxanthin are masked. No matter what color the lobster shell when raw, it will turn red when cooked. (6) By flipping its tail and swimming backward, a lobster can cover 25 feet in just under a second.

Lobsterman's Co-op, Boothbay Harbor, ME. On Atlantic Avenue near the aquarium you'll find an unpretentious wooden pier with outdoor picnic tables and a choice of hardshell or softshell lobster (defined on a hand-printed sign as SOFT SHELL = LESS MEAT, SWEETER TASTE). To that definition, we can add "easier to crack open." While fat herring gulls perched on the rail look on, you can devour lobsters with melted butter, a package of potato chips, corn on the cob, fried onion rings, steamed or fried clams, and jug wine by the glass or pitcher. Open mid-May to Columbus Day, lunch and dinner. ☎ 207/633-4900.

The Gloucester House, Gloucester, MA. At the Gloucester House, waitresses call you "dearie" and serve an inexpensive assembly-line clambake with lobster, clam chowder, corn on the cob, and watermelon at long wooden tables out back. Located on Rogers Street. ☎ 978/283-1812.

Harraseeket Lunch & Lobster Company, South Freeport, ME. Harraseeket is at a pier on the harbor and won't let RVs in their parking lot when they're busy. There is, however, a boatyard across the way that will

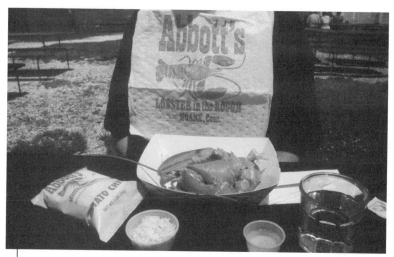

Abbott's Lobster in the Rough, Noank, CT

let you park briefly if you give them a dollar or two for the time it takes to fetch your steamed lobster, bring it back to the RV, and eat it. Open 11am to 7pm. ☎ **207/865-3535.**

Abbott's Lobster in the Rough, Noank, CT. Abbott's serves fresh boiled lobster with coleslaw and their own label potato chips at outdoor picnic tables by the water. You can get clams on the half-shell or in chowder, or a lobster roll, if you'd rather. Weekdays are less crowded, and there is adequate RV parking. Located at 117 Pearl St. in Noank (just south of Mystic on Route 217). ☎ **860/536-7719.**

The Old City Market, Saint John, NB. The Old City Market sells live or cooked lobsters to take out or ship home, as well as lobster rolls and cooked lobster tails. Everywhere you see paper bags of dark red flaky leaves, called *dulse,* dried seaweed that is a favored local snack and very much an acquired taste. The market dates from 1876 and is built to resemble the inverted keel of a ship. It's at 4951 Charlotte St. and is open 8am to 6pm. There's a glass-walled solarium next door if you want to eat your lobster here, or head for Billy's Seafood Company (11am to 10pm) in the north corner if you favor a sit-down meal. ☎ **506/672-FISH.**

The Lobster Shack, Cape Elizabeth, ME. The Lobster Shack occupies an incomparable setting by the sea at the end of Two Lights Road by the lighthouse in Cape Elizabeth, on the point south of Portland. A noted local landmark, it encourages you to "come as you are" and offers "eat in or take out" service. You can also choose between eating indoors or at picnic tables on the rocks at seaside. Open daily 11am to 8pm from April through mid-October. ☎ **207/799-1677.**

Mabel's Lobster Claw, Kennebunkport, ME. Mabel's, where George and Barbara Bush indulge in the peanut butter ice-cream pie, has softshell lobster in season (July to September) and lovely lobster rolls to eat in or take out. 124 Ocean Ave. ☎ **207/967-2562.**

The Clam Shack, Kennebunkport, ME. The Clam Shack is located by the bridge. There's nowhere nearby that is big enough for an RV to park, but if a passenger hops out and the driver goes on into town and parks for a while (there's often a wait), you can get fantastic lobster rolls to go or serious baskets of fried clams. It's open around 11am to 7pm. ☎ **207/967-3321.**

The Lobster Pot, Provincetown, Cape Cod. This funky but pricey restaurant in a two-story clapboard house serves classic clam chowder along with local clambake dinners, and has take-out chowder and lobster. You can sit inside or out on an open deck on the upper level, called Top of the Pot. Located at 321 Commercial St. ☎ **508/487-0842.**

TAKE-OUT (OR EAT-IN) NON-LOBSTER TREATS

Kitchen Little, Mystic Seaport, CT. On Route 27, 2 blocks east of the Mystic Seaport entrance (and a stone's throw from the Mystic Seaport Museum), is a tiny restaurant that serves breakfast and lunch only, but both are memorable meals, especially when taken in the little back garden by the water. We opted for an early lunch to miss the heavy breakfast rush and ate a cup (served in a coffee mug) of light and unique clam chowder in a thin clear broth redolent of fresh clam, followed by a fried scallop roll and a lobster roll. The late breakfasters around us were feasting on huge omelets, pancakes with fresh strawberries, and eggs with cheese and jalapeño peppers. Highway 27. ☎ **860/536-2122.**

Woodmans clam stand, Essex, MA. The first clam was fried and served at Woodmans back in 1916, so they say, and today in the same place you can get clams to take out or eat in by standing at a counter and watching them fried after you order them. This style of service is called "in the rough," but the delectable clams and their companion onion rings are silky inside, crunchily crusty outside. The clam fritters aren't bad, either. In fact, we defy you to drive out of the parking lot past the giant plaster clam without succumbing to the irresistible urge to taste at least one. We've been there a number of times and only once has the queue to get in defeated us (during Memorial Day weekend, 1999). 121 Main St. ☎ **978/768-6451.**

Farnham's, Essex, MA. To continue our tale from Woodmans, above, we drove down Eastern Avenue (also Route 133) toward Gloucester, and out on the edge of Essex we found Farnham's, a smaller, simpler, less crowded restaurant, where, like Woodman's, all the diners order from the counter, then take a seat in the restaurant or wait until the take-out is ready. The fried clams are crunchy, crisp, and luscious, the fish 'n chips light and delicious, and the clam chowder as rich and thin as any model's dream. In a moment of weakness, we also ordered the fried onion rings (the servings are enormous), and reheated both fried potatoes and onion rings the next day in a toaster oven without any loss of quality. You can call ahead for take-outs. 88 Eastern Ave. ☎ **978/768-6643.**

The Clam Box & The White Cap. Another pair of fried clam standbys awaits the aficionado just north of Essex in Ipswich, the center for great clam digging. The Clam Box, at 246 High St. (Route 133) on the north end of town (☎ **978/356-8707**), looks a little like a take-out box itself (be prepared for a wait), and the White Cap, in a strip mall at 141 High St. (☎ **978/356-5276**), also fries up some tasty morsels.

Durgin-Park, Boston, MA. Boston baked beans and Indian pudding are still the mainstays at Boston's Durgin-Park, now located in the gentrified confines of Faneuil Hall Market but still served at long family-style tables by brusque New England matrons. No reservations, no credit cards. North Market Bldg., Faneuil Hall. ☎ **617/227-2038.**

Arnold's Lobster & Clam Bar, Eastham on Cape Cod, MA. The fried onion rings at Arnold's are extra-special, and the steamed lobster, fried clams, steamers, and mussels not bad either. Prices are modest and there's little decor, but the open-air patio and nearby picnic tables among the pines are always filled with happy eaters. Beer and wine are available. 3580 State Hwy. ☎ **508/255-2575.**

Frank Pepe Pizzeria Napoletana, New Haven, CT. Frank Pepe's claims to have baked America's first pizza back in 1925. They still use the original brick ovens to turn out the famous white clam pie, a tomato-free pizza. Pepe's, at 157 Wooster St. (☎ **203/865-5762**), and its pizza-making neighbor a block down the street, **Sally's Apizza,** at 237 Wooster (☎ **203/624-5271**), are open at 4:30pm and through the evening. Sally's was a Bill Clinton favorite in his Yale days, and it makes a fresh tomato pie in summer and a broccoli-cheese pie year-round. Wooster Street, where the pizzerias are located, is in a residential area on the east edge of town (watch for signs) with adequate street parking for RVs early in the evening.

Louis' Lunch, New Haven, CT. It was also in New Haven that Louis Lassen made the first hamburger (so they say) back in 1900, and four generations later Louis' Lunch on Crown Street is still serving them plain on toasted bread, no hamburger buns, ketchup, mayo, mustard, or special sauce allowed. 261–263 Crown St. (downtown between Temple and College). ☎ **203/562-5507.**

Portuguese caldo verde soup. The classic Portuguese caldo verde soup, a luscious brew of potatoes, kale, and smoked garlic sausage, is one of many dishes brought to Nantucket by Portuguese immigrants. One good place to sample it is the upscale **Jared Coffin House,** 29 Broad St., open 9am to noon, 1pm to 5pm (☎ **508/228-2400**). **Juventino's Portuguese Bakery,** at 331 Commercial St. in Provincetown, Cape Cod, is an option for take-out (☎ **508/487-1803**).

Harlow's Bread & Cracker Company, Epping, NH. Harlow's is a rarity, a tiny bakery that makes its own crackers—and not just classic cream crackers and wheatmeal biscuits (perfect with cheese), but more than a dozen different flavors, from Cracked Pepper (seasoned with all the ingredients from a Bloody Mary except the vodka) to a slightly sweetened Benne Biscuit perfect with a cup of tea. They're all baked, not fried, and can also be ordered by mail. Call them at ☎ **603/679-8883** or show up in person between 6am and 6pm on Route 27 in Epping, New Hampshire, any day but Sundays, Labor Day week, and major holidays.

Harraseeket Lunch & Lobster, Freeport, ME. Harraseeket, on main street in south Freeport, serves the famous **whoopie pie,** a pair of big cakelike chocolate cookies sandwiched together with fluffy marshmallow cream. It's an old Maine treat, usually homemade and always wrapped and ready to go on the cafe counter. ☎ **207/865-3535.**

Moxie, the first carbonated soft drink, Lisbon Falls, ME. Sample the descendent of the first carbonated soft drink, Moxie, in its tiny Maine headquarters in the town of Lisbon Falls, between Brunswick and Lewiston. Developed in 1876 as Beverage Moxie Nerve Food, it pre-dated Coca-Cola by a decade, and lent its name to the slang vocabulary of the twenties, when "moxie" meant "a lot of nerve." Today the little company sells memorabilia and soft drinks from the store at 2 Main St. at the junction of Route 196. You can also have it shipped by the case. ☎ **207/353-8173.**

Jordan Pond Lodge, Acadia National Park, ME. Afternoon tea at Jordan Pond Lodge, on the Park Loop Road, begins at 11:30am and features popovers and strawberry jam in an old-fashioned garden filled with dahlias, sweet peas, and delphiniums. The island location is called Mt. Desert but pronounced "dessert." Think sweet thoughts, and call ahead to ☎ **207/ 276-3316.**

Cappy's Chowder House, Camden, ME. Cappy's ladles up clam chowder by the cup or bowl to eat in or take out, as well as serving bar drinks in Mason jars. This is the town where *Peyton Place* was set. Poet Edna St. Vincent Millay worked as a waitress at the nearby Whitehall Inn during the summer of 1912. ☎ **207/236-2254.**

The Portland Public Market, Portland, ME. This indoor fresh foods market also has snack bars and take-out prepared food, heaped counters of fresh seafood, farmhouse cheeses, and boutique butter made in Maine. Greengrocers carry more than one variety of Maine-grown potatoes. Located at 25 Preble St. on the corner of Cumberland, the market is open daily from 9am to 7pm, except Sundays, when the hours are 10am to 5pm. ☎ **207/ 228-2000;** www.portlandmarket.com.

Ganong's Chocolate Factory, St. Stephen, NB. Just across the border from Maine, Ganong's is where the candy bar was invented when the owner wrapped some slabs of chocolate in waxed paper to take on a fishing trip. Among their unique sweets are "chicken bones," crunchy white-striped, cinnamon-flavored logs with a bittersweet chocolate center. Early August the town celebrates a 6-day chocolate festival. The Chocolatiere on Water Street sells their candies by phone (☎ **506/465-5600**). They have a store in town at 73 Milltown Blvd. The factory itself is located on 1 Chocolate Rd. and hosts a tour once a year, in the first week of August.

Moosehead Brewery, Saint John, NB. In summer, tour the Moosehead Brewery, sample the highly praised brew, then drop by the Moosehead Country Store on Main Street to pick up a Moosehead cap or T-shirt. The brewery is at 89 Mainstreet West. Call ☎ **506/635-7000** for a tour appointment.

Little Malpeque oysters. Look for briny Little Malpeque oysters, a Prince Edward Island specialty, on menus throughout Canada's Maritime Provinces in season, and search out the fund-raising lobster suppers offered around PEI by churches and other community centers. You'll not only dine copiously and well, but you'll find the natives are friendly on their own turf.

WILDLIFE WATCHING

It always comes as a surprise to New England visitors when they learn that there are still plenty of **moose** in the woods up here, although the only people that seem to run into them do it literally, with their automobiles. Throughout New Hampshire, road signs give the running tally of how many moose have been hit by cars during the year.

White-tailed deer are plentiful throughout New England and the Maritimes, as are beavers, raccoons, porcupines, and skunks. **Black bear** are occasionally spotted. The red fox is common in Maine's Acadia National Park but rarely seen by visitors.

With all that ocean, you'll find an abundance of **marine life,** especially whales. Humpbacks, fin whales, and occasionally rare right whales (rare because they were the "right" whale for whalers and therefore virtually decimated) may be spotted, most easily aboard a whale-watching boat. You'll also usually see seals, porpoises, and dolphins. We've seen more **humpback whales** off Boston than in the Arctic, Antarctic, or anywhere.

Day cruises go out from Connecticut's Waterford; Maine's Bangor, Boothbay, Lubec, Northeast Harbor, and Portland; Massachusetts's Barnstable, Boston, Gloucester, Plymouth, Provincetown, and Rockport; New Hampshire's Rye Harbor; Nova Scotia's Cheticamp, Big Bras d'Or, and Westport; and New Brunswick's Grand Manan Island, near Campobello.

Pelagic seabirds, those that return to land only for breeding and raising their young, are frequently sighted along the coastline. Look for storm petrels, shearwaters, gannets, guillemots, razorbills, and puffins.

The National Audubon Society and the Canadian Wildlife Service have been working on a project since 1971 to return the **puffins** to Seal Island off Rockland, Maine. The once-thriving colony of birds was almost wiped out around the turn of the century by hunters.

On the Road

CAPE COD

The Pilgrims landed at the tip of Cape Cod, where Provincetown is located, before they reached Plymouth Rock, on November 11, 1620. They stayed there for 36 days before crossing Cape Cod Bay to Plymouth.

The famous rock, what's left of it, is shielded under a Grecian colonnade, and a replica *Mayflower* is staffed by costumed personnel.

Things are a bit more crowded these days. Try to avoid arriving on a summer weekend—or any time during the months of July and August—if you want easy driving and a place to park your RV within walking distance of kitschy little Provincetown. Autumn is a beautiful season on the cape and you can have the beaches to yourself.

Traffic on Route 28, the southernmost highway across the island, is very slow because the area is built up like a slightly quaint megalopolis. A far better route for RVers is smooth-running Route 6. Route 6A is the one to take if you like a slow-moving drive through villages with antiques shops and country inns.

For 30 miles of protected and beautiful beaches, but no camping, head for **Cape Cod National Seashore.** Unfortunately, they have only six parking lots, which fill up by midmorning in summer. Those at Nauset Light Beach and Wellfleet's Marconi Beach have steep stairways leading down to the beach. Hiking trails set out from Salt Pond Visitor Center in Eastham, where there's spacious parking for RVs, and Head of the Meadow Trailhead in Truro, both off Route 6. Bicycle trails run along both sides of the Cape Cod Canal, with parking available in the Sandwich Marina area.

Bayside beaches have warmer water and less turbulent surf than the ocean side. Low tide is best for beach hiking because the sand is packed; at high tide you'll be struggling through looser, deeper sand.

New England Coast Campgrounds

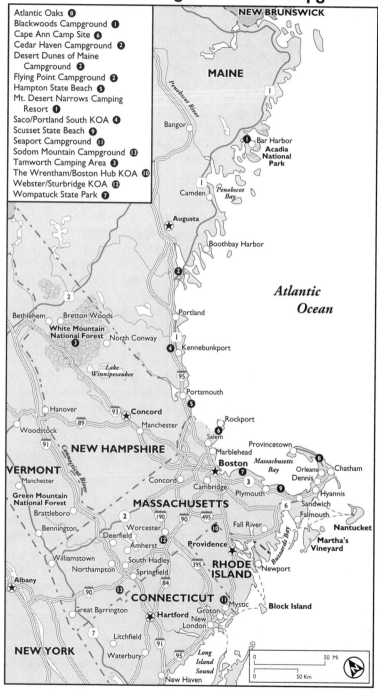

Atlantic Oaks **8**
Blackwoods Campground **1**
Cape Ann Camp Site **6**
Cedar Haven Campground **2**
Desert Dunes of Maine
    Campground **2**
Flying Point Campground **2**
Hampton State Beach **5**
Mt. Desert Narrows Camping
    Resort **1**
Saco/Portland South KOA **4**
Scusset State Beach **9**
Seaport Campground **11**
Sodom Mountain Campground **13**
Tamworth Camping Area **3**
The Wrentham/Boston Hub KOA **10**
Webster/Sturbridge KOA **12**
Wompatuck State Park **7**

NEW BRUNSWICK

MAINE

Penobscot River

Bangor

Bar Harbor
Acadia
National
Park

Camden

Penobscot
Bay

Augusta

Boothbay Harbor

*Atlantic
Ocean*

Bethlehem   Bretton Woods
White Mountain
National Forest
North Conway

Portland

Kennebunkport

Lake
Winnipesaukee

95

Portsmouth

Hanover   Concord

Woodstock   Manchester

Rockport

NEW HAMPSHIRE   Salem
Marblehead

Provincetown

VERMONT
Manchester   Concord

Green Mountain
National Forest
Brattleboro

Boston   *Massachusetts
Bay*   Orleans   Chatham
Dennis
Hyannis
Sandwich
Falmouth

Cambridge
Plymouth

MASSACHUSETTS

2   190   90   495

Worcester   Fall River

Deerfield

Nantucket

Amherst   Providence
South Hadley   **RHODE
ISLAND**   Newport   **Martha's
Vineyard**

Williamstown
Northampton   Springfield

Albany   84

CONNECTICUT   Mystic   **Block Island**

Great Barrington   **CONNECTICUT**

Hartford   Groton
New
London

NEW YORK   7   Litchfield

91

Waterbury   95   *Long
Island
Sound*

New Haven

Bennington

0   50 Mi

0   50 Km

GAMBLING AT FOXWOODS

Foxwoods High Stakes Bingo and Casino, generally considered the most profitable casino in the United States, is in Ledyard, Connecticut (☎ 800/PLAY-BIG), about 6 miles north of I-95 on Route 117 near Mystic Seaport on the Mashantucket Pequot Indian Reservation. The Pequots were virtually decimated in the 17th century by settlers and militia, but since the casino opened, their numbers, once down to one surviving resident on the reservation, have been increasing as news gets out about the profits.

For more information, contact **Cape Cod Chamber of Commerce,** 307 Main St., Hyannis, MA 02601 (☎ **888/33 CAPECOD;** www.capecod.com/chamber).

NANTUCKET

Leave your RV on the mainland and take a day trip on the ferry to the island of Nantucket from **Hyannis via Hy-Line Cruises** (☎ **508/778-2600**), daily year-round, then rent a bicycle when you get there. The free public beaches, seafood restaurants, and bright flowers blooming in front yards everywhere make this one of New England's prettiest places; plus, there's a Whaling Museum and some of the 11 other equally appealing museums.

Nothing built after the 1920s gets any comment or notice from the local guides. Walking tours meander through the main part of town looking at the shingled houses graying in the weather, the brick houses built by the whaling barons, and the newer Federal and Victorian houses. In the early summer, lupine, iris, and lemon lilies grow along the walkways, old-fashioned hollyhocks, alyssum, geraniums, hydrangeas, and nasturtiums bloom in pint-sized gardens, and rosa rugosa with its big red rose hips thrives in hedges everywhere.

Guides like to point out one house occupied by a writer who had traveled twice around the world before deciding that Nantucket was the best place; he nailed two pairs of shoes by the front door to show his traveling days were over.

Nantucket Island was purchased for 40 pounds by Thomas Mayhew in 1659 from Lord Sterling, who had been given it in a grant from Charles I. After holding onto the property for 18 years, Mayhew, a typical real-estate speculator, sold it for only 30 pounds and two beaver hats.

The early Nantucket sailing ships always carried a crew of four young boys ages 13 or 14 in each whale boat, along with a master and a harpooner. The boys did not necessarily choose to go whaling, but in Nantucket, they would not be acceptable suitors for a bride until they had been around Cape Horn and had taken a whale.

Rules like this probably contributed to the sheer islandness Nantucketers display, that quirky cantankerousness that dictates its idiosyncrasies. Here the world is divided into two simple camps—"on island," which is Nantucket, and "off island," which is everywhere else.

And that's where everybody else comes from, as many as 50,000 of them in summer, thronging the streets and filling the restaurants at lunchtime. So locals often partake of a midmorning meal, then splurge on a late dinner after the last of the day trippers have taken the ferry back to the mainland.

Nantucketers claim all the young people and rock stars go to trendier Martha's Vineyard. "We're happy in Nantucket that they're happy over there," one local told us.

For more information about Nantucket, contact **Nantucket Island Chamber of Commerce,** 48 Main St., Nantucket, MA 02554 (☎ **508/228-1700;** www.nantucketchamber.com).

Campground Oases in Connecticut, Massachusetts & New Hampshire

Seaport Campground. Located 3 miles from Mystic Seaport, the campground has 130 sites and is open March through November. Sites are fairly well spaced, with water and electric hookups and sanitary dump, hot showers, flush toilets, laundry, playground, and fishing. RVs over 34 feet are not permitted. To get there, take Exit 90 from I-95 to Route 184, at Old Mystic, CT. ☎ **860/536-4044** for reservations.

Scusset State Beach. Located at Sagamore on the Cape Cod Canal near the junction of Routes 3 and 6, the campground has 100 RV sites with 20- and 30-amp electricity and water hookups, a sanitary dump for registered guests only, a fishing pier, showers, flush toilets, and piped water. No reservations; open year-round. ☎ **508/888-0859.**

Atlantic Oaks. In Eastham, only ½ mile north of the entrance to Cape Cod National Seashore on U.S. 6, Atlantic Oaks has 100 pull-through sites with 30-amp electric, dump station, and cable TV. Sites are fairly wide for New England, but there are some pet restrictions. Call ☎ **800/332-2267** or log on to their Web site at www.capecamping.com.

Wompatuck State Park. Southeast of Boston at Hingham (1¾ miles on State Road 228 to Free Street, then 1 mile east to Union Street, then south 1½ miles on marked turnoff), Wompatuck has 400 grassy and shady sites, 150 of them with 30-amp electric hookups. We stayed there early in the season with very few neighbors, but in July and August it can get crowded, especially on weekends. Prices are very modest ($6 to $8), and there are rest rooms and showers, a sanitary dump station, and a 14-day camping limit. Call ☎ **781/749-7160** for information.

The Wrentham/Boston Hub KOA. Offers a good central location for the greater Boston area, with 140 wide sites (many of them big rig accessible),

30- and 50-amp electric, and free modem hookups in a cybercafe. Trust us, you do not want to take a motorhome into Boston during the current (and long-ongoing) road construction, so if you're not towing a car, you'll enjoy the convenience of nearby public transportation or the shuttle day tour into Boston or around Cape Cod that this campground offers. There are also lobster dinners and some free video games and miniature golf. It's off Exit 15 from I-495; call ☎ **800/KOA-2173** for reservations.

Cape Ann Camp Site. Listed under Gloucester but actually on the Cape Ann Peninsula off Exit 13 from Route 128, the Cape Ann Camp has 150 sites, some of them with great views of the water. Water and 30- and 50-amp electric are available in all sites, but only 50 also have sewer hookups. There is a dump station on the premises. We recommend anyone with a large motorhome or towing a long trailer or fifth-wheel to call the office at the top of the hill and let them send someone to meet you at the entrance, where some of the larger sites are located. Call ☎ **978/283-8683** or log on to www.cape-ann.com/campsite.

Webster/Sturbridge KOA. Near Old Sturbridge Village in the Worcester area off Exit 10 from the Massachusetts Turnpike. There are 97 sites, 25 of them pull-throughs, with a lot of shade, 20- and 30-amp electric hookups, cable TV, and a modem-friendly office. Call ☎ **800/KOA-1895** for reservations.

Sodom Mountain Campground. Located in Southwick, Massachusetts, Sodom Mountain has spacious, shaded sites plus a few floored teepees where campers (kids love this) can unroll sleeping bags. Open early May to mid-October, the campground is located near Springfield, 3 miles west of Route 57 from the junction of 57 and routes 10/202. ☎ **413/569-3930.**

Hampton State Beach. The state of New Hampshire likes RV campers, so you can find a state park—Hampton State Beach, right by the ocean in Hampton—that not only has 24 sites with full hookups (20- and 30-amps) but also imposes a 3-day minimum stay. There are some pet restrictions; call ☎ **603/926-8990** for details. It's open mid-June to late September. From the junction of I-95 and Route 101 (Exit 2), go east 3 miles on Route 101 to Route 1A, then south 2 miles. The entrance is on the left.

Tamworth Camping Area. On the edge of Tamworth, New Hampshire, this is a sprawling campground on a family farm complete with barn and farm animals. Some 100 spaces include secluded tent-sized sites by the Swift River and big rig sites in an open field with water and 15- and 30-amp electric hookups. Open mid-May to mid-October. Tamworth is a quiet New England village not far from bustling Conway and its factory outlet shopping. From the junction of highways 25-W and 16, go north ½ mile on Highway 16 to Depot Road, then west 3 miles. The entrance is on the left.

THE MUSEUM OF FAMILY CAMPING

Visit the Museum of Family Camping at Bear Brook State Park in Allenstown, New Hampshire, to walk through a free exhibit of the evolution of family camping from tents and bedrolls to today's modern RVs. Set indoors and out around a pine grove, the museum is open daily 10am to 4pm between Memorial Day and Columbus Day. Allenstown is located in Merrimack County on Route 28 between Epsom and Suncook, about 15 minutes from Concord. From the junction of routes 4 and 28 at the Epsom Traffic Circle, drive south 5.6 miles on Route 28 to the park entrance, then northeast 1.5 miles on Bear Brook State Park Road to the museum. Call them at ☎ **603/485-3782** or log on at www.channel1.com/users/brosius/museum.htm. 🚐

Call ☎ **800/274-8031** for reservations; e-mail at tamworthcampingarea@ rscs.net.

MOUNT DESERT ISLAND

Maine's Mount Desert Island (pronounced "dessert" by some, "desert" by others) is home to most of the serene and scenic **Acadia National Park** as well as the overcrowded summer streets of **Bar Harbor.** Even in August, the climate is fresh and cool.

Landscape painters from the group called the Hudson River School came here in 1844 to paint the scenery, then sold the pictures to wealthy northeast urbanites who in turn traveled to see the places depicted and, in typical robber baron fashion, ended up buying the real estate in their canvases to build elaborate 30-room summer "cottages" patterned after Tudor hunting lodges and Scottish castles.

Most of the grandiose cottages are gone now, victims of a 5-day fire that swept through Bar Harbor in 1947, changing the town's image considerably.

Summer residents of the island, many of them Boston millionaires, are responsible for preserving the 35,000 acres of land in Acadia National Park and handing it over to the government in 1916. John D. Rockefeller, who disliked automobiles and preferred driving through the parklands in a horse-drawn carriage, commissioned over 50 miles of gravel carriage roads to be constructed. Today hikers, bicyclists, and bird watchers are more in evidence than carriages in summer, and cross-country skiers use the roads in winter. The 27-mile **Park Loop Road** for automobiles is accessible for RVs.

Call **Acadia National Park** for more information about camping and hiking (☎ **207/288-3338;** www.nps.gov/acad).

Campground Oases in Maine

Saco/Portland South KOA. A comfortable, centrally located RV park with big wooded sites and a large heated swimming pool, plus Belgian waffle and blueberry pancake breakfasts on summer weekends, nightly desserts

THE BEANS OF FREEPORT, MAINE (AND MORE)

Freeport, formerly famous mostly as the home of **L.L. Bean,** has turned into the factory outlet capital of New England with around 100 shops, including a vast L.L. Bean emporium open 24 hours a day, 365 days a year. There are several RV campgrounds with hookups in the vicinity if you've shopped till time to drop (see "Campground Oases in Maine," below). Call ☎ **800/865-1994** for a free visitor guide, or log on to www.freeportusa.com. The main L.L. Bean showroom is on Main Street, and a smaller factory outlet store, adjacent to the town's RV parking lot, is open during regular business hours.

that include blueberry pie, a lobster cruise along the coast, and lots of scenery and nearby shopping. It's located off Exit 5 from the Maine Turnpike, then Exit 2B from I-195 and north 1½ miles. There are 120 sites in a wooded park, more than half of them pull-throughs, with city water and 20-and 30-amp electric. Call ☎ **800/KOA-1886** for reservations.

Flying Point Campground. In Freeport, Maine, heaven for shoppers and lobster lovers (not necessarily in that order), we like Flying Point Campground on Casco Bay, which has 45 oceanfront campsites with 30-amp electric hookups. It's a modem-friendly campground with rest rooms, pay showers, sanitary dump station, and mobile sewer service. From the junction of I-95 and U.S. 1 (Exit 19), go north 1 mile on U.S. 1 to Bow/Lower Flying Point Road, then east 3.75 miles. The entrance is on the left. For reservations, call ☎ **800/798-4569.**

Cedar Haven Campground. Also in Freeport and a tad closer to the shopping is Cedar Haven Campground, which purports to be the closest campground to L.L. Bean, only 2 miles away. It's also modem-friendly, with some 50-amp electric hookups and big rig capability, cable TV, camp store, and sanitary dump station. Located at 39 Baker Rd. Call them at ☎ **800/454-3403** for reservations or log on to their Web site at www.campmaine.com/cedarhaven.

Desert Dunes of Maine Campground. In Freeport you'll also find Desert Dunes of Maine Campground, with free shuttle service into Freeport (it's 2½ miles from L.L. Bean) so some family members can go shopping while others hike around the sand dunes. There are 45 sites with water and 20- and 30-amp electric hookups, a sanitary dump, swimming pool, store, and laundry. From the junction of I-95 and Desert Road (Exit 19), go west 2 miles on Desert Road. The entrance is on the left. For reservations, call them at ☎ 207/865-6962 or log on at www.desertofmaine.com.

Mt. Desert Narrows Camping Resort. On Route 3 (Bar Harbor Road) in Bar Harbor, Maine, this is a resort-style park on the ocean with some grassy, tree-shaded, fairly spacious sites. Swimming pool, video game room, playground, laundry, hot showers, and 239 sites with full and partial hookups. They even sell Maine lobster in July and August. Closed in winter. ☎ **207/288-4782;** www.narrowscamping.com.

Blackwoods Campground. Located in Maine's Acadia National Park, Blackwoods requires advance reservations for its 45 RV sites between June 15 and September 15. Toilets, sanitary dump, no hookups, 14-day maximum stay. Seawall, the park's other campground, is first-come, first-served. Call ☎ **207/288-3338.**

NOVA SCOTIA'S CAPE BRETON ISLAND

Cape Breton Highlands National Park in the wild and rocky Cape Breton Islands is the northernmost thrust of Nova Scotia into the Atlantic. The poetic headlands are dashed by the surf and softened by morning mists.

A 184-mile loop begins at Baddeck, a tranquil seaside village that was the longtime summer home of Alexander Graham Bell, who is buried here. The

Cape Breton Island near Bras d'Or

Alexander Graham Bell National Historic Park and Museum, 559 Chebucto St. (☎ 902/295-2069), shows the inventor's energetic and creative mind, which ranged far beyond the telephone into work with the deaf, early aircraft, and conversion of seawater to fresh.

Take the Cabot Trail, Canada Route 105, north of Baddeck in a clockwise direction for easier driving, especially if you begin in the morning, to the cluster of towns along the Margaree River that are named after the river. North East Margaree is home to the unique little **Salmon Museum** (☎ 902/248-2848) with its collection of hand-tied flies, fishing tackle, poaching equipment, and a study of the life cycle of the Atlantic salmon.

Follow the river to the coast and you'll encounter a series of French Acadian villages—Belle Cote, Terre Noire, St. Joseph du Moine, Grand-Etang—whose residents still speak the 18th-century French of their Norman ancestors. The Cape Breton Acadians show off their regional cooking and handicrafts at the **Cooperative Artisanale,** 15067 Main St., Cheticamp (☎ 902/224-2170), each summer between early May and the end of October. In the tiny downstairs restaurant, local women serve chicken fricot, potato pancakes, fish chowder, homemade pies, and gingerbread with syrup. In the craft shop upstairs, you can browse among the hooked rugs, wood carvings, handknit sweaters, and quilts.

From Cheticamp, you enter the park itself with its dazzling vistas of lonely beaches and stark cliffs sculpted by the wind and sea. Except for occasional campgrounds and picnic areas, you'll encounter no habitation until Pleasant Bay. Then the road turns inland to the sweeping grandeur of the highlands and distant vistas of the churning sea, interspersed with wooded valleys.

Note Neils Harbour, bright with colorful, painted houses and fishing boats, lobster pots, and fishnets. The cottages are usually daubed with whatever paint is left over from the boats by thrifty fishermen.

A few miles south at Ingonish Beach, a side road leads to the splendid **Keltic Lodge** (see "Ten Splurges," above; ☎ 800/565-0444). Moody, mist-clouded Cape Smoky lies south of Ingonish Beach, with Wreck Cove, Skir Dhu (Gaelic for "Black Rock"), and North Shore, from which you can sometimes see the Bird Islands, protected nesting area for cormorants, puffins, petrals, and terns. The park's Bog Trail is suitable for wheelchairs.

For more information about the island, contact **Cape Breton Island Tourism,** P.O. Box 1448, Sydney, NS, Canada B1P 6R7 (☎ 800/565-9464; www.cbisland.com).

CAMPGROUND OASES IN CANADA'S MARITIMES

Rockwood Park. This 2,200-acre park right in the city of Saint John, NB, welcomes RVers with 170 pull-through sites, 150 of them with water and 15- and 30-amp electric hookups, a dump station, flush toilets, showers, picnic tables, and fireplaces. Take Exit 113 from Highway 1 westbound or Exit 111

Canadian Maritimes Campgrounds

Baddeck/Cabot Trail KOA **2**
Broad Cove Campground **1**
Cavendish Campground **6**
Cavendish KOA Campground **5**
Fundy National Park **6**
Hartt Island Campground **8**
Louisbourg Motorhome RV Park **3**
Pine Hills RV Park **4**
Rockwood Park **7**

CANADA

Area of Detail

Atlantic Ocean

CAPE BRETON ISLAND

Ferry To Newfoundland

Cape North
Pleasant Bay
Ingonish
Ingonish Beach
New Waterford
Glace Bay
Sydney
Louisbourg
Cape Breton Highlands National Park
North Sydney
St. Ann's
Baddeck
Iona
Grand Narrows
Bras d'Or Lake
St. Peters
Chéticamp
Belle Côte
Margaree Harbour
Margaree Forks
Inverness
Whycocomagh
Port Hawkesbury
Chedabucto Bay
Canso
St. George's Bay
Mulgrave
Melrose
Antigonish
Liscomb
Port Dufferin

Gulf of St. Lawrence

Souris
Montague
St. Peters
High Bank
PRINCE EDWARD ISLAND
Prince Edward Island National Park
Stanhope
Charlottetown
Northumberland Ferry
Pictou
New Glasgow
Westville
Stellarton
Sheet Harbour
Ship Harbour
Tangier
NOVA SCOTIA
Truro
Stewiacke
Musquodoboit Harbour
Dartmouth

Tignish
Alberton
Eleanor's
Summerside
Confederation Bridge
Amherst
Cape Wolfe
Northumberland Strait
Oxford
Londonberry
Springhill
Parrsboro
Minas Basin
Bedford
Halifax
Windsor
Wolfville
Kentville
Chester
Mahone Bay
Lunenberg
Bridgewater
Liverpool
Lockeport
Clark's Harbour

Moncton
Fundy National Park
Middleton
Bridgetown
Annapolis Royal
Caledonia
Kejimkujik National Park
Shelburne

Newcastle
New Bandon
NEW BRUNSWICK
Fredericton
Saint John
Bay of Fundy
Digby
Meteghan
Sanford
Yarmouth

N
25 Mi
25 Km
0

1-0367

THE LOYALISTS & THE ACADIANS

By the end of the American Revolution, 40,000 Americans loyal to the British Crown had fled north to Canada. Some 14,000 arrived in what is now New Brunswick, with land grants for acreage along the Saint John River given to them by the Crown. In 1785, they incorporated their two settlements into the city of Saint John.

Meanwhile, to the south in the pretty village of St. Andrews-by-the-Sea, across the Passamoquody Bay from Maine, other Loyalists put their houses on rafts and towed them over the water to Canada. Kings Landing near Fredricton re-creates a Loyalist community from the early 1800s with costumed interpreters. (See "Living History Sites," above.)

The Canadian Acadians, settled in an area of Nova Scotia, New Brunswick, and Maine once called Acadia, are cousins of the Louisiana Cajuns. Descended from French peasant families who were the first European settlers in Canada, the Acadians in 1755 refused to swear allegiance to the British Crown and so were ordered deported. Some fled to other parts of the North Atlantic coast, others south to French-speaking Louisiana. Henry Wadsworth Longfellow dramatized the story in his poem "Evangeline."

Today the Acadians remaining in English-speaking Canada continue to speak French and to protect their cultural inheritance. The **Acadian Historical Village** near Caraquet re-creates their early settlements (see "Living History Sites," above).

and Route 100 eastbound. With fishing, swimming, a golf course, and a zoo, the park, only 5 minutes from central Saint John, makes a good stopover. No reservations. ☎ **506/652-4050.**

Fundy National Park. Located near Alma, NB, Fundy National Park has campgrounds with hookups and kitchen shelters. Chignecto Campground has 127 water and 30- and 50-amp hookup sites, and Headquarters Campground has 29 full-hookup sites with 30-amp electric. To get to headquarters, follow Route 114 for ½ mile northwest; to get to Chignecto, continue on the same road another 2 miles. ☎ **506/887-2000.**

Broad Cove Campground. Cape Breton Highlands National Park's Broad Cove Campground has 83 full-hookup sites (15- and 30-amp) with flush toilets and showers, fishing, swimming, and a playground. There's also a fine 18-hole golf course called Highland Golf Links inside the park. No campground reservations. Located 7 miles north of the East Park entrance on Cabot Trail. ☎ **902/285-2691.**

Louisbourg Motorhome RV Park. Located in the town of Louisbourg, NS, near the national historic park, the RV park has 49 sites, 36 of them with full hookups (15-amp). Despite the low amperage, the park is modem-friendly. Open mid-May through mid-October. Flush toilets, showers, sanitary dump, fishing, by the ocean. From the junction of Highway 22 and Harbour Front

Lighthouse along the New Brunswick coast

Crescent (in the town center), go northeast 200 feet on Harbour Front Crescent. The entrance is on your left. Reservations: ☎ **902/733-3631.**

The Baddeck/Cabot Trail KOA. Sitting off Trans-Canada Highway 105 at exits 8 or 9, this KOA lets you leave your RV in camp and take off to drive the Cabot Trail with your own car or truck or a rental vehicle. The campground also offers free fishing on a watery arm of the Bras d'Or Lake, access to a major 18-hole golf course, and guided tours to Fortress Louisbourg or the Cabot Trail. For reservations, call ☎ **800/KOA-7452.**

Hartt Island Campground. Near the New Brunswick capital of Fredericton on Route TCH 2, the Hartt Island Campground provides 90 campsites with water and 15- and 30-amp electric hookups. You can go freshwater fishing in the St. John River or visit King's Landing Historical Settlement. Call ☎ **506/452-9401** for information or reservations.

Cavendish Campground. The Prince Edward Island National Park was established to protect sand dunes, beaches, sandstone cliffs, saltwater

---

RV TRAVEL TIP

The 1997 opening of the Confederation Bridge across to Prince Edward Island from Cape Tormentine, New Brunswick, opened up the smallest and one of the most charming of Canada's provinces to much more vehicle traffic, increasing tourism by 51% in the first year alone. Go sooner, not later, to see this jewel of an island.

marshes, and freshwater ponds, as well as cultural and architectural treasures such as the Green Gables farm site and Dalvay-by-the-Sea Hotel. Its newest acquisition is the Greenwich Sand Dune System, officially opening in 2000. Cavendish Campground off Route 6 on Gulf Shore Parkway provides 80 full-hookup sites, 15- and 30-amp electric. Both the park and the campground are open from late June to early September and require a National Park personal use permit. For information on permits and camping reservations, call ☎ **800/213-PARK** or log on at www.gov.pe.ca/.

Cavendish KOA Campground. Located on Route 6, near Green Gables, Cavendish Beach, and Rainbow Valley, this KOA offers a good central location for PEI sightseeing and—good news for big rig drivers—some 50-amp electric hookups as well as a heated swimming pool. There are 230 grass sites, all with water and 148 with 30- and 50-amp electric. Call ☎ **800/ KOA-1879** for reservations.

Pine Hills RV Park. Located in Charlottetown, near the airport and 8 miles from the capital city, Pine Hills has 112 full-hookup sites with 15- and 30-amp electric. There are free daily hayrides and movies, a swimming pool, and a playground. Call ☎ **902/672-2801** for information.

Five Side Trips

1. **Visit Newport, RI.** Take a detour off I-95 in little Rhode Island along the coast on U.S. 1, across Route 138 and over the spectacular Newport Toll Bridge into the elegant city of Newport. This is where Jackie and Jack Kennedy got married, where Claus von Bulow's trial took place, and where various Vanderbilts, Astors, and Belmonts built 70-room "cottages" in dizzying excess, many of which are restored and open to the public. From here, it's an easy dash up to **Fall River, MA,** where Lizzie Borden may or may not have dispatched her parents with an ax. The relics from the trial, including the alleged murder hatchet, are on display at the **Fall River Historical Society,** 451 Rock St. (☎ **508/ 679-1071;** www.lizzieborden.org). Lizzie was acquitted and lived on in Fall River until her death in 1927. (Extra-wide and extra-long RVs and travel trailers should skip the trip into Newport since the streets can be narrow and congested with limited parking.) **Newport County Convention and Visitors Bureau,** 22 America's Cup Ave. (☎ **401/ 849-8048;** www.newportri.com).

2. **Follow the painters through Maine.** Maine's pristine beauty has drawn many artists over the years, including Andrew Wyeth. His famous *Christina's World* was painted at the Olson farm in Cushing, near Rockland. Winslow Homer painted at Prouts Neck, south of Portland, and Edward Hopper's Maine was captured in his lighthouse paintings at Two Lights in Cape Elizabeth. Hopper also painted with

fellow artists George Bellows and Rockwell Kent at Monhegan Island; they followed their former teacher Robert Henri there. Boat service to the island is provided by Hardy Boat Cruises in New Harbor (☎ **800/ 2-PUFFIN;** www.gwi.net/~hardy). Do bear in mind that the trip can be rough. It's said Winslow Homer got so seasick on the way over that he turned around and went back home without ever getting off the boat. Vehicles are prohibited on the island.

3. **Visit an FDR summer home.** Take the short detour from Whiting, ME, up Route 89 and across the bridge at Lubec to Campobello Island in Canada, famous as the summer home of Franklin D. Roosevelt, who was vacationing here in 1921 when he was stricken with polio. The house is evocative, even poignant, with FDR's austere bedroom, and the surrounding countryside has a number of wooded and beachfront walking trails where there's a chance of spotting deer, osprey, eagles, and, below the rocky ledges by the beach, seals. **Herring Cove Provincial Park,** with 91 campsites, is on the island; 40 of the sites have electrical hookups. Take an umbrella if you go walking. Campobello (☎ **506/752-2922**); Herring Cove (☎ **506/752-2396**).

4. **Visit the Acadian shore around northern New Brunswick.** Drive north from Moncton to Shediac, self-proclaimed "Lobster Capital of the World," where you can pick up a crustacean at a stall on the wharf and cook it yourself in the RV in a pot of boiling seawater, or pop into popular Fisherman's Paradise for table service. The town's annual lobster festival is in early July. Acadian towns in this region and the Acadian Historical Museum restaurants serve unique ethnic dishes like *fricots* (stews) based on potatoes and various kinds of meat. A *poulet fricot,* for instance, is a chicken stew; *rapure* is a pie with pork and a potato crust. Look for children selling blueberries by the roadsides in summer. **Tourism New Brunswick,** ☎ **800/561-0123.**

5. **Take the ferry from Hyannis to Martha's Vineyard.** The ferry takes walk-on passengers and their bicycles over to Martha's Vineyard, where summer weekends can see as many as 80,000 visitors and traffic and parking are nightmares. Chic shopping and fashionable restaurants give the impression of gentrification, but institutions like The Black Dog Tavern by the ferry landing, with its sought-after T-shirts, are still around. Bear in mind a couple of Vineyard peculiarities— beaches are privately owned down to the low tide mark, and Martha's Vineyard is dry except for drinks served at restaurants in Edgartown and Oak Bluff (you can take your own wine or beer when you're going out to dinner). Call ☎ **508/778-2600** for information about the ferry.

Travel Quiz: Name That Rock

In honor of New England's rockbound coast, we've gathered some notable rocks for you to match up with their geographic locations.

1. Actor Richard Dreyfuss sculpted this rock from mashed potatoes in the film *Close Encounters of the Third Kind.*

2. The inside of this rock was carved into a 14-room house in 1952 and occupied by the same family for 22 years before being turned into a tourist attraction.

3. This pair of rocks is famous for the automobile commercials filmed atop them.

4. Robert E. Lee and other Confederate heroes are carved into the side of this rock.

5. The Indian woman named Sacajawea, guiding Lewis and Clark's 1803 expedition, knew she was back in her home territory when she spotted a landmark that looked like an animal part.

6. An Indian maiden prayed to the God of the Winds to return her warrior, who had just fallen from this rock into the gorge below, so the winds came up and blew him back into her arms. Today's tourists are delighted when it also retrieves and blows back lightweight objects like handkerchiefs dropped over the edge.

a. Blowing Rock, near the town of the same name off U.S. 321 in western North Carolina

b. Beaverhead Rock, northeast of Dillon, Montana, on Route 41

c. Stone Mountain, Georgia, northeast of Atlanta off Route 10

d. Devil's Tower National Monument in northeastern Wyoming, off Route 24

e. Fisher Towers on Route 128 northeast of Moab, Utah

f. Hole 'N the Rock on U.S. 191 south of Moab, Utah

ANSWERS: 1 (d); 2 (f); 3 (e); 4 (c); 5 (b); 6 (a)

Harry & Shirley's RV Buying & Renting Guide

Just as with permanent homes, some people are RV buyers and some are RV renters. This section will provide the information you need, whichever profile you fit.

RV Types & Terms

AT THE BEGINNING, WE TOOK SOLEMN OATHS NOT TO REFER TO OUR motorhome as a "rig" (although we're not above calling her "Winnie" for Winnebago—but only in private). We also swore we'd never (a) wear visored caps (although they are handy to keep sun out of the driver's eyes), (b) display a carved wooden nameplate saying, "Hi, we're Harry and Shirley from LA," and (c) never refer to ourselves as "pilot" and "co-pilot," terms we considered unbelievably coy the first time we heard them.

However, like some New Year's resolutions, these proclamations have undergone a bit of acceptance and change. "Rig" has become "vehicle" (sometimes) and "co-pilot" is now "navigator." But we still haven't carved out the nameplate.

Just as we had to learn certain technical terms to work as film actors, then pick up a new set of terms as professional travelers, so we've had to adopt certain accepted terms from the RV world in order to correctly describe aspects of the vehicles. This chapter gives a few of the terms you'll need to know to get through the rest of this book. More glossary words will turn up from time to time in chapters 15 and 16 as they become necessary. Don't worry about memorizing them yet. All will be revealed, as we say to each other when we're stuck 5 hours in the Beijing airport or the ship we're waiting for in Ibiza never arrives or we're questioned by the Tunisian police, who suspect we're spies because we're carrying cameras.

> *"Look, Dad, it's got a TV and everything so the driver can watch television!"*
> —Child's comment on seeing a van camper at the LA RV Show

In the section following the glossary are full definitions and descriptions of the major varieties of RVs: type-A motorhomes, type-B van campers, and type-C mini-motorhomes (previously termed Class A, B, and C), truck campers, folding camping trailers, travel trailers, and fifth-wheel travel trailers.

The ABCs of RVs: A Glossary of Common RV Terms

Airbag: In RV terms, a sort of shock absorber positioned at the forward and rear axles of a motorhome.

Arctic Pack: Also spelled Arctic Pac and Arctic Pak, an optional kit to insulate RVs for winter camping.

Auxiliary battery: Extra battery to run 12-volt equipment.

Basement model: An RV that incorporates large storage areas underneath a raised chassis.

Bunkhouse: An RV area containing bunk beds instead of regular beds.

Cabover: The part of a type C mini-motorhome that overlaps the top of the vehicle's cab, usually containing a sleeping or storage unit.

Camper shell: Removable unit to go over the bed of a pickup truck.

Cassette toilet: Toilet with a small holding tank that can be removed from outside the vehicle in order to empty it.

Cockpit: The front of a motorized RV where the pilot (driver) and co-pilot (navigator) sit.

Coupler: The part of the trailer that hooks to the hitch ball.

Crosswise: A piece of furniture arranged across the RV from side to side rather than front to rear

Curbside: The side of the RV that would be at the curb when parked.

Curb weight: The weight of a basic RV unit without fresh or waste water in the holding tanks but with automotive fluids such as fuel, oil, and radiator coolant.

Diesel pusher: A motorhome with a rear diesel engine.

Drink holders: Fitted wood or plastic devices attached to the dashboard area designed to hold cups or cans steady while the RV is moving.

Dry weight or unloaded weight: Manufacturer's weight estimate with no passengers, fuel, water, or supplies.

Entry level: A price deemed attractive for first-time RV buyers.

GAWR (Gross Axle Weight Rating): The maximum allowable weight the axle is designed to carry.

GCWR (Gross Combination Weight Rating): The maximum allowable weight for the combination of vehicle, tow vehicle, passengers, cargo, and all fluids (water, fuel, propane, etc.)

'RITHMATIC

In addition to the verbiage in this section, you've got to learn a few numbers to talk the RV talk since most (but not all) RV manufacturers use as model numbers an abbreviated code that can give you basic information about the vehicle—28 RQ, for instance, will often mean a 28-foot vehicle with a rear queen bed, and 34 D may mean a 34-foot diesel pusher.

GTWR (Gross Trailer Weight Rating): The maximum allowable weight of a fully loaded tow vehicle.

GVWR (Gross Vehicle Weight Rating): The total allowable weight with passengers, cargo, and all fluids.

Garden tub: A bathtub angled into the bathroom so plants can be put on the wide edges against the corner walls.

Gaucho: Sofa/dinette bench that converts into a sleeping unit; a term less used now than formerly.

Generator: Small engine fueled by gasoline or propane that produces 110-volt electricity, built into many RVs but also available as a portable option.

Gooseneck: A colloquial name for fifth-wheel travel trailers.

Hard-sided: RV walls made of aluminum or other hard surface.

High profile: A fifth-wheel trailer with a higher-than-normal front to allow more than 6 feet of standing room inside the raised area.

Hitch: The fastening unit that joins a movable vehicle to the vehicle that pulls it.

Hitch ratings: The maximum amount of weight the hitch can handle— Class I up to 2,000 pounds, Class II up to 3,500 pounds, Class III up to 7,500 pounds, Class IV up to 10,000 pounds, and Class V up to 14,000 pounds. A fifth-wheel hitch can handle up to 25,000 pounds.

Holding tanks: Tanks that retain waste water when the RV unit is not connected to a sewer. The gray water tank holds waste water from the sinks and shower; the black water tank holds sewage from the toilet.

Inverter: A unit that changes 12-volt direct current to 110-volt alternating current to allow operation of computers, TV sets, and such when an RV is not hooked up to electricity.

Island queen: Not Hawaii's Queen Liliuokalani, but a queen-sized bed with walking space on both sides.

Leveling: Positioning the RV in camp so it will be level, using ramps (also called levelers) placed under the wheels, built-in scissors jacks, or power leveling jacks.

Pop-up: Foldout or raised additions to an RV that add height for standing room.

Porta-Potti: Brand name for a portable plastic toilet frequently used in folding camping trailers without facilities.

Self-contained: An RV that needs no external connections to provide short-term cooking, bathing, and heating functions and could park overnight anywhere.

Shore cord: The external electrical cord that connects the vehicle to a campground electrical hookup.

Slideout: A unit that slides open when the RV is parked to expand the living area.

Soft-sides: Telescoping side panels on an RV that can be raised or lowered, usually constructed of canvas or vinyl and mesh netting.

Solar panels: Battery chargers that convert sunlight to direct current electricity.

Streetside: The part of the vehicle on the street side when parked.

Tail swing: The rear motion of a motorhome built on a short chassis with a long rear overhang when the vehicle turns sharply; in simpler terms, the reason we knocked down that road sign when we came out of the driveway.

Telescoping: Compacting from front to back and/or top to bottom to make the living unit smaller for towing and storage.

Three-way refrigerators: Appliances that can operate on a 12-volt battery, propane, or 110-volt electrical power.

Towcar: A car towed by an RV to be used as transportation when the RV is parked in a campground.

Turning radius: The distance across the diameter of an arc in which a vehicle can turn.

Widebody: Designs that stretch RVs from the traditional 96-inch width to 100 or 102 inches.

Winterize: To prepare the RV for winter use or storage.

Types of RVs

There are two basic types of recreation vehicle based on locomotion—towable vehicles and motorized vehicles.

Towables, such as folding camping trailers, travel trailers, and fifth-wheel travel trailers, are living units that can stand alone in camp but are hitched to motor vehicles to travel. Truck campers, compact living units designed to travel atop the bed and cab of a pickup truck, are also part of the towable team.

Motorized vehicles include motorhomes and van campers, both of which are self-contained units built on a truck or van chassis with living, sleeping, cooking, and bathroom facilities accessible from the driver's area without leaving the vehicle. More and more, the dividing line is blurred between van camper and mini-motorhome as more compact units fitted with all the necessities for self-contained camping appear on the market. At the present time, however, the type-A motorhome, the type-B van camper, and the type-C mini-motorhome are still considered three different vehicle categories.

In most models and all price ranges, the buyer can specify interior colors and fabrics selected from a sample display board if the models on the lot are not to his liking.

TOWABLE RVS
Folding Camping Trailers
Think of it as a modern-day covered wagon, with your own team of oxen or horses already in your garage.

Folding camping trailer ready for the road

Affordable, open and airy, easy to store and tow, these lightweight units are the closest thing to tent camping, will fit into a carport or garage, and can usually be towed even by compact cars. From a traveling configuration that resembles a small U-Haul trailer, the RV unfolds to standing-room height with collapsible side walls to form two screened, covered wings, each containing a double bed area.

The center section has a solid floor that supports cooking, dining, and lounging areas, some converting to provide even more sleeping space, as well as optional toilet and shower facilities. Some models are equipped with heating and air-conditioning options, and most have a gas cookstove that can be used inside the unit or plugged into outside connections.

Generally the least expensive of the RVs, folding camping trailers are priced from $2,500 to $15,000, and may sleep as many as eight. The average

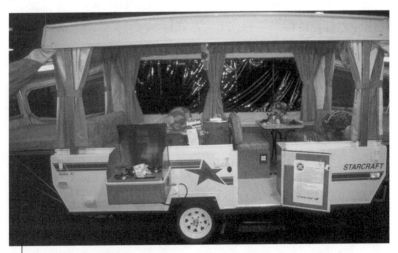

Folding trailer, unfolded

price is around $4,500. Whereas the original units had canvas and/or screen sides, newer models also offer the choice of vinyl or even lightweight aluminum hard siding.

Budget-minded young families with small children, tent campers who seek a bit more luxury without giving up the canvas-and-campfire ambience, and even veteran RVers seeking a simpler travel lifestyle enjoy these vehicles.

Average Cost of Using a Folding Camping Trailer

In a study commissioned by the Go Camping America Committee, the vacation costs for a family of four, traveling in their personal automobile towing a folding camping trailer, staying at campgrounds and preparing the majority of their meals in the RV, came to $149 for 2 nights, $483 for 7 nights, and $889 for 14 nights.

Folding Camping Trailers: The Plus Side

- **Ease of towing, with good gas mileage and lower wind resistance.** Even a compact car can handle most, and they can go anywhere the family car can go and can be left behind in camp while the family sets out to explore the area by car.

- **Economical both to purchase and operate.** Yet these units offer many options found in more expensive RVs, choices such as air-conditioning, heating, bathroom facilities, three-way refrigerators, awnings, and roof racks that can carry boats or bicycles atop the folded unit. Naturally, the more options added, the more expensive the unit is.

- **Easy to store.** Garage or carport storage capability of these small units eliminates the potential problems larger RVs create. Folded, they measure from 5 to 19 feet long and are usually less than 60 inches high.

Folding Camping Trailers: The Minus Side

- **Not always convenient.** Most folding camping trailers use a hand-cranked system for raising and lowering, simple enough when the operator is fit and the weather nice, but not always pleasant in the rain when you're trying to keep the wing mattresses dry.

- **Offers limited on-road access to stored items.** The unit is not usable when underway unless you crank it open at rest stops. Some models have front storage units that are accessible even when the unit is folded if you want to get to picnic items, toys, or bicycles. Access to kitchen and toilet facilities is available only when the rig is fully set up.

- **May mildew if left wet.** If a canvas unit is closed when wet, it has to be unfolded at home and dried out completely before storing or it can mildew. Vinyl units can simply be wiped dry.

- **Offers limited toilet facilities.** Some models do not contain toilet or shower facilities or offer them only as an option. Most contain a storage area for a portable toilet that has to be removed and emptied manually. So long as you're camping in areas that have public toilets and showers it won't be a problem, but self-contained camping is not feasible.

Truck Campers

For people who already own a pickup truck, the easiest and least expensive RV addition might be a truck camper, a unit that slides onto the bed of a pickup, sometimes overhanging the cab or the rear of the vehicle. Most models sleep two to six people and cost between $3,000 and $20,000, with the average price around $10,000. Since the unit is slid on and off, the truck continues to be useful as a hauling and transportation vehicle without the camper.

Sportsmen particularly like the rugged outdoorsy capability of truck campers because they can remove the camper and set it up in camp, then use the truck to go to and from the ski area, fishing hole, or trailhead. It is also possible to tow a boat, snowmobile, horse trailer, or Jet Skis behind a truck camper, something not permitted with other towables.

Low-profile pop-up models are available, as well as units that have optional electrical systems to load and unload the camper from the truck bed. They are often equipped with bathroom and kitchen.

Units range from 7 to 18 feet long, with a cabover bed extending over the pickup's cab. Sofa or dinette built-ins may convert to form a second sleeping area, but these are usually fairly short beds. A step leads from the lower floor area up to the cabover bed.

Truck Camper

Buyers of truck campers should plan to spend extra time matching camper to pickup. Some dealers may not be conversant with the precise details that make the combination work, so it is essential to be sure the camper's weight is compatible with the truck that will be carrying it. If an additional vehicle is being towed, the GCWR (Gross Combined Weight Rating) must also be considered.

Average Cost of Using a Truck Camper

On a cost comparison survey, a family of four traveling with a light-duty truck and truck camper, staying in campgrounds and preparing most of their meals at campsites, spent $152 for 2 nights, $492 for 7 nights, and $916 for 14 nights.

Truck Campers: The Plus Side

- **Economical.** Cheaper to buy, maintain, and operate than most other towables, with better gas mileage.

- **Versatile.** The camper unit can be removed and stored at home or set in place at the campground, and the truck used for utility. With a self-contained camper and a four-wheel-drive truck, you can go almost anywhere.

- **Durable.** Most models are made to endure tougher road conditions than other towables.

- **Offers passenger convenience.** In most states (except Maine, Mississippi, New Hampshire, New Mexico, North Dakota, Pennsylvania, and Wisconsin), passengers are permitted to ride inside a truck camper. California permits passengers to ride inside only if there is communication possible with the driver and if the door can be opened from both inside and outside. Several areas in Canada (Newfoundland/Labrador, Nova Scotia, Saskatchewan, and the Yukon) do not permit passengers to ride inside a truck camper.

Truck Campers: The Minus Side

- **Floor space is limited inside.** There's inadequate room for two adults to move around freely at the same time.

- **Hard to handle.** Weight distribution and higher center of gravity often mean more difficulty in handling these units on the road.

Travel Trailers

These soft- or hard-sided RVs can be towed by vans, autos, or pickup trucks, depending on the weight of the unit. They sleep from two to eight people and usually contain full bath and kitchen facilities. They range in length from 10 feet to 40 feet.

Exterior of a travel trailer

Models come in traditional box shape, an aerodynamic or teardrop shape, and a hard-sided telescoping travel trailer that can be lowered for towing and storage and raised for campground living. Prices range from $4,500 to $60,000, with an average cost of around $12,000.

"Slideouts" that are expanded at the campsite to add more walking-around room have greatly enhanced the comfort of travel trailers and fifth-wheels. Some models may have as many as three slideouts. There are, however, some campgrounds that prohibit RVs using slideouts.

Interior of a travel trailer

> INSIDER TIP
>
> Before selecting a travel trailer to be towed with a vehicle you already own, be sure to consider how much weight you'll be adding for traveling—food, water, clothing, books, sports gear—and be sure your tow vehicle is capable of handling it.

Travel trailers often have two doors with a sofa and dinette slideout area, which could be made into a second sleeping area. Sometimes the bath is split into two sides, and both linoleum and carpet are used on the floors, the former in the kitchen and bath, the latter in the bedroom and living room.

Average Cost of Using a Travel Trailer

A family of four traveling in their personal car or light truck towing a travel trailer and staying in campgrounds, where they prepare most of their meals, spend an average of $158 for 2 nights, $504 for 7 nights, and $924 for 14 nights.

Travel Trailers: The Plus Side

- **Easy to unhitch.** Travel trailers can be unhitched at the campsite, releasing the tow vehicle for local errands and touring.

- **Large selection of interiors.** Travel trailer interiors come in a wide variety of floor plans, with homelike furniture, full kitchens, and baths. Many models have two doors, and some offer a forward bedroom and rear bunkhouse design to sleep the whole family without converting other furniture into beds.

- **Can be pulled by most vehicles.** Today's travel trailers take a greater variety of tow package options, including 4×4s, light trucks, full and midsize cars, station wagons, and minivans.

Travel Trailers: The Minus Side

- **Can be hard to handle.** Some drivers find handling a travel trailer, especially when backing up, takes extra skill at the beginning.

- **Not always convenient and economical.** Wind resistance is greater with travel trailers, and hitching or unhitching can be a nuisance in bad weather.

- **Will cost you more in tolls.** For both travel trailers and fifth-wheels, road tolls based on axles will be higher.

Fifth-Wheel Travel Trailers

These are the most luxurious of the towables, particularly popular with full-timers who cite the ease of maneuvering and towing, the generous storage

Exterior of a fifth-wheel

areas, large living space, and homelike design. The raised forward section that fits over the truck bed allows a split-level design. This area is usually allotted to bedroom and bath, but is sometimes used as a living room or kitchen/dining area instead. By the time basement storage and slideouts are added, a fifth-wheel is comparable in comfort to a condo or a home in the suburbs.

There are numerous bedroom options as well as living, dining, and bath choices in a 36-foot fifth-wheel. The slideout contains sofa and dining furniture, while a second optional slideout in the bedroom area can add more room there as well. There's often space for a washer/dryer, bedroom TV, entertainment center, and large sitting area.

Fifth-wheels sell from $10,000 to $75,000 and up, with an average cost of around $19,420. They are from 22 to 40 feet long.

Interior of a fifth-wheel

Average Cost of Using a Fifth-Wheel
For average expenditures on vacations, see "Travel Trailers."

Fifth-Wheels: The Plus Side
- **Maneuverability and towability.** These are major assets; fifth-wheels are easier to handle than a travel trailer because the hitch is in the bed of the truck, with less vehicle trailing behind. This also creates a shorter turning radius.

- **Easy to unhitch.** Like the other towables, the fifth-wheel can be unhitched and left at the campsite while the truck is available for touring or shopping in the area.

- **Allows storage in your pickup.** The truck bed can still be used for storage with the addition of a pickup bed cover.

Fifth-Wheels: The Minus Side
- **Can't carry passengers on the road.** Because a truck is the obligatory tow vehicle and passengers are not permitted to ride in the fifth-wheel in 29 states and 8 Canadian provinces, large families might find them inconvenient for long trips.

- **Limited headroom.** In many forward bedroom models, except those labeled "high profile," there is not quite enough headroom for anyone over 6 feet tall to stand up straight.

- **No entry from towing vehicle.** As with all towables, you have to exit the towing vehicle and go outdoors to enter the RV, an inconvenience in bad weather.

MOTORIZED RVS
Type-B Van Campers
Also called type-B motorhomes, these conversions are built within the framework of a van, but with raised roofs or lowered floor sections to allow passengers to stand upright, at least in the center of the vehicle. Galleys, fresh-water hookups, sleeping and dining areas that convert to beds, even toilets and showers are readily available in these versatile vehicles.

Ranging from 18 to 22 feet in length, van campers sell from $25,000 to $65,000 (on the upper end comparable in price to an entry-level motorhome), with an average cost of around $40,000. Most sleep two to four people, but also can carry four to six adults as a weekday commuter vehicle. They typically sleep four people, two in the overhead bunk and two on the convertible sofa. A drop-in table fits in front of the sofa for dining.

One enterprising man we met at the Los Angeles RV show was buying a camper van with four swivel passenger seats to use on weekend family trips,

Van camper

but hoped to pay for it by carrying weekday commuters who appreciate having a toilet, microwave, and TV set on the daily run.

Custom van conversions are also readily available from a number of manufacturers at an average price of around $25,500. For a complete list of manufacturers who make van conversions, contact RVIA, P.O. Box 2999, Reston, VA 22090.

Average Cost of Using a Van Camper

A family of four using their own van camper or van conversion, staying in campgrounds and preparing most of their meals in camp, spend at average of $155 for 2 nights, $501 for 7 nights, and $924 for 14 nights.

Van Campers: The Plus Side

- **Multipurpose use.** These RVs double as a second car to use around town or for carpooling.

- **Easy to drive and park, with good gas mileage.** Van campers can go anywhere a passenger car can, including areas in national parks where larger RVs may be restricted.

- **Cozy (the good kind).** Self-contained van campers mean there's no need to leave the vehicle to use any of the facilities.

- **Easy to park.** Unlike other motorized or towable RVs, the camping van can fit into almost any spot left in a campground, so it's good for TGIF getaways and late arrivals.

Van Campers: The Minus Side

- **Cozy (the bad kind).** While most van campers can sleep four people, they'd have to be very good friends, or, more likely, a couple with one or two small children. The living area is extremely compact for a family spending a rainy day inside.

- **Susceptible to wear and tear.** Because it doubles as a second car, the greater mileage accrued by selling time may make it harder to sell or trade than a larger motorhome.

- **Not always easy to set up.** Making up some of the optional beds in these vans could knock your back out—even before you lie down.

- **Limited storage space.** You'll have to carry fewer clothes and supplies than in other RVs, meaning more frequent laundry and grocery stops. Also the mini-refrigerator inside rarely has a freezer compartment.

Type-C Mini-Motorhomes

Familiar, convenient, and affordable, the type-C (think cabover bed) motorhome packs a lot of living in a compact space. Also called mini-motorhomes, the units are built on a truck or van chassis, and usually range in length from 19 to 31 feet long. Widebody designs up to 102 inches across and diesel engine options are available, as well as low-profile models that can be telescoped for travel and storage to under eight feet high. Type-Cs are priced from $26,000 to $75,000 or more, with the average price around $42,000. Some models offer slideouts that increase the usable living space.

Normally, a cabover bed is above the driver's seat, while a sofa provides additional sleeping area. A dinette, rear galley, and bathroom complete the interior. In some models, the cabover may be turned into an entertainment center with a double bed in back and dining on a drop-in table by the sofa.

Average Cost of Using a Type-C Mini-Motorhome

A family of four traveling in their own personal motorhome, staying in campgrounds and preparing most of their meals in camp, spends an average of $188 for 2 nights, $590 for 7 nights, and $1,059 for 14 nights. Compare this to a family traveling in their personal car and staying at motels or hotels and eating most of their meals in restaurants, and you find the latter spends an average of $339 for 2 nights, $1,169 for 7 nights, and $2,257 for 14 nights.

Mini-Motorhomes: The Plus Side

- **Easy to drive.** Type-Cs are more maneuverable for beginning RV drivers than most type-A motorhomes.

- **Comfortable and compact.** Mini-motorhomes are as livable as larger motorhomes but take up less parking and campground space.

Exterior of mini-motorhome

Mini-Motorhomes: The Minus Side

- **So-so sleeping accommodations.** The cabover bed is not appealing for claustrophobic adults, but kids love it. In general terms, the sleeping accommodations, except where there is a rear bedroom, are less private than in the type-A motorhomes when more than two are traveling together.

- **Limited driving visibility.** Because of the overhang from the "cabover" bed, visibility is limited to a normal-sized windshield, while most type-A motorhomes provide large, panoramic windshields.

Interior of mini-motorhome with entertainment area replacing cabover bed

INSIDER TIP

Despite its generally smaller size, in our experience, the type-C gets no better gas mileage than a small type-A, except in the Lite models.

Type-A Motorhomes

A self-propelled motor vehicle chassis with a living unit built on it, the type-A motorhome offers the widest range of choices in the entire RV fleet, from small, 22-foot, fully equipped entry-level vehicles to enormous, 45-foot, bus-like widebody coaches with slideouts, icemakers, washer/dryers, richly appointed furnishings, and marble bathrooms. They're priced from $40,000 all the way up to $725,000 for the most deluxe models, with the average around $82,000.

Decor can vary from the old-fashioned but tough velour fabrics in slate blue or green in the lower-priced vehicles to Bluebird Wanderlodge's cushy white leather furniture, brass trim, wood parquet floors, and sculpted area rugs.

A fairly standard entry-level 28-foot model will contain cockpit seats that swivel; a choice of a sofa with drop-in tables or a dinette, either of which can be made into a bed; a bath; and rear island queen bed with an option of twin beds.

Average Cost of Using a Type-A Motorhome

For a cost comparison of traveling in a motorhome and staying and cooking in campgrounds versus traveling in the family automobile, staying in hotels and eating in restaurants, see "Type-C Mini-Motorhomes."

Type-A Motorhomes: The Plus Side

- **Always accessible from the front seats without going outside.** The type-A motorhome lets you pull over to fix lunch, use the bathroom, or take a quick nap by the side of the road or in a parking lot.

- **Bigger windshield and windows than the type-C.** You'll have greater visibility when traveling and better vantage points for photographs.

- **Livability.** A big, open sense of space and luxury makes the type-A the most livable of the motorized RVs for most people.

- **No setup required.** In most type-As, all the living areas are set up and ready for two people, not requiring any additional conversion on site. (For sleeping more than two people, however, a sofa or dinette usually has to be made up.)

Exterior of a type-A motorhome

Type-A Motorhomes: The Minus Side

- **It's your only wheels.** Unless you're towing a car, a type-A has to be unplugged and moved anytime you need to go out shopping or sightseeing away from the campground.

- **Tough to maneuver.** The larger type-A motorhomes can offer maneuvering problems in narrow city streets with heavy traffic, as well as parking problems almost everywhere except mall and supermarket parking lots. Height and width limitations prohibit entering most parking garages and can present problems in clearing low overhanging roofs and narrow tunnels or bridges.

- **Low mileage.** Gas mileage is quite low, usually under 10 miles to the gallon.

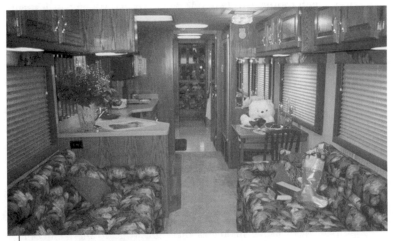

Interior of a type-A motorhome

• **Sometimes too big for parks and campgrounds.** Choosing a size to match your travel style is critical in this category, since larger units cannot be accommodated in some rustic campgrounds and are not permitted to enter certain narrow or winding roadways in national parks such as Glacier, Big Bend, and Zion.

TEN QUESTIONS TO ASK YOURSELF WHEN SELECTING AN RV

1. **How often will I use the vehicle?** Some RV owners in cold climates have to winterize and store the RV, while others use it year-round, either going south for the winter, going skiing or winter camping, or just living in or near mild climates. If you think you may use it only once a year for a 2-week family vacation, it might be cheaper to rent rather than buy.

2. **Where will I store the vehicle?** City-dwellers like us have to rent storage space elsewhere because there's nowhere to store our motorhome on our property. But even suburbanites may face parking regulations that preclude keeping an RV in the driveway or on the street in front of the house. Owners with a large garage might consider folding camping trailers, truck campers, or telescoping travel trailers that are compact enough to store inside. Some travelers who like to visit the same park or campground year after year might want to store the vehicle permanently at the vacation location.

3. **Do I already have part of an RV unit?** If you have a pickup, for example, depending on its size, you're already capable of handling a towable, such as a travel trailer, truck camper, or fifth-wheel. Most family cars can pull a small travel trailer or folding camping trailer.

4. **How much money can I spend?** Budgeters and young families starting out often begin by buying an entry-level RV in whichever type category they want. With sticker shock a strong factor these days, more and more manufacturers are offering lower-priced models in all categories. Previous RV owners often, but not always, look to buying a larger, newer, more expensive model. A few choose instead to downgrade for a simpler travel lifestyle. In many cases, interest paid on your loan to purchase an RV is tax deductible as a second home.

5. **How many people does the RV need to accommodate on a routine trip?** There's a big difference between a salesman's estimate of how many people a vehicle can sleep and the reality of the number of adults and children it can comfortably and conveniently accommodate. Some people dislike the idea of making a bed out of a sofa or dinette night after night during a vacation. Others don't want someone climbing over them in the middle of the night to go to the bathroom. A major consideration is how many seat belts are in the vehicle if it's a

motorized RV. All states but New Hampshire now require that all passengers in the moving vehicle be secured by seat belts, and will not authorize more passengers inside than there are seat belts provided.

6. **How will I be using the vehicle?** People who like to stay in one place, say a country-club–type private campground with swimming pools and putting greens, will want a more luxurious vehicle than campers who want to go out in the woods in a national park or forest, build a campfire, and cook outdoors. Travelers who want to stop at a different campground every night while touring a large region need to give priority to ease of setting up camp and fuel efficiency, while snowbirds who want to stay cheaply all winter on BLM desert lands or other self-contained camping should look for vehicles with greater capacity in water storage and holding tanks.

7. **Which is more important, generous living space in the vehicle or more flexible handling, parking, and roadway options?** In making a decision on vehicle size, 1 foot in length or 4 inches in width can make a tremendous difference. Spend a lot of time mentally moving around in the floor plan, or even physically moving around in the vehicle at the dealer's or the RV show, to assess its livability. Know your size requirements before setting out to look at vehicles, especially if you are considering a motorhome; you'll save a lot of time on the lot.

8. **How important is personal privacy?** Some types of RVs offer more solid-door privacy areas than others. In particular, the shower and toilet facilities in folding camping trailers or camping vans, when they are provided at all, may offer minimum privacy, while travel trailers, fifth-wheels, motorhomes, and some truck campers provide facilities in a completely closed-off area. Sleeping facilities as well may be open or shielded with curtains rather than doors, as in many folding camping trailers, truck campers, and even type-C mini-motorhomes.

9. **What kind of fuel do I want the vehicle to burn, gasoline or diesel?** The general consensus is that diesel engines cost more on initial purchase but less in the long run to operate. One disgruntled RVer, however, has gone on record complaining about the high cost of oil and filters for diesel engines. Diesel engines usually seem quieter in the cockpit than gasoline engines because they are positioned in the rear of the vehicle.

10. **Will I be happy with a standard "off-the-rack" model RV, or do I want some special features and options?** The section below discusses new trends, choices, and options in RVs, and chapter 16, "RV Manufacturers: Who Makes What," gives a rundown on the leading North American RV manufacturers and the various types of RVs they produce.

15

To Rent or Buy?

FOR A FIRST-TIME RV TRAVELER, RENTING A UNIT OF THE SAME TYPE you're thinking of buying can be an invaluable help in making up your mind. Just be sure to allow enough time—a week is the minimum, 2 weeks are better—to get comfortable with the day-to-day logistics of handling it on the road and hooking it up in the campground.

Our own first RV experience was a 6-week lease on a 27-foot motorhome because of a book assignment that required us to visit more than 100 remote ski areas all across the United States. If we'd been renting it for only a few days, we'd probably have turned it back in and said RVing was not for us. (See chapter 1, "Life on the Road: A Personal & Public History of RVing.")

When they heard about our plans, well-meaning friends regaled us with their experiences. A West Los Angeles bookstore owner took her family out for a month, but they used the RV only for travel and sleeping. "We never cooked a single meal inside," she said. "It seemed too complicated."

A couple from San Diego had tried a rented motorhome for 2 days, then, frustrated by slow road speeds, turned it back in and set out in their Mercedes 300 SL instead.

But even that's a record compared to a short-tempered D.C. lawyer and his wife, who rented an RV for a weekend and gave it up less than an hour into the trip.

Note that in none of these cases did the user give the vehicle the old college try.

Three Ways to Check Out Campground Life Without an RV

1. **Check into a Kamping Kabin or Kamping Kottage at a nearby KOA (Kampgrounds of America) campground.** Kamping Kabins, one- and two-room rustic log cabins with porches and double beds plus bunk beds, can sleep four for $20 to $30 a night. Kamping Kottages offer a kitchenette, dining area, bathroom with shower, and sleeping quarters for four, with porch swing and sometimes fireplaces

<u>INSIDER TIP</u>

Reserve a rental RV at least a month in advance, 3 months during peak vacation time. If planning to rent in Alaska, reserve 6 to 12 months ahead.

and air conditioners. It's a good introduction to camping, especially for families with kids. The fee includes use of the campground's toilet and shower facilities, pool, playground, laundry, and store. The Kabins do not have bathrooms, but an outdoor grill and picnic table are provided. You need to bring your own bedding, lantern, and cooking utensils. Get a full list of locations from KOA, free at any KOA campground or by sending $3 to KOA Directory, P.O. Box 30558, Billings, MT 59114. You can call their administration offices at ☎ **406/248-7444.**

2. **Call around to the campgrounds in your area or the area you'd like to visit and ask if they have any rental RV units available.** Sometimes a popular area may offer RVs already in place and hooked up and available for rent by the night. See the "The Best Campground Directories," in chapter 3 for a listing of campground guides.

3. **Book the family into Fort Wilderness at Walt Disney World in Orlando.** Lodging is available in Fleetwood park trailers with full kitchens and baths, similar to travel trailers but set in place for a season or longer. Although you won't be able to road-test the vehicle, you can determine how well your family fits into an RV. The cost—with air-conditioning, swimming pool privileges, cable color TV, cookware, and housekeeping services—is around $200 a night for a party of six with two adults. It's a good idea to reserve well ahead (☎ **407/934-7639** or 407/WDW-CAMP).

Renting

WHEN TO RENT RATHER THAN BUY

- When setting out on your very first RV journey.

- When considering replacing your current RV with a totally different type.

- When you and your family can take only a 2-week vacation once a year but want to do it in an RV. That way you can test-drive different models every year, and when the time comes to buy, you'll have plenty of experience.

- When you want to travel several weeks far from home—say, in a distant part of the United States—or take a camping trip in Europe. Popular fly-and-drive packages are available from many rental companies.

- When you want to drive the Alaska Highway (see chapter 7, "RVing the Alaska Highway") or down Baja (see chapter 5, "Baja Bound: From Tijuana to Los Cabos") in one direction only and/or without subjecting your own vehicle to inescapable wear and tear.

WHERE & HOW TO RENT

A great many rental RVs are booked by European and Australian visitors to the United States who want to be able to see our national parks or drive along the coast of California.

The most common unit available for rental is the motorhome, either the larger type-A or the type-C mini-motorhome, which accounts for 90% of all rentals. Prices begin at around $725 a week.

Use of the generator is not usually included in the fee. You would need it only for operating the ceiling air-conditioning, microwave oven, and TV in a place without electrical hookups, and the dealer will know how much time you've logged by reading the generator counter, usually located by the on/off switch.

When you find a company that rents travel trailers, you'll find they usually require that you furnish your own tow vehicle, hitch, and electrical hookups on the tow vehicle.

Some companies offer a furnishings package with bedding, towels, dishes, cooking pots, and utensils for a flat price of around $85 per trip. Other add-on kits are those containing power cords and hoses, plastic trash bags, toilet chemicals, and a troubleshooting guide.

Be sure you're provided with a full set of instruction booklets and emergency phone numbers in case of a breakdown. Best of all is to have a 24-hour emergency 800 number in case of a problem.

When in doubt, ask a fellow RVer what to do. They're always glad to help, but sometimes hesitant to offer for fear of offending. No matter how much you bustle around like you know what you're doing, the veterans in the campground can spot a goof-up a mile away.

Before setting out, be sure the dealer demonstrates all the components and systems of your unit. Take careful notes, and, just as with rental cars, check for dents and damage from prior use before leaving the lot.

Several helpful publications that list rental companies all over the United States and Canada are available from Recreation Vehicle Rental Association

INSIDER TIP

Get a detailed list of what furnishings are included in your rental so you'll know what necessary items you have to supply. It may be easier to bring things from home than spend vacation time searching for them on the road.

(RVRA) at ☎ **800/336-0355.** *Who's Who in RV Rentals* is a 62-page annual directory that lists addresses, phone numbers, and prices for European, Canadian, and U.S. companies listed by city and state or province. Accompanying the $7.50 publication is a companion booklet, ***Rental Ventures,*** with additional helpful information. Write to them at RVRA, 3930 University Dr., Fairfax, VA 22030-2525.

Your local yellow pages should also carry a listing for rentals under "Recreation Vehicle—Rentals."

Cruise America (☎ **800/327-7799**), the largest rental company with more than 100 outlets, has added budget items such as camping vans, fully equipped travel trailers, and fold-out truck campers with compact pickups to tow them, to answer the requests from European campers in America, who are responsible for one-half to two-thirds of the company's rentals.

Carl's Acres of Trailers in Ontario, California, claims to have the largest trailer rental department in the United States, offering folding camping trailers from $250 a week and travel trailers from $400 a week. No rentals are made to anyone under 25 years of age. Renters supply tow vehicle, hitch, and electrical connections. A cleaning deposit is required and forfeited if the vehicle is not returned clean; the company has its own dump stations for emptying holding tanks. Call them at ☎ **909/983-9647** for details.

Altman's Winnebago in Carson, California (☎ **310/518-6182**), has type-A and type-C new motorhomes for rent. A typical rental charge for a small type-C motorhome with 60 miles a day included would be $113 a day plus 38¢ a mile beyond the 60. A 7-day rental would give a 10% discount. Additional charges would be a $74 prep fee, $12 a day insurance, $6 a day generator fee, and optional charges for kitchen kit (pots, dishes, glasses; $42 per trip) and bedroom kit (sheets, etc.; $26 a person per trip).

Many rental companies offer free **airport pickup** and return, so long as you notify them ahead of time of your flight number and estimated arrival time.

Finally, if you fall in love with your rental vehicle (as we did ours), you might be able to negotiate a purchase price that would subtract your rental fee from the total. If the vehicle is a couple of years old, the price should be even lower, since most dealers get rid of vehicles after 2 or 3 years.

One source for low-priced **used RVs** is Cruise America's RV Depots, lots that sell previously rented units at discounted prices, along with a 12-month, 12,000-mile warranty and free emergency road assistance for a year. Call ☎ **800/327-7799** and ask for national fleet sales.

FIVE MONEY-SAVING RENTAL TIPS

1. **Check prices with several companies before making a decision.** Establish exactly what the lowest-priced rental will include, such as free miles, amenities like dishes and linens, and breakdown service.

INSIDER TIP

Normally, **insurance on a rental RV** is not covered on your personal automobile insurance, so ask your insurance agent for a binder that extends your coverage to the RV for the full rental period. Many dealers require the binder before renting you a vehicle.

2. **Try to plan your trip for shoulder season or off-season.** This may vary seasonally, depending on the rental area.

3. **Check in advance to see if your own automobile insurance agent will cover your rental insurance.** He can usually do it more cheaply than the rental company.

4. **Try to plan a loop trip from the area where the rental unit is based to avoid drop-off charges.** On long, major journeys such as Alaska or Baja California, you might want to pay the drop-off charge and fly back rather than repeat the arduous drive back to the beginning.

5. **Negotiate based on selection.** The more units a rental company has, the wider your range of choices, but if you're flexible about what sort of rig you rent, you may be able to negotiate a better price if the selection is limited.

TEN BIG RENTAL COMPANIES

1. **Cruise America,** 4,000 units nationwide (☎ 800/327-7799)

2. **Trip Makers Inc.,** Walpole, MA (☎ 800/427-9807)

3. **El Monte RV Center,** Orlando, FL (☎ 800/367-2120); Santa Ana, CA (☎ 800/367-2201), with 950 units.

4. **Carl's Acres of Trailers,** Ontario, CA (☎ 909/983-2567)

5. **Moturis Inc.,** 300 units in Hawthorne, CA, near LAX; 400 units in San Francisco. Call central reservations, toll-free, at ☎ 877/**MOTURIS** for both locations.

6. **Road Bear Intl.,** 100 units in Agoura Hills, CA (☎ 818/865-2925)

7. **Nolan's RV Center,** 120 units in Denver, CO (☎ 800/232-8989)

8. **Western Motor Coach,** 95 units in Lynnwood, WA (☎ 800/800-1181)

9. **Canadian RV Rentals,** 120 units in Vancouver, BC (☎ 604/530-3645)

10. **Altman's Winnebago,** 45 units in Carson, CA near LAX (☎ 310/518-6182)

INSIDER TIP

Read your instruction sheets and checklists through at least once before setting out, then daily before hooking up and unhooking until you know the whole routine. Otherwise, you may—as we did that first time—drive miles out of your way to an RV dealer to find out why your generator doesn't work, only to learn it never works when your gas level drops below one-quarter of a tank.

Buying

SHOPPING AT RV SHOWS

Dozens of national and regional RV shows are held annually, most during the winter months. They make especially safe hunting grounds for three types of people: looky-loos who have no idea what they want but are not about to succumb to the first smooth-talking salesman they encounter; well-researched potential buyers who know exactly what they want and are ready to make a deal; and RV owners who want to see the latest technical and design innovations but are basically happy with their existing rig.

The action gets hot and heavy during the last day or two of a show, when it's possible to stumble across an offer you can't refuse. On the other hand, if you're susceptible to super-salesmen, tread carefully or you may be driving a brand-new rig home from the show.

Besides acres of new RVs to explore, a show usually presents seminars on how to "full-time" or where to travel, an oriental bazaar of esoteric gadgets from no-snore pillows to salad-makers (as well as a lot of helpful and practical items), and entertainment from Dixieland or country music musicians to a walk-through virtual reality module.

For a free listing of RV shows, contact the **Recreation Vehicle Industry Association (RVIA),** Dept. SL, P.O. Box 2999, Reston, VA 22090 (☎ **703/ 620-6003;** www.gorving.com or www.rvia.org), or watch your local newspapers for a show in your area.

SHOPPING AT RV DEALERS

Check the yellow pages for local RV dealers and spend an afternoon walking around the lot looking at various types of vehicles and mentally moving

INSIDER TIP

Just as with car rentals, be sure to establish how many free miles you get and what the cost per mile is beyond that daily or weekly limit.

into them. The dealer can usually give you a brochure to take home and study, which details all the features, along with floor plans and specifics about the vehicle's features.

Every dealer has a number of previously owned vehicles that they have taken in as trade-ins or RVs they are brokering for the owners. You can figure the used vehicle could be one-third to half the price of a new model. Purchasing from a reputable dealer ups the chances that the RV will be in good condition and also gives you some place to come back to if there's a problem later.

Don't worry about taking up time if you're not ready to buy yet. Sooner or later you will be, and dealers are accustomed to the allure of a new and unfamiliar RV both to wannabe and veteran owners.

Expect the best buys in December and January, when dealers want to get the previous year's still-new models off the lot to make room for the new year's models.

WHERE *NOT* TO SHOP FOR AN RV

Avoid parking lot and campground "distress" sellers who give you a spiel about bad luck and desperate need for cash. A nationwide group of con artists who call themselves Travelers make a big profit selling cheaply made travel trailers, which also serve as living quarters and office headquarters for numerous other scams.

Be extremely careful buying from any private party unless you know a great deal about the RV you're considering and can make a clear-eyed evaluation of it before signing the deal. If it looks beat up and shows wear and tear inside and out, walk away. Chances are, if the owner has treated the superficial areas badly, the critical working systems you can't see are also flawed. Remember, with motorized vehicles, you're buying both a used car and a used house.

RV PRICES

Prices (entry, mid-range, upscale, and luxury) vary according to the type of RV. Motorhomes range from $45,000 at entry-level to $350,000 and up for

---

INSIDER TIP

RVs that carry the **RVIA Seal** clearly affixed to the vehicle in the vicinity of the doorway are certified by the manufacturer to comply with 500 safety specifications for fire and safety, plumbing and electrical systems, and LP gas systems established under the American National Standards Institute. The Recreation Vehicle Industry Association, representing builders of more than 95% of all RVs sold in the United States, makes periodic unannounced plant inspections to ensure members maintain an acceptable level of compliance.

luxury. Type-C mini-motorhomes range from $35,000 to $65,000, fifth-wheels from $15,000 to $85,000, travel trailers from $12,000 to $45,000, van campers from $35,000 to $50,000, truck campers from $5,000 to $20,000, folding camping trailers from $2,500 to $15,000.

FINANCING

Because RV buyers are generally considered more reliable for a loan than car buyers (only 1.39% of all RV loans are delinquent), loans are easier to get. Check with banks, savings and loan associations, finance companies, credit unions, or the RV dealer. Loans for big new RVs typically range from 10 to 12 years, even 15, with many asking a 20% down payment or less. A few lenders may require a 25% down payment. Financing packages for used RVs are usually for up to 8 years. Interest on the loan is deductible as second home mortgage interest, so long as the unit contains basic cooking, sleeping, and toilet accommodations. To get free **IRS publications** detailing interest information, call ☎ **800/829-3676** and request Publication 936, "Home Interest Deduction," and Publication 523, "Selling Your Home." *The RV Money Book* by Bob Howells (Trailer Life Books, 1992, $29.95; also available from RVIA, address previously given) offers detailed information on buying, selling, financing, and insuring RVs.

FIVE PRECAUTIONS BEFORE BUYING A USED RV

1. **Take a long test drive.** Watch gauges closely, and check out all systems personally from toilet flush to water pump and heater. Look particularly for dry rot in any areas with wood, or water stains that may be signs of leaks.

2. **Ask questions.** Ask the owner very direct and specific questions about all systems in the vehicle.

3. **Have the RV inspected.** Ask a knowledgeable friend, or better still, hire an RV mechanic to a look at the vehicle.

4. **Check the book value of the rig.** Check out the current value in a Kelley or NADA blue book; your bank loan officer should have current copies.

5. **Shop around.** Check comparable models and prices at another dealer's lot to have a price comparison.

INSIDER TIP

Renting out your own RV to others to help defray costs of ownership may appeal to you. If you decide to try it, check the costs of upgrading your insurance policy to cover any liability, and see if a local dealer might add it to his rental fleet for a share of the profits.

16

RV Manufacturers:
Who Makes What

THE FOLLOWING ARE THE LEADING NORTH AMERICAN MANUFACTURERS of type-A motorhomes, type-B van campers, type-C mini-motorhomes, travel trailers, fifth-wheel trailers, truck campers, and folding camping trailers.

If there is a manufacturer in your vicinity who produces an RV type you're interested in seeing, you might want to call and ask if it's possible to tour the plant. You could also request brochures from the company, or get the name of a dealer in your area so you can visit the lot and see the latest models. Some manufacturers also provide a video of their travel products for a modest fee or deposit.

In addition to the following, there are a number of van conversion specialists. To get a list of them, write to the **Recreation Vehicle Industry Association (RVIA),** 1896 Preston White Dr., Box 2999, Reston, VA 22090 (☎ **703/620-6003**).

Action RV Specialists. 239 Juan Tabo NE, Albuquerque, NM 87123. ☎ **505/ 294-1654.** Type: travel trailers. Models: Action Leisure. Price range: mid-range. Tours: no.

Airstream, Inc. 419 West Pike, Jackson Center, OH 45334. ☎ **937/596-6111;** www.airstream-rv.com. Type: travel trailers, motorhomes. Models: Land Yacht. Price range: mid-range to upscale. Tours: call.

Aero Manufacturing Inc. 1018 W. Brooklyn St., Syracuse, IN 46567. ☎ **219/ 457-8787;** www.aero-rv.com. Type: travel trailers, fifth-wheels. Models: Aerolite. Price range: mid-range. Tours: call.

Alfa Leisure, Inc. 13501 5th St., Chino, CA 91710. ☎ **909/628-5574.** Type: travel trailers, fifth-wheels. Models: Alfa. Price range: mid-range to upscale. Tours: call.

American Travel Systems. 21746 Buckingham Rd., Elkhart, IN 46516. ☎ **219/ 294-2117;** www.americantravelsystems.com. Type: travel trailers, fifth-wheels.

Models: Backwaters, Capri, Coach Craft, Ledger, Royal Voyager, VacationAire, Vagabond. Price range: moderate/expensive. Tours: call.

Auto-Mate Rec. Prod. Inc. 150 W. G St., P.O. Box 831, Los Banos, CA 93635. ☎ **209/826-1521.** Type: travel trailers, fifth-wheels. Models: Auto-Mate. Price range: mid-range. Tours: call.

Beaver Motor Coaches, Inc. 20545 Murray Rd., Bend, OR 97701. ☎ **800/ 423-2837.** Type: motorhomes. Models: Marquis, Monterey, Patriot, Contessa. Price range: luxury. Tours: Mon–Fri, 10am and 2pm.

Bigfoot Industries, Inc. 4114 Crozier Rd., RR#3 Comp 44 Palisades, Armstrong, BC, Canada V0E 1B0. ☎ **250/546-2155.** Type: travel trailers, type-C, truck campers. Models: Bigfoot. Price range: entry/mid-range. Tours: Tues, Wed, Thurs, after 2:35pm.

Blue Bird Wanderlodge. P.O. Box 1259, One Wanderlodge Way, Ft. Valley, GA 31030. ☎ **912/825-2021.** Type: motorhomes. Models: Blue Bird, Wanderlodge. Price range: luxury. Tours: call ahead for appointment.

Bonair Leisure Products Ltd. 2885 Smith Blvd. N., Thetford Mines, Quebec, Canada G6G 6P6. ☎ **418/335-5259.** Type: folding camping trailers. Models: Bonair, Master Coach. Price range: entry/mid-range. Tours: call.

Carriage, Inc. #5 Industrial Park, P.O. Box 246, Millersburg, IN 46543. ☎ **219/ 642-3622.** Type: travel trailers, fifth-wheels. Models: Carri-Lite, Carriage, Royals International. Price range: entry to upscale. Tours: Mon–Fri, 10am and 2pm.

Centurian Vehicles, Inc. 69651 U.S. 131 South, P.O. Box 715, White Pigeon, MI 49099. ☎ **616/483-9659.** Type: van campers. Models: Advantage, Cobra, Rockwood. Price range: mid-range. Tours: call.

Classic Manufacturing Ltd. 10026 Marquis Ave., North Battleford, Saskatchewan, Canada S9A 3W2. ☎ **306/445-5510.** Type: folding camping trailers, truck campers. Models: Explorer, Sundance. Price range: mid-range. Tours: call.

Coach House. 3480 Technology Drive, Nokomis, FL 34275. ☎ **941/485-0984.** Type: van campers. Price range: mid-range to upscale. Tours: no.

Coachmen Industries, Inc. 2831 Dexter Dr., P.O. Box 3300, Elkhart, IN 46515. ☎ **219/262-0123;** www.coachmen.com. Type: travel trailers, motorhomes, fifth-wheels, folding camping trailers, van campers, truck campers, type-C. Models: Catalina, Countess, Cross Country, Cruiseair, Crusader, Dearborn, Encounter, Epic, Santara. Price range: entry to upscale. Tours: Middlebury Plant, Tues and Thurs 11:50am.

Columbia Northwest, Inc. Main St. Kecksburg, P.O. Box 131, Mammoth, PA 15664. ☎ **412/423-7440;** www.aliner.com. Type: folding camping trailers. Models: A-Lite, Aliner. Price range: entry/moderate. Tours: call.

Country Coach. 135 E. First St., P.O. Box 400, Junction City, OR 97448. ☎ **541/ 998-3720;** www.countrycoach.com. Type: motorhomes, type-C. Models: Country Coach, Affinity, Allure, Concept, Magna, Intrigue. Price range: upscale/luxury. Tours: 9 and 11am, 1:30 and 3pm, Mon–Fri.

Crossroads RV Inc. 1115 W. Lake St., Topeka, IN 46571. ☎ **219/593-3850;** www.crossroadsrv.com. Type: travel trailers, fifth-wheels. Models: Crossroads. Price range: mid-range. Tours: call.

Cruiser RV Corporation. 13861 County Rd. #4; Bristol, IN 46507. ☎ **219/ 825-1558.** Type: travel trailers, fifth-wheels, truck campers. Models: Shadow Cruiser. Price range: mid-range/upscale. Tours: call ahead.

Custom Interiors. 207 Buffalo St., P.O. Box 526, Caddo, OK 74729. ☎ **580/ 367-2603;** www.redriverok.com/custominteriors. Type: travel trailers. Price range: mid-range. Tours: call.

D. M. Conversions, Ltd. 12651 W. Silver Spring Dr., Butler, WI 53007. ☎ **414/ 781-1170.** Type: van campers. Price range: moderate/upscale. Tours: no.

Damon Corporation. 2958 Gateway Dr., P.O. Box 2888, Elkhart, IN 46515. ☎ **219/262-2624;** www.damonrv.com. Type: motorhomes, travel trailers, type-C, fifth-wheels. Models: Challenger, Escaper, Hornet, Intruder, Magnum, Ultrasport. Price range: entry to upscale. Tours: call for appointment.

Exiss Aluminum Trailers. 1505 E. Rock Island, El Reno, OK 73038. ☎ **405/ 262-6471.** Type: fifth-wheel. Models: Cargo. Price range: mid-range. Tours: no.

Featherlite Mfg., Inc. 816 7th St. W., Erickson Industrial Park, P.O. Box 380, Cresco, IA 52136. ☎ **319/547-2600.** Type: fifth-wheels. Models: Econolite, Featherlite. Price range: entry, mid-range. Tours: call for time and location.

Fleetwood Enterprises, Inc. 3125 Myers St., Riverside, CA 92503. ☎ **909/ 351-3500;** www.fleetwoodrv-info.com. Type: motorhomes, type-C, travel trailers, folding camping trailers, truck campers. Models: Avion, Bounder, Discovery, Jamboree, Oak Park, Pace Arrow, Prowler, Southwind, Terry, Tioga, Wilderness. Price range: entry to upscale. Tours: call for appointment.

Forest River. 3010 College Ave., P.O. Box 124, Goshen, IN 46527. ☎ **219/ 533-5934.** Type: motorhomes, fifth-wheels, travel trailers, type-C, van campers. Models: Cardinal, Flagstaff, Rockwood, Salem, Sandpiper, Veri-Lite, Wildwood, Cherokee, Georgetown, Windsong, Sierra, Spinnaker, Sunseeker, Real-Lite. Price range: entry to upscale. Tours: Mon, Wed, Fri, 1:30pm.

Foretravel, Inc. 1221 NW Stallings Dr., Nacogdoches, TX 75964. ☎ **409/ 564-8367;** www.foretravel.com. Type: motorhomes. Models: Grand Villa, GTC, Travco. Price range: upscale to luxury. Tours: Mon–Fri, 3:30pm.

Franklin Coach Co., Inc. South Oakland Avenue, P.O. Box 152, Nappanee, IN 46550. ☎ 219/773-4106. Type: travel trailers, fifth-wheels. Models: Franklin. Price range: mid-range. Tours: yes.

Georgie Boy Manufacturing, Inc. 69550 M 62, Edwardsburg, MI 49112. ☎ 800/521-8733; www.georgieboy.com. Type: motorhomes. Models: Cruise Air, Cruise Master, Encounter, Swinger, Pursuit. Price range: entry to upscale. Tours: Mon–Fri, 1:30pm.

Glendale Recreation Vehicles. 145 Queen St., Strathroy, Ontario, Canada N7G 3J6. ☎ 519/245-1600. Type: travel trailers, fifth-wheels, type-C. Models: Presidential, Golden Falcon, Royal Classic. Price range: mid-range to upscale. Tours: call.

Great West Van Conversions, Inc. 329 Parkdale Rd., St. Andrews, Manitoba, Canada R1A 3N9. ☎ 204/338-9303. Type: van campers. Models: Classic Sport, Classic Royale, Classic Supreme. Price range: mid-range to upscale. Tours: no.

Gulf Stream Coach, Inc. P.O. Box 1005, 503 S. Oakland Ave., Nappanee, IN 46550. ☎ 800/289-8787; www.gulfstreamcoach.com. Type: motorhomes, travel trailers, fifth-wheels, type-C, van campers. Models: Ameri-Lite, Conquest, Friendship, Gulf Stream, Innsbruck, Palm Breeze, Scenic Cruiser, Sea Hawk, Sun Sport, Sun Voyager, Tour Master. Price range: entry to upscale. Tours: Mon–Fri, 3pm.

Harney Coach Works. P.O. Box 5639, Bend OR 97708. ☎ 541/573-8800. www.smccorporation.com. Type: motorhomes, type-C. Models: Renegade, Riata, Desperado. Price range: mid-range. Tours: Mon–Thurs, 9am and 2pm.

Hi-Lo Trailer Co. 145 Elm St., Butler, OH 44822. ☎ 419/883-3000; www.hilotrailer.com. Type: travel trailers. Models: Hi-Lo, Tow-Lite, Bon Voyage, Fun Chaser, Fun-Lite, Fun Maker, La Grand, Tele Casa, Voyager. Price range: entry to mid-range. Tours: Mon–Thurs, 10:30am and 2pm.

Holiday Rambler Corp. 606 Nelson's Parkway, P.O. Box 465, Wakarusa, IN 46573. ☎ 219/862-7211; www.holidayrambler.com. Type: motorhomes, travel trailers, fifth-wheels. Models: Alumna-Lite, Alumascape, Endeavor, Imperial, Navigator, Vacationer. Price range: entry to upscale. Tours: 10:30am and 1:30pm.

Home & Park Motorhomes. 100 Shirley Ave., Kitchener, Ontario, Canada N2B 2E1. ☎ 519/745-1160. Type: van campers. Models: Roadtrek. Price range: mid-range/upscale. Tours: no.

Hy-Line Enterprises Inc. 21674 Beck Dr., Elkhart, IN 46516. ☎ 219/294-1112. Type: travel trailers, fifth-wheels. Models: Hy-Line. Price range: mid-range. Tours: Mon–Fri, 9am to 4pm.

Isata. 3733 Lexingron Dr., Elkhart, IN 46514. ☎ 888/295-7859. Type: motorhomes, type-C. Models: Touring Sedan, Sport Sedan. Price range: mid-range to upscale. Tours: Mon–Fri, 8am–5pm. Tours: call 1 day ahead for appointment.

Itasca. 605 West Crystal Lake Rd., P.O. Box 152, Forest City, IA 50436. ☎ **219/ 825-5861;** www.winnebagoind.com. Type: motorhomes, type-C. Models: Sunflyer, Suncruiser, Sunrise, Spirit, Sundancer. Price range: entry to upscale. Tours: Mon–Fri, 9am and 1pm in summer, 1pm only in winter.

Jayco Inc. 903 S. Main St., P.O. Box 460, Middlebury, IN 46540. ☎ **219/825-5861;** www.jayco.com. Type: travel trailers, fifth-wheels, type-C, folding camping trailers, truck campers. Models: Jayco, Starcraft, Heritage, Eagle, Camper, Jay, LeisureStar, LumaStar, Sportster. Price range: entry to mid-range. Tours: Mon–Fri, 9:30am and 1:30pm summer only; 1:30pm winter.

K-Z, Inc., Sportsmen. 9270 W US 20, Shipshewana, IN 46565. ☎ **219/ 768-4016;** www.kz-rv.com. Type: travel trailers, fifth-wheels, truck campers. Models: Sportsmen, New Vision. Price range: entry to mid-range. Tours: Tues and Thurs, 3pm.

Keystone RV Company. 17400 Hackberry Dr., Goshen, IN 46526. ☎ **219/ 642-4590;** www.coled@keystone.com. Type: travel trailers, fifth-wheels. Models: Sprinter, Springdale Lite. Price range: entry to mid-range. Tours: Tues, 10am.

King of the Road. 553 S. Front St., P.O. Box 553, Russell, KS 67665. ☎ **913/ 483-2138;** www.kingoftheroadrv.com. Type: travel trailers, fifth-wheels. Models: King of the Road. Price range: mid-range to upscale. Tours: Mon–Fri, 10:30am and 3:30pm.

Kit Manufacturing Company. 412 S. Kit Ave., P.O. Box 990, Caldwell, ID 83606. ☎ **208/454-9291;** www.kitmfg.com. Type: travel trailers, fifth-wheels. Models: Sportsmaster, Companion, Cypress, Elite, Hillcrest, Monterey, Road Ranger, Sun Chaser. Price range: entry to mid-range. Tours: call for appointment.

Komfort Corporation. 3701 SE Naef Rd., P.O. Box 68305, Milwaukie, OR 97268. ☎ **503/653-1160;** www.komfort-rv.com. Type: travel trailers, fifth-wheels. Models: Komfort. Price range: entry. Tours: no.

Lance Camper Mfg. Corp. 43120 Venture St., Lancaster, CA 93535. ☎ **661/ 949-3322;** www.lancecamper.com. Type: truck campers. Models: Lance Camper, Squire. Price range: entry to upscale. Tours: call ahead for Wed.

Lazy Daze, Inc. 4303 Mission Blvd., Montclair, CA 91763. ☎ **909/627-1103.** Type: type-C. Models: Lazy Daze. Price range: mid-range to upscale. Tours: Mon–Fri, 9am to 4pm.

Leisure Travel Vans Ltd. Box 1208, Highway 3 East at Road 28 West, Morden, Manitoba, Canada R6M 1B1. ☎ **204/822-3990;** www.leisurevans.com. Type: van campers. Price range: mid-range. Tours: no.

Marathon Coach Inc. 91333 Coburg Industrial Way, Coburg, OR 97408. ☎ **800/234-0001;** www.marathon-marathon.com. Type: motorhomes. Models: Marathon. Price range: luxury. Tours: Mon–Fri, 11:30am.

Marathon Homes Corp. 4420 Pine Creek Rd., P.O. Box 1302, Elkhart, IN 46515. ☎ 219/294-6441; ww.marathonhomes.com. Type: travel trailers, fifth-wheels, type-C. Models: Marathon, Olympian. Price range: mid-range. Tours: call for appointment.

Monaco Coach Corporation. 91320 Coburg Industrial Way, Coburg, OR 97408. ☎ 800/634-0855; www.monaco-online.com. Type: motorhomes. Models: Windsor, Diplomat, Dynasty, Executive, Signature, McKenzie, La Palma. Price range: luxury. Tours: Mon–Fri, 10am to 2pm.

Mountain High Coachworks. 4750 Zinfandel Court, Ontario, CA 91761. ☎ 800/977-0797. Type: motorhomes. Models: Residency, Summit, Traveleze, Pinnacle. Price range: mid-range. Tours: Thurs, 2pm.

Nash Travel Trailers and Fifth Wheels. Northwood Manufacturing Corp., 59948 Downs Rd., P.O. Box 3359, LaGrande, OR 97850. ☎ 541/962-NASH; www.northwoodmfg.com. Type: travel trailers, fifth-wheels. Price range: mid-range. Tours: Mon–Fri after 3:30pm.

National RV Inc. 3411 N. Perris Blvd., Perris, CA 92571. ☎ 909/943-6007; www.nrvh.com. Type: motorhomes, fifth-wheels. Models: Dolphin, SeaBreeze, Tropi-Cal. Price range: entry to mid-range. Tours: Mon–Fri, 3pm.

Newmar Corporation. 355 N. Delaware St., P.O. Box 30, Nappanee, IN 46550. ☎ 219/773-7791; www.newmarcorp.com. Type: motorhomes, travel trailers, fifth-wheels. Models: American Star, Dutch Star, Kountry Aire, Kountry Star, London Aire, Mountain Aire. Price range: mid-range to upscale. Tours: Mon–Fri, 10am and 1pm.

Nu Wa Industries. 3701 Johnson Rd., Chanute, KS 66720. ☎ 316/431-2088; www.nuwa.com. Type: travel trailers, fifth-wheels. Models: Hitchhiker, Nu Wa, Snowbird. Price range: mid-range to upscale. Tours: Mon–Fri, 9:30am.

Overland Motor Coach. 2208 Middlebury St., Elkhart, IN 46516. ☎ 219/293-0595; www.overlandmotorcoach.com. Type: motorhomes. Models: Lorado, Osprey. Price range: upscale. Tours: call for appointment.

Phoenix USA Inc. 52400 N. State Rd. 15, Bristol, IN 46507. ☎ 219/848-0207. Type: type-C, van campers. Models: Phoenix. Price range: mid-range. Tours: Mon–Fri, 9am to 4pm.

Play-Mor Trailers, Inc. Highway 63 South, P.O. Box 128, Westphalia, MO 65085. ☎ 573/455-2762. Type: travel trailers, fifth-wheels. Models: Play-Mor. Price range: entry to mid-range. Tours: no.

Pleasure-Way Industries Ltd. 302 Portage Ave., Saskatoon, SK, Canada S7J 4C6. ☎ 306/934-6578. Type: van campers. Models: Pleasure-Way. Price range: mid-range. Tours: no.

R-Vision, Inc. 700 E. Beardsley, P.O. Box 4538, Elkhart, IN 46514. ☎ **219/ 268-2111;** www.trail-lite.com. Type: travel trailers, fifth-wheels. Models: Beachcomber, Sandcastle, Trail Lite. Price range: mid-range. Tours: Mon–Fri, 9 to 11am and 1 to 3pm.

Rexhall Industries, Inc. 46147 7th St. W., Lancaster, CA 93534. ☎ **805/ 726-0565.** Type: motorhomes. Models: Aerbus, Airex, RexAir, Vision. Price range: mid-range. Tours: Tue, Wed, Thurs, 1:30pm (reservations required).

Safari. 30725 Diamond Hill Rd., Harrisburg, OR 97446. ☎ **800/458-8735.** Type: motorhomes. Models: Trek, Sahara, Serengeti, Ivory, Continental. Price range: mid-range to upscale. Tours: Mon–Fri, 10am and 2:30pm.

Shasta Industries. 14489 U.S. 20, P.O. Box 631, Middlebury, IN 46540. ☎ **219/ 825-8555;** www.shastaind.com. Type: travel trailers, fifth-wheels, type-C. Models: Shasta, Phoenix, Sprite, Cheyenne, Flite, Travelmaster. Price range: entry to mid-range. Tours: Mon–Fri, 1pm.

Skyline Corporation. 2520 By-Pass Rd., P.O. Box 743, Elkhart, IN 46515. ☎ **219/294-6521;** www.skylinecorp.com. Type: travel trailers, fifth-wheels, truck campers. Models: Aljo, Layton, Nomad, WeekEnder. Price range: entry to mid-range. Tours: arrange through dealer.

Sooner Trailer Manufacturing Co. Inc. 1515 McCurdy, Cuncan, OK 73533. ☎ **405/255-6979;** www.soonertrailers.com. Type: horse trailers, fifth-wheels. Price range: mid-range to upscale. Tours: no.

Sportsmobile Inc. 250 Court St., Huntington, IN 46750. ☎ **219/356-5435.** Type: van campers. Price range: mid-range. Tours: Mon–Fri, 9am to 5pm.

Starcraft Corporation. 2703 College Ave., P.O. Box 1903, Goshen, IN 46526. ☎ **219/533-1105;** www.starcraftcorp.com. Type: van campers, truck campers. Models: Starcraft. Price range: mid-range. Tours: no.

Starcraft RV Inc. 536 W. Michigan St., P.O. Box 458, Topeka, IN 46571. ☎ **800/ 945-4787;** www.starcraftrv.com. Type: travel trailers, fifth-wheels, truck campers, folding camping trailers. Models: Starcraft, Venture, StarLite. Price range: entry to mid-range. Tours: no.

Sunline Coach Company. 245 S. Muddy Creek Rd., Denver, PA 17517. ☎ **717/ 336-2858;** www.sunlinerv.com. Type: travel trailers, fifth-wheels. Models: Sunline. Price range: entry to mid-range. Tours: Mon–Thurs, 9am to 4pm.

Sun-Lite, Inc. 28868 Paul Dr., Elkhart, IN 46514. ☎ **800/327-7684;** www. sunliteinc.com. Type: travel trailers, fifth-wheels,. truck campers, folding camping trailers. Price range: mid-range. Tours: Mon–Fri, after 2:30pm.

Sunnybrook RV, Inc. 201 14th St., Middlebury, IN 46540. ☎ **219/825-5250;** www. sunnybrookrv.com. Type: travel trailers, fifth-wheels. Price range: mid-range to upscale. Tours: Mon–Fri, 2:30pm.

Teton Homes. P.O. Box 2349, Mills, WY 82644. ☎ **307/235-1525**; www. tetonhomes.com. Type: fifth-wheels. Models: Royal, Grand, Prestige. Price range: upscale. Tours: no.

Thor Industries. 419 W. Pike St., Jackson Center, OH 45334. ☎ **937/596-6849**; www.thorindustries.com. Type: motorhomes, travel trailers, fifth-wheels, type-C, van campers. Models: Airstream, Aristocrat,. Bambi, Chateau, Citation, Corsair, Cutter, Dutchmen, Excella, Fifth Avenue, Four Winds, Fun Mover, Hurricane, Infinity, Komfort, Land Yacht, Limited, Park Avenue, Prism, Safari, Signature, Skamper, Tahoe, Wanderer, Wind. Price range: entry to upscale. Tours: Mon–Fri, 2pm.

Ticom Corp. 6881 Chicago Rd., Warren, MI 48092. ☎ **810/978-7875.** Type: truck campers. Price range: mid-range. Tours: no.

Tiffin Motor Homes, Inc. West 4th St., P.O. Box 596, Red Bay, AL 35582. ☎ **256/356-8661**; www.allegromotorhomes.com. Type: motorhomes, type-C. Models: Allegro, Allegro Bay, Allegro Bus. Price range: mid-range. Tours: Mon–Fri, 8am to 3pm.

Tow-Lite, Inc. 500 S. Main St., P.O. Box 577, Bellville, OH 44813. ☎ **419/886-0066**; www.towlite.com. Type: travel trailers. Models: Tow-Lite. Price range: entry to mid-range. Tours: no.

Trailmanor, Inc. 304 Church St., P.O. Box 130, Lake City, TN 37769. ☎ **423/426-7426.** Type: travel trailers. Price range: entry. Tours: call.

Trail Wagons, Inc. 607 E "R" St., P.O. Box 2589, Yakima, WA 98907. ☎ **509/248-9026**; www.trailwagons.com. Type: type-C, van campers, truck campers. Models: Chinook. Price range: mid-range. Tours: Mon–Fri, 10:30am and 2:30pm by appointment.

Travel Line Enterprises, Inc. 25876 Miner Rd., Elkhart, IN 46514. ☎ **219/264-3127.** Type: travel trailers, fifth-wheels. Models: Astro Star, Celebrity, Country Charm, Elite, Impala, International, Kountry Comfort, Royal Stewart, Spartan, Sun Aire, Whispering Pine. Price range: entry to mid-range. Tours: no.

Travel Supreme, Inc. 66149 State Road 19, P.O. Box 610, Wakarusa, IN 46573. ☎ **219/862-4484**; www.travelsupreme.com. Type: travel trailers, fifth-wheels. Models: Travel Supreme. Price range: entry to mid-range. Tours: Mon–Fri, 9 and 10:30am, 1 and 3pm.

Triple E Canada Ltd. P.O. Box 1230, Winkler, Manitoba, Canada R6W 4C4. ☎ **204/325-4361**; www.triplerv.com. Type: motorhomes, travel trailers, fifth-wheels, type-C. Models: Commander, Embassy, Empress, Senator, Topaz, Topaz Touring Edition. Price range: mid-range to upscale. Tours: no.

Turtle Top, Div. of Independent Protection Co. Inc. 67895 Industrial Drive, New Paris, IN 46553. ☎ **219/831-5680.** Type: van campers. Models: Turtle Top. Price range: mid-range. Tours: no.

Vanguard Industries of Michigan Inc. 31450 Mich. 86 West, P.O. Box 802, Colon, MI 49040. ☎ **616/432-3271.** Type: folding camping trailers, truck campers. Models: Palomino. Price range: mid-range. Tours: no.

Veri-Lite, Inc. 2323 Middlebury St., Elkhart, IN 46516. ☎ **219/295-8313.** Type: truck campers. Models: Veri-Lite, Real-Lite. Price range: mid-range. Tours: call, Mon–Fri, 8am to 3pm.

West Coast Leisure Homes. 316 Sawson Ave., Penticton, BC, Canada V2A 3N6. ☎ **250/493-1535.** Type: travel trailers, fifth-wheels, truck campers. Models: Okanagan. Price range: mid-range. Tours: no.

Western Recreational Vehicles, Inc. P.O. Box 9547, Yakima, WA 98909. ☎ **509/457-4133;** www.wrv.com. Type: motorhome, travel trailers, fifth-wheel, truck campers. Models: Alpine Coach, Alpenlite. Price range: moderate to upscale. Tours: call.

Wide Body R.V. Ind., Ltd. 5 Station Rd., Bishop's Falls, Newfoundland, Canada A0H 1C0. ☎ **709/258-5951;** www.exploitschamber.nf.ca/islander. Type: van campers. Models: Islander, Malahat, Islander Supreme. Price range: mid-range. Tours: no.

R. C. Willett Co., Inc. 3040 Leversee Rd., Cedar Falls, IA 50613. ☎ **319/233-3461;** www.rewillett.com. Type: folding camping trailers, truck campers. Models: Northstar. Price range: entry to mid-range. Tours: call Mon–Fri, 9am to 3pm.

Winnebago Industries, Inc. 605 West Crystal Lake Rd., P.O. Box 152, Forest City, IA 50436. ☎ **515/582-3535;** www.winnebagoind.com. Type: motorhomes, type-C, van campers. Models: Itasca Spirit, Suncruiser, Sundancer, Sunflyer, Sunrise, Rialta, Adventurer, Brave, Chieftain, Minnie Winnie, Freedom. Price range: entry to luxury. Tours: Mon–Fri, 9am and 1pm summer only; 1pm winter.

Xplorer Motor Home Division, Frank Industries, Inc. 3950 Burnsline Rd., Brown City, MI 48416. ☎ **810/346-2771.** Type: motorhomes, van campers. Models: Xplorer. Price range: mid-range. Tours: no.

INDEX

FROMMER'S® COMPLETE TRAVEL GUIDES

Alaska
Amsterdam
Arizona
Atlanta
Australia
Austria
Bahamas
Barcelona, Madrid &
  Seville
Beijing
Belgium, Holland &
  Luxembourg
Bermuda
Boston
British Columbia & the
  Canadian Rockies
Budapest & the Best of
  Hungary
California
Canada
Cancún, Cozumel &
  the Yucatán
Cape Cod, Nantucket &
  Martha's Vineyard
Caribbean
Caribbean Cruises & Ports
  of Call
Caribbean Ports of Call
Carolinas & Georgia
Chicago
China
Colorado
Costa Rica
Denmark
Denver, Boulder & Colorado
  Springs
England
Europe

European Cruises & Ports
  of Call
Florida
France
Germany
Greece
Greek Islands
Hawaii
Hong Kong
Honolulu, Waikiki &
  Oahu
Ireland
Israel
Italy
Jamaica
Japan
Las Vegas
London
Los Angeles
Maryland & Delaware
Maui
Mexico
Miami & the Keys
Montana & Wyoming
Montréal & Québec City
Munich & the Bavarian
  Alps
Nashville & Memphis
Nepal
New England
New Mexico
New Orleans
New York City
New Zealand
Nova Scotia, New Brunswick
  & Prince Edward Island
Oregon
Paris

Philadelphia & the
  Amish Country
Portugal
Prague & the Best of the
  Czech Republic
Provence & the Riviera
Puerto Rico
Rome
San Antonio & Austin
San Diego
San Francisco
Santa Fe, Taos & Albuquerque
Scandinavia
Scotland
Seattle & Portland
Singapore & Malaysia
South Africa
Southeast Asia
South Pacific
Spain
Sweden
Switzerland
Thailand
Tokyo
Toronto
Tuscany & Umbria
USA
Utah
Vancouver & Victoria
Vermont, New Hampshire
  & Maine
Vienna & the Danube Valley
Virgin Islands
Virginia
Walt Disney World &
  Orlando
Washington, D.C.
Washington State

FROMMER'S® DOLLAR-A-DAY GUIDES

Australia from $50 a Day
California from $60 a Day
Caribbean from $70 a Day
England from $70 a Day
Europe from $60 a Day

Florida from $60 a Day
Hawaii from $70 a Day
Ireland from $60 a Day
Italy from $70 a Day
London from $85 a Day

New York from $80 a Day
Paris from $85 a Day
San Francisco from $60 a Day
Washington, D.C.,
  from $60 a Day

FROMMER'S® PORTABLE GUIDES

Acapulco, Ixtapa &
  Zihuatanejo
Alaska Cruises & Ports of Call
Bahamas
Baja & Los Cabos
Berlin
California Wine Country
Charleston & Savannah
Chicago

Dublin
Hawaii: The Big Island
Las Vegas
London
Maine Coast
Maui
New Orleans
New York City
Paris

Puerto Vallarta, Manzanillo
  & Guadalajara
San Diego
San Francisco
Sydney
Tampa & St. Petersburg
Venice
Washington, D.C.

FROMMER'S® NATIONAL PARK GUIDES

Family Vacations in the
  National Parks
Grand Canyon

National Parks of the
  American West
Rocky Mountain

Yellowstone & Grand Teton
Yosemite & Sequoia/
  Kings Canyon
Zion & Bryce Canyon

FROMMER'S® MEMORABLE WALKS

Chicago
London

New York
Paris

San Francisco
Washington D.C.

FROMMER'S® GREAT OUTDOOR GUIDES

New England
Northern California

Southern California & Baja
Southern New England

Washington & Oregon

FROMMER'S® BORN TO SHOP GUIDES

Born to Shop: China
Born to Shop: France

Born to Shop: Italy
Born to Shop: London

Born to Shop: New York
Born to Shop: Paris

FROMMER'S® IRREVERENT GUIDES

Amsterdam
Boston
Chicago
Las Vegas

London
Los Angeles
Manhattan
New Orleans

Paris
San Francisco
Seattle & Portland
Vancouver

Walt Disney World
Washington, D.C.

FROMMER'S® BEST-LOVED DRIVING TOURS

America
Britain
California

Florida
France
Germany

Ireland
Italy
New England

Scotland
Spain
Western Europe

THE UNOFFICIAL GUIDES®

Bed & Breakfasts in
  California
 Bed & Breakfasts in
  New England
Bed & Breakfasts in
  the Northwest
Beyond Disney
Branson, Missouri
California with Kids
Chicago

Cruises
Disneyland
Florida with Kids
Golf Vacations in the
  Eastern U.S.
The Great Smoky &
  Blue Ridge
  Mountains
Inside Disney

Hawaii
Las Vegas
London
Miami & the Keys
Mini Las Vegas
Mini-Mickey
New Orleans
New York City
Paris

Safaris
San Francisco
Skiing in the West
Walt Disney World
Walt Disney World
  for Grown-ups
Walt Disney World
  for Kids
Washington, D.C.

SPECIAL-INTEREST TITLES

Frommer's Britain's Best Bed & Breakfasts and
  Country Inns
Frommer's Britain's Best Bike Rides
The Civil War Trust's Official Guide
  to the Civil War Discovery Trail
Frommer's Caribbean Hideaways
Frommer's Food Lover's Companion to France
Frommer's Food Lover's Companion to Italy
Frommer's Gay & Lesbian Europe
  ommer's Exploring America by RV
     ging Out in Europe
       ast & Present

Mad Monks' Guide to California
Mad Monks' Guide to New York City
Frommer's The Moon
Frommer's New York City with Kids
The New York Times' Unforgettable
  Weekends
Places Rated Almanac
Retirement Places Rated
Frommer's Road Atlas Britain
Frommer's Road Atlas Europe
Frommer's Washington, D.C., with Kids
Frommer's What the Airlines Never Tell You